Essentials of Pharmacy Management

Essentials of Pharmacy Management

SECOND EDITION

Dennis H. Tootelian PhD

Professor of Marketing, College of Business Administration, California State University, Sacramento, CA, USA

Albert I. Wertheimer PhD

Professor of Pharmacy, Department of Pharmacy Practice, Temple University School of Pharmacy, Philadelphia, PA, USA

Andrey Mikhailitchenko DBA

Assistant Professor of Marketing, College of Business Administration, California State University, Sacramento, CA, USA

London • Philadelphia Pharmaceutical Press

Published by Pharmaceutical Press
1 Lambeth High Street, London SE1 7JN, UK

University City Science Center, Suite 5E,
3624 Market Street, Philadelphia, PA 19104,
USA

Pharmaceutical Press is the publishing division of the
Royal Pharmaceutical Society

First edition published 1993
Second edition published 2012

Typeset by River Valley Technologies, India
Printed in Great Britain by TJ International, Padstow, Cornwall

ISBN 978 0 85711 018 3

Contents

Preface

Background

Prior to the late 1970s, very few pharmacy schools offered courses in business management, and few students in these schools wanted to "waste" time on such courses. Students focused on the clinical aspects of the profession as that was, and still is, their passion.

Unfortunately, back in those times most students did not fully appreciate that they would be working in a business world, whether in an independent or chain community setting or a hospital inpatient pharmacy. And they did not realize the extent to which the business world would impact the provision of pharmacy services and, ultimately, their careers.

Robert C. Johnson, former CEO of the California Pharmacist Association (CPhA) and later CEO of Prescription Card Services, Inc. (PCS) was among the very first modern day executives to recognize the importance of business management to the profession of pharmacy. He was a visionary in understanding that sound business practices were essential if community pharmacies were to survive and grow. He knew that the provision of good clinical services and the use of good business practices go hand-in-hand instead of being contradictory in all practice settings.

Accordingly, in the late 1970s he retained me to start developing continuing education programs for the CPhA that were designed to help train pharmacists to better manage their pharmacies. At the onset we focused on independent community pharmacies, but we quickly added programs for employee pharmacists as well. Our rationale was that owners and managers needed to be good business people, and employee pharmacists were increasingly going to have to practice in a "business of pharmacy" environment.

The programs we created for the CPhA became widely recognized not only within the state, but across the country. The American Pharmacists Association (APhA) and state pharmacy associations included a variety of management programs at their annual and other meetings. Support for the development of our programs quickly came from pharmaceutical manufacturers and drug wholesalers.

Today, there is nearly universal recognition within the profession of the importance of sound business practices. In community settings, competition is keen for consumer patronage because customers have a multitude of delivery systems available to them. Not only do community pharmacies have to be concerned about each other, but they have intense competition from "mail order" pharmacies that are increasingly using the Internet as a means of serving customers. In essence, no individual community pharmacy is safe from a competitor seeking to attract its patients. Nearly all aspects of a pharmacy manager's job and a staff pharmacist's work environment are decided partly or mainly from a business perspective.

And no hospital inpatient pharmacy is safe from draconian cuts to their resources (e.g. budgets) unless they provide excellent and efficient services to patients and the other medical staff. Hospital administrators watch every aspect of the organization to ensure that each is providing appropriate levels of patient care, is efficient, and is cost effective. An inpatient pharmacy that is not achieving all three is likely to see a change in its management and receive fewer hospital resources. In fact, every operating division within a hospital "competes" with all others for funds, space, and personnel. How much of a hospital's scarce resources are provided to the pharmacy will be directly dependent on how well it is managed. As is the case in community settings, decisions as to staffing levels, equipment, range of services offered, and many other aspects of a staff pharmacist's daily life are made as

PART I

Pharmacy practice in perspective

1

The evolving nature of pharmacy practice

Learning objectives

The objectives of this chapter are to assist you to be able to explain:

- the development of community pharmacy in the USA
- the development of professional pharmacy education in the USA since 1800
- the array of healthcare spending categories in recent years in the USA
- issues between independent and chain-owned pharmacies as well as with supermarket-based operations
- future trends in community pharmacy direction and policy.

Key terms

Chain pharmacy battles
Chain pharmacy growth
Community pharmacy development
Early US pharmacy education
Future possibilities for community pharmacy
Healthcare expenditures
History of retail pharmacy
Mail service pharmacy
National pharmacy expenditures
Payment for pharmacy services
Pharmacy management

History of pharmacy and drugs

For well over a thousand years there have been people who have grown and prepared medications and who have sold them. The names of the products have changed over time, as have the names used to describe these persons. Today, those persons are referred to as "pharmacists," and they usually practice their profession in a pharmacy. The products are not often grown any longer as a giant industry has developed that synthesizes chemical compounds and sells finished dosage forms to the pharmacy.[1] The development of the US Pharmacopeia in the mid-1850s standardized formulations throughout the country, but was not in a position to improve compounding accuracy.

Throughout the last thousand years, the physician, or the apothecary, or chemist, druggist, or pharmacist has stored medications and dispensed them to patients with precise instructions. Payment for medications has changed as well. Once, the physician dispensed drugs as a portion of their visit services. Later, pharmacists bartered goods or collected a fee that was estimated to be affordable by that specific patient. This "what the traffic will bear" pricing scheme allowed the pharmacist to charge higher fees to wealthy patients and essentially subsidize the less affluent who might be charged a lesser fee. Today, essentially all pharmacies are paid for medication dispensing via a standard professional fee.

Early community pharmacies were solo practices that were often family enterprises. The pharmacist— along with his wife and children and sometimes with the addition of cousins, brothers, and sisters— operated a community pharmacy that sold mostly prescribed drugs, over-the-counter (OTC) drugs and some limited cosmetics and fragrances. By the 1950s, the corporate-owned chain store was growing rapidly in numbers and market share. At this point, professional management was introduced into the pharmacy business.

Everyone has seen photos of early twentieth-century pharmacies, then called "drugstores," with a long soda fountain where patrons would have anything from a soft drink, or ice cream item to a snack or complete dinner. Now we know that the resources and floor space required by the soda fountain cannot be justified by the revenues it generates. Such management decisions are commonplace, if not standard today.

Let us pause here and examine the pharmacy sector as a component of the overall healthcare market or industry. While pharmaceuticals and pharmacy services account for only about 10 percent of the total healthcare expenditures in the USA, that is an important 10 percent. It is estimated that 70 percent of physician visits result in the writing of one or more prescriptions, and it is difficult to find anyone who has not taken an OTC drug within the last two weeks.

While some prescribed drugs are obtained directly from the physician or clinic, or from a hospital pharmacy, the vast majority of drugs are dispensed through community pharmacies (see Figures 1.1 and 1.2).

The study of management is complex and built upon a foundation of numerous disciplines. You might not think that the efficient operation of a community pharmacy/retail establishment requires knowledge of organizational behavior, the process of influence, and modern management science, but you would be wrong. A successful manager must be knowledgeable and experienced in planning, leadership, interpersonal communications, evaluation techniques, accounting and financial controls, negotiation, purchasing, promotion, pricing, fundraising, public relations, forecasting, and advertising. A knowledge of history, law, and psychology can also be useful.

Neither is management prowess confined to the USA and the developed world. A pharmacy practice management book by an early expert in the area, Dr. Frederick Adenika, was published in Nigeria in 1975. The book reads like any management book used in North America. It discusses the functions and tasks of the pharmacist, the legal organization of pharmacies, location analysis, the marketing process, finance and administration, layout and design of a pharmacy, personnel management, purchasing, turnover and inventory control, pricing options and techniques, fiscal management, planning for profitability, financial analysis, and legislation.

Pharmacy as a component of the healthcare system

Early in the history of the USA pharmacists had come from Germany or England and it soon became recognized that a domestic supply of pharmacists for the future had to be developed. In the 1820s, pharmacy schools in Philadelphia, Massachusetts and in large cities in the northeast began operation. The instructors were practicing pharmacists, and the students took classes part-time for a period of about six months in between their work at a pharmacy. Prior to that time, pharmacists were educated by a practicing pharmacist agreeing to take a student as an apprentice into his practice. There was no standard curriculum and the "student" was ready for graduation when the preceptor said so.[2]

Next came the one-year curriculum where the Pharm.D. degree was granted. Following that was a period where the Pharmaceutical Chemist (Ph.C.) was awarded, followed later by a three-year program terminating with the granting of the Ph.G. degree. A four-year Bachelor's degree was begun in the early 1930s, with a five-year B.S. in 1965 and the Pharm.D., again, in the 1990s.

Management courses were introduced into the curriculum of US pharmacy schools in the 1950s. The course work emphasized retailing and basic management principles. Scientific management became quantitative and well accepted at that time.

In the 1950s community pharmacies sponsored their own credit programs. The patron would say "charge it" or tell the pharmacy clerk to add that purchase to their monthly bill. Consumers would write many checks at the end of the month; one for the grocer, one to the pharmacy, one to the department store. The introduction of the Visa card which could be used at numerous retailers made individual store charge accounts obsolete. With that change in credit policy a little bit of the older store loyalty died and personal relationships were lost. The consumer could now obtain the same credit privileges from any pharmacy, even if they were totally unknown. Moreover, shopping behaviors and patterns began to migrate from small neighborhood outlets to the larger suburban shopping malls with the "one-stop" possibility. Independent community pharmacists tried to portray the chain pharmacies as inferior, but that was never proven. Big box stores in the 1970s (K-Mart, Woolco, followed later by Target and WalMart) carried everything that customers could get at a community pharmacy with the exception (for a while) of prescription drugs.

The other societal change that occurred in the 1960s and subsequently was the arrival of two-car families. Now while the breadwinner had the car parked all day at the office or plant, the spouse could go shopping at the nearest mall and was no longer tethered to the little neighborhood community pharmacy, where there was no convenient parking availability.

The external environment

It would be unrealistic to think that pharmacies were not concerned about their viability and profits from the earliest days. However, the ability of a community pharmacy to promote itself and its prices were quite limited during the first half of the twentieth century by conventional norms and by the code of

ethics of the American Pharmaceutical Association. A number of events, both individually and in the aggregate, forced the independent community pharmacy owner to take a more aggressive stance in defending their businesses. Following a number of price wars and hostility, two antitrust laws were passed in the USA and there was acceptance of something called "fair trade pricing." The Fair Trade Acts enabled contracts requiring a retailer to sell at or above a resale or retail price set by the supplier. There was also a non-signer clause which required compliance by all retail establishments, including pharmacies, if anyone signed such a contract even if that store did not participate. During the ensuing years, fair trade had been challenged in the courts and in the marketplace and finally it became too difficult and costly a chore for manufacturers to defend their fair trade suggested retail prices everywhere in the USA. That emboldened chain grocery stores to sell very popular OTC drugs at deeply discounted prices, to create a low price image.[3]

Owners of community pharmacies fought back by purchasing full or partnership status in two or three additional community pharmacies for the purpose of gaining better quantity discounts. In addition, independent community pharmacy owners in a substantial number of cities created coop (cooperative) wholesaling operations where the owners each purchased a share of the company and that same share of the net profits from the operation of the wholesale business at the end of the year. They passed along the best prices they were able to negotiate as well.

That idea spread in the 1940s with the development of voluntary advertising cooperatives. For example, some of the pharmacies in Buffalo, New York, created a "Leader Drug" trademark. Advertising and other promotional expenditures aimed at directing traffic to independently owned "Leader" stores were shared by the member pharmacies. A similar concept occurred next with the development of franchise pharmacies. Some of the earliest of these were the Rexall drugstores, which by 1947 had 553 units and more than 10,000 franchised Rexall drugstores. Both the franchise concept and the voluntary advertising cooperative presented an advantage to the independent community pharmacy owner to compete with the growing number of chain pharmacies that were expanding throughout the USA in the 1930s, 1940s, and 1950s.[4]

During this same period, we notice a change in the assortment of products available at community pharmacies. Through World War II (1939–1945), independently owned community pharmacies carried in inventory as many of the needs identified in that neighborhood. Housewives preserved fruits and vegetables at the harvest time and consequently, pharmacies sold the bottles and seals used in this process. Similarly, women and girls made some of their own clothing, so pharmacies sold dress patterns, cloth, sewing supplies, and ribbon. In those years black and white television was introduced using lightbulb-like tubes prior to the invention of transistors and chips. Persons carrying a big bag very carefully could be identified as heading to the tube tester machine at the pharmacy to test their tubes, hoping to find a faulty one and thereby avoid a costly service call from the TV repair person.

Using the concept of mimicking the chain stores, independents resisted their incursions into the marketplace. For example, chain stores featured and promoted store brands that would compete with the nationally known brand-name products. The independents in the buying groups and voluntary advertising cooperatives did the same thing, and thereby offered patrons the choice of the advertised, branded product or a lower priced equivalent that would have to be replaced at one of the cooperative member shops.

As chain stores began to dominate certain markets in the 1950s and 1960s, state boards of pharmacy, which were dominated by independent community pharmacy owners, attempted to introduce legislation and regulations that would serve as hurdles or barriers for the chain stores.

One argument was the requirement that a pharmacy must be owned by a licensed pharmacist, which gained little or no traction since the chains offered to appoint a responsible supervising pharmacist for each location, even though that individual might not be an owner of the corporation. As we all know, the chain stores prevailed and during the ensuing 50 years, have grown enormously to where they command more than 50 percent of the retail pharmacy market in the USA today. After a number of mergers, purchases, and other consolidations there are three enormous chains—Walgreens with over 8,000 stores, CVS with over 6,000 stores, and RiteAid with another 6,000

stores—which dominate the retail pharmacy scene. In addition there are hundreds of smaller chains and many thousands of successfully operated independent community pharmacies.[5]

Typically, the chain-owned pharmacies were giant compared to the square footage of much smaller independents. To fill this space, we began to see large school supplies sections, and the pharmacies began to sell convenience foods and dairy products, toys and gifts, auto parts, tools, housewares, leisure-time goods and sports equipment, magazines and books, minor appliances such as clocks, radios, toasters, irons, picnic and party supplies, luggage, and even sickroom supplies such as crutches, walkers, wheelchairs, and canes.

In neighborhoods populated by seniors, one might find magnifying eyeglasses, adult diapers, and a wider selection of supplements and herbal products. In neighborhoods with a younger clientele with new families, there would be baby foods, infant formula, cribs, strollers, playpens and diapers of every description. More affluent locations had fancier cameras, recorded music, and pricier toys. Less affluent locations featured generic brands to save money and might accept utility payments and issue money orders for customers without checking accounts.

Competition

It was the chain stores that brought professional or scientific management to the retail pharmacy sector. Most of the chain pharmacies are publicly owned corporations and therefore are required to report just about every aspect of their commercial operations to their shareholders and the investment community as well as to the Securities and Exchange Commission (SEC) of the federal government.

Now we are able to learn about sales by category, rents and all of the other expenses of a chain pharmacy. Other pharmacies can compare their operations and benchmark them against the more successful market entrants, and employ the analyses that the largest and most successful corporations are using to modify their price policies, promotional strategies and product mix, among numerous other variables. The era of scientific management had arrived.[6]

Now in the second decade of the twenty-first century even the smallest, most remote pharmacy in northern Maine or in rural New Mexico has the ability to examine its return on investment per square foot of selling space, just as the giant chains undertake this effort. A valuable tool that was used widely through the 1980s was the *Lilly Digest*. This financial tool was sponsored by the Eli Lilly Company every year and community pharmacists could submit their operating information and receive an analysis of their operation conducted by skilled accountants and others. The information was de-identified and aggregated and Lilly representatives distributed the annual report to community pharmacists.

With the help of this resource, pharmacists had the ability to compare their expense for rent or any other expense category with a large number of similar pharmacies in similar sales and situational categories. In the most recent years, the digest has been published by other pharmaceutical manufacturers and, unfortunately, is used by far fewer pharmacies and therefore the data available to pharmacists is of much less value.[7]

The marketplace

In 2012 there are about 60,000 community pharmacies in the USA. Chain stores represent slightly less than half of this number although in dollar sales, they lead.

Many if not most stores are open 24 hours a day, 7 days per week. Such operating hours create serious stresses to a community pharmacy, since clearly there is not a high volume of prescription business after midnight at most locations. These opening hours require at least three full-time pharmacists for staffing purposes, which adds to the overhead of that pharmacy. For the last 30 years, the number of independent community pharmacies has been declining, with a slow but continuous growth in the number of chain operations. In the most recent years, it appears as though the situation is stable and that existing well-located community independent pharmacies will be viable for the foreseeable future (Figure 1.1).

Just when the independent community pharmacists and the chain pharmacy owners thought that they had arrived at a period of tranquility and stability, supermarket and mail service pharmacies gained popularity. Supermarket pharmacies actually make a great deal of sense since the patient may leave the prescription at the pharmacy counter, conduct their shopping and later return to pick up the dispensed

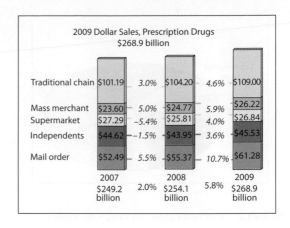

Figure 1.1 2009 Dollar sales, prescription drugs, $268.9 billion. (Source: Adapted from 2010 World Drug Market Report, IMS Health, Towanda, NJ.)

medication without having to drive anywhere else or park the car for a second time.

Mail service pharmacy has grown enormously over the last few years for two major reasons. First, it adds even further to the convenience, since a prescription can be sent to a mail order address and the medication will be received in one's mailbox several days later. The second driving force is the requirement that certain medications used for maintenance of chronic conditions must be dispensed by participating mail service pharmacies in certain managed care or other health insurance programs. Mail service continues to be a rapidly growing trend.

In order to compete and maintain profitability, community pharmacies of all types and ownerships must become prudent purchasers, discerning cost cutters and efficiency experts and skilled marketers, in addition to remaining up-to-date clinical practitioners. The competition has now increased with the sale of OTC drugs, vitamins and supplements, cosmetics and fragrances available at department stores, specialty stores, convenience stores, gift shops and hotels and restaurant cashier counters, numerous mail order and websites among numerous other types of purveyors (Figure 1.2).

By making shrewd decisions and maintaining a careful and thorough vigilance on sales and cost figures, a community pharmacy manager should be able to steer his or her operation to minimum costs while expanding sales and profit numbers. "How is this done?" one might ask, and the answer lies in paying

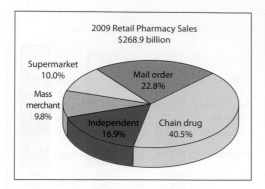

Figure 1.2 2009 Retail pharmacy sales, $268.9 billion. (Source: Adapted from 2010 World Drug Market Report, IMS Health, Towanda, NJ.)

attention to every aspect of community pharmacy operation. For example, employees should be carefully trained and observed with feedback provided to the new hire. In addition, the use of automation and robotics has increased as a cost-cutting effort. And the use of technicians and other para-professionals further helps to contain costs.

Incentives should be provided for pharmacy personnel who are especially cordial and responsive to patient needs and requests. Similarly, management should frequently observe any change in the patterns or mix of sales. If there is an increase in the sale of diapers or baby foods, this is a clue that one may choose to expand the array and variety of products for infants and children. If, on the other hand, the sales of greeting cards decline because of the increasing use of email, the pharmacy manager should consider replacing some of the floor space in the card department with other merchandise. Promotional and marketing programs should be monitored and tested, with the successful ones being repeated and the less successful ones being discarded. Doing all of this does not guarantee a successful pharmacy operation because there is no end point. The marketplace and the environment as well as technology and the overall economy will always continue to present challenges which must be met by a well-informed manager acting prudently. For example, since the 1970s, pharmacists have been allowed to dispense a generic version of a drug instead of the specified brand product, unless the physician expressly prohibits it. The pharmacist should know which patients might appreciate the cost savings of a generic drug.

International healthcare comparisons

Community pharmacies exist to serve the medicine and pharmaceutical counseling needs of ambulatory patients, a statement which is true throughout the world. However, the means that different countries go about fulfilling these needs varies greatly. Canada, the USA, and a small number of other countries permit pharmacies to be established at any location where the prospective community pharmacy owner chooses to establish a licensed community pharmacy.

Throughout most of the developed world, Ministries of Health award community pharmacy licenses based upon distance or population criteria. For example, in nearly all of the countries of Western Europe, one may apply for a license to open a pharmacy if one can demonstrate a need for community pharmacy services by a minimum of 5,000 unserved or underserved residents. This would permit new pharmacies to be established only in new suburban residential developments or in center cities where new apartments add to the existing population density. Some countries require a metric more easily measured: a minimum distance of 500 m (approx. 500 yards) from the nearest existing community pharmacy. Governments know of the temptation to cut corners and act unprofessionally when pharmacies are located too close to each other, permitting none of them to earn a decent profit.

In most of those same Western European countries, there is a single payor financing system, where the wholesale and retail prices are established along with the granting of Food and Drug Administration (FDA) marketing authority. This means that all pharmacies will charge the identical payment or co-payment for a drug product. Since the prices are identical, this encourages pharmacies to compete on the basis of the extent and quality of professional services.

Pharmacies offer other services as the traditions and customs in each country dictate. Some pharmacies offer clinical analysis services for cholesterol testing, pregnancy determination, blood glucose testing, etc. Pharmacists in England make house calls to deliver tanks of oxygen, and in earlier times some "chemist shops" performed refractions for eye glasses. This last function is rarely found in 2012. Pharmacies in Germany and in Northern Europe maintained a chemical laboratory in the back of the store where analysis was supposed to be conducted on ingredients purchased by that pharmacy for compounding purposes. These days, most pharmacists trust the quality control activities mandated by the regulatory authorities, and that lab is used as a meeting or lunch room.

Rules in those countries set the range of merchandise sold in various types of retail outlets. For example, pharmacies may sell medications, first aid supplies, some limited cosmetics and health and beauty products. Other types of stores can sell anything but only a very restricted selection of OTC drugs, often limited to the cough and cold, constipation and fever areas.

Recent developments

We are in the midst of important changes affecting pharmacy practice through the community pharmacy. Most of these changes are recent, occurring between 1990 and today, but the first evidence of the profession flexing its muscle happened in the 1970s when pharmacists demanded the right to substitute an FDA-approved generic drug in place of a prescribed brand-name product. Such state "anti-substitution" laws were eventually overturned in all of the USA and territories/districts. It was a battle between the powerful pharmaceutical industry and local community pharmacy associations that played out in the individual states. In some jurisdictions, this was permissible only if there were monetary savings to the patient, while in others the patient and/or physician had to approve of the change.

Today, pharmacists offer generics to patients to save them money and also usually to gain a greater profit. After the 20-year patent period for drugs, these generics become available. Most drugs are on the market for about 12 or more years before generic competition arises. While the patent was granted for 20 years, the first years had the drug awaiting regulatory approval. This translates into the pharmacist being able to tell a patient that any drug on the market is deemed by the FDA to be safe and effective.

More recently, with the support of the American Pharmacists Association (APhA), the major professional society for all types of pharmacists, and schools of pharmacy, pharmacists have gained the right to administer immunization injections to patients. Several progressive states went first, followed by a gradual number of other states, and the final 10 states took

many more years to be convinced as to the safety of the proposal and the obvious cost-benefit numbers, not to mention convenience and accessibility.

At isolated practices, mostly in smaller towns, we have seen local community pharmacists enter into joint practice agreements with local primary care physicians, where the community pharmacist is authorized to dispense refill medications and to modify the dosage within certain pre-specified parameters. Hypertension control is a good example of this type of practice cooperation.

From the usually brief consultation at the time of dispensing, some community pharmacists have pioneered a service referred to as "medication therapy management," where the patient makes an appointment for 45–60 minutes (usually) and brings all of his or her prescribed and OTC drugs, and other herbals and supplements. The pharmacist reviews the need for each item and its potential for interactions with the others, checks to determine whether each product is still needed today, and finally adjusts the daily medication schedule to maximize favorable outcomes and to minimize the possibility for adverse events and other problems. Sometimes, a call to the patient's physician is called for, to request authorization for a therapy change from one drug to another within the same therapeutic category. An "ARB" for an "ACE inhibitor" to stop a drug-induced cough might be a typical scenario. Medicaid, Medicare, and some private insurers will pay a fee for such services upon being invoiced in the proper format.

Other demonstrations and pilot studies are ongoing for the community pharmacy-based pharmacy practitioner to pursue additional efforts to enhance patient compliance with prescribed medication regimens, to counsel and educate patients about the administration and storage of products and in the use of less-commonly used dosage forms, such as metered dose inhalers, suppositories, self-injections, ostomy care, and wound care.

In the United Kingdom, the community pharmacies negotiate their dispensing fees, payment structure and other professional policies through a non-governmental organization, the Pharmaceutical Services Negotiating Committee (PSNC), which negotiates with the Ministry of Health on behalf of all British community pharmacies. One of the foundations for a basic payment for each pharmacy is a fee for the provision of education and advice to persons located adjacent to the practice. This public health function to endorse and educate on screening, prevention and wellness is seen as a valuable service, giving people the opportunity to seek help without the necessity of an appointment and without the need for a purchase, with the assumption that it might eliminate the need for some number of general practitioner physician visits.

Future developments

Community pharmacists and their professional associations have been advocating for a third class of drugs to be sold only in pharmacies. As is generally known, in the USA, there are presently two categories of drugs: *OTC*, which may be sold via any outlet including vending machines, door-to-door, mail service and at a wide array of retail establishments, and *prescribed drugs* sold only in pharmacies. The decision of whether a product may be sold OTC or only by prescription is made by the US Food and Drug Administration. As the movement of some long-available and safely used prescription drugs to OTC status continues, pharmacy groups have posited the opinion that these "switched" drugs might be sold OTC only in pharmacies for a limited period until their safe, unsupervised use may be validated in practice. The temporary period of 2 years is often mentioned.

Increasingly, new drug launches are in the biotechnology category. These agents are peptides or proteins that must be injected because they would not maintain their effectiveness through oral administration. So cancer patients and others, including osteoporosis, rheumatoid arthritis, and hemophilia patients requiring frequent injections could receive those injections at the community pharmacy conveniently and inexpensively.

Specialization

Most community pharmacies are very much like the general practitioner physician, open to all patients without knowing what the next patient might need, from head to toe. In recent years there have sprung up a small number of specialized pharmacies. This is an intriguing concept with a high probability of further development and success in certain circumstances. There are some pharmacies that serve long-term care facilities and hospices where common oral dosage forms are converted into syrups or elixirs for those

with swallowing difficulties, or where high concentrations of opiate narcotics are prepared for pain relief in terminal patients. For many years, community pharmacies located at or near pediatric hospitals have learned how to make pediatric dosage forms even when they are not commercially available. The same situation is present for women's hospitals and orthopedic and cancer treatment hospitals with nearby pharmacies.

Other community pharmacies have chosen to specialize in compounding, in veterinary pharmacy practice, in dealing with ostomies and with post-trauma care with a huge array of bandaging supplies, tapes, gauze and related products.

The ultimate control of home health is still not decided. Some non-pharmacy firms do this as well as some specialized community pharmacies that deliver injectable drugs for chemotherapy, total parenteral nutrition (TPN), post-surgical antibiotic treatment, among others. We can expect that some pharmacies will specialize in this space and gain market recognition via contracts with home health and visiting nurse organizations.

Every city has a certain pharmacy that is *the* place to go for sickroom supplies due to its knowledgeable staff and outstanding product selection. Surely, there has to be room for more of such pharmacies, especially considering that sicker patients are being discharged sooner and sooner due to managed care organization pricing pressures at hospitals.

Access to information

The last topic in this section to be mentioned probably holds the greatest level of opportunity for community pharmacies. With the near total use of electronic medical records (EMR) within the next few years, the community-based pharmacist will finally have access to lab values and other more extensive patient clinical information to be used in making clinical decisions and providing better, more precise, knowledge-based recommendations to patients.

It is hoped that the pharmacist will be able to see what medications were used during hospitalizations, and what medicines were dispensed at other community pharmacies in the past. Clearly, superior guidance is possible with this information at the community pharmacist's finger tips. With this information available real-time and recent pharmacy graduates having an excellent clinically focused education, one may expect the community pharmacist of the future to venture more opinions and to provide more advice to patients of practical value.

Forecasting the future is a most difficult task, and even so-called experts would not get good grades for accuracy most of the time. We still do not have the weather-controlled bubble-covered cities that were predicted 100 years ago or the jet cars to avoid road congestion suggested 50 years ago, What we do know with certainty is that the community pharmacy of 20 years from now will be very different from what we know as a community pharmacy today. But that poses no problem for a skilled manager.

The skills, areas of importance, and evaluative tools will very likely remain the same, even if the pharmacies are dispensing and selling new technologies of therapeutics unthought-of today. Our financial analysis tools, our location analysis tools, and good human resource (HR) skills will carry us through then as they will today. The greeting cards and photo labs may go the way of the soda fountain, but there will be merchandise to replace them that will require purchasing, placement and pricing expertise.

Retail store management can be fun and exciting as well as challenging and problematic. But as one becomes more experienced and skilled in using the tools available to a community pharmacy manager, the task becomes easier and more predictable. The following chapters provide a most thorough review of the various topics requiring internalization by a successful manager, whether in pharmacy or in the operation of a restaurant or any type of other merchant activity.

Summary

- British trained pharmacists were the original pharmacists in the USA. They taught younger persons through the apprenticeship method.
- The need for standardization and sustainability resulted in the first pharmacy schools.
- Chain pharmacies developed in the mid-1900s and were resisted by independent store owners.
- Chains proved their equality and exist safely today.
- Economies of scale now favor the chain store for profitability and success.
- Today, nearly all medications are prefabricated in factories.

- Pharmacists are paid via a fixed professional dispensing fee.
- Automation and the use of paraprofessionals have kept costs low.
- Pharmacy accounts for about 10 percent of total annual health expenditures.

Questions for discussion

1 What was the argument against chain/corporate-owned pharmacies?
2 Why did chains win that battle?
3 Is it good or bad that pharmacy consumes nearly 10 percent of the health budget?
4 How can pharmacists widen their role in the marketplace?
5 Should OTC drugs be sold only in pharmacies as is the case in much of the rest of the world?
6 What features in European community pharmacy might be beneficial if adopted in the USA?

Self-test review

True/false statements

1 Independent pharmacies welcomed chain pharmacies.
2 There is evidence that chain pharmacy practice is of a lower quality.
3 The earliest pharmacy schools were in California.
4 The official compendia led to an end to compounding errors.
5 Independent, small neighborhood pharmacies are the trend for the future.
6 Pharmacists must dispense branded drugs if the doctor writes for a specific brand.
7 The patent period for drugs is 20 years.
8 After the first 12 years, generic drugs can come on the market.
9 Someday in the future, pharmacists will give immunizations and other injections.
10 The US Food and Drug Administration guarantees that all drugs on the market are safe and effective.

Multiple choice questions

1 The first pharmacy school was located in

(A) Nevada.

(B) Montana.

(C) Pennsylvania.

(D) Oklahoma.

(E) Idaho.

2 In colonial times students apprenticed with a pharmacist for

(A) Three months.

(B) Six months.

(C) Nine months.

(D) Twelve months.

(E) Until the preceptor thought the student was ready.

3 A growing trend is

(A) Use of branded products.

(B) Home delivery of drugs.

(C) Mail service pharmacy.

(D) In-pharmacy compounding.

(E) Mini photo labs in pharmacies.

4 The major professional society for all pharmacists is the:

(A) National Pharmacists Assocation.

(B) American Pharmacists Association.

(C) Society of Professional Pharmacists.

(D) National Druggists Guild.

(E) Academy of Licensed Pharmacists.

5 The decision of whether a drug product is OTC or requires a doctor's prescription is made by:

(A) Federal Trade Commission.

(B) Food and Drug Administration.

(C) US Justice Department.

(D) Pharmaceutical Manufacturers Association.

(E) The World Health Organization.

References

1. Sonnedecker, Glenn (Ed.) *Kremers and Urdang's History of Pharmacy*, 4th edn. Philadelphia: JB Lippincott, 1976.
2. Smith MC and Knapp DA. *Pharmacy, Drugs and Medical Care*, 3rd edn. Baltimore: Williams and Wilkins, 1981.
3. Fincham JE and Wertheimer AI. *Pharmacy and the US Health Care System*, 2nd edn. Binghamton, NY: Pharmaceutical Products Press, 1998.
4. Smith MC and Worthen D. *The Rexall Story: A history of genius and neglect*, Binghamton, NY: Pharmaceutical Products Press, 2004.
5. National Association of Chain Drug Stores. www.NACDS.org.
6. US Securities and Exchange Commission. www.sec.gov.
7. Varnell, M (Ed.) *Lilly Digest*, Indianapolis: Eli Lilly and Co., 1991.

2

The role of business in pharmacy practice

Learning objectives

The objectives of this chapter are to assist you to be able to explain:

- the misconceptions about the role of business in pharmacy practice
- why a business perspective is important
- challenges for community and hospital pharmacies
- how to integrate different managerial functions
- the functional areas of business.

Key terms

Accounting function
Controlling
Directing
Finance function
Human resources
Human resource management function
Input–output system
Marketing function
Material resources
Monetary resources
Operations management function
Organizing
Planning
Remaining competitive
Staffing
Utilization of resources

Changes in the demography of the USA

Many factors have helped to bring about an evolution in the practice of pharmacy. Among the more important ones from a business perspective are the changes in the demography of the USA, healthcare usage and providers, and attitudes toward the traditional role of the pharmacist and pharmacy.

One of the most important factors affecting modern healthcare is the changing demography of the USA. Most notably, there has been a massive distortion of the age distribution of the population, a general aging of the population, and a changing racial composition.

Age distribution of the population

The effects of the "baby boom" period following World War II coupled with the "birth dearth" in the early 1970s, when fertility rates declined dramatically, caused a pronounced shift in age distributions. The effect has often been called a "pig in a python," similar to what happens to the shape of a large snake after it swallows a whole pig. As the pig moves through the snake's body, it distorts the shape of the snake in much the same manner as the baby boom group has altered the demography of the USA as it moves through its life cycle.

The change in the distribution of the population can be seen in Table 2.1. The 25- to 44-year-old age group is declining as a percentage of the total population starting from 1990, while 45 and older is increasing as baby boomers move through this category.

For pharmacy managers, it is difficult not to target the baby boom group as it heads toward senior status. No doubt, it will be a major concern for businesses and insurance companies in their formulation of policies for payment of their prescription drug costs. As described later in this chapter, the costs of healthcare have grown significantly in recent decades, and as more of the baby boomers begin to reach age 65, drug costs and usage could skyrocket. Pharmacies can expect a restructuring of their payment systems as government and the private sector try to cope.

Additional implications of the distortion of the demography are the fact that healthcare services will be refocused on the 45- to 65-year-old age group. The types of services and products they need will take on greater importance with the sheer increase in numbers of people. Competition among pharmacies for their business will become more intense, not only because of the immediate dollar potential but because loyalties developed now may extend into a time when the baby boomers become seniors.

The aging of the population

The aging, or "graying," of America is also quite evident. Within the population group aged 65 or more years, those 80 and older are making up a larger percentage. This is shown in Table 2.2. From 1980 through the year 2009, the percentage who are 85 or older increased from 8.8 to 14.2 percent.

People are living longer, and this aging process is expected to continue further. As shown in Table 2.3, life expectancies for both females and males have risen by 8.6 years from 1970 to 2010, and are expected to increase even more by the year 2020.

As would be expected, the healthcare implications of this are quite significant. Seniors have more and different needs for health services than do other members of the population. They visit physician offices more frequently, require more hospital stays, use more prescription and non-prescription drugs, and have a greater number of multiple medical problems.

In addition, seniors require different services. Many have hearing or sight impairments, diminished cognitive skills, are physically limited, etc. A community pharmacy targeting an elderly market, for example, may need wider aisles, larger signs, improved

Table 2.1 Age distribution of the US population

Age group	Unit	1980	%	2000	%	2005	%	2009	%
	1,000	226,546	100	282,172	100	295,753	100	307,007	100
9 years and under	1,000	33,048	14.6	39,679	14.1	40,116	13.6	41,909	13.7
10–24 years	1,000	60,729	26.8	60,022	21.3	63,038	21.3	63,051	20.5
25–44 years	1,000	62,716	27.7	84,995	30.1	83,257	28.2	83,096	27.1
45–64 years	1,000	44,503	19.6	62,402	22.1	72,638	24.6	79,379	25.9
65 years and older	1,000	25,550	11.3	35,074	12.4	36,704	12.4	39,571	12.9
Median age	Years	30.0		35.4		36.2		36.8	

From US Census Bureau. *Statistical Abstract of the United States: 2011. Resident Population by Sex and Age: 1980 to 2009.*

Table 2.2 Population age 65 years and older

Age group	Unit	1980	%	2000	%	2005	%	2009	%
65–74 years	1,000	15,581	61.0	18,375	52.4	18,666	50.9	20,792	52.5
75–84 years	1,000	7,729	30.3	12,429	35.4	13,176	35.9	13,148	33.2
85 years and over	1,000	2,240	8.8	4,271	12.2	4,862	13.2	5,631	14.2
TOTAL		25,550		35,074		36,704		39,571	

From US Census Bureau. *Statistical Abstract of the United States: 2011. Resident Population by Sex and Age: 1980 to 2009.*

Table 2.3 Life spans

Year	Total	Male	Female
1970	70.8	67.1	74.7
1980	73.7	70.0	77.4
1990	75.4	71.8	78.8
2000	76.8	74.1	79.3
2005	77.4	74.9	79.9
2010	78.3	75.7	80.8
2020 (projection)	79.5	77.1	81.9

From US Census Bureau. *Statistical Abstract of the United States: 2011. Resident Population Projections by Race, Hispanic-Origin Status, and Age: 2010 and 2015.*

lighting, and a staff that understands how to cope with the mannerisms of seniors. Similarly, the types of prescription drugs and non-prescription products are different from those needed to care for a younger group of patients. And pharmacies in the future will likely target more of their efforts and resources on the over-65 market.

Changing racial composition of the population

A third major change that is taking place within the American population is the shift in racial composition. Non-White populations are expected to grow rapidly, and much of the growth within the "White" category is Hispanic. This can be seen in Table 2.4.

The implications of the changing racial composition of the marketplace are quite pronounced. For some groups, there are differences in culture, language, and product and service needs. Historically, however, it has not been economically feasible for pharmacies to target their efforts partly or completely on a particular ethnic group. In the next several decades, however, some ethnic groups will be sufficiently large and geographically concentrated that it will become financially attractive to do so. This means, for example, ensuring that pharmacy staff can speak a language other than English, the pharmacy carries non-prescription merchandise that is desired by the particular ethnic group, and signage in the pharmacy is in a second language.

Aside from the possible growth of specialty pharmacies, nearly all community and hospital pharmacies need to become more attuned to unique cultures, languages, etc. Having staff that can speak Spanish or some dialects of Chinese, carrying a range of non-prescription merchandise used predominantly by an ethnic group, and understanding a group's attitudes toward the administration of drug products is

of those resources would be achieved when organizations fought among themselves. If this were to occur, he reasoned, only those organizations which operated efficiently would be able to survive.

This laissez faire doctrine has had far-reaching implications. If an organization, whether public or private, could not become efficient from a cost-benefit standpoint, and appeal to a sufficiently large group of people, it had no right to exist.

While a free-for-all fight among organizations does not exist, the fact remains that they must compete for the nation's precious human, financial, and material resources. Thus, individual community pharmacies, hospitals, skilled nursing facilities, and the rest, must fight for their survival. Inefficient organization wastes resources which could be put to better use by other pharmacies, hospitals, or other organizations.

How does an organization become efficient? How can it fight for its share of the available resources? This is the role of business and professional management.

Utilization of resources

A business focus helps to utilize the pharmacy's monetary, human, and material resources in an effective way. In the high-cost and highly competitive environment that exists, there is little room for waste and error. For example, an average independent pharmacy in 2010 generated 26.8 percent gross profit (i.e. net sales minus costs of goods sold). With operating and other expenses reaching 23.9 percent, it leaves profit before taxes on the level of 2.9 percent of net sales.[2] If costs rise by 3.0 percent, all profits would be lost. As shown in Table 2.6, this margin was relatively stable over time.

Financial figures for hospital inpatient pharmacies are not readily available. However, hospital profits over the years have also remained on modest level. An average hospital in 2010 generated a profit before taxes of 5.2 percent of net sales.[2] The margins, although somewhat higher than in the case of community pharmacies, are still thin. As described later in this chapter, the functional aspects of business help pharmacies to improve revenues, control costs, and monitor operating performances. Through the use of business tools, specific activities that are not operating profitably can be examined to determine if they can be

corrected before the pharmacy's survival is placed in jeopardy.

Remaining competitive and adapting to change

A business perspective centers on the ability of the pharmacy to compete. Every pharmacy faces competition for patients and resources. In community settings, pharmacies must fight for their share of the market. In hospitals, directors of pharmacy must compete with other organizational units for shares of the budget.

Through carefully developed marketing efforts, the pharmacy can show its "customers" (e.g. patients, hospital administrators, hospital boards of trustees) the benefits of its services. Since customers have so many choices for how and where they spend their funds, pharmacies must take the initiative in demonstrating their values.

Equally important, a business focus helps the pharmacy keep abreast of changes occurring in the environment, such as those shown in Table 2.7. Social and cultural shifts, changes in law, technological advances, shifts in economic conditions, and other variables can be monitored and assessed through a business framework. Pharmacy practice does not operate in a vacuum. As the world changes, the profession must adapt if it is to remain useful.

Deciding on roles for pharmacists

As the role of the pharmacy has changed over the past decade, so too has that of the pharmacist. During the last part of the twentieth century and early part of the twenty-first century, there have been evolutions in the profession, in the pharmacist's position within the healthcare delivery system, and in the pharmacist's role within the community. Each of these has affected the way pharmacists view their positions and the activities they engage in on a day-to-day basis.

Evolution of the profession

The pharmacy profession has made several transitions since the seventeenth century. At times, the pharmacist has been a primary source of medical information and products. The pharmacist was looked upon as a

Table 2.6 Trends in pharmacy profitability

Percentage of net sales	2006	2007	2008	2009	2010
Gross profit	25.8	24.9	26.0	25.2	26.8
Operating expenses	23.2	22.6	23.9	22.7	23.7
Other expenses	0.2	0.1	0.3	0.2	0.2
Profit before taxes	2.3	2.2	1.7	2.2	2.9

Data from RMA's *Annual Statement Studies, 2010–2011*.[2]

Table 2.7 Environmental forces affecting the practice of pharmacy

Environmental force	Components
Competition	Chain
	Independent
	Mail order
	Physician dispensing
	Alternative therapy (e.g. surgery)
Demographics of possible patients	Age, gender, income, employment
Geographic location	
Economic conditions	Employment
	Inflation
	Savings
Healthcare coverage	Extent of coverage
	Private pay
	Health maintenance organization
	Capitation
	Discounted fee for service
Political/legal environment	Federal and state licensing requirements
	Food and Drug Administration regulations
	Drug Enforcement Administration regulations
	Healthcare Financing Administration payment schedules
	State payment schedules
Social attitudes towards healthcare	Self-diagnosis
	Trust in providers
	Trust in healthcare services
	Preferences for delivery system
Social attitudes towards medications	Brand-name vs. generic drugs
	Self-medication
Technology	Biotech drugs
	Computer systems for delivery
Methods of claims verification and processing	Methods for monitoring patient care

healthcare specialist who often was more accessible than the physician. And the pharmacist's expertise in compounding medications was critical to good healthcare.

From being a key adviser in healthcare matters, the pharmacist at times has assumed more of a role of a provider of products than a provider of professional services. During much of the twentieth century, for example, payments to the pharmacist were based on the provision of product—prescription drugs—to patients. Pharmacists were not compensated for their expertise. They were considered to be persons who would "count and pour, lick and stick."

During the early part of the 1990s, however, a transformation began to take place. This was the result of the high costs of healthcare, the growing complexity of products, potentials for drug interaction, incidents of prescription errors, and other factors. The profession was looked to as a means of controlling the costs of care. These included point-of-sale activities to make generic substitutions when such actions would prove to be therapeutically appropriate and cost-effective, identification of possible drug interactions, intervention when it was proper not to dispense a prescription suspected to be erroneous, and monitoring patient drug therapy, and consulting with patients about their drug therapies.

As a result, the pharmacist's knowledge of clinical drug therapy became a more critical component of the healthcare delivery system. Many of those involved in healthcare services, such as insurance companies and employers, recognized that pharmacists were in a key position to affect patient outcomes. Their knowledge of drug therapy plus their position at the point of service refocused the profession on the clinical aspects of practice.

To help make this possible, technicians were allowed to assist in the prescription-filling function. The concept was to free the pharmacist of routine and repetitive activities, and provide more time and opportunity to engage in the more professional activities in which he or she was trained.

These efforts served to return to the profession a major role in healthcare delivery. By separating the provision of products from the provision of professional expertise, the profession was elevated. The movement toward medication therapy management (MTM) has been advanced because of this.

The role of pharmacists as healthcare professionals

In the early years of pharmacy practice, the pharmacist was responsible for much of the manufacture and dispensing of medicines. Many products were compounded, and the pharmacist's role was to ensure that proper medications were produced.

Over the years, the role of the pharmacist in the manufacture of prescription drugs has diminished significantly. There are relatively few instances where compounding is necessary. Repackaging medications into smaller units that coincide with appropriate days of therapy has grown but not at an exceptionally rapid rate, even though the population is aging.

There are some areas in which the pharmacist's role in the preparation of medications is still highly significant. Examples are the preparation of intravenous (IV) solutions for home healthcare and the creation of unit doses in skilled nursing facilities and hospital settings.

While the role of the pharmacist in the manufacture of medications may have diminished somewhat over the centuries, other roles have taken its place. As the complexity of products has grown, especially with the advent of biotech drugs, the pharmacist's knowledge of drugs and drug therapy has become more important in healthcare delivery. The same is true as more powerful drugs are converted from prescription to over-the-counter status. In some respects, then, the pharmacist has become more of a specialist who is valued for technical knowledge of drug therapy.

This also can temper the tremendous amount of information available over the Internet. As people increasingly seek information about medical care and medicines, the pharmacist can provide a professional level of expertise needed to adapt the information to individual situations.

As drugs become more complex in both their form and usage, it is likely that the role of the pharmacist as a healthcare professional will continue to grow. Both physicians and patients will need the expertise pharmacists can provide to ensure correct initial drug therapy, continued compliance, appropriate monitoring, and satisfactory therapeutic outcomes.

The role of the pharmacist within the community

Historically, pharmacists have maintained a high degree of respect within their communities. In consumer polls, the pharmacist consistently has been rated among the most, if not the most, respected professional.

There are a variety of reasons for this. First, the pharmacist is one of the most accessible healthcare professionals. Pharmacists can be reached either in person or by telephone, and appointments have not been needed.

Second, they tend to be able to converse with patients on the patient's level. Pharmacists have experience in consulting with patients about medications, and can focus on the major issues of concern to patients (e.g. drug administration, side-effects).

Third, historically, they have not charged directly for their services. Patients believe they can ask questions of the pharmacist without being charged a fee—unlike physicians who are expected to charge for advice. This has both positive and negative implications since charging for such services as MTM has met with resistance.

Fourth, pharmacists tend to be less intimidating to patients than physicians. Patients are more comfortable in retail stores than in the physician's office, and it is not usually the pharmacist who provides the patient with bad news.

Finally, pharmacists are viewed as being members of the community to a greater extent than are other healthcare professionals. They are perceived to be both healthcare professionals and business people and employees. This makes pharmacists closer to being "regular" people who live and work within the community.

In the future, this role of the pharmacist within the community is likely to change. To the extent that pharmacists become more involved in point-of-sale activities such as MTM, intervention, consultation, monitoring, and so on, their professional activities will take on added emphasis. This will serve to alter the "regular people" perception of pharmacists. The pharmacist may be the bearer of bad news, and have more authority over the healthcare that is provided.

In addition, as payments for cognitive services increase in usage, the public perception of pharmacists will change. To the extent that patients are personally charged for cognitive services, economic barriers to accessibility will arise. Patients will no longer feel free to seek advice, and the view that pharmacists are "out to make money" is likely to grow. Overall, pharmacists will have to demonstrate the value of their advice, showing that the benefit patients receive from counseling is commensurate with the fee being charged.

The pharmacist as a clinical purist

Perhaps as a culmination of the other misconceptions, there are some who believe that a good pharmacist is one who focuses only on the clinical aspects of the profession. One reason for this perspective relates to the fact that the complexities of modern drug therapy do not allow time to be concerned about other matters. Another reason relates to questionable practices that have occurred.

As never before, pharmacists must understand the business and economic environments within which they work. Many aspects of clinical services are affected by these environments. In order to successfully practice pharmacy, the pharmacist must know how to operate within the constraints that are placed on modern healthcare by government, employers, insurance companies, and others. This applies to everything from understanding new healthcare regulations, making generic substitutions, to counseling patients on drug therapy compliance, to intervention, and to recommending companion over-the-counter products to counter minor side-effects of prescription drugs. In an era of cost management, a good pharmacist is one who can provide the best quality of care possible with the resources, and restraints, at hand.

Identifying the challenges for community pharmacies

This evolution of the profession creates both challenges and opportunities. The profession itself is not in danger, but its role in healthcare delivery is continually being redefined.

A business world orientation

Perhaps the most significant challenge facing pharmacists in all practice settings is accepting that they are operating in a business as well as a healthcare world. The days of "care at any cost" are gone and it is now "the business of healthcare."

In its place is the recognition that the USA cannot afford unrestricted healthcare. As distasteful as this may be, government and the private sector have come to believe that there must be some balance between the costs of care and its accessibility.

In community settings for both independent and chain pharmacies, decisions about what to offer, how much to charge, etc., are being made increasingly on a business basis. Indeed, the managers of many pharmacies are professional business people rather than healthcare professionals. Government and the private sector are simply unable and unwilling to support pharmacies in any practice setting that is operating inefficiently.

In hospital settings, administrators are professional managers who may or may not have healthcare backgrounds. Large hospital organizations are businesses that are guided by the economics as well as the clinical issues of healthcare. Within this context, the inpatient pharmacy is being viewed as a cost-conscious as well as a profit center. The attention it receives from administrators and boards of trustees will be directly related to how well the pharmacy can help the hospital increase its revenues or reduce its costs as well as improve patient outcomes.

Accordingly, the first challenge confronting pharmacists is to become more business-oriented. They need to understand the world of business and professional management. For employers, it will be absolutely essential if they are to remain competitive and viable. For employees, it will be absolutely essential if they are to cope well in their future working environments.

Challenges in community settings

In community settings, pharmacy owners and managers will face five major challenges in the early twenty-first century. These are revenue retention, preservation of market share, cost containment, legal considerations, and technological change.

Retaining revenues in an environment where the emphasis is on control over healthcare expenses will be a major challenge. The pressures to reduce reimbursement rates for prescription drug products and dispensing fees mean that pharmacies have to build volume. They can no longer rely on price increases and stable sales volume to bring more revenues into the pharmacy. The continued conversion of many prescription drugs to over-the-counter status may also influence the numbers of prescriptions being dispensed.

An offsetting consideration, of course, is the aging of the USA. Since the elderly tend to use more prescription drugs, this will help to support prescription volume. Nevertheless, pharmacies will continue to be confronted with the evolution from "low

volume, high margin," to "high volume, low margin" operations.

A second major challenge will be to preserve market share. Within this area are two major considerations. First, as competition continues to become more sophisticated, there will be added pressures on independent pharmacies to become better managed. Chain pharmacies often can afford to hire specialized managerial expertise in marketing, finance, human resource management, etc. Independent pharmacy owners and managers have to develop their own skills in these areas.

A second consideration in market share retention will be the exclusive and preferred provider networks that have evolved. Maintaining market share when contracts for services are provided to only a select few pharmacies (whether chains or independents) requires creative and sophisticated management skills.

A third challenge will be cost control. The profitability of any pharmacy will be highly dependent on controlling its costs of goods and operating expenses. As expensive new medications, such as biotech drugs, continue to come into the market, the pharmacy's management will be challenged to keep inventory costs to acceptable levels. In addition, it will be difficult to manage labor and other service-related costs while increasing the quality and amount of services provided to patients and physicians.

A fourth major challenge concerns potential legal problems. While pharmacists have always been held accountable for errors in dispensing, their expanded roles in the delivery of healthcare will increase their exposure. Patient counseling, MTM and other forms of patient monitoring, drug therapy, intervention, and managing technicians are but a few of the areas where legal issues can arise.

Finally, pharmacists will face the challenge of keeping up with a rapidly changing technology. The computerization of the dispensing function, much more complex drugs and their potential interactions and side-effects, on-line patient insurance verification, and claims adjudication are changing the world in which the pharmacist operates. The technological advances that might arise over the next 10–20 years may significantly alter the way in which drug therapy is made available. While this type of change has always been occurring, it tends to do so at an ever-accelerating pace.

Challenges in hospital settings

The challenges facing pharmacists in hospital settings are no less significant than those occurring in community settings. Some of the major challenges will be to remain effective and efficient in an eroding economic climate for hospitals, coping with hospital management that is more business-oriented, becoming more involved in assisting the hospital in strengthening its market position, controlling costs of goods and operating expenses, and gaining and retaining an acceptable share of the hospital's financial resources.

One of the more difficult challenges facing directors of pharmacy and staff pharmacists will be to remain focused and efficient if hospital profits continue to deteriorate. Opportunities to improve and expand the services of the pharmacy will be increasingly difficult to justify unless hospital pharmacists can demonstrate that their services can either generate additional revenues or reduce operating costs. Pharmacists in hospital settings may find it challenging to maintain the quality and volume of care under these conditions.

Closely related to this will be the challenge to work within a more business-oriented environment, and directly for business-oriented managers. While quality of care will remain an important consideration in daily operations, so too will the economic issues. In some instances, management will be focusing predominately on how the hospital can survive economically. Pharmacists will need to show how high quality of care and use of their professional services can contribute to this survival.

This need to contribute to the economic survival of the hospital may necessitate pharmacists being more actively involved in building the hospital's image and market share. Outreach programs, such as drug information and drug abuse lectures, can enhance the hospital's marketing efforts.

As in the case of pharmacists in community settings, there will be a major challenge to control operating costs. As costs of goods and labor rise, it will be difficult for the pharmacy to keep its expenses within budgetary limits—especially when budgets are likely to remain somewhat stable.

Finally, directors of pharmacy will face significant challenges to retain appropriate budgets for their operations. Hospital administrators will remain under continuous pressures to focus their attention on recruiting physicians and maintaining their affiliation, keeping the hospital's equipment and facilities technologically advanced, and maintaining a market presence.

Accordingly, a majority of hospital budgets will be allocated to these endeavors. A director of pharmacy will have to compete for funds with others who may be in better positions to have the administrator's attention. Demonstrating the contributions the pharmacy can make to the hospital's quality of care and its economic well-being will be critical.

How to integrate different managerial functions

Bringing all business functions together into a unified whole, and integrating them with the clinical activities of the pharmacy is a complex process. It requires a focused, organized effort that can be sustained over the long term. This is what "managing" a pharmacy is all about: bringing together all of the resources available and uniting them in such a way that, collectively, they achieve the goals of the pharmacy in the most efficient manner possible.

Managing an organization effectively is more difficult than it may initially seem. With limited resources, tradeoffs must be made in terms of how they will be used. Furthermore, given the uncertainties in the environment, it is hard to accurately project whether the use of the resources will achieve all that is intended. Finally, as was indicated earlier in the chapter, some activities tend to work in opposite directions (e.g. increasing sales while controlling costs).

As an example, again consider a community pharmacy that is trying to generate more sales, but this time wants to increase its cash position. To do this, it may lower prices in the hope of bringing in more patients to purchase private pay prescriptions and non-prescription merchandise. Telling people that prices have been lowered will take advertising, and there is an expense to that. Assuming that the advertising is successful—and there certainly are no guarantees that it will be—the pharmacy's volume increases. Accordingly, an additional part-time pharmacist and another sales clerk are hired to ensure that patients do not have to wait too long for service.

What has happened here? Sales have increased, but so have the costs of advertising, and wages and fringe benefits. If the pharmacy's lease is based on a percentage of sales, its rent also will rise. Since prices have been reduced, there is less gross profit on each sale—the difference between the selling price and the cost of the merchandise.

Will the incremental gross profit cover the additional expenses? The answer is maybe. But, what happens if most or all of these patients charge their purchases? The pharmacy has had to spend more dollars, but does not receive the inflow of cash until the patients, the private third-party payers, or the governmental agency pays. Is it possible for the pharmacy to find itself in a worse cash position than it had prior to doing this? The answer is yes.

A manager cannot always determine in advance what will be the final consequences of decisions pertaining to the activities of the pharmacy. But a very good manager will prepare plans, organize the resources at his or her disposal, staff the pharmacy in such a way as to bring together those persons with the talents necessary to achieve desired objectives, direct their activities, and control their actions. While management is as much an art as a science, many potential mistakes can be avoided if the process of managing is undertaken correctly. Thus, as shown in Table 2.8, planning, organizing, staffing, directing, and controlling form the core of the management process.

This text considers these management processes in this chapter. The business functions of accounting, finance, marketing, organizing and staffing, and operations management were used as the format for the remaining sections of this text.

Planning

The most critical element of the management process is planning. Without a business plan, the pharmacy's operations will have no purpose and no direction. As a result, it will be nearly impossible to achieve any efficiency in its daily activities.

As described in Chapter 4, developing a business plan can be a rather time-consuming and tedious process. What makes the planning process so difficult is the fact that it focuses on an unknown future. Planning for the next 1–3 years requires assumptions that may or may not come true. Despite this problem, however, plans establish a basic structure for guiding the pharmacy. Plans can be changed as conditions warrant, but part of the objective of a plan is to influence conditions and turn them to the pharmacy's advantage.

Planning requires the pharmacist to take an introspective look at the pharmacy's current strengths and weaknesses. It also requires an evaluation of the environment within which the pharmacy operates, and the strengths and weaknesses of its competitors.

Based on all of these and other considerations, the manager or owner will have to decide on a set of objectives. Given the state of the pharmacy's internal and external environments, what can and should it achieve? This decision should be made for both the short and long term, with achievement of the short-term objectives moving the pharmacy closer to its longer term goals.

The planning process is essential to pharmacies in all practice settings. For example, the manager of an inpatient pharmacy must assess what its resources are, and what the pharmacy is and is not capable of doing. How many prescriptions can it dispense per hour? To what extent are staff pharmacists available to counsel patients, physicians, and nurses? Does the pharmacy have adequate equipment to prepare complex medications for innovative drug therapies? With respect to the "competition," what other organizational units will be vying for the hospital's funds and space? What are the strengths and weaknesses of their arguments for additional funding or space? Based on all of these considerations, what should the pharmacy try to achieve for the next year, and for the next 3 years?

The most valuable part of business planning is the process itself. It forces the manager to examine a wide range of issues that tend not to be considered on a day-to-day basis. It also requires the manager to develop a set of strategies, using the business functions and clinical activities that can be put in place to achieve established goals.

Organizing

Once objectives have been established, and the resources of the pharmacy delineated, they must be organized in some fashion. Typically, this is done by identifying all of the tasks to be performed within the pharmacy, and then grouping them in some logical way. The process of organizing the pharmacy is described in Chapter 12.

There are, of course, many ways of organizing the financial, human, and material resources of the pharmacy. And no single organizational structure is

Table 2.8 The management process

Planning	Assess internal resources
	Establish goals
	Develop general policies and procedures
	Develop business strategies
Organizing	Identify tasks to be performed
	Arrange tasks in logical order
	Combine tasks into appropriate groups
	Assign employees to groups
	Designate employees to manage groups
	Provide authority and responsibility
	Define methods for evaluation, accountability
Staffing	Determine position to be filled
	Prepare job description
	Identify sources of potential applicants
	Search for applicants
	Interview applicants
	Select applicant(s)
	Orient new employee to job
	Train new employee
	Evaluate new employee's performance
Directing	Set personnel goals
	Establish work standards
	Develop leadership style
	Motivate personnel
	Train and retrain personnel
	Evaluate personnel
	Discipline and dismiss personnel as necessary
	Promote personnel
Controlling	Establish points for periodic monitoring of pharmacy
	Measure pharmacy performance
	Examine strategies and recommend changes as appropriate
	Develop annual performance measurement
	Evaluate annual performance of pharmacy

best for all pharmacies. Much depends on what is to be achieved and how it is to be accomplished.

The key to successfully organizing, however, is to divide the tasks to be performed as clearly as possible, assign personnel to manage and undertake the tasks, and then to hold them accountable for their achieving the tasks in an efficient manner. This process is essen-

tial in both large chain and hospital inpatient pharmacies as well as independent community pharmacies.

A common mistake in smaller pharmacies is for the manager to assume that, because there are only a few employees, everybody knows the tasks for which he or she is individually held accountable. Unless the pharmacy is formally organized, some tasks invariably will not be assigned to employees and will not be completed.

Staffing

One of the more difficult management processes is staffing the pharmacy. As is described in more detail in Chapter 12, this involves determining the human resource needs of the pharmacy, identifying sources of possible employees, screening applicants, and selecting the one(s) most qualified.

While there are many steps that can be taken to minimize the errors in selecting personnel, this is an inexact process at best. Many factors affect how well the manager matches the needs of the pharmacy with the talents of the potential employee. Even the most exhaustive staffing process may result in mistakes.

For example, while a manager can quantitatively measure the speed at which a pharmacist fills a prescription, he or she cannot precisely evaluate the quality of the counseling process for every type of medication and every type of patient. In addition, the evaluation of a job applicant during an interview does not provide adequate information on how well the person will fit into the overall work environment. Will he or she relate well to other employees? Will he or she be able to cope with the pressures of the job, or with difficult patients or physicians?

In many respects, staffing is a highly qualitative process. As such, the manager must have both technical knowledge of the jobs to be performed and a feel for the "human" element of how people will fit into their work environments.

Directing

Planning and organizing the pharmacy, and acquiring a good labor force are essential to the management process. But, no pharmacy will be successful if the resources are not directed properly on a daily basis. Directing involves keeping personnel and other resources focused on the goals of the pharmacy and ensuring that they are used in a manner consistent with the policies established by the owner.

While planning, organizing, and staffing are management processes undertaken periodically, directing goes on continuously. Consequently, most managers spend the bulk of their time involved in this management process.

As is described in Chapters 13 and 14, directing personnel and other resources (e.g. cash) is especially difficult because it must be undertaken from both short- and long-term perspectives. For example, a director of pharmacy in a hospital inpatient setting can keep staff pharmacists focused on what is to be accomplished for a day or a week through a variety of positive (e.g. compliments) and negative (e.g. threats of dismissal) actions. But, how can this be accomplished over long periods of time? How can morale and productivity be maintained if pharmacy budgets are tightly restricted for successive years?

Finding different ways to keep personnel productive and motivated to achieve the goals of the pharmacy is a challenge. For this reason, directing is one process that often separates the highly competent from the less skilled managers.

Controlling

The most often overlooked management process is controlling clinical and business activities. It is commonly assumed that the directing process is sufficient to ensure that the pharmacy is operating effectively and efficiently. However, this simply is not the case. Embroiled in day-to-day activities of the pharmacy, it is easy for even the most skilled manager to lose an overall perspective of whether the objectives are being accomplished and whether the strategies developed during the planning process are still appropriate.

Accordingly, the controlling process involves periodic assessments of the status of the pharmacy. Is it achieving its goals? Are the business strategies working properly? Would changes in the organization, staff, or method of directing provide better operating results?

There are a variety of ways in which control can be maintained over operations, and these are described in Chapters 4, 7, 16 and 17. Some are quantitatively based, such as reviews of financial statements to determine if revenues and expenses are within budgeted limits. Others are more qualitative, as with evaluating levels of patient satisfaction and employee performance.

The most important consideration in the control process is to monitor the pharmacy's progress as it moves through the fiscal year. It makes little sense to wait until the year is over to determine whether the pharmacy achieved or did not achieve its goals. By then, it is too late.

A common example of the control process relates to monitoring revenues. In both community and hospital settings, it is critical that the manager periodically determine whether revenues are progressing in the planned manner. If they are below expectations, what corrective actions in marketing strategies can be taken to increase them? In hospital settings, it would be important to determine if reductions in the volume of prescription activity were due to a lower census, a change in the mix of patient admissions for which drug therapy is appropriate, lower utilization of drug therapy which might have improved patient outcomes and reduced hospital stays, etc.

If it is found that revenues cannot be increased, then steps may need to be taken to reduce costs so that the profitability is preserved. Similarly, if revenues are well above projections, what is the cause? Can revenues be increased even more? What changes are necessary in the budget to ensure that sufficient resources (e.g. staff, inventory) are available to preserve the quality of patient care?

When used properly, the control process is the manager's "fail-safe" mechanism. It identifies problems and opportunities in their early stages so as to provide time to take appropriate actions. In this way, many problems can be eliminated or at least alleviated, and opportunities can be taken advantage of while they still exist.

Recognizing the functional areas of business

If the input–output process illustrated in Table 2.5 were to be examined under a microscope, the analyst would be able to identify a rather wide range of activities. In some respects the various activities are like pieces of a jigsaw puzzle. Unless they all fit into their proper places, the picture will not make sense. Similarly, if all of the functions that must be performed in a pharmacy are not meshed perfectly, the operations will be inefficient at best.

A pharmacy, however, is much more complex than even a very large puzzle because some facets of its operations do not blend smoothly. In fact, they often work in opposite directions.

This was described previously, but this example is worth another look. If a community pharmacy wanted to increase profits, it might try to lower some prices on merchandise and advertise in a local newspaper. The objective would be to bring in more customers and sell in higher volume but at lower profit margins. But if the advertisements are effective and more people come in, the pharmacy will need more sales personnel, incur more credit card or charge sales, have more wear and tear on the equipment, etc. Newspaper advertisements are expensive; additional personnel means more labor expenses; credit card sales cost the pharmacy a percentage of the selling price; and equipment may have to be repaired sooner than normal.

The effort to increase sales also results in higher costs of operations. How can the manager balance the effects of efforts to increase sales with the countervailing pressures on additional expenses? In this example, it is possible to increase sales but reduce profits.

To manage these sometimes divergent variables, the manager must understand the various functions of business and how they interact. While the functions of business can be categorized in many ways, those most important for the pharmacy can be grouped as accounting, finance, human resource management, operations management, and marketing. These are illustrated in Table 2.9.

Accounting function

One of the more important functions of business involves monitoring and reporting on the pharmacy's financial resources. Every pharmacy is involved in some manner in the purchase and sale of materials, products, and services. In community settings, this is accomplished through the transfer of products and services for cash or promises to pay (i.e. accounts receivable). In hospitals, purchases are made with cash, and the sales are made through hospital billings to patients or their insurance companies.

As is described in Chapters 6 and 7, the accounting process is used to keep track of the inflow–outflow process in dollar terms. When designed properly, the accounting system can keep the manager abreast of the current status of the resources and what is available for use. In particular, it will monitor the pharmacy's cash position so the manager will know how much can be purchased. The system also will show how well the pharmacy is controlling its expenses, collecting its accounts receivable, and achieving its profit goals.

Table 2.9 The functions of business

Accounting	Develop set of financial "books"
	Record business transactions
	Prepare financial statements for internal use
	Prepare financial statements for external use (e.g. bank)
	Compute federal and state tax liabilities
Finance	Determine financial needs
	Identify sources of borrowed funds
	Identify sources of equity capital
	Develop operating budgets
	Invest excess funds
	Evaluate financial position
	Manage current assets (e.g. cash, accounts receivables)
	Manage fixed assets (e.g. computer, dispensing equipment)
Human resource management	Prepare job description
	Hire personnel
	Train personnel
	Manage personnel
	Evaluate personnel
	Determine compensation levels
	Terminate employment (e.g. retire, dismiss)
Operations management	Determine pharmacy layout
	Define jobs to be performed
	Define work flow
	Purchase inventory and equipment
	Complete work flow (e.g. dispense prescriptions)
Marketing management	Assess internal strengths and weaknesses
	Identify competitors and their respective strengths and weaknesses
	Identify possible target markets
	Evaluate and select target market(s)
	Product strategy development
	Distribution strategy development
	Price strategy development
	Promotion strategy development

Financial function

Some people consider accounting and financial functions to be the same. In fact, they are highly interrelated but separate activities. While accounting focuses on monitoring the state of the pharmacy's resources expressed in dollar terms, finance seeks to get the maximum benefit from those that are or could be converted to monetary units.

Included in the financial function are such activities as obtaining needed capital for the pharmacy, managing cash, managing receivables, and investing in inventory. As described in Chapters 6 and 7, the pharmacy may need funds to make major purchases of equipment and fixtures, compensate for inequities when cash inflow is less than outflow, and support special projects (e.g. begin durable medical equipment sales or rental).

In addition, financial activities relate to the use of excess cash through short-term investments. This may be to purchase bank certificates of deposit, invest in inventory, etc. And financial management involves controlling the level of accounts receivable, and ensuring that private patients and insurance companies pay for pharmacy services.

Human resource management function

Perhaps the greatest deficiency in accounting and finance functions is that they do not take into consideration the most important asset of the pharmacy—the personnel it employs. The human resources are not shown in the financial statements. But they are critical because they usually have the most direct contact between the pharmacy and the patient, and because they are a very expensive part of the pharmacy's operations. In an average community pharmacy, labor costs consume from 15 to 40 cents of every sales dollar generated.[3] In both hospital and community settings, labor expenses are second in magnitude only to cost of goods.

Managing this most precious asset is essential if the pharmacy is to provide a high quality of care and control its cost of operations. The critical question facing a manager is how to find, develop, motivate, and retain people who will work in the pharmacy's best interests over the long term.[4] Getting a group of people who have diverse personal objectives and professional skills to focus on achieving goals other than their own is no simple task. The complexity of these tasks is described in detail in Chapters 12, 13 and 14.

Operations management function

The internal operations of the pharmacy center on the process of converting inputs into outputs. It involves everything from purchasing inventory and equipment to the actual collection of accounts receivable. As such, it closely interacts with the accounting, finance, and human resource management functions.

Developing an efficient method for purchasing and converting inputs into outputs that benefit the patient involves a wide variety of tasks. Not only must the proper medications and supplies be available, but the equipment needed to make the con- version must be right. And these all need to be spatially arranged to allow the conversion to take place efficiently. The implications of a poorly designed internal operation are significant: wasted time adds to the costs of labor, excessive inventory reduces cash resources that could be invested or used elsewhere, and inefficient conversions cause delays in serving patients.

Portions of the operations function are treated in several chapters. However, Chapter 16 focuses on specific aspects of internal operations.

Marketing function

Even the most efficient pharmacy will be of little consequence if it has no patients. The marketing function is the pharmacy's primary and most direct link to the "outside." It is through the marketing efforts that patients, physicians, hospital administrators, and others are targeted for pharmacy services.

Unfortunately, marketing is the most often misunderstood business function. Usually equated with advertising or personal selling, marketing involves a far more diverse set of activities. To ensure that the pharmacy satisfies the needs of patients, marketing activities include identifying and assessing possible target markets, developing an appropriate mix of products and services to satisfy the needs of selected target markets, ensuring that those products and services are made available conveniently, pricing products and services, and promoting the pharmacy to target markets.

In many respects, the marketing function is like a conductor. If the pharmacy is to serve its patients well, it needs direction with respect to what to do, when to do it, etc. As the pharmacy's link to the patient, the marketing function provides the necessary guidance to what must be done to achieve the objective of customer satisfaction.

Marketing efforts are not only focused on patients. They also are targeted to physicians and hospital administrators. Marketing plays a crucial role in building physician relations for referrals and improving patient care through drug therapy. In addition, marketing is useful in targeting hospital administrators to demonstrate the value of the pharmacy in improving therapeutic outcomes and thereby reducing the length of the hospital stay. The many activities associated with marketing in all practice settings are described in Chapters 8, 9, 10 and 11.

Summary

- In the most basic sense, every organization is an input–output system. It takes monetary, human, and material resources, and converts them into an output that is useful to a target group of people.
- In a very simplistic sense, the role of business and the function of management are to ensure that this input–output system operates smoothly.
- There are many misconceptions about the role of business vis-à-vis the practice of pharmacy.
- One of the more common misconceptions is that the practice of pharmacy is ethically inconsistent with good business. Good business and good pharmacy practice, however, have a common objective: to serve the patient's needs with the resources available.
- Another misconception is that in business, the quality of patient care is secondary to the generation of profits. In fact, the generation of profits is closely linked to the quality of care. The real issue, however, is one of what level of quality is necessary or desirable.
- Because there have been many abuses of good business practices by some firms, the entire realm of business has been criticized as not having professional standards of conduct. But many laws and trade and professional standards of practice regulate business activities.
- There are some who believe that a good pharmacist is one who focuses only on the clinical aspects of the profession. However, pharmacists must understand the business and economic environments within which they work.
- The laissez faire doctrine developed by Adam Smith established a public policy that, by allowing organizations to fight for available resources, the best utilization of those resources would be achieved.
- The role of business and professional management is to help an organization become efficient and fight for its share of available resources.
- A business focus ensures that the pharmacy's monetary, human, and material resources are used most effectively.
- Through carefully developed marketing efforts, the pharmacy can show its "customers" the benefits of its services.
- Without some guidelines that direct the pharmacy's activities, consistency will suffer, and there will be no direction to the pharmacy's efforts.
- While the functions of business can be categorized in many ways, the most important for the pharmacy can be grouped as accounting, finance, human resource management, operations management, and marketing.
- The management process involves planning, organizing, staffing, directing, and controlling.

Questions for discussion

1 Why can a pharmacy be viewed as an input–output system?
2 How did the various misconceptions about the role of business in pharmacy practice arise?
3 What are the benefits to pharmacy practice of having an interrelationship with business?
4 Why is it important for pharmacists to have a business perspective?
5 How does the doctrine of laissez faire influence pharmacy practice?
6 What are the functions of business, and why is each important?
7 How do the functions of business interrelate? Why do they sometimes work at cross-purposes?
8 What are the elements of the management process, and why is each important?
9 How do the elements of the management process interrelate?
10 Why is planning so important?

Self-test review

True/false statements

1 A pharmacy should not be considered an input–output system because of its clinical functions.
2 Good business and good pharmacy practice have the same objective: to serve the patient's needs with the resources available.

3 There are many laws regulating business, but no self-regulation by trade or professional organizations.

4 One benefit of having a business perspective, remaining competitive, has little application in a hospital inpatient pharmacy.

5 Business plans provide the vehicle for establishing rules of conduct with respect to pharmacy operations, and help keep them focused on the goals.

6 In both hospital inpatient and community settings, labor expenses are second only to costs of goods in magnitude.

7 Developing an efficient method for purchasing and converting inputs into outputs is a finance function.

8 The most often misunderstood business function is accounting.

9 The management process that occurs on a daily basis is planning.

10 The most often overlooked management process is controlling.

Multiple choice questions

1 Which of the following is not a misconception about business?

(A) The practice of pharmacy is ethically consistent with business.

(B) Business cares more about profit than the quality of care.

(C) Business is not guided by a set of standards of practice.

(D) A good pharmacist is a clinical purist.

2 The laissez faire doctrine can best be equated with which of the following?

(A) Quality care at any cost.

(B) Regulation of business is important to ensure proper conduct.

(C) Survival of the fittest generates the best utilization of the nation's resources.

(D) None of the above.

3 Which of the following is not a benefit of having a business perspective in the practice of pharmacy?

(A) A business focus ensures that resources are used effectively.

(B) A business perspective helps the pharmacy remain competitive and capable of adapting to change.

(C) A business focus ensures a continuity of purpose and organization.

(D) All of the above are benefits of having a business perspective.

4 Which of the business functions is the pharmacy's primary and most direct link to the outside?

(A) Accounting.

(B) Finance.

(C) Human resource.

(D) Marketing.

5 Which element of the management process is the most critical?

(A) Planning.

(B) Organizing.

(C) Staffing.

(D) Controlling.

References

1. Smith A. *The Wealth Of Nations*, New York: Modern Library, 1917: 250.
2. Risk Management Association. *Annual Statement Studies, 2010–2011*, Philadelphia, PA: RMA, 2011.
3. Eli Lilly Drug Co. *Lilly Digest*, Indianapolis: Eli Lilly Drug Co., 1991: 3.
4. Tootelian DH. Wage and benefit programs: Meshing employers' and employees' needs. *California Pharmacist*, November, 1989: 24–25.

3

Going into "business" in independent, chain, and hospital pharmacy settings

Learning objectives

The objectives of this chapter are to assist you to be able to explain:

- what motivates prospective owners to go into business
- why some pharmacists do not go into business for themselves
- how business and personal objectives must mesh if a pharmacy is to succeed
- what personal characteristics are essential for business success
- how to make an appraisal to determine personal readiness to go into business.

Key terms

Adaptation to change
Conceptualization and planning
Family involvement
Financial loss
Financial readiness to become an owner
General management readiness to become an owner
Impact on the family
Independence and power
Lack of security
Managing others
Managing time and learning
Marketing readiness to become an owner
Meshing personal and business goals
Personal readiness to become an owner
Personal satisfaction
Profit and wealth
Social status
Uncontrollable environment
Work and time demands

Objectives of going into a pharmacy "business"

Careers in pharmacy practice offer a number of options. While most pharmacists initially work for others, there comes a time for serious decision-making: Should I remain an employee pharmacist, or should I embark upon a career of becoming an owner and entrepreneur? Today, this could involve owning a community pharmacy, owning a specialty pharmacy for specific types of patients (e.g. hemophilia, pain management), a consulting pharmacy service, etc.

Even if the pharmacist remains an employee, it is important to understand the forces affecting the owner and the motivations for entrepreneurship. After all, every pharmacy is owned by someone or a group of people who have particular desires for being "in business."

Going into business can be an exciting and at times a depressing experience. Opportunities and challenges associated with entrepreneurship make it exciting, but risks of loss and fear of the unknown in attending to all of the details will be troublesome. Because this is such an important step, the decision to start or buy a pharmacy, or be an employee, should be made deliberately and objectively. The emotional aspects of fulfilling a long-held ambition of becoming

an employer rather than an employee should not supersede a realistic assessment of one's entrepreneurial skills and what is needed to be successful.

Many people have dreams of being an entrepreneur and becoming a modern-day Horatio Alger hero. The achievements of people such as Steven Jobs (Apple Computer) and Ray Kroc (McDonald's) illustrate that it is possible to do well as an entrepreneur.

However, owning a pharmacy is not for everyone. Some pharmacists mistakenly believe they cannot practice in a professional manner and operate a pharmacy as a business. Not understanding that good business practices are consistent with good professional practices, they have little interest in working in a community setting either as an owner or an employee. After careful thought, other employee pharmacists will not want to put in the time and effort necessary to build profitable pharmacies. They do not like the challenges and uncertainties that go with ownership. Still other pharmacists will find that they do not possess the appropriate skills to be successful.

Before making a decision to start or buy a pharmacy, therefore, the pharmacist needs to: (1) have clear objectives as to what is to be gained; (2) examine the possible drawbacks to ownership; and (3) assess personal skills and abilities to become successful both now and in the future. Many successful independent pharmacy owners are more business people than pharmacists. Making this a formal process provides an opportunity to fully understand what it takes to be successful, and determine whether entrepreneurship is as rewarding as it may initially appear to be (Figure 3.1).

The most important issue facing the prospective pharmacy owner is what is to be achieved by going into business. This will have a significant impact on the eventual decision as to whether to become a pharmacy owner, and the goals will provide the basis for future management decisions. As shown in Figure 3.2, among the many objectives people have for going into business are profit and wealth, personal satisfaction, family involvement, independence and power, and social status.

Profit and wealth

One of the main reasons for starting or buying a pharmacy is the potential for profits and the accumulation

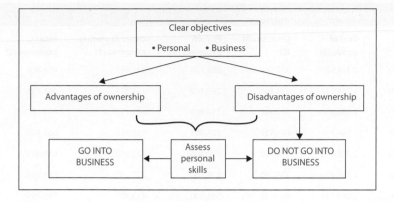

Figure 3.1 The entrepreneurial decision process. From Gaedeke RM and Tootelian DH. *Small Business Management*, 3rd edn. Boston: Allyn and Bacon, 1991: 72. Used with permission.

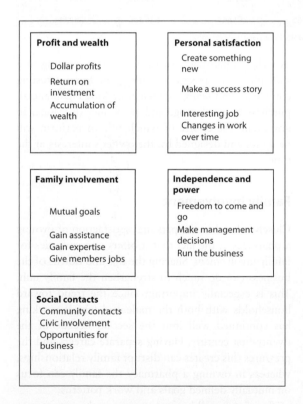

Figure 3.2 Reasons for going into business. From Gaedeke RM and Tootelian DH. *Small Business Management*, 3rd edn. Boston: Allyn and Bacon, 1991: 73. Used with permission.

of wealth. Many prospective owners believe the adage that "you never get rich by working for someone else." Faced with the prospects of remaining as an employee pharmacist who receives wage increases that are only commensurate with inflation, it is easy to understand why many people view ownership as one of the few ways to really become wealthy.

The well-publicized success stories of Henry Ford, Frank Perdue (Perdue chickens), Sam Walton (Wal-Mart), and Marilyn Fields (Mrs. Field's Cookies) illustrate that it is possible to become rich by starting a business. Even though millionaires are the exception rather than the rule in small business tales, pharmacy ownership can offer reasonable levels of profits. Shown in Table 3.1 are some average profits for pharmacies over a 10 year period. While most owners may not become extremely wealthy, they can earn returns on their investments that provide for enjoyable lifestyles.

A key issue for the prospective entrepreneur, therefore, is what level of profits is needed to make pharmacy ownership personally worthwhile. There is a big difference between the desire for a comfortable living and a life of luxury. How much profit the entrepreneur needs will influence whether to start or buy a pharmacy and nearly all future management decisions, since higher returns are usually associated with greater risk.

Consequently, profit must be evaluated in relation to the amount of risk that is acceptable and the time frame desired to achieve the profit goal. The prospective owner has to balance the profit objective with other aspects of ownership. As an article in *Fortune* reported: "The easiest way to make a small fortune? Start with a large one."[1]

Table 3.1 Averages of pharmacy operations

Year	Sales ($)	Cost of goods ($)	Gross profit ($)	Payroll expenses ($)	Other operating expenses ($)	Total expenses ($)	Net operating income ($)
1999	1,967,000	1,494,920	472,080	251,776	149,492	401,268	70,812
2000	2,296,000	1,761,032	534,968	280,112	181,384	461,496	73,472
2001	2,480,000	1,909,600	570,400	310,000	171,120	481,120	89,280
2002	2,855,000	2,184,075	670,925	374,005	188,430	562,435	108,490
2003	3,244,000	2,465,440	778,560	428,208	220,592	648,800	129,760
2004	3,580,000	2,788,820	791,180	436,760	225,540	662,300	128,880
2005	3,745,000	2,861,180	883,820	501,830	243,425	745,255	138,565
2006	3,612,000	2,788,464	823,536	491,232	231,168	722,400	101,136
2007	3,604,000	2,767,872	836,128	493,748	234,260	728,008	108,120
2008	3,881,000	2,980,608	900,392	523,935	252,265	776,200	124,192
2009	4,026,000	3,067,812	958,188	567,666	257,664	825,330	132,858

From *2010 NCPA Digest*, sponsored by Cardinal Health, National Community Pharmacists Association.

Personal satisfaction

Building a successful pharmacy from scratch or taking over one that is experiencing difficulties and turning it into a great success is personally satisfying. For many prospective owners, the desire to be the key element in the development and growth of a pharmacy is an exciting prospect and powerful motivator. It provides a sense of accomplishment that is difficult to achieve as an employee.

A supplemental benefit to the entrepreneur is that managing the pharmacy is likely to be personally interesting. Given the fact that close to 25 percent of an average person's life span is consumed earning a living (assuming an 8 hours workday), most people would like to be doing something they enjoy.

Starting a business provides an opportunity to create the "perfect" job for oneself. Many pharmacists find that by being their own bosses, they can provide greater patient service than would be possible if they worked for others. They believe that their concerns for patients and the community can best be served by having more control over the way they practice their profession.

Of course, the perfect job may well change over time, depending on how successful the pharmacy becomes. The initial role of being both a manager and staff pharmacist will evolve into becoming more manager and less pharmacist as the business grows. However, most owners find that their interests change

as well. Dispensing prescriptions, once exciting in a staff pharmacy position, tends to be less interesting compared with being a manager making big financial, purchasing, marketing, and personnel decisions. In any event, the choice of which role to perform will be up to, and designed by, the owner's interests at the time.

Family involvement

Closely related to the personal satisfaction of owning a pharmacy is the fact that it offers opportunities for family involvement. Sharing the ups and downs of the business can do much to strengthen the family unit. This is especially important since the trend toward households with both the male and female working has continued well into the second decade of the twenty-first century. Having separate careers and the pressures this creates can disrupt family relationships, whereas in owning a pharmacy the family can focus on mutually defined goals and work patterns.

In many small business ventures, the spouse provides much-needed part- or full-time assistance. The spouse can serve in this supporting role to keep records, purchase non-prescription merchandise, manage non-prescription departments, and so forth.

Irrespective of whether the husband or wife is the real entrepreneur, the efforts of the spouse can contribute to overall family life and the future success of the pharmacy. The spouse can provide added expertise and be a source of cheap labor, which reduces expenses and maintains the funds for business operations. Employing children of the family not only provides them with jobs but, more importantly, also gives them opportunities to mature and gain valuable experience.

A small pharmacy, for example, contains many types of jobs that can bring a family together. One member of the family may be especially adept at selecting non-prescription merchandise that is in fashion and displaying it in a manner that will attract attention. Another family member may keep the financial records and manage receipts and disbursements. Others may be involved in sales, delivery, claims processing, etc.

While family involvement can be an important motivator, it is seldom the prime reason for opening or buying a pharmacy. Only about one in three businesses is passed on to children. As described later in this chapter, there also are some potentially significant disadvantages to the family unit stemming from entrepreneurship.

Independence and power

Being one's own boss can be an especially appealing aspect of going into business. In hospital and chain pharmacies, the ability to come and go as one pleases, make important decisions, and not report to a superior is limited to the relatively few who achieve upper-level management positions. Even then, however, a director–manager of pharmacy operations is likely to report to a professional manager who has more of a business than a healthcare orientation.

An owner of a small medical pharmacy, for example, will have the ultimate responsibility for deciding what to sell, how many people to employ, whom to buy from, what prices to charge for prescription and non-prescription merchandise, etc. Many of these decisions cannot be made by staff pharmacists without approval from superiors or committees. Entrepreneurship provides opportunities to make a variety of critical decisions.

Unfortunately, some of these desires prove to be unattainable in the short term. Even though the pharmacy owner can decide to go to work at noon rather than 8 o'clock in the morning, the likelihood of success is closely tied to the amount of time and energy committed to the pharmacy. Owners who spend little time at the business tend to quickly fail.

Nevertheless, there is psychological value in the fact that the owner can decide what to do and when to do it. Even though in reality there are few options available to those who want to succeed, the choices are still theirs.

Social status

On becoming a pharmacy owner, a person opens up a whole new realm of social contacts. The movement from working for somebody else to being the owner–manager typically generates community contacts and respect from people in other pharmacies as well as other businesses. Many civic functions are based on support from the business community, and as an owner, the pharmacist gains access to a variety of events and organizations.

For many pharmacists who like and are comfortable in social settings, the new-found status is an important ingredient to success. Membership in such community groups as the Chamber of Commerce, Rotary, and others is an excellent vehicle for developing name recognition for oneself and the pharmacy. These contacts with key business and civic leaders are not usually as easy for staff pharmacists.

Reasons for not going into business

Going into business for oneself carries with it drawbacks that at times outweigh the advantages (Figure 3.3). It has been said, and probably correctly, that entrepreneurship is not for the faint of heart. A person who enjoys an orderly and scheduled environment, for example, may find owning a small business, with its seemingly daily crises, intolerable. Accordingly, the prospective owner must evaluate the benefits of having a business against possible financial loss, lack of job security and control over the environment, work and time demands, and impact on the family.

Financial loss

Any pharmacy, new or old, chain or independent, carries the risk of financial loss. While some pharmacies are highly profitable, many either are operating at a loss or just breaking even.

It is estimated, too, that as many as 50 percent of all smaller businesses are only breaking even or are losing money. This is especially common among those that are in their first year or two of operation. Even

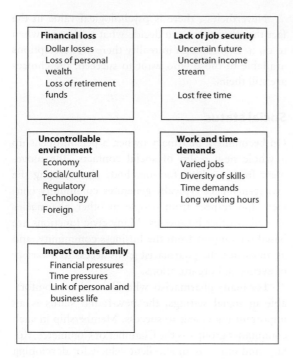

Financial loss	**Lack of job security**
Dollar losses	Uncertain future
Loss of personal wealth	Uncertain income stream
Loss of retirement funds	Lost free time

Uncontrollable environment	**Work and time demands**
Economy	Varied jobs
Social/cultural	Diversity of skills
Regulatory	Time demands
Technology	Long working hours
Foreign	

| **Impact on the family** |
| Financial pressures |
| Time pressures |
| Link of personal and business life |

Figure 3.3 Reasons for not going into business. From Gaedeke RM and Tootelian DH. *Small Business Management*, 3rd edn. Boston: Allyn and Bacon, 1991: 78. Used with permission.

potentially profitable businesses tend not to make money at the start, forcing the entrepreneur to use private funds or debt to meet operating and personal living expenses.

Financial loss also includes risks to the entrepreneur's personal wealth. If the business is formed as a proprietorship or partnership, creditors can seek payment from the owner's personal assets. Corporate forms of ownership provide protection from such creditor claims. However, most owners who seek financing for their new pharmacies either will have to invest considerable personal sums into the business or secure the debt with personal guarantees. Thus, this risk is seldom avoided.

A pharmacist must be prepared financially and emotionally to cope with business loss, at least in the short term and possibly for quite some time. Many prospective owners either are unwilling or unable to make these financial commitments.

The risks involved in starting and managing a pharmacy have effects even into retirement. Many nest eggs have been lost because of unsuccessful pharmacies. A good pension plan may be given up when

an employee makes the transition to entrepreneurship, and often has to use some of the money previously set aside for retirement just to get the business going.

It takes considerable courage to forfeit financial security in retirement years for the decision to go into business for oneself. Being employed allows a person to predetermine the approximate amount of money that will be available in later years, and to plan for additional savings.

With small business ownership, funds available for future retirement are much more difficult to predict. Initial profits during the firm's infancy usually are put back into the operation, and later profits may be used to expand. Many pharmacists mistakenly believe that they can sell their businesses, and use that money to enjoy the good life. As a practical matter, however, many large and small pharmacies are not easy to sell. Finding a buyer who has adequate cash takes time, and most owners are reluctant to carry loans on the business and allow new owners to take over. Furthermore, many long-time owners experience some negative emotions when it comes time to sell. It's like losing a member of the family.[2]

Lack of security

There is much to be said for the job and income security that goes with working for a large chain, hospital, pharmaceutical manufacturer, or government agency. Although even large organizations have had their problems, employment is relatively constant, work hours well defined, and income dependable. Vacations can be planned, and the staff pharmacist can be away for extended periods.

Relatively few owners would dare leave their pharmacies for more than several days or a week. They simply do not have staff they can rely on to manage their businesses for two or more weeks. Even within this relatively short period of time, irreparable damage could be done to a small pharmacy's fragile professional, financial, and market position.

The entrepreneur must be ready to substitute at least some of the pleasures of stable employment for the business-related satisfaction described earlier in this chapter. Possibilities of business downturns or failure have to be accepted as threats to self-employment and income. Business crises also can disrupt time available for family and friends. Thus, the owner loses the security of working and having defined leisure times.

Despite the stigma often attached to wanting security, it is a comfortable feeling that allows the staff pharmacist to plan and make the best use of time. Thus, the normalized nature of being employed offers many advantages to people who derive much of their satisfaction from activities other than work. And many chain and hospital pharmacies encourage creativity with respect to practicing the profession and improving patient relations and outcomes.

Uncontrollable environment

The prospective owner must be aware of the external environment and the factors that could affect the business. It is quite possible for a business to fail due to factors beyond one's control. The economic recession in the early part of the twenty-first century, for example, has dealt death blows to many firms, while economic prosperity has kept marginal firms alive. The rise in unemployment during this time caused many people to lose their jobs and the healthcare insurance coverage they previously enjoyed. The high costs of drugs coupled with low margins afforded by many managed care programs also caused many pharmacies to suffer.

Social and cultural, and legal and regulatory forces can make or break smaller businesses. For example, the growth of the senior population has made it necessary to provide greater levels of care, thereby increasing the amount of time pharmacists must spend with their patients. Similarly, the rise in minority populations increased the need to have pharmacists who could speak a second language.

Overcoming these forces is very difficult for large companies with greater resources. Smaller pharmacies with very limited resources have even less chance of coping with a changing buyer.

Technological change can significantly affect pharmacy practice. Innovations in drug therapy, such as biotech drugs, expand the need for patient consultations, as well as increase the expenses associated with carrying an inventory of these expensive drugs.

Similarly, innovation can render a pharmacy's existing computer system obsolete. New computer hardware and software also has changed the dispensing and filling processes. Potential drug interactions and other warnings are much easier to identify and assess given the state of software available on most pharmacy computers.

Many smaller pharmacies do not have the financial resources or expertise to keep abreast of changes. As a consequence, they may not have the latest equipment that allows them to provide the range of pharmacy services or generate the same quality of internal reports as can their larger competitors.

Many prospective owners have difficulty coping with the fact that the success or failure of their businesses may be determined by uncontrollable economic, social–cultural, legal–regulatory, or technological forces. In some respects, this directly conflicts with an entrepreneurial desire to have greater influence over one's destiny. Being at the mercy of environmental forces can tarnish the attractiveness of ownership.

Work and time demands

One of the distinguishing characteristics of pharmacy ownership is the varying nature of the tasks to be performed by the owner–manager (Table 3.2). During

Table 3.2 Job changes over time			
	Importance of management task		
Owner tasks	**Early years**	**Middle years**	**Later years**
Accounting	Primary	Primary	Primary
Administrative	Primary	Secondary	Secondary
Clerical	Secondary	Secondary	Secondary
Financial	Secondary	Primary	Primary
Personnel management	Secondary	Secondary	Primary
Operations	Primary	Secondary	Secondary
Sales and marketing	Primary	Primary	Primary

From Gaedeke RM and Tootelian DH. *Small Business Management*, 3rd edn. Boston: Allyn and Bacon, 1991: 82. Used with permission.
primary = of major importance as a management task; secondary = of somewhat less importance as a management task.

the early years, and when cash and profit margins are low, the owner will have to do many of the managerial and non-managerial jobs him- or herself in order to control expenditures. In effect, it takes hard work, a willingness to do every job in the pharmacy, a high degree of integrity when dealing with customers and employees, help from friends and acquaintances, and a bit of luck.

While attractive to those who like new challenges, being continually confronted with new and different tasks can make the work physically and mentally taxing. Little time is available to become comfortable with all of the unique problems and opportunities that arise. A new pharmacy owner, for example, will have to assume several roles. They include dispensing prescriptions, deciding on sale items in the non-prescription departments, purchasing prescription and non-prescription inventory, buying supplies, establishing work schedules, greeting customers, processing claims, maintaining financial records, etc. Similar broad ranges in tasks face nearly all owner–managers of retail and industrial businesses.

In many respects, being employed often means less demanding work. As a staff pharmacist in a larger pharmacy, hospital, or governmental agency, the job usually is well defined and somewhat routine. Specialization of labor, for example, is one of the strengths of larger companies, even though repetition also has its drawbacks.

Some prospective owners, of course, would thrive on the newness of each workday, while others would find it too demanding. Many people are uncomfortable with the combination of possible financial loss and the diversity of tasks to be performed. They prefer to have the opportunity to become highly skilled in a narrower range of tasks.

Time pressures placed on entrepreneurs are also a drawback to going into business. An owner's time is demanded by many people: customers want to talk to the boss; suppliers want to deal directly with those who have the authority to purchase goods and services; employees want access to their superiors; and family members would like personal time. The entrepreneur who believes that going into business will mean days off work and time for movies or golf is in for a rude awakening.

Being employed for 8 hours a day, 5 days a week, can be very attractive. Home, leisure, and vacation time are well defined. Successful ownership means long hours and little vacation time, especially in the pharmacy's early life. What work is not finished at the end of the day must be taken home. It will not be completed by somebody else, nor will there be time for it the next day. And it simply may cost too much to hire others to perform the tasks the owner does not want or have time to do.

Impact on the family

The risks of financial loss, lack of job security, and work and time demands also take their toll on the entrepreneur's personal life. While small business ownership brings a family closer together because of the commonality of purpose, the pressures can serve to tear it apart. Periods when the pharmacy is losing money or is beset with cash shortages, or has just lost a key employee, create pressures on the family. Personal budgets may have to be trimmed, time with the family sacrificed, etc.

As already described, a staff pharmacist's income stream and work schedule is better defined. Earning a living tends not to place the same types of strains on family life, and there are fewer crises to deal with.

To be successful, the owner must have the support of the family. It is nearly impossible to separate the business from personal life, so a prospective owner needs the commitment of his or her family before proceeding to start a venture.

Appraising readiness to become an entrepreneur

Although prospective owners of community or consultant pharmacy practices are the principal source of their pharmacies' management expertise and labor, relatively few owners have all of the necessary skills when they go into business. They tend to learn over time and on an as-needed basis.

While this is to be expected, prospective owners should nevertheless try to determine how well prepared they are, and what talents they need immediately and what talents they can develop in the future. If the list of needed skills is too long, or some critically important ones are lacking, the prospective owner may decide to build them prior to going into business. In general, an assessment of readiness focuses on personal, financial, marketing, and managerial considerations.

Personal considerations

The skills and personality of the owner play an important role in a small business. The successful entrepreneur is one who:

- has clear goals that are reasonable given the resources available
- has the personal abilities described earlier in this chapter
- has some management experience, training, or both
- is willing to work long and nontraditional hours
- has the ability to work hard without adversely affecting his or her physical and mental health
- is self-confident, but understands his or her weaknesses
- can make decisions, quickly when necessary, and is right most of the time
- is a self-starter and likes to take the initiative
- is willing to perform every job within the pharmacy, from the highest level management decisions to cleaning the windows
- likes people and feels comfortable in dealing with them as customers, employees, etc.
- enjoys learning to do new things even though they take time
- is willing to alter his or her lifestyle to meet the needs of the business
- has the ability to keep business and professional problems from overly affecting his or her personal and family life
- has family support
- does not get discouraged easily, yet is realistic about future options.

A prospective small business owner should begin the pursuit with energy and optimism. Nevertheless, the reality of entrepreneurship must be faced. It requires total personal and family commitment, and even then it may result in failure. The person who has the personality that can cope with these facts of business life is much better prepared for ownership than one who naively takes the plunge.

Financial considerations

Every small business owner must be able to determine the financial position of the business and understand the financial implications of alternative management decisions. How much capital is needed to start and run the business? What expenses will be incurred? How much profit is needed to sustain the owner's lifestyle and provide for business growth? What will happen to sales and profits if investments are made in inventory, remodeling, a new computer, or a promotional campaign? Such questions are addressed continually by entrepreneurs.

In addition to evaluating decisions based on financial issues, the owner–manager has to be able to convert theoretical business plans into dollars in the form of budgets. It has been said that "money is the language of business," and that is true for much of the management process. Since businesses need profits to survive, most of the pharmacy's operations eventually have to be translated into dollar terms.

With respect to financial attributes, an entrepreneur should be one who:

- has extra funds available so that not all financial resources are being used to open or buy the pharmacy
- can project revenues, expenses, and profits with reasonable accuracy
- can do all of the bookkeeping, and can prepare financial statements and use them in making management decisions (while the entrepreneur may not do all of this, she or he should have the capabilities to do so and understand how financial statements are created and what they mean)
- can prepare budgets and adhere to them (while the entrepreneur may not always prepare a budget, she or he should have the capability to do so and understand how the budget was developed and the implications of committing resources in the way defined in the budget)
- has estimated all of the costs of going into business, and the extra expenses that will be incurred during the first few months of operation
- knows how to prepare a loan package to meet initial, growth, or emergency capital requirements
- understands the differences between using personal funds and debt to finance the business
- knows how much money is needed to maintain an acceptable lifestyle, and what expenses can be trimmed if necessary.

Although they recognize the importance of the financial aspects of owning and operating a pharmacy, many owners do not like dealing with budgets, bookkeeping, and financial statements. This is unfortunate because few owners or managers succeed unless they have an understanding of, and control over, this critical component.

Marketing considerations

A pharmacy's marketing efforts are its direct link with the buying public. Through its product, price, distribution, and promotional efforts, the pharmacy attracts customers and sells them merchandise and services to satisfy their needs. Being able to evaluate the marketplace and the existing and potential competition is a key element to survival.

It is rare to find a pharmacy with nothing distinctly different from its competitors enjoying any measurable degree of success. Customers do not seek out new pharmacies. They must be told that the business exists, what it offers to satisfy their needs, and why they should patronize it rather than one of its competitors. Too often, new owners open their doors and expect to be besieged by buyers. The high failure rate among small businesses, generally considered to be at least 50 percent in the first 5 years of life, attests to the fact that it just does not happen that way.

In terms of marketing attributes, the successful owner is one who:

- knows how to evaluate the marketplace in terms of identifying the needs of different groups of potential patients
- can identify the major competitors, define their relative strengths and weaknesses, define who their customers are, and isolate the marketing strategies they are using
- appreciates the importance of product, price, distribution, and promotion strategies, and how they interrelate
- understands what motivates buyers to purchase goods and services, and their reasons for patronizing one pharmacy as opposed to another
- is always looking for new strategies to reach potential customers and better satisfy their needs
- understands customer perceptions of the relationship between price and value of a product or service
- appreciates how to exhibit non-prescription merchandise attractively
- knows how to conduct simple marketing research to better define possible markets and needs for products and services.

General management considerations

Managerial skills in planning and dealing with people will be developed as the business grows. However, the entrepreneur should possess at least some talent for organizing and operating the various facets of the pharmacy before going into business.

In general, the management skills needed are defined in terms of planning operations; organizing the financial, personnel, and material resources; staffing; directing the workforce to achieving the goals; and controlling operations to ensure that the goals are achieved.

In terms of general managerial attributes, a successful entrepreneur is one who:

- has an ability to develop policies for the pharmacy's operations, and can design procedures to ensure that they conform to those policies
- understands the various specialized skills needed to effectively manage a pharmacy through periods of growth and decline
- knows how to delegate authority to make decisions, and can be comfortable in letting others make decisions even though there might be occasional mistakes
- can develop methods of making personnel feel that they are participating in the success of the pharmacy
- understands how to select competent personnel and give them jobs commensurate with their skills and personal objectives
- knows how to motivate personnel to achieve short- and long-term goals
- can develop means for evaluating both personnel and the overall performance.

Whether to start a practice or buy an existing one

Opening a pharmacy or consulting practice from scratch is a common method of getting into business. As is the case when evaluating an established pharmacy, much investigation and analysis is required to increase the new venture's probability of success. It may be prudent to incur some expense to obtain help in areas where one lacks experience or knowledge in starting a pharmacy.

Starting a new pharmacy or consultant practice allows the pharmacist greater freedom in selecting the business location, physical facilities, equipment, suppliers, products, and services. It allows the owner to be truly innovative. The pharmacist is not bound to the established policies and practices of a going pharmacy or hampered by existing legal commitments. In addition, possible ill-will from customers, suppliers, employees, and creditors is not inherited.

On the other hand, a pharmacist launching a new pharmacy or consultant practice must be willing to work at zero wages for a year or two. Except that, as a rough guide, a capital investment of at least $2 for every $5 in estimated annual sales should be anticipated.[3]

Innovative methods of operation should be tried when existing businesses do not adequately satisfy market needs and wants. Customers may be dissatisfied with the availability, distribution, or prices of products and services. On the other hand, rapid market expansion, changing customer needs, and new government regulations may have created new opportunities that established pharmacies have not exploited.

Starting a pharmacy

In the complicated process of starting a pharmacy, the following steps need to be addressed:

1. Plan the business
2. Choose the legal form of the business
3. Obtain financing
4. Select a location
5. Obtain licenses
6. Set up records
7. Insure the business
8. Promote the business
9. Manage the business.

Advice and assistance are available for each of these steps. Owners starting a new venture can obtain advice from numerous sources. Among the most important are accountants, bankers, other business owners, suppliers, family and friends, and lawyers (Figure 3.4).

Planning the pharmacy

Regardless of the nature of the proposed pharmacy, the prospective pharmacy owner needs a comprehensive plan in order to transform an idea into a successful business operation. The business plan should describe, in writing, the proposed pharmacy and its products and services. It should include an assessment of the market, a marketing strategy, an organizational plan, and measurable financial objectives.

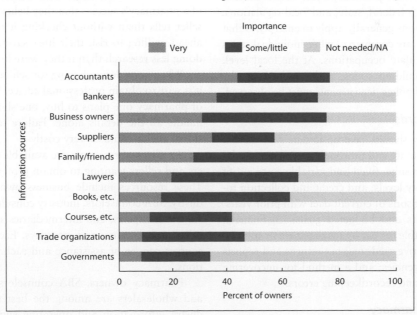

Figure 3.4 Importance of information sources used in forming a business. From Gaedeke RM and Tootelian DH. *Small Business Management*, 3rd edn. Boston: Allyn and Bacon, 1991: 101. Data developed and provided by The NFIB Foundation and sponsored by the American Express Travel Related Services Co., Inc. Used with permission.

Choosing the legal form of organization

A prospective pharmacy owner should consult an attorney to clarify technical aspects of the different forms of business organization. The major legal forms of business are a sole proprietorship, general partnership, limited partnership, subchapter S corporation, limited liability corporation (LLC), and corporation.

Obtaining financing

Most beginning pharmacists lack the necessary financial resources to launch a new pharmacy. In addition to using their own savings, they must secure funds from other sources, such as family members, bank loans guaranteed by the Small Business Administration (SBA), and venture capital firms.

Selecting a location

The location decision involves selection of the trade area and selection of a site from which the business is conducted. One important question to ask is: How strategic is the particular site in terms of number and types of available clientele and number and types of competitive enterprises? A related question is the number and types of prescribers in the area.

Obtaining licenses

The owner of a new pharmacy must obtain licenses and comply with federal, state, and local regulations. Federal regulations generally apply to enterprises that engage in interstate commerce, while individual states license and regulate occupations. At the local level, zoning laws, building codes, and standards set by health, fire, and police departments must be observed.

Setting up records

Every pharmacy should have up-to-date records that provide: (1) accurate and thorough statements of sales and operating results, fixed and variable costs, profit or loss, inventory levels, and credit and collection totals; (2) comparisons of current data with prior years' operating results and budgeted goals; (3) financial statements suitable for use by management or submission to prospective creditors; tax returns and reports to regulatory agencies; and a method for uncovering material waste and recordkeeping errors.

Insuring the pharmacy

An insurance agent or broker needs to be consulted before opening a pharmacy. A comprehensive insurance plan should be designed which might include fire insurance, liability insurance, crime coverage, automobile insurance, workers' compensation insurance, business interruption insurance, employee health insurance, and "key person" insurance.

Promoting the pharmacy

A new pharmacy owner must be prepared to inform potential customers. Few establishments can count on word-of-mouth alone to bring in customers. Advertising is needed to inform, persuade, and remind people about the pharmacy.

Managing the pharmacy

As the prime initiator of the pharmacy, the new owner must be involved with planning, staffing, directing, and controlling the entire operation. The pharmacy has to be firmly managed and operated in order to succeed.

Buying an established pharmacy

Buying a pharmacy can be one of the most stressful experiences in a pharmacy owner's career. Buyers of pharmacies are more vulnerable to making costly mistakes because they frequently lack sophistication and do not know where to seek advice. Many believe they do not need it. Others get so caught up in the aura of a pharmacy's success that they believe anything the seller tells them without checking it out. They rush ahead, willing to risk their life's savings while often doing less research than if they were buying a house.

When considering buying (or selling) a pharmacy, it is wise to obtain professional advice. Whatever type of pharmacy one plans to buy, one should not try to handle all the details alone. Failure to seek professional advice could be very costly.

A variety of resources are available for those buyers and sellers wanting to obtain professional advice. These resources include business owners in the industry, SBA counselors, industry consultants, business valuation experts, and intermediaries such as wholesalers, accountants, and attorneys. Each of these resources can be of assistance and each has its limitations.

Pharmacy owners, SBA counselors, consultants, and wholesalers are among the best sources of industry information and operating suggestions. SBA counselors provide their services free of charge and can be reached through local SBA offices. Pharmacy owners may be able to give free advice, and they are often the best source of information. No one knows more about a particular pharmacy than someone who is successfully operating one.

Pharmacy valuation experts can independently appraise a pharmacy's value. It should be remembered, however, that they rely on the representations of the seller. They render a conditional opinion based on the assumption that the financial statements are accurate and complete. They will attempt to independently verify only certain information.

Accountants are best used to perform an audit, if one is needed. They can help interpret financial statements and provide advice in structuring the transaction to minimize tax consequences for the buyer and seller. They also can arrange to have inventory valued prior to the transfer of title.

Probably the most often consulted adviser in the purchase or sale of a pharmacy or drugstore is an attorney. Attorneys are asked to do everything from assessing the viability of a pharmacy and appraising its value to negotiating the purchase price and preparing the necessary documents. The primary function of an attorney is to prepare the purchase and sale documents as negotiated by the parties.

Advantages of buying an established pharmacy

There are a number of possible advantages in buying an established pharmacy. These should be thoroughly evaluated before a decision is made to start a new pharmacy.

- Buying a pharmacy will save the time, cost, and effort of finding a location. A major difficulty in starting a new pharmacy is finding the right place to locate. An existing pharmacy has already demonstrated the value of its location.
- An established pharmacy can be evaluated to determine its ability to attract customers. In buying a going pharmacy, one normally acquires customers who are accustomed to trading with the pharmacy.
- Uncertainties regarding physical facilities, inventory requirements, and personnel needs are reduced. The existing owner can also share the benefit of his or her experience in the pharmacy and in the community.
- An existing pharmacy may be available at a bargain price. For personal reasons, an owner

may be willing to make a quick sale and offer favorable terms.

In short, a pharmacy that is already established and operating has a track record that can be evaluated and compared with others in the industry.

Disadvantages of buying an established pharmacy

A number of factors might rule against the purchase of an existing pharmacy. Indeed, on close examination the advantages just cited may turn out to be disadvantages.

- The pharmacy location may no longer be convenient to customers. Parking problems, deterioration of the neighborhood, and shifts of pedestrian and traffic flows plague many existing pharmacies.
- The current owner or pharmacy may have a poor reputation and image. A new owner would be faced, at least initially, with the prejudices and skepticism of former customers, and perhaps of suppliers.
- The physical facilities may be outmoded, in need of repair, or inefficient. Fixtures, equipment, and additional space can be costly to acquire.
- Too much of the front-end inventory on hand may be obsolete, poorly selected, or slow-moving. Yesterday's breadwinners may be tomorrow's dead stock.
- The price of the pharmacy may be too high because of the former owner's misrepresentation or the buyer's inaccurate appraisal.

All these factors are potentially serious disadvantages to buying an existing pharmacy. A careful and timely evaluation of the pharmacy is a must.

The nature of pharmacy management to employee pharmacists

The term "management" can be and often is used in several different ways. For example, it can refer to the people who guide and direct the organization; to a body of knowledge that furnishes insights on how to manage; or to the process that managers follow to accomplish organizational goals. It is this last use that is commonly associated with the term.

Management can thus be defined as: "The process of reaching organizational goals by working with and through people and other organizational resources."[4] This definition shows that management has three main characteristics: (1) it is a process of continuing activities; (2) it involves and concentrates on reaching organizational goals; and (3) it reaches these goals by working with and through people and other organizational resources. Management tries to encourage individual activity that will lead to achieving organizational goals. "There is no idea more important to managing than goals. Management has no meaning apart from its goals."[5]

Misconceptions about pharmacy management

Many employed pharmacists are fully satisfied with their employers, their work environment, and their particular functions. Still, it is not uncommon to hear the following comments: "All they [managers] care about is profit!" "I'm filling a tremendous number of prescriptions a day, and they still complain about low profits." "How would they know what's going on? They are up in their offices—they don't have to work here and deal with these customers."

There can be no doubt that some of these comments are valid, and that others are rooted in significant problems. Yet, the general thrust of the ones cited above transcends nearly all industries and professions, and stems from a misunderstanding of what management means and what managers do.

The management of a pharmacy is a much more complex process than it might appear. In general, what is involved is synthesizing organizational resources—people, money, materials, and equipment—into a cooperative and efficiently working system and balancing the desires and demands of numerous "stake holders," including the owners, employees, and governmental agencies. This is illustrated in Figure 3.5.

The owners expect profits from the pharmacy's operations since they have invested money in it. If profits were not expected, this money would be better placed in a financial institution or some other interest-bearing repository. Employees expect to share in the revenues generated by operations and various governmental agencies want a share of the monetary

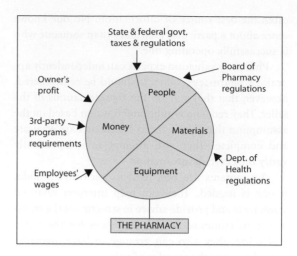

Figure 3.5 Demands on the pharmacy. From Gaedeke RM and Tootelian DH. *Essentials of Pharmacy Management.* St. Louis, MO: Mosby-Year Book, Inc., 1993: 88. Used with permission.

resources as well. The government and other regulatory commissions, and third-party programs also impinge upon the pharmacy in terms of limitations on the use of these resources. Juggling these conflicting interests is part of the pharmacy management process.

Reasons underlying management actions

Employees often fail to understand the rationale underlying specific management actions and concerns. Pharmacists may wonder: Why does management think only of revenues and profits? While some managers may appear to be overly concerned about monetary resources vs. the employees who work in the pharmacy, it must be recognized that profits are the hub of any pharmacy's operations. As shown in Figure 3.6, no business could exist without generating a profit. Thus, profit becomes the bottom line for most business activities and enterprises.

Contrary to popular belief, profits are not ends in themselves. Profits are used for a multitude of purposes, and not necessarily to fill the owner's pockets. If there was no money, inventory could not be purchased, rent could not be paid, and perhaps most importantly, wages could not be paid.

Assuming that there is a profit left over after all the bills are paid, it is common for much of that to be put back into the pharmacy to improve its operations. Such reinvestments may be for more extensive inventories, modern equipment, new fixtures, and the like. Typically, it is expected that this will generate additional profits and help to assure stable growth. If realized, the end result for employed pharmacists is continued employment, and the likelihood of better salaries, benefit programs, and working conditions.

The consequences of profitability in a pharmacy are all-encompassing. Virtually every aspect of pharmacy operations, from supplier credit and employee salaries to customer credit and store advertising, is contingent on profits. As a result, management must give profitability its maximum consideration.

Employer–employee relations

Does management care about the employees? There is simply no justification for or benefit in mistreating or taking advantage of employees. Pharmacy managers who abuse the employer–employee relationship typically find themselves with less qualified workers, higher levels of personnel turnover, lost customers, and lower profits (Figure 3.6).

Yet management often makes decisions and takes actions that seem unfair or excessive. Lack of communications, salaries that are perceived to be too low, benefits that appear less than adequate, and obsolete equipment are often considered indicative of disregard of employees. In some instances these may be signs that employee relations are not a high-priority item to management. Most often, however, this is not the case.

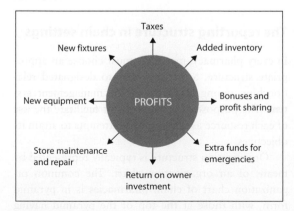

Figure 3.6 Uses for revenues and profits. From Gaedeke RM and Tootelian DH. *Essentials of Pharmacy Management.* St. Louis, MO: Mosby-Year Book, Inc., 1993: 89. Used with permission.

A critical function of management is to make decisions about all the resources of the pharmacy. Trade-offs must be made both in terms of the manager's time and the pharmacy's money. In general, managers spend much of their time trying to resolve problems or take advantage of opportunities for the good of the pharmacy. So long as employee relations are running smoothly, the tendency is to direct attention to the crises. Consequently, communication may suffer. The employer–employee relationship is most susceptible to apparent inattention since most managers try to strike a balance between no communication and too much communication. The latter may be interpreted by employees as being "too closely managed." Unfortunately, a proper balance is difficult to achieve.

The way financial resources are used, of course, is frequently a sore spot in employer–employee relations. Since higher expenditures in one area must be balanced by reduced expenditures in others or by increased sales, part of the management process involves making these evaluations. Coming to grips with these problems and reaching the proper balance between all the potential users of management time and pharmacy funds is indeed a difficult process. Unfortunately, this management function too often appears colder and more impersonal than it actually is.

Good employer–employee relations can be achieved only through the mutual efforts of all parties involved. The traditional premise of a "natural conflict" must be discarded in favor of an attitude of understanding the positions and functions of both managers and employees.

The business of chain pharmacies

A chain pharmacy is generally defined as a store that fills prescriptions and is part of a group of four or more stores operating together under common ownership.

One major advantage that chain operations have over independent stores is economies of scale. Centralized volume purchases for the entire chain allow chains to buy at lower prices than independents. Administrative functions are performed by the corporate organization rather than by each store. This means that large chains can afford to use merchandising and layout specialists, sales training, and computerized merchandise ordering, inventory control, and accounting systems to increase efficiency. In addition, the large sales volume and wide geographical coverage of many chains enable them to advertise in a variety of media, including television and magazines.

Compared with independent pharmacies, chain pharmacies or drugstores tend to realize higher dollar sales per store; occupy more store space; feature more departments and deeper assortments of front-end merchandise; depend more on merchandise sales than prescription sales; stay open more hours per week; employ more pharmacists; spend more on advertising and sales promotion; and tend to have lower prices.

Classification of chain drugstores

Chain drugstores can be classified into four distinct types: (1) the pharmaceutical center, (2) the traditional drugstore, (3) the bantam store, and (4) the superstore. These types of chain drugstores differ from one another in terms of store size, type of services offered, and variety of products offered for sale.

- The *pharmaceutical center* usually has less than 6,000 square feet of floor space. The primary emphasis is on pharmaceutical services and merchandise items related directly to healthcare.
- The *traditional drugstore* normally operates stores averaging about 10,000 square feet. The services and merchandise lines are consistent with those of a neighborhood drugstore.
- The *bantam store* tends to have about 3,000–6,000 square feet. These stores emphasize prescription services and health and beauty aids.
- The *superstore* often covers 25,000 square feet or more and carries a much wider variety of merchandise lines than the other types of chain drugstores. Merchandise lines may include hardware items, sporting goods, automotive goods, soft goods, and other items normally associated with large, regional, or national retailers. The pharmacy is typically a separate department located within the larger unit.[6]

The role of the pharmacist in chain settings

The professional practice of pharmacy itself is virtually identical in chain operations and independent pharmacies.

The pharmacist dispenses the same prescription drugs from a department that is more or less constant in size. The same over-the-counter medications and health and beauty aids are recommended and sold. And to a large degree, the same techniques and governmental regulations influence the way in which the pharmacist goes about practicing his or her profession.

Professional and technical work activities of pharmacists consist largely of dispensing prescriptions, counseling patients, and consulting with physicians. The traditional service of dispensing prescriptions involves numerous tasks, including: checking or developing patient medication profiles; calling the prescriber in reference to refills; filling prescriptions; screening for drug interactions; checking for allergic reactions; verifying insurance program eligibility; and verifying acceptability of the drug insurance program.

Patient counseling may include answering routine questions in reference to both prescriptions and over-the-counter drugs. Other patient services may consist of taking blood pressure readings and developing and disseminating patient information sheets. Pharmacists may consult with physicians in such areas as intervention, ways to lower the cost of medicine, and patient complaints concerning drug side-effects.

In addition to providing clinical services and patient counseling, pharmacists may be involved in various routine managerial activities. These activities can involve purchasing, inventory control, stocking shelves, and supervising clerks and technicians.

The reporting structure in chain settings

In every pharmacy, managers must choose an appropriate structure. Structure refers to designated relationships among resources of the management system. The purpose of structure is to facilitate the use of each resource as management attempts to attain its objectives.

Organization structure is typically represented by means of an organization chart. The common organization chart of chain pharmacies is in pyramid form, with those at the top of the pyramid having more authority and responsibility than those at the bottom. The organization chart depicts relationships of people and jobs and shows the formal channels of communication between them.

In a typical chain drugstore, the reporting structure is for pharmacists to report to a pharmacy department manager, who in turn either reports to the store manager or a district pharmacy manager. The store manager, who can be either a pharmacist or a person with background in business, reports to a district manager. Drug clerks and technicians report either to the staff pharmacists or to the pharmacy department manager.

It is common in chain pharmacies for the areas of responsibility between the assistant manager and the pharmacy manager to be divided. The pharmacy manager controls the prescription department and over-the-counter drugs, while the assistant manager controls the other "front-end" merchandise.

Pressures affecting chain pharmacists

Pharmacists employed in chain pharmacies may experience various pressures associated with employment in a large organization. Compared with independent pharmacies, the structure of chain operations tends to be more complicated and areas of responsibility and authority may become more fractionated as well. This, in turn, may cause problems in communication and decision-making. For example, pharmacists may be held accountable for pilferage by both customers and store employees, yet they may lack the authority to control such events.

Pharmacists in chain pharmacies may experience job pressures due to:

- relatively inflexible work schedules
- the possibility of job transfers
- the amount of time devoted to non-clinical services
- more overtime work due to chains' inability to hire enough full-time pharmacists
- salaries peaking after a relatively few years in practice.

It should be pointed out, however, that pharmacy chains are addressing longstanding workplace issues for pharmacists. For example, the value of the pharmacist is being recognized publicly by highlighting pharmacists in advertising and promotion efforts. One chain has mounted prominent signs over all its prescription departments with the motto, "Ask the Pharmacist," while other chains feature the availability of pharmacists in their advertising. These types of actions provide the pharmacist with a sense of being not only an employee but also a professional.

The business of hospital pharmacies

Hospital pharmacies are the primary employer of pharmacists involved in institutional practice. The limits to hospital pharmacy practice are continuously expanding and new responsibilities, new drugs, and new corporate relationships ensure that the profession will continue to flourish in the coming years.

There are some distinct differences between the hospital pharmacist and the community pharmacist. First, hospital pharmacists primarily serve inpatients. Second, their professional relationship involves mainly physicians and nurses, while patient involvement is often indirect, through the nurses. Third, they are largely employed in non-profit hospitals, although there are many for-profit hospitals. The distinction between profit and non-profit hospitals, however, is less and less important because hospital administrators often expect the director of pharmaceutical services to generate a profit or "surplus" in order to offset losses in other departments.

Clinical pharmacy services in hospital settings

Clinical pharmacy services have developed in recent years because of the deficiencies in traditional medication systems, the lack of effectiveness of drug information services, and the need to improve the level of drug therapy to patients. Major clinical services that a pharmacist, practicing in the patient care area, might provide include the following (personal communication, Adrian Lee Bal, PharmD., Methodist Hospital, Sacramento, CA):

- interpreting physician drug orders
- checking orders against transcriptions on pharmaceutical service records
- medication reconciliation at discharge
- processing intravenous (IV) orders
- preparing IV admixtures and IV piggybacks
- interviewing patients and discussing drug therapy with them
- monitoring drug therapy

- answering and discussing nurses' and clerks' questions
- contacting physicians concerning drug orders and therapy
- suggesting drug therapy changes or laboratory tests as appropriate
- answering and discussing physicians' patient-related drug therapy questions
- participating in patient care rounds.

Additional duties may involve work on special projects; supervisory responsibilities, and procurement and preparation of drugs. Work on special projects may include patient drug therapy research activities, preparing, reviewing, and auditing medication dosing guidelines, and drug utilization review activities. Supervisory responsibilities may include giving on-the-job directions to technicians, as necessary; teaching new skills to technicians; processing pharmacy drug notices; and coordinating pharmacy activities.

The reporting structure in hospital settings

The reporting structure or chain of command is relatively straightforward in most hospitals. Staff pharmacists either report to the assistant director of pharmacy (if there is one) or to the director of pharmacy. The assistant director reports to the director of pharmacy who, in turn, reports to the hospital administrator. Technicians report either to staff pharmacists or to the director of pharmacy.

The director of pharmacy usually has ultimate authority to hire and fire pharmacists and technicians and to formulate pharmacy policy. Pharmacists' conflicts with nurses, physicians, and patients are ultimately resolved by the hospital administrator.

The basic components of a pharmacy department organization providing drugs and drug information to the hospital generally include the following:

- organizational management: planning, budgeting, departmental goals
- business management: purchasing and bidding, receiving and issuing, charging systems
- drug information services: referral questions, pharmacy and therapeutic committee, newsletters
- outpatient services: clinics; discharge, bedside, and pass prescriptions; surgery; emergency room

- inpatient services: pharmacists, technicians
- manufacturing and packaging: manufacturing, unit dose packaging, prepackaging
- narcotics control: intra- and inter-departmental transactions.

Major issues facing hospital pharmacists

The external and internal forces affecting the hospital pharmacy are increasing. Internal forces, such as the concern for quality patient care and the desire to assimilate the increasing body of knowledge, and external forces, such as cost containment, medical liability, and healthcare regulations by government, are mounting.

Pharmacy standards mandated by the Joint Commission Accreditation of Healthcare Organizations (JCAHCO) have to be implemented. For example, JCAHCO standards contain a statement concerning the pharmacy's responsibility to participate in a program that relates to drug use and effectiveness by determining use patterns for each drug and assisting in the setting of drug use criteria. To be sure, the scope of the drug use evaluation (DUE) process is included in the Joint Commission's standards.

Most of the major issues facing the profession are common to all hospital departments, not only the pharmacy department. They include the need to (personal communication, Adrian Lee Bal, PharmD., Methodist Hospital, Sacramento, CA):

- reduce operating costs through cost containment, cost avoidance, cost reduction, and managed care
- increase productivity and demonstrate leadership
- improve patient safety from both a prescribing and a dispensing perspective through development of sound quality assurance programs and compliance with JCAHCO standards
- improve the understanding of, and response to, medical–legal and ethical issues
- maintain and motivate a well-trained staff through good human resource management
- expand the application of computers and new technologies.

It is apparent that these needs can present enormous challenges, pressures, and frustrations for hospital pharmacists.

Summary

- Before making a decision to start or buy a pharmacy, the prospective entrepreneur needs to have clear goals, examine the disadvantages of ownership, and assess personal skills and abilities to become successful in business.
- The reasons for starting a pharmacy are varied, but often relate to profit and wealth, personal satisfaction, family involvement, independence and power, and social status.
- Going into business carries with it disadvantages such as possible financial loss, lack of job security and control over the environment, work and time demands, and impact on the family.
- The costs and benefits of starting a pharmacy must be weighed carefully—entrepreneurship is not for everyone.
- In a small pharmacy, it is especially important that the goals of the owner and the business be compatible.
- To achieve success, the entrepreneur needs to develop strong managerial skills because most failures have been attributed to lack of good management.

Questions for discussion

1 What objectives do people have for going into business, and how could they be prioritized?
2 What are the reasons for not going into business, and how important are they in deciding whether to open a pharmacy?
3 What are the characteristics someone needs to own and manage a pharmacy and how do those characteristics differ from being an employee pharmacist?
4 How can someone assess whether she or he is ready to become an entrepreneur?
5 What are the steps to starting a pharmacy and how important is each?
6 What are the advantages and disadvantages of buying an established pharmacy?
7 What are the advantages and disadvantages of starting a new pharmacy?
8 What are the misconceptions about pharmacy management and why are they believed?
9 What roles do pharmacists have in chain pharmacy settings and how do those differ from roles in independent community pharmacy settings?

10 What roles do pharmacists have in hospital pharmacy settings and how do those differ from roles in community pharmacy settings?

Self-test review

True/false statements

1 Business ownership provides an opportunity to create a "perfect job" for oneself right from the beginning.
2 Spouses and other family members tend to be of little help to entrepreneurs, and, in fact, are a major obstacle to success.
3 Greater and more speedy profit expectations often mean higher levels of risk.
4 One common disadvantage to ownership is the lack of job stability and security.
5 Compared with employees of chains, hospitals, and governmental agencies, entrepreneurs generally face fewer work and time demands.
6 In small businesses, the goals of the entrepreneur most often are separated from those of the business.
7 The entrepreneur must be able to conceptualize and plan if the pharmacy is to have a real chance of success.
8 A person who was a good employee will also be a good employer.
9 As a business grows, its owner must be ready and willing to step away from day-to-day operations.
10 An understanding of bookkeeping is not an important characteristic of a successful entrepreneur since there are specialists available to do this work.

Multiple choice questions

1 Which of the following "advantages" of ownership is mostly an illusion in the short term?

(A) Interesting work.
(B) Social status.
(C) Independence and power.
(D) Ego satisfaction.

2 Which of the following is not a major consideration when setting profit objectives for the pharmacy?

(A) Level of wealth desired.

(B) Amount of risk that is acceptable.

(C) Amount of time in which to achieve the profit goal.

(D) All of the above are major considerations.

3 A disadvantage of business ownership is:

(A) Lack of family involvement.

(B) Lack of power.

(C) Lack of social status.

(D) Lack of job security.

4 Which of the following is not a skill needed for success?

(A) Ability to mesh personal and business goals.

(B) Ability to remain the same over time.

(C) Ability to manage time.

(D) Ability to manage others.

5 Which of the following is not a personal attribute of a successful entrepreneur?

(A) Willing to perform every job within the pharmacy.

(B) Has some managerial experience or training.

(C) Makes all decisions slowly and carefully.

(D) Can work hard without having it adversely affect one's health.

References

1. Great fortunes lost. *Fortune*, July 18, 1988: 75–77.
2. Eli Lilly Drug Co. *Lilly Digest*. Indianapolis: Eli Lilly Co., 1991: 14–24.
3. Emshmiller JR. Handing down the business. *Wall Street Journal*, May 20, 1989: B-1.
4. Certo SC. *Modern Management*, 5th edn. Boston: Allyn and Bacon, 1992: 8.
5. Albanese R. *Management*, Cincinnati: Southwestern Publishing Company, 1988.
6. McGee KA and Pinto D. An overview of chain drugstore operations, in Marion Laboratories, Inc. in *Effective Pharmacy Management*, 3rd edn. Kansas City: Marion Laboratories, 1986: 458.

Cases for Part I*

Short cases

Case I.1 Uptown Community Hospital

Bonnie Conner, director of pharmacy at Uptown Community Hospital, just returned from yet another budget meeting. Present at this meeting were the hospital administrator, the chairman of the board of trustees of the hospital, the chief financial officer (CFO), the chief of the medical staff, director of nursing, vice president of marketing, vice president of human resources, and the manager of Uptown Pharmacy—the hospital's outpatient pharmacy. This particular session had been especially difficult, and Dr. Conner had asked Dr Robert Gwinn, the manager of Uptown Pharmacy, to meet over lunch to discuss the roles of the inpatient and outpatient pharmacies in relation to other hospital operating units.

The 200-bed hospital had just recorded another net loss on operations of more than $100,000 for the past month. The administrator and CFO both thought this level of loss would continue if some changes were not made. Not only was the census below projections, but the mix of patients was not favorable. A very high percentage of admissions were state Medicaid patients, and payments for these patients' services usually were insufficient to cover operating costs.

Because of the hospital's financial position, the administrator, Gene Davis, immediately froze all hiring, and asked each operating department to prepare plans to reduce its operating expenses by 10 percent.

This came on top of a 5 percent budget reduction requirement just two months ago.

The only area that was not included in this round of budget cuts was the marketing efforts to recruit and retain physicians, and the budget of the chief of the medical staff. The administrator and the chairman of the board of trustees were adamant that these reductions would not affect the quality of care or damage physician relations. They insisted that the physicians were critical, and that no actions be taken that could jeopardize their affiliation with the hospital.

Upon hearing these actions taken by the administrator, Dr. Conner knew that she would be in a very difficult situation. In order to reduce expenses, she could not replace some antiquated equipment, would have to reduce purchases of inventory, and might have to lay off some technicians.

She was very concerned about what all of this would do to the performance of the inpatient pharmacy, and the morale of the pharmacists. There already had been some dissatisfaction with working conditions, the lack of salary increases, and the quality of the equipment. Dr. Conner was afraid that further reductions in expenditures would cause some staff pharmacists to quit—and it was already difficult to find qualified people. How could she keep the inpatient pharmacy going with less money, and still provide satisfactory service to the physicians and patients?

In discussing her situation with Dr. Gwinn, she began to feel a little better. His situation appeared to be worse than hers. The outpatient pharmacy was not only over budget on operating costs but its revenues were below projections.

---

*Names of the organizations, individuals, and locations of all cases are fictional. Any likeness to actual organizations and/or individuals is purely coincidental.

While the number of prescriptions had grown over the last 2 years, the profit margins had declined significantly. In order to compete, Uptown Pharmacy agreed to participate in a managed care contract that offered very little profit. Dr. Gwinn indicated that on a prescription costing $75.00 for the drug, the pharmacy was selling it in this program for $68.50. The $6.50 margin was supposed to cover the costs of the pharmacist's time, the container, label, claims processing, etc., and still provide a profit. Had he not accepted this contract for services, nearly 10 percent of the pharmacy's current patients would have been lost. There also was a health maintenance organization in the market area that was becoming increasingly aggressive during open enrollment periods.

In addition, like Dr. Conner, Dr. Gwinn was having trouble hiring staff pharmacists at salaries and benefits that were competitive in the marketplace. Furthermore, the pharmacy computer was out-of-date and needed to be replaced. Several physicians wanted to have their computers link directly to Uptown Pharmacy's. The current pharmacy computer did not have the capacity to do this, but there was no room in the budget for a new system. Two of the physicians indicated that they were considering referring their patients to other pharmacies that already had these capabilities.

Over lunch, Dr. Conner and Dr. Gwinn began discussing the reasons why they were in these difficult situations. It was apparent that their respective pharmacies were not as important to the hospital administrator and chairman of the board of trustees as were other operating units. They wondered if they could change this condition before having to make what would be major budget cuts.

Questions

1 What are the similarities and differences in the situations faced by the inpatient and outpatient pharmacies?

2 How can Dr. Conner and Dr. Gwinn enhance the stature of their pharmacies so that they can get their fair shares of the hospital's budget?

Case I.2 Value Drugs, Inc.

Alfred Lim just walked out of a meeting with the regional manager for Value Drugs, Inc., and he was in a state of shock. The regional manager of this chain of 52 discount pharmacies informed Dr. Lim that the pharmacy department manager for the store in which he worked had been dismissed, and that Alfred was being promoted to that position. Although Dr. Lim had previously indicated a desire to assume some managerial duties, he had not expected it to occur so quickly, or under these circumstances. The initial excitement of the promotion had been tempered with his own concern about whether he was able and ready to assume the role of a manager rather than remain a staff pharmacist.

Value Drugs, Inc. was a relatively new chain of stores that emphasized both prescription and non-prescription merchandise. Each store had a pharmacy which occupied approximately 1,200 of the 11,000 feet of total floor space.

The company strategy used by the chain was to compete on both price and promotional bases. Many high-profile non-prescription drugs were priced very competitively, to encourage repeat business. Heavy advertising was used to guarantee low prices, and it was hoped that the additional foot traffic would enhance the sales of other non-prescription merchandise. One of the policies of the chain was that patients should wait between 15 and 30 minutes to have a prescription filled. It was hoped that during this time they would shop for other items.

Upon graduating from pharmacy school nearly 5 years ago, Dr. Lim had been hired by the chain. During his time as a staff pharmacist, Dr. Lim worked closely with the pharmacy department manager, but he had never been given any managerial responsibilities. His business background consisted of one pharmacy management course taken in school.

The regional manager for Value Drugs, Inc. indicated to Dr. Lim that the company had some concerns about his lack of managerial experience. However, he said that because Dr. Lim had been a very good employee, it would not take him long to become acclimated to his new responsibilities. The company thought that under the circumstances, it would be best for the pharmacy department to have one of its own promoted to manager. Since Dr. Lim had been with the store longer than the two other staff pharmacists, two technicians, and three sales clerks (one being part-time), he was considered to be the best suited for the job.

Of particular concern to the regional manager was the financial performance of the pharmacy department. Revenues were 15 percent below projections, and the ratio of pharmacists and technicians to number of prescriptions dispensed was very high—in effect, the department had too many employees for the amount of prescription volume generated. As a result, patients were waiting less than 10 minutes for a prescription. It was thought that they did not have enough time to do other shopping. In addition, the inventory level was too high, especially for the slower moving drugs.

Deciding that the company could wait no longer, the previous manager was offered the option of taking a staff pharmacist position at another store located in a different region or resigning from the company. He chose the latter.

In concluding the meeting, the regional manager indicated that he would be available to help Dr. Lim during the first few weeks of the transition, and that the company was willing to send him to several seminars on pharmacy management. However, he also made it clear that he expected Dr. Lim to assume control of the department immediately and begin to bring operating performance back in line with the desires of the company.

Questions

1 What do you think of the business strategies employed by Value Drugs, Inc.?
2 If you were Dr. Lim, what would you do as a first step in assuming control over the pharmacy department?

Case I.3 Phil's Pharmacy

Ron Sterling has been a successful pharmacist and manager of the pharmacy department in a major hospital for the past 15 years. Now he was thinking of going out and pursuing his dream of being his own boss and owning and managing a community pharmacy.

During the first 10 years that Dr. Sterling has worked for Stanton Medical Center Hospital, his primary responsibility has been filling prescription orders within the hospital. For the last 5 years, he headed the department that consisted of eleven pharmacists and six technicians. In his management role, he became well acquainted with the various suppliers of prescription drugs and some of the contracts that were offered by private insurers.

Furthermore, he has acquired some knowledge of front-end merchandise when he worked for a commu-

nity pharmacy while going to school, and his closest friend was a manager of a national chain drugstore in the same city. When they got together, it seemed to Dr. Sterling, that all they talked about was contracts, front-end merchandise, and the healthcare profession overall. All of this made Dr. Sterling want to be an entrepreneur rather than continue working for someone else. While his friend also discussed the advantages and disadvantages of being an owner, the negatives did not seem to discourage Dr. Sterling.

Dr. Sterling wanted to locate in the growing town of about 15,000 people which was only 15 miles from his current residence. He felt more comfortable with the small-town atmosphere with growth prospects than trying to go stay in the much larger city in which he currently worked. There were only two pharmacies in the small town, and one supermarket and two local grocery stores. The supermarket already had a pharmacy, but he was not sure that the two local grocery stores would ever do so because they had very limited space. To place pharmacies in their stores, both would have to relocate to larger facilities, and that didn't seem to be likely in at least the near future.

One of the two pharmacies in town, Phil's Pharmacy, has been in business for 15 years. The pharmacy enjoyed a solid reputation for quality service, performed largely by Phil Franklin and his son Michael. But, Michael Franklin was about to move to a neighboring city to start his own pharmacy. His father had wanted to turn over the business to Michael, but there are hard feelings between father and son and the working arrangement was never comfortable for either one. For that reason, Michael decided to go out on his own.

Phil's Pharmacy is on the eastern edge of town, an area that has not been in the growth area in the past 3 years. Nevertheless, patrons have been willing to drive to Phil's because they liked Michael and him and the service they provided.

Unfortunately, though, the physical facilities for the pharmacy were old and the store's fixtures and equipment needed costly repairs. Because Phil Franklin wanted to retire, he was not especially interested in investing a minimum of $150,000 in the pharmacy to make it more modern. He knew that sooner or later the run-down appearance of the pharmacy would impact customer patronage. He assumed that as the town grew, more modern buildings would be erected and that would make his look even worse.

Table I.3.1 Summary from Phil's Pharmacy income statement for this year and last 2 years

	This year	Last year	2-year average
Net sales	$1,531,666	$1,494,514	$1,478,090
Cost of sales	$1,038,470	$1,001,324	$975,539
Gross profit	$493,196	$493,190	$502,551
Expenses	$428,866	$413,980	$406,475
Net income	$64,330	$79,209	$96,076
Percent of net sales			
Cost of sales	67.8%	67.0%	66.0%
Gross profit	32.2%	33.0%	34.0%
Expenses	28.0%	27.7%	27.5%
Net income	4.2%	5.3%	6.5%

Given his son's imminent departure and the need to spend money to modernize Phil's Pharmacy, Phil approached Ron Sterling. He had met Dr. Sterling several years ago at a local function when Dr. Sterling's best friend introduced them. Subsequently, the three would occasionally get together for golf or tennis.

In discussing the possibilities of Dr. Sterling buying Phil's Pharmacy, Phil Franklin provided a summary from his income statement for this year and last 2 years. Mr. Franklin thought this would serve as a basis for considering the sale and arriving at a sales price. These are presented in Table I.3.1.

Dr. Sterling was excited about Franklin's offer. He knew that to start a new pharmacy in town would require lots of hard work which he could avoid if he took over Phil's Pharmacy. Starting new would require finding a suitable location, obtaining the necessary licenses, investing in inventory, and advertising the pharmacy's opening. Various other headaches would surely occur. Furthermore, Dr. Sterling knew that Mr. Franklin would help out during the first several months of operations and be available for advice on small business management, about which Dr. Sterling knows relatively little.

Dr. Sterling faces a major decision. He knows that he can fulfill his dream almost immediately if he buys Phil's Pharmacy. On the other hand, he has a relatively secure job at the hospital and his income is good and growing.

Questions

1 What are the advantages and disadvantages of Dr. Sterling staying in his present position working for a hospital versus owning a pharmacy?

2 If Dr. Sterling decided to own a pharmacy, what are the advantages and disadvantages of buying Phil's Pharmacy versus starting a new pharmacy?

Major cases

Case I.4 Haig's Pharmacy

Nathan and Jake Haig, owners of Haig's Pharmacy, were in the process of reviewing their financial statements for the most recent calendar year and making plans for the future. The past year had been somewhat of a disappointment because profits had been about the same as they have been for the last 3 years despite their efforts to better control costs. As they pondered the future, Nathan noted:

This pharmacy has been in our family for more than 30 years and it has always provided us with a good living. We know that the healthcare environment is changing and we have tried to adopt, but some of the dynamics are difficult to cope with when you are a relatively small business. Last year, we tried to make some serious cuts in expenses, but it really didn't have as good a result as we had hoped. We were always told that it is easier to cut costs than to grow revenues, so that is where we started. We need to consider what we want to do in the next year or so to ensure that our families are able to enjoy reasonable standards of living.

History of Haig's Pharmacy

Haig's Pharmacy was started 42 years ago by H.S. Haig, Nathan and Jake's father, in a large city in the southwest. The pharmacy had originally been a convenience store located near a hospital that was situated in a largely residential area. Mr. Haig purchased the store and converted it to a pharmacy that could cater to the medical needs of the residents and provide various sundries to people who were visiting patients in the hospital.

Over the years, the pharmacy provided a good living for Mr. Haig and his family. Although there were not many medical office buildings immediately surrounding the hospital, Mr. Haig had spent time meeting with and building strong relations with physicians who had hospital privileges. This gave him a good prescription business as those doctors recommended Haig's Pharmacy to their patients not in the hospital.

Mr. Haig also realized that the hospital drew a lot of visitors because it was well known for its cardiac care unit. The hospital also had a large rehabilitation unit and a skilled nursing facility (SNF) that was used primarily as a transition facility for patients who needed time for more intense medical care before either going home or to a permanent SNF or assisted living facility. Mr. Haig thought that the number of visitors to the hospital coupled with the residential areas surrounding the facility made it attractive for building a large gift and card area within the front-end of the pharmacy. Accordingly, he spent considerable time merchandising the entire front-end to appeal to hospital visitors who would buy gifts and cards for patients. While this proved to be successful, Mr. Haig also discovered that by carrying some unique items, he also became a "go to" place for residents who wanted to find gift items that would not be available in mass merchandise stores.

Ultimately, the front-end gift section grew beyond Mr. Haig's capabilities to continually find unique items. After considerable searching, Mr. Haig hired a merchandising manager, Agnes Tulan, whose responsibilities were to find and display relatively expensive gift items. Ms. Tulan had been working in an up-scale gift shop in the city's downtown area, and was looking for an opportunity to work closer to home. She has been with Haig's Pharmacy for more than 20 years.

After each had completed pharmacy school, Nathan and Jake Haig worked for national chain pharmacies for 5 years. Mr. Haig believed that it was important for his sons to gain experience working for someone else before coming to the family pharmacy. Nathan, who was nearly 3 years older than Jake, was

the first to do this and come back to work for Haig's Pharmacy. Jake did the same and has been back for about 4 years.

Once Jake returned to the pharmacy, Mr. Haig retired and sold the pharmacy to his sons for a nominal sum. While he was still a licensed pharmacist, Mr. Haig was not involved in the operations of the pharmacy except to fill in as a staff pharmacist when the need arose—primarily when the sons took time off for vacations.

Organization of the pharmacy

When Mr. Haig sold the pharmacy to his sons, he made the sale conditional on them deciding ahead of time how responsibilities would be divided between them. He wanted the family to stay close and not let the pharmacy be a source of conflict between his sons.

As a result, it was agreed that Nathan, as the oldest, would be president of the company. He was responsible for the pharmacy overall and for the prescription department in particular. Jake was the vice president and treasurer. While he worked as a pharmacist in the prescription department along with Nathan, he also oversaw the front-end and kept all financial records. Each managed the staff in their respective departments. A condensed organization chart is presented in Figure I.4.1.

As Jake indicated:

> Our father is a great guy, very progressive and insightful. We have no serious management problems. Nathan and I discuss the pharmacy's operations all of the time and there have been no major disagreements. We also talk to our father from time to time about what we are doing, but he wants us to run things and do what is best for our two families.
>
> Both Nathan and I have one pressing concern. Agnes has indicated that she does not want to work full time for much longer. I think she is ready to retire, but hates to quit because she has been with us for so long and feels like she is a member of the family. I am not sure what we will do when she is not around. She has had a great feel for gift purchases and merchandising the pharmacy, and neither Nathan nor I know quite how to replace her. Of course, sales of gifts have declined in recent times, but I guess that is partly due to customers shopping at mass merchandise stores, discount warehouses, and

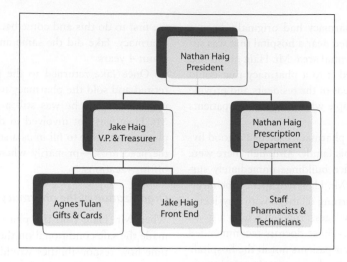

Figure I.4.1 Haig's Pharmacy organization chart.

other places. When it comes down to it, I am not sure whether Agnes has lost her touch, is just burned out, or the market has changed so much that this big a space for gifts is just not viable anymore.

Description of the pharmacy

Haig's Pharmacy is located on a corner of a busy avenue. It has about 12,500 square feet of interior space and a parking lot for about ten cars. Although the building is old, the store has been remodeled several times, the last of which occurred 3 years ago. As such, it has a modern appearance both inside and out. As Nathan noted:

> We may not do everything right, but we do try to maintain the exterior and interior of our pharmacy. We are in a relatively affluent neighborhood, sell fairly high-priced items, so our patients and other customers want something nice. Besides, the value of this land and building is probably the greatest asset we own.

The departments within Haig's Pharmacy and their approximate square footage are shown in Table I.4.1. The sizes include aisles and not all space has merchandise. The storage area is used primarily for non-prescription merchandise, although some space is used for medications when needed.

Haig's Pharmacy is open seven days a week, but is closed on major holidays. Its hours of operation are shown in Table I.4.2.

Table I.4.1 Sizes of Haig's Pharmacy's departments

Departments	Approx. sq. feet
Prescription department	1,500
Gifts and cards	3,000
Home health products	750
Cosmetics	750
Over-the-counter medications	750
Personal care products	500
Sundries (miscellaneous)	500
Candy	350
Checkout registers	150
Office	500
Storage	3,750
Total	12,500

With respect to staffing, two pharmacists are usually on duty, with at least one of them being either Nathan or Jake. The pharmacy department also employs two technicians who perform a variety of duties. During the 9 hours of operation during weekdays, Nathan and Jake relieve the one full-time pharmacist for mandatory breaks. Haig's Pharmacy employs two part-time pharmacists on weekends, with each working half-days on both weekend days. Nathan felt that this gives the pharmacy greater flexibility to staff the pharmacy in the event that one part-time person cannot work on a weekend. Occasionally, too, the part-time pharmacists assist during the week if either the full-time pharmacist or Nathan or Jake is not available.

Table I.4.2 Hours of operation of Haig's Pharmacy

Days of operation	Operating hours
Sunday	11 a.m. to 4 p.m.
Monday	9 a.m. to 6 p.m.
Tuesday	9 a.m. to 6 p.m.
Wednesday	9 a.m. to 6 p.m.
Thursday	9 a.m. to 6 p.m.
Friday	9 a.m. to 6 p.m.
Saturday	10 a.m. to 5 p.m.

Staffing in the front-end consists of Ms. Tulan and eight other employees who work on part-time bases. Ms. Tulan works weekdays from 9 a.m. to 5 p.m. The part-time employees have varying work schedules and are paid prevailing retail clerk wages. According to Jake:

Nathan and I decided some time ago that we would pay fair wages to our staff, but use part-time people only. By doing this, we can minimize the benefits we need to pay, and can mix and match their hours as needed. At first, this didn't work perfectly because we had considerable turnover of people and they wanted set schedules. So, we set schedules and now everything seems to be ok.

Over half of the part-time employees have been on staff for more than 5 years. They consist primarily of older people who just want to work some hours to keep busy and make extra money. Jake notes:

This has worked out well because these people stay with us and get to know how we operate and our customers. Nearly every employee knows who our regular customers are and can call them by name. We could get by cheaper by hiring from the local high school and community college, but there would be much more turnover and our customers would not get the recognition they do now.

Haig's Pharmacy tries to be price competitive with all of the other pharmacies in the immediate area. It runs advertisements in newspaper circulars once every two weeks on Sundays with sale items. These circulars only are distributed to the immediate geographic area. It also does some "door hangers" with information on both pharmacy services and coupons for discounts on non-prescription products. Door hangers are dis-

tributed about once a month to the 10,000 households in the area. Neither Nathan nor Jake wants to use television advertising, as Nathan commented:

We tried television for two weeks. We ran about six advertisements during a local 6 p.m. newscast and it didn't do a thing for us. I guess we should have run more advertisements, but we hate to spend that kind of money when we can do circulars less expensively. Besides, after 30 years, I think people know us by now.

The neighborhood and the competition

The neighborhood immediately surrounding Haig's Pharmacy was older and relatively affluent. While many of the homes were at least 30 years old, most had been remodeled and were valued considerably higher than many other parts of the city. The main factor in their value was the central proximity to downtown and nearly every other part of the city. As Jake indicated:

The homes in our area are somewhat like the old saying of "$100,000 homes on $600,000 lots." The real value is in the location. People in this area tend to stay here and have considerable equity built into their homes. With the ages of these homes, I sometimes wish we were a hardware store rather than a pharmacy. These people are always doing something to their houses. Actually, that is one reason for our success with gifts. Many of our customers buy our "gifts" for themselves. Decorations we sell almost fly off the shelves, and we have not been shy about pricing them at a premium.

Selected demographic characteristics of the immediate area are presented in Table I.4.3. As both Nathan and Jake noted, the characteristics have not changed much over the years, except that even in difficult economic times, housing values have not declined to the extent found in other parts of the city.

The main competition in the area consisted of four other pharmacies (see Table I.4.4). One of these, Bakers Drugs, is a national chain drugstore, and another, Standard Pharmacies, is a local chain of nine pharmacies. In addition, there are two independent pharmacies that are more traditional medical pharmacies, with relatively small front-ends.

Bakers Drugs is a national chain that has been in the city for about 8 years, but only opened a store

Table I.4.3 Selected demographic characteristics of surrounding area

Gender	
Male	47.3%
Female	52.7%
Total population	23,355
Age	
Under 20 years	24.3%
20–34 years	13.2%
35–54 years	31.2%
55–64 years	10.6%
65–74 years	9.7%
75 years and over	11.0%
Household income	
Less than $10,000	4.0%
$25,000–$49,999	13.8%
$50,000–$74,999	22.6%
$75,000–$99,999	12.1%
$100,000–$149,999	14.2%
$150,000–$199,999	15.8%
$200,000 or more	17.6%
Education (25 years and older)	
Less than 9th grade	2.3%
9th–12th grade, no diploma	3.9%
High school graduate	15.7%
Some college, no degree	22.6%
Associate degree	6.9%
Bachelor's degree	28.3%
Graduate or professional degree	20.3%
Total	100.0%
Home value	
Less than $50,000	0.5%
$50,000–$99,999	3.7%
$100,000–$149,999	5.3%
$150,000–$199,999	16.8%
$200,000–$299,999	20.4%
$300,000–$499,999	26.4%
$500,000–$999,999	16.7%
$1,000,000 or more	10.1%
Total	100.0%

within the immediate area 4 years ago. It tends to focus on low prices and heavy television and newspaper advertising to sell its front-end merchandise. While it takes most insurance plans for prescription drugs, less than one-third of its sales come from the pharmacy department.

Standard Pharmacies is a local chain that has been in existence for 7 years. Initially, it was a network of independent pharmacies that formed to make group purchases of prescription drugs. In time, it started joint advertising and then the nine owners decided to merge and form a chain. The pharmacy in the immediate vicinity of Haig's Pharmacy had been an independent store within this network. Its orientation is similar to Haig's in terms of its mix of prescription and non-prescription sales, but the smaller size has kept it from benefiting from the moderately heavy radio advertising done by the other eight stores in the chain.

A & D Pharmacy and Medical Drugs are independently owned and focus mostly on prescriptions and medical supplies (e.g. home health products and durable medical equipment). Both also offer compounding services and have tried to separate themselves by preparing specialty medications. Neither has a large front-end, and sales of non-prescription products are quite small. Both also rely on working relationships with physicians as a means of generating prescription volume.

Haig's Pharmacy financial information

Condensed financial statistics for Haig's Pharmacy for the last 3 years are presented in Table I.4.5. Of particular concern to both Nathan and Jake was the decline in profits from which they draw their salaries and retain funds for future renovations to the building and any new business ventures they want to pursue. As Jake summarized:

Nathan and I are concerned about the financials. Clearly, the year before was much better than last year in terms of both revenues and profits. We realize, of course, that there will be ups and downs in sales, but our two big sections of the pharmacy were down last year. And, our gross margins are only holding steady because we were able to better control our costs of goods. A question, however, is whether the lower costs of goods for all other areas of the pharmacy than prescriptions led to the decline

Table I.4.4 Comparisons with competing pharmacies

	Haig's	Standard	Bakers	A & D	Medical
Characteristics					
Ownership	Independent	Local chain	National chain	Independent	Independent
Size of pharmacy (total square feet)	12,500	9,500	18,500	5,500	4,000
Years in business in this area	32	3	4	12	18
Number of full-time pharmacists	3.0	3.0	3.0	2.0	2.0
Prescription department					
Compounding services				X	X
After-hours prescription services	X			X	
Automatic prescription refill service	X				
Prescription bubble-pack service	X				
Prescription delivery	X	X		X	X
Non-prescription products/services					
Personal care products	X	X	X	X	X
Over-the-counter medications	X	X	X	X	X
Cosmetics	X	X	X	X	X
Gifts	X				
Greeting cards	X	X	X		
Home health products	X			X	X
Durable medical equipment				X	X
Candy	X	X	X		

in sales in gifts and cards—we may be cutting in the wrong places and buying the wrong things.

Jake indicated that inventory turns in the prescription department remained between 10 and 14, which he considered reasonable. Inventory turns for the other sections of the pharmacy are shown in Table I.4.6.

Prices of some items have risen, but it was difficult to control prices on prescriptions since nearly all were under insurance contracts. For the front-end merchandise, the brothers tried to hold the lines on prices in order to remain competitive. As Nathan pointed out:

> Even though we are in an affluent neighborhood, the residents are not stupid. They still shop in mass merchandise stores, warehouse discount outlets, and other places like supermarkets that compete strictly on a price basis. They are not going to pay too much more for the convenience of our location when they have to go to those stores anyway for most

of their needs. So, Jake and I have taken the position that we need to be as competitive with our prices of non-prescription merchandise as possible. This builds customer loyalty and helps drive the prescription business to us. If our customers think our prices for aspirin are much too high, they probably think that our prescription prices are high also.

The future

Even though Nathan and Jake felt that Haig's Pharmacy was doing "ok," they believed that they needed to plan for the future before things got worse. In the past few weeks, Nathan and Jake had identified some options that they felt were worthy of consideration.

About two weeks ago, Nathan was approached by a statewide chain pharmacy about selling Haig's Pharmacy to it. This chain was not in the local area and wanted to establish an entry point to the city. The management of this chain felt that the reputation and location of Haig's Pharmacy would be an ideal starting point. The general terms of the informal offer

Table I.4.5 Financial summaries for Haig's Pharmacy

	Last year	Two years ago	Three years ago
Revenues			
Prescription department	$4,528,800	$4,695,535	$4,387,871
Gifts and cards	$816,000	$885,950	$826,560
Home health products	$204,000	$190,820	$135,608
Cosmetics	$408,000	$306,675	$376,472
Over-the-counter medications	$476,000	$368,010	$516,600
Personal care products	$272,000	$313,490	$244,739
Sundries (miscellaneous)	$170,000	$170,375	$180,810
Candy	$68,000	$68,150	$64,575
Total	$6,942,800	$6,999,005	$6,733,235
Cost of goods sold			
Prescription department	$3,306,024	$3,521,651	$3,194,370
All other (front-end)	$1,665,660	$1,520,290	$1,665,208
Total	$4,971,684	$5,041,941	$4,859,579
Gross margin			
Prescription department	$1,222,776	$1,173,884	$1,193,501
All other (front-end)	$748,340	$783,180	$680,156
Total	$1,971,116	$1,957,064	$1,873,657
Operating expenses			
Employee wages and benefits	$833,136	$803,486	$767,589
Legal and professional	$150,000	$150,000	$135,000
Advertising	$128,000	$130,000	$120,000
Utilities and insurance	$240,700	$227,980	$225,740
Supplies and repairs	$108,465	$107,995	$109,545
Other	$248,750	$252,100	$249,150
Total	$1,709,051	$1,671,561	$1,607,024
Net profit before taxes	$262,065	$285,503	$266,633

were that a selling price for the pharmacy would be agreed upon and Nathan and Jake would continue running the pharmacy as employees for a period of 5 years. During that 5-year period, they would be paid managerial salaries plus bonuses to help cover the "goodwill" value of the pharmacy that the chain would pay. After 5 years, the chain would decide whether to retain the services of Nathan and Jake. During the 5 years, it was expected that both brothers would do what they could to retain the goodwill with the physicians and current customers. The chain had used this strategy in other parts of the state and been reasonably successful.

Another option the brothers considered was just continuing doing what they were doing. As both

agreed, they were making a reasonable living and even if things went downhill, they did not think it would do so quickly.

A third option was to totally revamp front-end operations. This would involve retiring Ms. Tulan and starting over with respect to how the space in the pharmacy was utilized. Nathan thought that the trends in purchasing gifts and cards may have burned out, and that the future was in other areas such as more home health products and services. Jake was not as sure about this, but thought it was worth considering.

Finally, Nathan wondered about starting a "medication therapy management" (MTM) program in the pharmacy. This would involve trying to get selected

Table I.4.6 Inventory turns by department

Departments	Turns last year	Turns 2 years ago	Turns 3 years ago
Prescription department	12.8	13.1	11.9
Gifts and cards	4.8	4.9	6.0
Home health products	3.0	2.9	3.3
Cosmetics	6.6	6.7	6.4
Over-the-counter medications	4.5	4.0	4.3
Personal care products	2.8	3.0	2.9
Sundries (miscellaneous)	3.1	3.0	3.0
Candy	2.6	2.7	2.9

patients to pay the pharmacy on a monthly basis for consults on their medications and their lifestyle habits (e.g. diet, exercise). Since this was an affluent area, he felt that customers might want this service and would be willing to pay some fee. He doubted that the insurance companies would cover this, so he thought it might be best to do it on their own and see how it would work. To implement this, however, they thought they would have to hire another pharmacist to cover the time Nathan and Jake would spend in MTM consultations. A concern was how the physicians would respond to this—would they consider it a valuable service for their patients or an infringement on what they did?

In summarizing the options, Nathan commented:

> We are not sure what to do, but think we need to do something. This was instilled in us by our father. It is a "grow or die" perspective. The offer from the chain is somewhat interesting because it would take the pressure off us and we know that chains have and will continue to make inroads into the market. But, starting an MTM program would be invigorating. We don't know the types of patients for which MTM would be most suitable, but think that those with chronic medical issues might be the place to start, or those with the highest cost medications. In any event, we need to figure out what to do and think it all depends on what the future healthcare marketplace will be like.

Possible discussion questions

1 What will the market for pharmacy services be in the next 5 years? How will that impact Haig's Pharmacy?

2 What are the advantages and disadvantages of each option being considered? Are there other options to consider?

3 If Haig's Pharmacy is not sold to the chain, what changes, if any, should be made in operations?

4 What would it take to build a strong consulting program, such as MTM or some other service?

Case I.5 Middlefield Medical Center Pharmacy

Susan Chu, Vice President for Pharmacy Services at Middlefield Medical Center (MMC), was in the process of reviewing the minutes of the last executive committee (committee) meeting at MMC. The committee, made up of the president of MMC, the chairman of the MMC board of directors, the three vice presidents, and the medical chief of staff, had been discussing ways to make every aspect of the Center's operations more profitable and more responsive to patient needs.

Of particular concern to Ms. Chu was the general feeling that Pharmacy Services should open a satellite outpatient pharmacy on the Center's campus. It was thought that this would be a way to generate greater income for the center and better utilize the services of the inpatient pharmacy staff.

As Ms. Chu noted:

> There is no question that each unit within MMC needs to do a better job of generating profits, whether it be by increasing revenues or reducing costs or both. I think our pharmacy within the hospital is doing about as good as it can, but the executive committee wants to take a more aggressive approach to pharmacy services being a profit center. I know this is the

Table I.5.1 Population characteristics of the city

Total population	
Male	11,287
Female	13,713
Total	35,000
Population by age	
Under 5 years	7.3%
5–14 years	8.1%
15–19 years	7.7%
20–34 years	16.9%
35–54 years	24.0%
55–64 years	12.0%
65–74 years	9.9%
75–84 years	8.3%
85 years and over	5.9%
Household income	
Less than $10,000	4.8%
$10,000–$14,999	16.5%
$15,000–$24,999	13.5%
$25,000–$34,999	14.7%
$35,000–$49,999	14.4%
$50,000–$74,999	17.2%
$75,000–$99,999	7.6%
$100,000–$149,999	6.9%
$150,000–$199,999	1.9%
$200,000 or more	2.5%
Number of households	10,521
Education of population 25 or older	
Less than 9th grade	4.9%
9th–12th grade, no diploma	9.2%
High school graduate (includes equivalency)	30.4%
Some college, no degree	22.9%
Associate's degree	10.6%
Bachelor's degree	14.9%
Graduate or professional degree	7.1%

(continued)

Table I.5.1 *(continued)*

Civilian labor force	
Management, professional, and related occupations	16.1%
Service occupations	28.7%
Sales and office occupations	17.8%
Farming occupations	16.1%
Construction occupations	10.9%
Other	10.4%
Health insurance[a]	
Not covered	16.7%
Covered by private insurance	63.9%
Covered by employment based	55.8%
Covered by own employment based	29.5%
Covered by direct purchased insurance	8.9%
Covered by government health plan	30.6%
Medicaid	15.7%
Medicare	14.3%
Military	4.1%

[a] Percentages do not total to 100% due to multiple insurance.

but that was on an exception basis only. Typically, the attending physician would ask the patient or her or his family which pharmacy they wanted to use and any necessary prescriptions would be forwarded electronically to that pharmacy. In cases where it was extremely inconvenient for the patient to obtain needed medications, the inpatient pharmacy would provide just a sufficient supply to ensure that patient care was not compromised. According to Ms. Chu:

> Our job in the pharmacy is to provide the correct medications needed by physicians attending to patients in hospital beds and those being treated in the emergency department. The staff spend considerable time consulting with both physicians and the nursing staff to determine the proper course of medication therapy, and then dispense the medications as directed. We have not been an outpatient pharmacy as that is an entirely different ball game.

Competition for pharmacy services

There are 12 pharmacies located within the city. Ten of these are independent and chain community pharmacies and the other two are located in a grocery chain and a mass merchandise store. Of the ten community pharmacies, seven are independently

Five full-time pharmacists plus support staff worked within the pharmacy, which was located on the second floor of the hospital's three floors.

The primary responsibilities were to provide medications to patients in the hospital. On occasion, prescriptions were filled for patients being discharged

Table I.5.2 Healthcare activity

Average number of prescriptions per person per year	
Ages 0–18	4.5
Ages 19–64	13.2
Ages 65 and older	33.4
Where prescriptions are dispensed	
Traditional chain	47.9%
Independent	20.3%
Mass merchant	11.7%
Supermarkets	13.5%
Other	6.6%
Average spending on healthcare per person	
Total	$2,976
Drugs	$727
Average prescription sales per year	
Community independent	$2,380,000
Community chain	$4,950,000
Supermarket	$3,150,000
Mass merchandiser	$3,950,000
Average charge per prescription	
Traditional chain	$66.30
Independent	$65.59
Mass merchant	$65.40
Supermarkets	$61.25

owned and three are owned by chains with one chain having two outlets and the other having one pharmacy.

Ms. Chu provided a brief summary of what she considered the key attributes of the pharmacies in the city:

> Of the seven independent community pharmacies, five have been in existence for at least 10 years. The other two just opened within the last 3 years. It seems strange for independent pharmacies to be opening up in this environment with competition from the chain drugstores, grocery chains, and mass merchandisers becoming more intense in most parts of the country. But, the newest two seem to be doing ok. The five that have been here for a long time plus one of the new ones have relatively large front-ends and try to sell an array of non-prescription merchandise as well

as some durable medical equipment. The other new pharmacy is almost exclusively a prescription shop and has a very limited selection of other merchandise. Unlike the other six, it is located next to the largest physician office complex in the city.

Although we have not analyzed these pharmacies to a great extent yet, I think their main advantages are that some of the owners have built good relations with the physicians in this town. Having been in business for some time, and this being a small town, it seems like everybody gets to know everybody. The owners of two of these pharmacies really go out of their way to help the physicians and their patients. These two will open their pharmacies in the middle of the night and deliver prescriptions to patients of some physicians, special order merchandise, make sure to consult with every patient either in person or over the telephone, and so on. They are very service oriented. The owners of the other independent pharmacies are not this responsive most of the time, but they also have tried to build good relations with the physicians.

The chain drugstores are like what you would find in most cities. They operate on volume. They take contracts that have very low co-payments and hope that patients will purchase non-prescription merchandise while waiting for their prescriptions. I don't want to give the impression they do a poor job, because they are fine. Their focus, however, seems to be to use their prescription department as the attraction to generate store traffic.

The one grocery chain and the one mass merchandiser that have pharmacies do much the same as the chain drugstores. They focus on convenience and the "one-stop shopping" concept. I think both have been quite successful overall, but I am not sure how much volume their pharmacies do. I have heard a few complaints that it takes a long time to get a prescription filled at these pharmacies, and that would be consistent with the image that they want patients to wander the store aisles for a period of time. I'm not sure how true this is, but I've heard it from a couple of physicians who told me of the experiences of the patients.

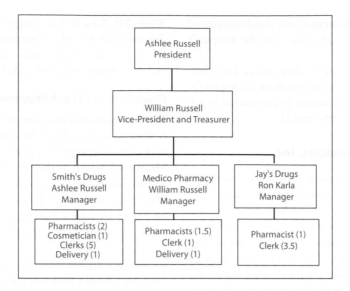

Figure I.6.1 Organizational structure of Park Pharmacies, Inc.

headaches. Besides, this store tends to cater to very low income clientele. These people are hard for me to deal with, especially with all the Medicaid claims. Each store does its own billing to insurance companies and to the state under the Medicaid program.

We also had considerable problems with shoplifting, and we were robbed twice this year by drug addicts. It just wasn't worth the additional $2,000.

As Mr. Karla noted, each pharmacy was managed independently of the others. Since they were nearly 7 miles apart, Ms. Russell and Mr. Russell felt that they were not competing with one another for customers, so they could operate autonomously. By doing this, they could each run their store as they saw fit, avoiding some of the common problems associated with partnerships. Not wanting to cause any new troubles, they agreed when they purchased Jay's Drugs that each would take an interest in overseeing its operations on a time-available basis. They left the day-to-day operations to the pharmacist–manager. Normally, Ms. Russell would stop by the store once a week, and Mr. Russell once every three weeks.

The market

Located in a city of nearly 350,000 people, the three pharmacies faced moderate to intense competition from both chain and independent drugstores located

nearby. Within the city there were 17 chain drug outlets, over 40 independent pharmacies, and outpatient pharmacies in the four local hospitals (see Tables I.6.1 and I.6.2).

Smith's Drugs faced the greatest amount of competition, since three chain stores and two independent pharmacies were located within 2 miles of the store. Being well established, the pharmacy was thought to have a loyal clientele, who were older and had higher incomes. Accordingly, these customers were not considered to be especially price sensitive or overly concerned with comparing chain store prices with those of Smith's Drugs for front-end items such as over-the-counter medications (OTCs) and health and beauty aids (HBAs). Ms. Russell believed that her customers were primarily interested in service rather than price. Although the store's growth had slowed down as new competition entered the area and the total population in the immediate area declined, both Ms. Russell and Mr. Russell thought that the store was doing very well.

Medico Pharmacy was a small pharmacy with limited front-end merchandise. It sold more home health supplies than most any other non-prescription merchandise. The pharmacy was situated in a medical center located near one of the larger hospitals in the city. Being the only pharmacy in the center gave Medico Pharmacy a significant advantage. However, there were four other independent pharmacies and one chain outlet located within 1.5 miles.

Table I.6.1 Selected demographics of the market area

	Smith's	Medico	Jay's
Gender			
Female	53.0%	54.0%	45.0%
Male	47.0%	46.0%	55.0%
Age			
Under 21	9.0%	12.0%	16.0%
21–35	17.0%	23.0%	31.0%
36–50	24.0%	28.0%	19.0%
51–64	31.0%	26.0%	18.0%
65 or older	19.0%	11.0%	16.0%
Household income			
Under $10,000	5.0%	2.0%	16.0%
$10,000–$25,000	12.0%	5.0%	35.0%
$25,001–$50,000	25.0%	18.0%	32.0%
$50,001–$75,000	25.0%	32.0%	15.0%
$75,001–$100,000	18.0%	25.0%	2.0%
$100,000–$150,000	10.0%	12.0%	0.0%
Over $150,000	5.0%	6.0%	0.0%
Employment			
Blue collar	19.0%	14.0%	39.0%
White collar	41.0%	43.0%	21.0%
Professional	21.0%	24.0%	10.0%
Unemployed	7.0%	5.0%	14.0%
Retired	11.0%	13.0%	14.0%
Other	1.0%	1.0%	2.0%
	100.0%	100.0%	100.0%

While Mr. Russell considered convenience to be a critical factor in selecting a pharmacy among those operating within his area since contract prices and co-payments were all about the same, he refused to compete on price because he considered price cutting to be unprofessional. As he noted:

> We are all about the same on prescriptions, except that I don't accept some insurance plans because reimbursements are too low. I grudgingly accept Medicaid, but prefer not to fill those scripts. If customers are going to patronize Medico Pharmacy for prescriptions or on home health supplies strictly because we offer the lowest prices, I don't want them. After all, how long will they remain our customers? I'll tell you, just until one of the other pharmacies offers them a better deal. There's no

> future in that type of activity. I offer my customers good service and convenience, and I expect them to pay for it. And, they do!

Jay's Drugs was located on the outskirts of the city in a relatively depressed area, along with one chain and two independent pharmacies. Incomes tended to be lower and a significant level of unemployment was evident. A much greater percentage of this store's customers were under the Medicaid and other third-party programs than in either Smith's Drugs or Medico Pharmacy. As Mr. Karla commented:

> The Medicaid program is a real issue here. This program only accounts for about 15 percent of Smith's Drugs' total revenues and 30 percent of those for Medico Pharmacy. For us, it represents about 60 percent of total revenues.

Store operations at Medico Pharmacy were much simpler. The pharmacy was open from 9 a.m. to 6 p.m., Monday through Friday. Mr. Russell ordinarily remained in the store throughout that time, even during normal lunch hours. He employed a delivery person on a part-time basis, and a semi-retired pharmacist during times he had to be away from the pharmacy. He had one technician working from 10 a.m. to 4 p.m., the pharmacy's busiest hours.

Jay's Drugs employed a pharmacist–manager, one full-time pharmacist, one technician, and three clerks. Because so many of its prescriptions were Medicaid and carried low profit margins, delivery service was not offered. Both Ms. Russell and Mr. Russell felt that the costs of delivery were too high to justify this service, and that delivery costs could not be passed on to store customers as an added charge. Store hours were 9 a.m. to 7 p.m., Monday through Saturday. The store manager, unlike other employees, was paid a straight salary. In addition to the management responsibilities for hiring and firing, the manager was expected to fill in as a backup pharmacist during peak times. Typically, the manager would work 5.5 days per week and receive $2,000 more in salary than the employee pharmacist earned in hourly wages for a month.

Financial position

As Ms. Russell and Mr. Russell reviewed the financial statements for each pharmacy (see Tables I.6.3 and I.6.4), it became apparent that the businesses had

not grown to the extent that Ms. Russell had hoped. Although both Smith's Drugs and Medico Pharmacy had always been profitable, the former generated considerably more sales and profits than did the latter. Nevertheless, the owners divided the profits equally, and tried to maintain a policy of retaining 20 percent of the net profits before taxes in the company. Believing that the acquisition of Jay's Pharmacy would increase their sales to more than $4 million and profits to $375,000, Ms. Russell expected Park Pharmacies, Inc. to continue to grow, possibly with the purchase of another pharmacy.

Mr. Russell, on the other hand, seemed quite content with the level of sales and the income he was receiving. Although he agreed that the profitability of the corporation was not up to expectations, he noted that the business still provided him with a comfortable living. However, he did express one major concern:

> Despite the fact that I am happy with my income from the business, I am not happy that Jay's has not turned out to be as good a pharmacy as Ashlee said it would.
>
> I'm also worried about the future need for more money. Smith's Drugs is getting pretty old, and will need some extensive modernization within the next 2 years. I expect that this will cost approximately $200,000. And, I would like to have a new computer system for my store. Ashlee has a new one and

Table I.6.3 Financial statements for pharmacies in last year			
	Smith's	**Medico**	**Jay's**
Sales			
Prescription	$1,162,007	$1,618,899	$1,071,750
Non-prescription	$1,259,083	$180,601	$357,250
Total	$2,421,090	$1,799,500	$1,429,000
Costs of goods sold	$1,646,225	$1,245,983	$900,179
Gross margin	$774,865	$553,517	$528,821
Operating expenses			
Manager's salary	$131,790	$131,790	$109,223
Employee wages	$338,023	$160,100	$268,506
Advertising	$65,396	$9,762	$24,575
Rent	$56,386	$68,450	$64,624
All other	$80,431	$96,320	$43,234
Total	$672,025	$466,423	$510,162
Net profit before taxes	$102,840	$87,094	$18,659

Table I.6.4 Consolidated financial statements Park Pharmacies, Inc. for last 3 years

	Last year	Two years ago	Three years ago
Sales			
Prescription	$3,852,656	$3,839,645	$3,829,585
Non-prescription	$1,796,934	$1,699,426	$1,701,018
Total	$5,649,590	$5,539,071	$5,530,603
Cost of goods sold	$3,792,387	$3,600,415	$3,602,013
Gross margin	$1,857,203	$1,938,656	$1,928,590
Operating expenses	$1,648,609	$1,724,890	$1,720,103
Net profit before taxes	$208,594	$213,766	$208,487

I would like to put the present one I have in the other store and get a new one for myself. I am not sure what this would cost, but it will certainly be a considerable expense. When we take these expenditures into account, we don't have all the money we think we do. Neither of us particularly likes to borrow money, so we could have some trouble here.

The future

In considering Ms. Russell's comments regarding the problems they were facing, Mr. Russell was both concerned and amused:

Ashlee was the one who wanted to jump into the "Jay's" deal. I was reluctant to change the good thing we had going; I just wanted to keep everything the way it was. She wanted to grow and get rich and be the big businesswoman. Unfortunately, I don't think that we can sell Jay's Drugs without losing a lot of money.

Before even considering the possibility of selling Jay's Drugs, Ms. Russell wanted to review the entire operation of Park Pharmacies, Inc. She knew that the poor operating performance of Jay's Drugs over the past 4 years would make it very difficult to sell the store. Furthermore, she did not want to give up, feeling that there must be ways to solve the problems they faced:

I don't think we have done all that we could to make Jay's successful. Our advertising hasn't been consistent and the store is not well merchandised. Some of the strategies I have used in my store should work well in Jay's, but William has not agreed. The effect has been a sporadic effort and the operating results show this to be true.

Possible discussion questions

1 How well run a business is Park Pharmacies, Inc.? What could be done to improve current operations?

2 How well positioned is each of the pharmacies relative to the competition?

3 In terms of how Park Pharmacies is organized and managed, how ready is it for a future role in healthcare?

4 What should be done with Jay's Drugs? How could operations be improved?

PART II

Planning and risk management

4

Developing business plans and policies

Learning objectives

The objectives of this chapter are to assist you to be able to explain:

- the importance of objectives, plans, policies, and procedures to successful business operations
- the types of goals a pharmacy may have
- the steps in the strategic planning process
- the major obstacles to planning
- when and on what basis reviews of goals, plans, policies, and procedures should be undertaken.

Key terms

Earning power
Goals
Growth
Plans
Policies
Profit
Strategic plan development

Business plans

Small business statistics show that 95 percent of the 400,000 annual small business failures can be attributed to poor management.[1] Pharmacists who know only the clinical aspects of dispensing prescriptions are likely to lead their pharmacies to the small business graveyard. To be successful, owners and managers must not only provide good professional services, they must be able to plan their pharmacies' future courses of action and develop policies and procedures for moving them toward their predetermined goals. This is illustrated in Figure 4.1.

Successful pharmacy management in any practice setting begins with an identification of goals, and a recognition of the need to develop plans for their achievement. A manager in any practice setting must recognize that it is important that the pharmacy has a direction in terms of whom to target as patients, what prescription and non-prescription products to offer,

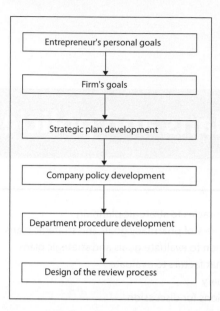

Figure 4.1 The process of planning. From Gaedeke RM and Tootelian DH. *Small Business Management*, 3rd edn. Boston: Allyn and Bacon, 1991: 168. Used with permission.

what services to offer, what prices to charge, how to grow, and so on.

Some managers, of course, have become successful without utilizing sound planning processes—everybody gets lucky now and then. The idea, however, is to become successful "because" rather than "in spite" of one's efforts.

Those who sit down with a road map to plot the best route for a vacation without first deciding where they want to go quickly realize the folly of their efforts. It is impossible to decide the best route until a destination has been decided upon. The same holds true for a pharmacy manager. Decisions must first be made about where the pharmacy is headed, and then a business plan can be prepared.

Every pharmacy needs to have strategic plans and direction. A strategic plan helps the manager:

- focus on and take advantage of the pharmacy's strengths
- eliminate or reduce the pharmacy's weaknesses
- capitalize on opportunities and emerging trends in the marketplace, and take defensive steps to reduce potential threats to the pharmacy's existence
- bring together all of the resources and direct them toward specific goals in areas like prod-

uct quality, healthcare, sales, profitability, and growth

- to arrange and list in order of importance all of the owner's objectives over the next 1–3 years, and assign responsibilities and timetables to ensure that they are accomplished.

For an existing pharmacy, the plan can build on past activities and performance. This makes the planning activities somewhat easier because the pharmacy manager has something with which to work. For a start-up pharmacy, planning is more difficult because there are a greater number of unknowns relative to future revenues, costs, and internal operating activities.

Nevertheless, the processes for both existing and start-up pharmacies are quite similar. The main difference is that there needs to be more flexibility in developing plans for a start-up pharmacy due to the unknowns. Accordingly, plans for a start-up could include preparing options for goals, organizing, staffing, and operating controls based on different scenarios that might occur (e.g. greater than expected demand, less than expected demand, changes in the services to be provided).

Business goals

In any practice setting, business goals can take many forms. However, they all tend to fall within three broad categories: survival, profit, and growth. The synthesis of these three categories into a single set of goals for the pharmacy establishes the basis for future planning. For example, if the owner's objectives lean heavily to survival, extreme caution will prevail in creating business strategies and risks will be minimized. On the other hand, if the objective is high profits or high rates of growth, more speculative strategies may be necessary. An owner of a pharmacy who wants to retire in 3 years may have very different goals from one who wants to stay in business for another 20 years.

Goals are set for both the short and long term. Short-term goals are for periods of 1 year or less, while long-term goals range for periods of 1–5 years. The owner or manager should begin by setting objectives for the long term and then create a series of short-term goals, which, when accomplished, will lead to achievement of the long-term ones.

Survival

The primary objective of most pharmacies, whether in community or institutional settings, is to survive. All managers in community pharmacies must confront the question: What actions will be necessary just to keep the business going for the desired amount of time? In hospital pharmacies, the question is: What has to be done to ensure that the pharmacy receives adequate resources to do its job, and preserve its role in delivering quality healthcare?

In community settings, the survival objective may conflict with other goals such as profits or growth. For example, it may be necessary for a pharmacy to be more price competitive if it is to keep its market position. And, in doing so, profit margins may suffer and not provide the funds necessary to invest in activities that could cause the pharmacy to grow. Given the general rule that greater profits and more rapid rates of growth require greater risks, management must make tradeoffs between this survival goal and other objectives (Figure 4.2).

Profit

Certainly one of the most common reasons cited for opening and continuing a pharmacy is the hope of profits. Establishing a goal "to make money" is not sufficient when it comes to planning the pharmacy's operations. If, for example, the pharmacy generates $1 in profit at the end of its fiscal year, has the profit objective been attained? Does a profit of $50,000 or $500,000 satisfy the owner's or hospital administrator's desire "to make money?"

As should be evident, profit objectives need to be stated in quantitative terms. A goal of earning $50,000 for the fiscal year provides greater direction than does "making money." Each business decision can be made in terms of how it will help the pharmacy earn $50,000.

Profit goals also must be realistic in the sense that they can be achieved without incurring unacceptable levels of risk. Wanting to achieve $500,000 profit when the best the pharmacy has ever done is $50,000 does not give management a good perspective in planning since the goal is nearly impossible to achieve.

Owners and hospital administrators can establish quantitative goals on the basis of "net revenues," "net profits," "market share," and return on investment. Net sales and net profits are defined in absolute dollar terms, such as revenues of $5,000,000 or net profits before or after taxes of $150,000. Market share in community settings is measured in percentage terms based on the pharmacy's sales in relation to its total sales and those of its competitors. For example, a 25 percent market share for prescriptions means the pharmacy's revenues from prescriptions are 25 percent of those for all prescription sales within the market area.

Although these first three profit goals are widely used, better ones are return on investment (ROI) and return on assets (ROA). ROI is measured by dividing the net profit of the pharmacy, typically before taxes, by its net worth (total assets minus total liabilities). The attraction of ROI is that it examines profits in relation to how much the owner has to invest to generate those profits. For example, if two pharmacies—A and B—each were to earn $50,000 in profits, would they be equally profitable?

The answer is no if the owner of A invested $500,000 and the owner of B had to invest $1 million. The ROIs would be 10 percent (i.e. $50,000 divided by $500,000) and 5 percent (i.e. $50,000 divided by $1 million) respectively.

In hospital settings, it is difficult to use ROI because net worth is difficult to compute. Accordingly, ROA (i.e. net profit divided by net assets) is preferable because the assets of the pharmacy are more easily determined. The computation is similar to that of ROI. However, with ROA, the issue is how much is being earned on all of the investments—those of the owner and those of the creditors.

Growth

One of the more important goals for a pharmacy is growth. Too often, management focuses only on survival and profits, and neglects the fact that most successful pharmacies need to grow over time. A key to the growth objective is to define rate and consistency. Every effort should be made to ensure that the business grows in a stable fashion rather than haphazardly. Only in this way can management plan and utilize the available resources to maximum advantage.

For example, it would be more difficult to plan for the type of growth when sales or profits rise and fall radically. It is hard to know when to buy more inventory and equipment, hire more pharmacy personnel, obtain more space, and so forth.

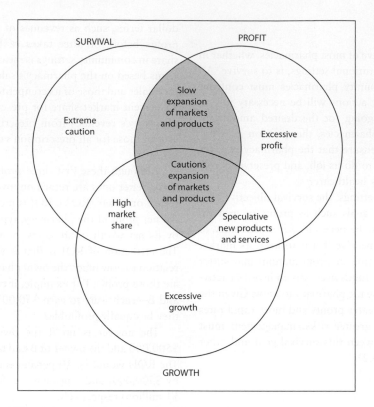

Figure 4.2 Business goals and their interactions. From Gaedeke RM and Tootelian DH. *Essentials of Pharmacy Management.* St. Louis, MO: Mosby-Year Book, Inc., 1993: 105. Used with permission.

Growth, like profits, must be quantified and realistic, and typically focus on increases or stability in the profit goals. Generally, they are defined in percentage terms over some specified time period. For example, management may want a 5 percent average growth in sales, a 2 percent increase in market share, or a 1 percent rise in return on investment or return on assets over a one-year period.

Strategic planning within a pharmacy

Strategic planning is a process by which management and other key people within the pharmacy:

- define the pharmacy's mission
- assess its current situation
- decide what the pharmacy is to look like in 1–3 years
- design a course to bring the pharmacy from where it is now to where it should be, recog-

nizing its strengths and weaknesses, and the opportunities and threats confronting it.

When conducted properly, a strategic plan is a means of combining separate marketing, financial, production, human resource, and other plans. In this way, management can better integrate and utilize the resources available to achieve a predetermined set of objectives. In very small pharmacies where there is just the owner and a few employees, plans often are developed by the owner and then passed on to employees.

However, in somewhat larger chains and hospital pharmacies where there are middle managers, the planning process should be undertaken throughout the organization. Most plans, of course, ultimately are decided upon by the owner and key managers. The top level of management (e.g. owner, hospital administrator) needs to establish broad, long-range goals and the necessary framework for policies and procedures. Lower levels of the organization (e.g. pharmacy manager, district manager) will develop specific policies and procedures oriented to what is to be done and how it is to be done. The emphasis will be on short-term perspectives necessary to support and blend with the long-range plans. Particular concern needs to be given to ensuring that all of the operating, marketing, and financial activities are included in the plan.

Some managers start with short-term plans and build up long-term plans (the "build up method") accordingly. After deciding what is to transpire in 1 year, the owner can then identify what is to be achieved over a 2- to 5-year period. For many pharmacies, however, this approach has serious pitfalls. Most important, the result of this type of effort is that management often focuses on what *can* rather than what *should* be accomplished over the long term. In addition, there is greater likelihood that in the long term the pharmacy evolves from a disjointed series of decisions rather than a conscious effort to model it into something specific.

A preferred approach is one where long-term objectives and plans are established and used as guidelines for short-term ones. Sometimes known as the "breakdown method," this technique forces the owner to identify where the pharmacy should be over time and then implement the necessary short-term policies and procedures to ensure achievement of those goals. Each decision, then, is viewed with this perspective and provides a better way for management to identify and plan for the future.

The strategic planning process

The planning process is one of the many responsibilities that rests ultimately with the pharmacy owner or hospital administrator and board of trustees. The process itself can be both challenging and time-consuming depending on how well-defined the goals are, what is to be accomplished, the complexity and size of the pharmacy's operations, and the state of the environment (e.g. governmental regulations, number of competitors, economic conditions, potential for technological advances).

In general, for owners, managers, and hospital administrators who know what they want their pharmacies to be and do, and who have some degree of management expertise, planning the course of operations can be an enlightening experience. For pharmacies in community and hospital settings, the planning process should follow the steps described below.

Steps in strategic planning

Actual planning involves working through a series of questions designed to examine how the pharmacy operates and how current decisions will affect future actions. By addressing six major questions that form the planning process, management should be able to develop a set of strategies to guide the pharmacy's future activities.

1. What is the current status of the pharmacy?

It is impossible for management to develop a set of plans and strategies for the future without assessing the present situation. Management must analyze the present status with respect to the pharmacy's goals, financial position, operating capabilities, management and labor expertise, and market position and marketing capabilities (Table 4.1).

Complementing this evaluation of the present should be an examination of "why" and "how" the pharmacy came into its present position. Experiences of the past can assist in future planning. Decisions that turned out to be good and those that were poor (in retrospect) often provide a sound basis for plotting future operations.

Past actions are not always indicative of the future, however. Given changes in goals and the highly volatile business environment (e.g. new regulations and new biotech products), what was good or bad in the past may not be so in the future. Consequently, management also should evaluate how well the past coincides with the present and what can be expected over the next year.

Enough emphasis cannot be placed on this first step of the planning process. Not only does it establish the initial framework for business planning, but such an analysis can prove to be an excellent learning experience for management.

2. Where should the pharmacy be at the present?

Realistic assessments of the present status also demand that consideration be given to where management and the pharmacy "should" be. Of particular concern are the financial, management, and marketing positions. What should be the sales level? What should be the mix of private pay, government, and other third-party prescriptions? Within which third-party programs should the pharmacy participate? How much profit should it generate? How many employees should the pharmacy have?

Table 4.2 Sample business plan outline

I. Summary	A. Description of the pharmacy	1. Name
		2. Address
		3. Telephone number
		4. Products and services sold
		5. Market area and competitive position
	B. Goals of the pharmacy	1. Long-term goals
		2. Short-term goals
	C. Summary of financial position	1. Cash situation
		2. Accounts receivable situation
		3. Sales and profit patterns
		4. Funding needs for future growth
II. Market analysis	A. Description of the market area	1. Geographic characteristics
		2. Demographic characteristics
		3. Operating characteristics
	B. Nature of the market	1. General situation
		2. Trends from the past
		3. Expectations for the future
	C. Economic conditions	1. Income
		2. Employment
		3. Disposable spending
		4. Overall prosperity
	D. Technology	1. Areas of development
		2. Long-term prospects for change
	E. Political and legal situation	1. Political climate
		2. Applicable laws
III. Competitive analysis	A. Number of competitors	
	B. Competitors' strengths	
	C. Competitors' weaknesses	
	D. Competitors' target markets	

(continued)

for the manager who desires a more streamlined and efficient operation. Conflicting or overlapping programs do little to strengthen the pharmacy.

6. What controls should be built into the plans?

It is often thought that sound management includes a yearly review of plans to determine whether the goals have been achieved. While such reviews are useful for future planning, they are insufficient because at that point it is too late to take corrective action. An evaluation at the end of a fiscal year provides no vehicle to assure goal achievement.

Consequently, checkpoints at one-, three-, or six-month intervals need to be established within the plan itself. By examining these periodically, problems can be identified and remedied before they hinder achievement of business goals. Examples of these checkpoints include:

- quality control checks on prescription dispensing
- quarterly market share calculations for prescription and non-prescription lines.
- quarterly profitability tests through such ratios as ROI and percent profits on sales.

Table 4.2 (*continued*)

IV. Target market and competitive advantages	A. Target market	1. Characteristics
		2. Sales and profit potential
	B. Competitive advantages	1. Tangible advantages
		2. Intangible advantages
V. Products and services	A. Product-service mix	1. Number
		2. Consistency between types
		3. New offerings
	B. Characteristics	1. Physical characteristics
		2. Benefits provided
		3. Advantages over those offered by competitors
VI. Marketing strategies	A. Product-service strategies	
	B. Distribution strategies	
	C. Price strategies	
	D. Promotion strategies	
VII. Management strategies	A. Business organization chart	
	B. Number of employees, by areas of expertise	
	C. Description of management team	
	D. Primary duties and responsibilities of individual managers	
VIII. Financial strategies	A. Evaluation of financial condition	
	B. Income statements	
	C. Balance sheets	
	D. Cash flow statements	
	E. Capital budgets	

Modified from Gaedeke RM and Tootelian DH. *Small Business Management*, 3rd edn. Boston: Allyn and Bacon, 1991: 180. Used with permission.

Consequently, policies and procedures should be developed to include the types of controls, how and when they are to be implemented, and who is to be responsible. As part of the established strategic plan, they will serve to keep the pharmacy on a proper course and minimize differences between expected and attained results.

Obstacles to strategic planning

The planning effort essentially allows the manager to decide in definitive terms what the pharmacy should accomplish in the future. Given the great importance of planning business operations, however, it is difficult to understand why so few managers do so.

The inexact nature of planning is the most common excuse for not engaging in this activity. Many

pharmacists think that planning is a waste of time because the future is so uncertain. Since plans must deal with the unknown, the possibility of errors in definitive plans is a problem.

Nevertheless, planning provides opportunities to study these ambiguities and develop contingency plans to prepare for various possible situations. The successful pharmacy owner or manager recognizes that plans are not etched in stone, and can and should be revised. Flexible plans are a must. They need to be adaptable to uncontrollable environmental and market changes.

Some managers couple the inexactness of planning with the fact that the healthcare and business worlds are in a constant state of flux. While there is considerable variability in these environments this, too, is a poor excuse. To the extent possible,

Examples of this abound. Companies that are the victims of fire, earthquakes, tornadoes, and such often do not have adequate insurance to cover their losses. Even when the owner becomes ill and cannot manage the business for an extended period of time, the pharmacy can suffer irreparable damages. Factors well beyond personal control can have a significant impact on the survival and success of the pharmacy.

Pharmacy owners and managers in all practice settings must plan and prepare for risks within and beyond their personal control. In most cases, business risk cannot be eliminated completely. Some risks are unavoidable, and others would be too costly to fully protect against.

Risk management, therefore, does not mean risk avoidance. Rather, it implies that risk be assessed, measured, and reduced to the extent economically feasible. Perhaps the key lies in making sure that some unexpected or uncontrollable circumstances cannot unilaterally destroy the venture.

Non-crime-related business risks

The more common types of non-criminal business risks that can be guarded against include (Figure 5.1):

- fire
- natural disasters
- personal liabilities
- economic downturns
- business interruptions
- loss of key personnel.

Fire

Threat of fire is probably the first fear that comes to the mind of every manager. Many owners seek to allay this fear solely through the purchase of fire insurance. They mistakenly assume that such protection will fully cover their losses.

While fire insurance can cover most of the monetary costs, it cannot completely protect against lost customers, records, and so on. Consequently, fire insurance should be viewed as a fail-safe mechanism supplemental to a sound fire safety program. The goals here are to reduce both the threat of fire and the losses should fire occur.

A program of fire protection essentially is a set of procedures for making sure that the physical premises, employees, and customer practices do not create unnecessary fire hazards. The pharmacy should be inspected periodically for faulty construction or wiring. Use of fire-resistant materials and insulation also serves to reduce the likelihood of fire. In addition, employees and customer activities should be closely scrutinized. Smoking should not be permitted indoors, and care must be taken in storing flammable products such as cleaning supplies, etc.

Natural disasters

High winds, floods, earthquakes and tsunamis (e.g. Japan in 2011), tornadoes (e.g. record numbers in the Midwest in 2011), and hurricanes (e.g. Katrina in New Orleans in 2005) are other calamities that can affect business activities. Usually unpredictable,

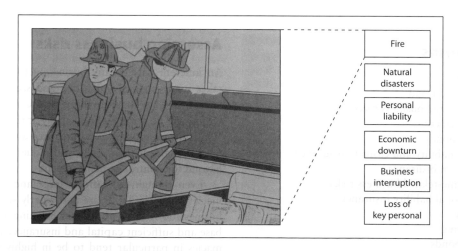

Figure 5.1 The different types of non-crime-related risks. From Gaedeke RM and Tootelian DH. *Small Business Management*, 3rd edn. Boston: Allyn and Bacon, 1991: 272. Used with permission.

they can quickly destroy or damage business establishments. The earthquake and resulting tsunamis that hit Japan in 2011 is clear evidence of how natural disasters can destroy not only individual businesses, but entire cities. That same year, a record number of tornadoes touched down in various Midwestern and Southern states, destroying homes and businesses in their sometimes mile-wide paths. And, of course, Hurricane Katrina devastated New Orleans in 2005, and many businesses never recovered from the winds and subsequent flooding.

Depending on the geographic area, management must identify which disasters are more likely. For example, California is more prone to earthquakes, parts of Texas and the Midwest have a considerable number of tornadoes, and the Southeastern seaboard is commonly in the path of hurricanes. Purchasing insurance frequently is a good hedge against some risks and may be the only protection available.

Personal liabilities

Pharmacies incur risks from injury to third parties caused in the course of business activities. If a customer is injured in the store or is injured while using a prescription filled by the pharmacy, damage suits may result. Similarly, if the delivery vehicle becomes involved in an injury accident, the pharmacy may be liable. And, of course, if the wrong drug is dispensed, liability will be very high.

For most pharmacies the greatest risks consist of possible injury to customers. Prescription errors by the physician, dispensing errors by the pharmacy, and injury within the store expose the pharmacy and its pharmacists and technicians to considerable risk.

Even though most businesses carry insurance to protect against major lawsuits, they still need to safeguard their products and premises. With respect to product safety, pharmacies must be alert to possible compounding and dispensing errors, and adhere to stringent processes and quality control standards. In addition, how products are stored and rotated to ensure freshness must be clearly specified for employees. The extent to which a pharmacy and its employees need to delineate the do's and don'ts of product usage to patients has increased. However, there is always the question of how far the pharmacy has to go to protect consumers from their own stupidity. In general, the answer is to do all that is necessary to ensure customer safety.

Economic downturn and social/cultural shifts

Changes in the business economy loom as a significant risk, but are largely beyond the control of management. Such was the case with the recession worldwide and in the USA in the latter part of the first decade in the 2000s and early part of the second decade (i.e. 2010s).

Economic factors create problems for all businesses. Efforts to control the costs of healthcare have caused many employers to seek third-party contracts that contain discounted fees for pharmacy services. Unemployment brings a loss of private health insurance, and people tend to visit physicians only when they have to do so, thereby reducing the number of prescriptions generated.

Economic changes cannot be controlled, but they can be prepared for to some extent. Building financial reserves during prosperous times enhances stability during economic downturns. Increasing the owner's equity and working capital positions through increased current assets can act as a buffer against business fluctuations.

Shifts in social and cultural patterns also cause economic changes. Greater acceptance of mail order dispensing in the 1900s and 2000s had a significant impact on both chain and independent pharmacies. Similarly, the growth of health maintenance organizations with their own pharmacies has had a pronounced effect on prescription sales in independent and chain settings.

Social and cultural changes can be prepared for if management maintains a reasonable degree of flexibility and does not become tradition-bound. The ability to adapt quickly to changing market conditions is especially important for small pharmacies because they usually can adjust more rapidly than can larger chains. For example, to the extent that they can modify their non-prescription merchandise to new items and those appealing to their very local markets, they can develop competitive advantages when seeking to attract new customers. Although not always true, larger chains can get caught up in bureaucratic structures which slow their reaction time during highly volatile times.

Business interruptions

Management must be concerned about disruptions in business due to labor actions, building renovations, street work, and other factors that can limit potential

Table 5.1 Protection from shoplifters

Business policy	Prosecute shoplifters
	Have the pharmacy "shopped" by a professional security firm periodically
Employees	Acknowledge customers when they enter the pharmacy
	Be alert for unusual customer dress
	Monitor customers' movement in the pharmacy
	Watch groups of customers who disperse after entering pharmacy
Store layout	Keep low end displays
	Use low shelving
	Have mirrors for hard-to-watch areas
	Provide ample lighting in all areas of the store
	Use surveillance cameras
	Keep expensive merchandise in locked cases

Modified from Gaedeke RM and Tootelian DH. *Small Business Management*, 3rd edn. Boston: Allyn and Bacon, 1991: 278. Used with permission.

in the summer), bags, boxes, or briefcases, should be watched closely.

Trained salespeople are alert to shoplifters' early warning signals. Employees should be on the lookout for customers carrying concealment devices such as bulky coats and large shopping bags or purses. They also should watch groups of shoppers who enter the store together, and then break up and go in different directions. A customer who attempts to monopolize a salesperson's time may be covering for a companion who is stealing elsewhere in the store.

Ordinary customers want attention; shoplifters do not. When busy with one customer, the salesperson should acknowledge others who are in the store. This will make legitimate customers happy and shoplifters uneasy.

Customers who handle considerable amounts of merchandise but take unusually long periods of time to make decisions may be viewed with suspicion. Shoplifters often linger in one area, loiter near stockrooms or other restricted areas, or wander aimlessly through the store.

Aside from the efforts of employees, the general layout of the premises can be designed to minimize opportunities for shoplifting. A key to preventing shoplifting is to maintain adequate lighting in all areas. By keeping protruding "wings" and end displays low, not more than 3 feet high, visibility by salespeople is enhanced. In addition, small items of high value are often kept behind counters, or locked in special cases. Finally, protective devices such as one-way mirrors, closed-circuit television, and convex wall mirrors can be utilized.

Credit card fraud and bad checks

Losses to business through the use of stolen or fake credit cards and bogus checks pose a continuous risk to pharmacies. In many cases, however, these risks can be reduced significantly through proper control and common sense (Table 5.2).

Credit card problems typically occur when a business accepts expired cards, stolen or otherwise invalid cards, and cards for purchases above the maximum established by the issuer. Simple care in observing pictures on licenses and matching names to the card usually eliminates a portion of the problem. The electronic verification of transactions and instant authorizations for purchases by credit card companies also have resolved many problems associated with credit cards.

Close examination of signatures to assure that the one on the card is similar to the one on the receipt, and inspections of other forms of identification, serve to reduce the more flagrant abuses.

Modern electronic credit card verification and insurance systems are a relatively quick way to protect against credit card fraud. While they must be paid for, these systems can ensure that the pharmacy does not sustain large losses.

With the growth in use of debit cards and credit cards, checks are not used to as great an extent as in the past. However, in some geographic areas and among some population groups, checks are still a preferred method of payment.

Acceptance of bad checks, like credit card frauds, often is the result of poor business practices by management. Winning the battle of wits against criminal

Table 5.2 Protection from credit card fraud and bad checks

Business policy	Seek collection of all bad checks
	Establish policies concerning which checks and credit cards to accept
	Establish limits for check cashing and credit card acceptance by employees without manager's approval
	Do not allow split-ticketing for credit cards
Employees	Train employees to examine checks and credit cards
	Require at least two pieces of identification that have pictures and signatures
	Watch for inconsistencies between customer appearance and type of merchandise purchased
	Keep records on the number of bad checks and fraudulent credit cards employees accept, and include this information as part of their evaluations

From Gaedeke RM and Tootelian DH. *Small Business Management*, 3rd edn. Boston: Allyn and Bacon, 1991: 279. Used with permission.

check passers is a matter of knowledge and vigilance. A business on occasion might receive five different types of checks and money orders:

- Personal check—written and signed by the person offering it; the check is made out to the pharmacy.
- Two-party check—issued by the maker to a second person, who endorses it so that it may be cashed by a third party. This type of check is most susceptible to fraud because the maker can stop payment before it is cashed by the third person.
- Payroll check—issued to employees for services performed. Usually, the check contains the printed name of the employer, an imprinted identification number from a check writing machine, and a signature. The employee's name is either typed in or printed on the check by the machine. In general, it is risky to accept payroll checks that are hand-printed, rubber-stamped, or typewritten.
- Government check—issued by a local, state, or federal agency. Managers should be particularly cautious with government checks since they are often stolen and the endorsement forged. In some areas, this is such a problem that banks refuse to cash welfare, relief, or tax refund checks unless they know the customer or the customer has an account with the bank.
- Money order—a "check" that can be purchased for a specified amount and sent to another party. Typically, money orders are bought to send in the mail by people who do not have checking accounts. Most retailers do not accept them for payment in face-to-face transactions, and pharmacies that sell money orders should never

accept personal checks for payment. There is little need for money orders if the person has a checking account.

Bad check artists can fool all but the best detection available, and as such find smaller businesses in general relatively easy prey. While some protective measures are possible, they add to the cost and complexity of completing a transaction. Use of check verification services, photographic equipment, and other devices often wards off criminals.

Of equal importance is guarding against forgers. Careful examination of the check can identify poorly forged or altered checks. In addition, properly signed identification cards should be requested to provide more protection.

The pharmacy owner should develop specific policies regarding two-party checks, out-of-state checks, checks for amounts above the purchase, etc., and discuss them with all sales employees. These policies ensure that employees know what should and should not be accepted, and keep them on notice that this is a critical concern.

Insurance eligibility cards

Historically, one of the more common problems faced by pharmacies is filling prescriptions for those who are ineligible for insurance coverage. Customers can have insurance cards or other forms of documentation that indicate they are eligible for coverage when, in fact, they are not.

On-line claims processing helps protect pharmacies from most of these problems. Most of this is now done automatically before a prescription is dispensed. However, some pharmacies still use older computer programs that require verification where the systems are not rapidly updated.

Employee theft and embezzlement

Most pharmacy owners take some precautions to guard against external factors such as robbery, burglary, and fraud. Unfortunately, they tend to neglect protection from internal theft. Employee theft and embezzlement are two of the greatest risks faced by all business owners (Table 5.3). According to some experts, small pharmacies are more vulnerable. They tend to have relaxed accounting systems, preferring to sacrifice some control for the cost savings. In addition, with relatively few employees there is not as much segregation of duties. One employee may do several jobs, which in larger pharmacies, chains, and hospital organizations would be separated for security purposes.

Employee crime can be costly. A few examples reported over the years include a bookkeeper who deposited $750,000 in bill payments to her own bank account, and a trusted employee of 28 years who was an expert at filling orders for himself and never reporting the shipments to the billing department. Losses were estimated to have run into the hundreds of thousands of dollars.

The Department of Commerce estimates that 8–10 percent of all employees are hardcore pilferers and that 15–80 percent of all retail shortages are caused by employee theft. The ready availability of cash and merchandise can tempt even the honest employee. Consequently, management must take steps to minimize this type of risk.

The process of reducing internal theft must begin with a careful assessment of where opportunities for theft are most prevalent. Storage rooms, cash registers, and open desks where payment invoices and blank checks are kept are especially vulnerable. A simple tour of the premises with the idea of trying to steal something will help pinpoint trouble spots.

Although specific safeguards will depend on the areas most likely to be vulnerable to internal theft, some standard precautions are as follows:

- Segregate duties related to payments, receipts, purchasing, inventory control, inventory receiving, etc. When employees are allowed to handle two or more of these functions, the opportunities for theft and embezzlement increase greatly.

- Maintain good records and review them both periodically and at random times. This makes it more difficult for employees to steal and makes it easier to track down any shortages.

- Make sure that the paperwork ties in with the bookkeeping. For example, payments should be made only when all the paperwork has been completed and everything tallies correctly.

Table 5.3 Protection against employee theft and embezzlement

Preventing employee theft	Prosecute all employees caught stealing
	Segregate duties that allow funds to come into and go out of the pharmacy
	Keep good records that create proper trails of revenues and expenses, and review them periodically
	Use outside auditors/accountants to review the books once per year
	Minimize access to cash, checks, and purchase and receipt documents
	Keep valuable inventory under special security
	Inspect incoming and outgoing shipments, employee lunch boxes, etc., on a periodic basis insofar as there is compliance with all local, state, and federal laws
Clues to embezzlement	Unusually high levels of sales returns
	Unusually high bad-debts and write-offs
	Reductions in cash sales that appear unexplainable
	Cash register shortages or overages
	Inventory shortages of items that are easily marketable
	Increases in expenses that are not explainable
	Employees who appear to be living beyond their means
	Imbalances between cash receipts and cash deposits
	Checks being issued to unknown or unusual suppliers

Modified from Gaedeke RM and Tootelian DH. *Small Business Management*, 3rd edn. Boston: Allyn and Bacon, 1991: 282. Used with permission.

- Use special safeguards such as locked cabinets and screened-in areas to protect valuable inventory, just as for controlled substances. Watch expensive non-prescription merchandise closely or place it in locked displays.
- Be especially watchful of the most trusted employees. These are the people who receive less attention and are provided with more opportunities to commit crimes.
- Prosecute employees who are caught stealing—settling for restitution and an apology is inviting theft to continue.
- At random times, check incoming materials to ensure that there is no collusive activity between drivers and employees who are in charge of receiving inventory.

What distinguishes embezzlement from pilferage and other internal theft is that it is "the fraudulent appropriation of property by a person to whom it has been entrusted." The embezzler is typically a trusted employee, and therefore is not viewed with suspicion until extensive theft is evident. Common clues to embezzlement include:

- a decline or unusually small increase in cash or credit sales that might mean some sales are not being recorded
- inventory shortages caused by fictitious purchases, unrecorded sales, or employee pilferage
- profit declines and increases in expenses, which can be a sign that cash is being siphoned off illegitimately.

There are many ways to reduce the possibility for losses through embezzlement. The owner, or manager, should check the background of all prospective employees. This may involve making telephone calls or writing letters to past employers, or turning the matter over to a credit bureau or similar agency which can conduct background checks. To help control internal theft, managers are increasingly making criminal background checks on potential employees and requesting that employees take drug tests.

The pharmacy owner or manager also should attempt to get to know employees well enough to recognize signs of financial or other personal problems that could make it more likely that the person would need money in a hurry. Some pharmacy owners prefer to have a post office box for receiving mail to ensure that checks that do come in can be picked up

by a designated person. When mail comes into the pharmacy directly, more people have access to letters and envelopes. Other safeguards to protect against embezzlement include the following:

- Prepare daily cash deposits with a record of the cash and checks received.
- Arrange for bank statements and other correspondence from banks to a post office box. The pharmacy owner or manager should reconcile the statements personally, or have an outside accountant do so to ensure the propriety of all transactions.
- Examine canceled checks for any that appear unusual or where too many are written to a particular person.
- Employees who are in positions to misappropriate funds should be bonded as a matter of policy.
- Managers should personally approve unusual discounts and bad-debt write-offs.
- The owner or manager should personally sign all checks and approve all cash disbursements to the extent that this is possible. Periodically, the owner or manager should examine invoices and supporting data before signing checks. Special attention can be directed to possible fictitious purchases from unknown companies.

Pharmacy practice risks

Aside from the traditional non-criminal and criminal risks faced by pharmacies, some risks are very specific to the profession. Of particular concern are risks associated with malpractice, improper use of pharmacy technicians, improper recordkeeping, inadequate patient consultation, etc. While these vary on a state-by-state basis, the manager must consider them to be real potential threats to the operation of the pharmacy.

Typically, well-established policies and procedures help to reduce these types of risk. For example, the risk of dispensing an inaccurate prescription can be minimized by ensuring that checks are made in the filing, and that pharmacists and technicians are performing only their assigned tasks.

Another type of risk associated with pharmacy practice is that associated with denied reimbursement on government and other third-party contracts. The risks include serving patients whose program eligibility has been discontinued, dispensing medications that are not approved on a drug formulary, etc. As the practice of pharmacy moves more into electronic claims management, these types of problems will be reduced.

What insurance to carry

While some risk is inherent in any business situation, it can be controlled or reduced with a little extra care. One means of reducing the threat of significant loss is by purchasing insurance. Used as a hedge against major losses that could endanger survival, insurance is a means of reducing uncertain losses for relatively certain costs. As such, insurance allows the owner or manager to direct more attention and resources to other operations.

Unfortunately, many owners and managers believe that insurance provides them with a risk-free environment. The statement, "I'm not worried, I have insurance," often is used by the unknowing owner. Policies typically are written with deductible clauses and limitations on coverage. Full (no deductible) and comprehensive insurance are very expensive and usually not warranted except in extraordinary situations. Consequently, most pharmacy owners use insurance as a fail-safe program to augment standard risk-reduction precautions.

Risk coverage

The most commonly carried types of insurance include:

- fire and natural disaster
- general liability and casualty
- professional liability
- workers' compensation and liability
- fidelity and surety bonds
- business interruptions
- life and key person insurance.

Whether any or all of these areas need coverage and the extent to which they should be insured are complex issues. Insurance should not be taken out for trivial risks. It makes little sense, for example, to safeguard a $50 asset. Similarly, the pharmacy owner should not spend inordinate sums for premiums whose total coverage is unnecessary. In most instances, it would be foolish to have a $50 deductible

policy when a $200 deductible is available at reasonable savings in premiums. The extra $150 is not likely to have a major impact on survival.

Management must carefully weigh the costs of the policy with the potential amount of loss and its probability of occurring. Threats to survival take on special importance, and often make some insurance justified even though the likelihood of its being needed is remote.

Fire and natural disaster

Fire insurance is one of the most common types of policy purchased. This covers all or part of the losses resulting from fire and lightning. Additional coverage also may be purchased to protect the business against hail, windstorms, riot, explosion, smoke, and auto and aircraft damage. In some cases, these types of protection may be quite necessary.

General liability and casualty

General liability and casualty insurance policies basically cover automobiles, crime, and injury to others. While these policies are expensive to maintain, they should be considered a normal cost of doing business. This is especially true for automobiles used in the course of business and general protection from injury to others. Automobile accidents and injury to customers often turn into lawsuits, which can result in very expensive attorney fees and judgments against the business.

Crime insurance to protect the business against burglary, robbery, and theft also is warranted in many cases. This depends heavily on the location of the business. In a high crime area, this insurance becomes a must. On the other hand, for the pharmacy located in a high-rise medical office building within a low crime area, the need for crime insurance is reduced somewhat.

Unfortunately, insurance in high crime areas is very expensive, if it can be obtained at all. If no policies are available, some states have Fair Access to Insurance Regulations (FAIR) plans in which the federal and state governments work in cooperation with insurance companies to make crime insurance available to businesses operating in selected locations.

Professional liability insurance

Errors happen in the practice of pharmacy that expose the business and pharmacist to considerable risk. Dispensing the wrong medication, making errors in label instructions, failing to check for possible drug interactions, and so on, can result in lawsuits.

To protect the pharmacy and pharmacist from these types of liabilities, professional liability insurance must be purchased. Often, the owner of the pharmacy will pay for this partly or entirely for each employee pharmacist. While the premiums can be high, it usually is viewed as an essential cost of doing business.

Workers' compensation and employer liability

Business owners are required by common law to provide a safe working environment for employees and to warn them of any unavoidable hazards. Even if management fully conforms to Occupational Safety and Health Act (OSHA) regulations, accidents can occur and employees can sue the business. Despite the best employer–employee relationships, this risk is too great to leave uncovered because court judgments can be high.

The type and extent of coverage varies on a state-by-state basis since the benefits to be paid are determined by the individual state. In general, these benefits will include payments for medical care, death, disability, and income payments to the disabled or surviving dependents.

Fidelity bonds

Fidelity bonds are a specialized form of insurance designed to protect the pharmacy from dishonest employees. They typically are purchased to protect the pharmacy from internal theft. Employees who are in contact with considerable sums or very expensive merchandise can be covered in this way. Such insurance should be considered in terms of its costs vs. potential losses through theft, embezzlement, and other internal crimes.

Business interruption

Losses resulting from the disruption of business due to fire or other disasters can be protected against by business interruption insurance. This reduces the risks of a prolonged downtime when no revenues are being generated and some fixed costs are still being incurred. Normally, these policies cover loss of profits as well as fixed expenses.

While losses from a disaster itself may be high, it is possible that disruption to the business will be even greater. Over an extended period of time, the interruption could threaten the survival of the pharmacy because customers will find other pharmacies to patronize. For this reason, many owners add this coverage to their policies to hold them over until they can build a new patient base.

Life and key person insurance

What would happen to the business if one or more key persons died? In the case of a sole proprietorship, the death of the owner may seriously reduce the value of the business for the heirs. For partnerships and some closely held corporations, the death of one partner can so disrupt business that it may cease.

Consequently, many partnerships have life insurance on each partner to provide the surviving partner with funds to buy out that portion of the deceased's estate. The Small Business Administration has developed a list of suggestions on life insurance for various types of business ownership, such as business life insurance for the sole proprietor, business life insurance for the partnership, or corporate business life insurance.

Business life insurance for the sole proprietor. Life insurance protection provides an owner–manager's dependants or heirs with cash representing the sound valuation of the business at death. Such insurance also can assure business continuity. The policy should meet the conditions of a will or trust agreement if selling or liquidating the business is desired. In addition, thought should be given to selecting an appropriate beneficiary and determining who is to pay the insurance premiums.

A most important consideration is who takes custody of the business in case of death. If the family is continuing the business and nobody in the family has the necessary training, experience, or licenses, someone will probably have to be hired to manage the pharmacy. The business will need working capital, at least for a period of readjustment. If employees take over the business, they will need funds to purchase the pharmacy.

Business life insurance for the partnership. Unless the partners have provided otherwise, a partnership dissolves when one partner dies. For practical purposes, the business is finished. The surviving partners become "liquidating trustees." The only business allowed is that of winding up the affairs of the partnership. If the business is continued, the surviving partners become personally liable for any losses incurred should assets not cover losses.

One way to avoid these difficulties is an adequately financed buy-and-sell agreement. Such an agreement provides for the purchase at a prearranged valuation of the deceased partner's interest. A better way, however, is to agree on a method for valuing the pharmacy rather than just a dollar value. The value of the pharmacy will change over time, and these agreements are seldom updated as often as they should be. By agreeing on a valuation method, the parties ensure that the correct value will be placed on the pharmacy when the time comes for such action.

An attorney can prepare the necessary papers carrying out the wishes of the partners. If a buy-and-sell agreement is decided on, the next step is to fund the arrangement. This can be done through a life insurance policy that enables surviving partners to reorganize at once and continue in business. Such insurance liquidates the interest of a deceased partner without loss. It also enables the beneficiaries of a deceased partner to secure full, fair value for the interest in the pharmacy if the policy is kept up to date and commensurate with the increasing value.

There are various ways of establishing a partnership insurance plan, each with advantages for particular requirements. One plan involves the purchase by each partner of a policy on the life of the other partners. Each partner pays the premiums. Another plan, where there are three or more partners, is to have the business buy a policy on the life of each. The questions of how much each partner should pay, the amount of insurance needed, the beneficiary arrangements, the tax effects, and the necessary policy assignments are only a few of the questions involved.

The valuation of the partnership is a vital problem to be met in setting up a partnership insurance. A formula needs to be set up under which full value is to be paid to the deceased partner's heirs at some future time. The formula must be equitable and must satisfy all partners or it could become the basis of lengthy controversy and litigation.

Corporate business life insurance. Because the success of a corporation depends largely on the skills and talents of those who run it, the death of any one executive may lead to financial loss to the corporation. Life insurance can protect the corporation against the loss of the services of its executives. It also can provide funds for their replacement.

Death of the principal stockholder in a close corporation (one with a few stockholders, all of whom usually are actively engaged in the management of the business) may lead to management or personnel clashes that might seriously affect the business. It can result in credit impairment, direct loss of business, or damage to employee morale. Unless otherwise provided, the deceased stockholder's stock becomes a part of the estate and passes into the hands of the administrator of the estate during the period of settlement. The administrator can vote the stock, and if it is a controlling interest, the administrator could even name a new board of directors and take over full control.

Many hazards can be eliminated through a stock purchase-and-sale agreement with life insurance written into it to guarantee the funds for carrying out the process. Such an agreement determines in advance just what will be done upon the death of a major stockholder. It also makes funds immediately available for accomplishing the objectives of the plan.

There are many benefits to using insurance. Continuity of management without interruption is guaranteed. No outsiders can come into the business unless this is agreed to in advance. The cash needed to carry out the purchase of the stock is automatically provided on a basis previously agreed to as fair. The common causes of friction between heirs and surviving stockholders are removed. Finally, widows or heirs are not burdened by business responsibilities or worries. Having a guaranteed price, they are protected against shrinkage of stock values.

In addition to life insurance on the owner, key person insurance also should be considered. The death of a highly valued employee–pharmacist might seriously disrupt the ability to continue "business as usual." This is especially true in times when good employees are difficult to find, and the time to locate a replacement may be prolonged.

Group life and health insurance

A final area of consideration should be group life and health insurance. Some aspects of health insurance are mandated by federal and state laws. In any case, making provisions for employees often is worth the cost since it can improve employee morale and loyalty. Such decisions, however, need careful planning and cost-benefit evaluations.

Selecting the insurance company

Because insurance is important and can be a relatively high cost item, sound insurance management is essential. This involves selecting an insurance company, purchasing insurance economically, and managing the insurance.

Even though there are many types of insurance companies, management most likely will buy from either a mutual or a stock company. While both are chartered by the state, the former is a non-profit organization owned by the policyholders, and the latter is a profit-seeking enterprise. There is no inherent advantage to either. Each prospective company should be evaluated on the basis of the types of insurance offered, its financial stability, its adaptability of policy coverage to the pharmacy owner's needs, the premium costs, and the company's willingness to pay benefits.

Since many insurance companies specialize in specific types of coverage, some may not be appropriate. Similarly, companies differ in the flexibility of the programs they offer. Some tailor policies to the pharmacy's specific needs, while others are not able or willing to do this. Management, of course, will want to have and pay for only the needed coverage.

Insurers differ greatly in their financial stability. A relatively simple check of Best's Insurance Reports will provide an assessment of the financial positions of various companies. A financially weak insurer may not be able to help if and when the need arises, and such weakness may be indicative of forthcoming increases in policy costs.

Of equal importance to the stature of the company is the skill and reputation of the agent. Since the owner or manager typically deals exclusively with the insurer's representative rather than the company itself, management must select an agent who is fair and will work with the policyholder.

How often to evaluate insurance needs

Choosing the most economical insurance for a business involves a number of elements:

- Decide which kind of risk protection will work best and most economically. Commercial insurance is only one way of handling risk. Investigate the other methods, such as loss prevention, self-insurance, no insurance, risk transfer, to see if they better meet specific needs.

- Cover the largest loss exposure first, and then the less severe one as the budget permits. Use the premium dollar where the protection need is greatest. Some pharmacies insure their automobiles against collision loss but do not purchase adequate liability insurance. Collision losses seldom bankrupt a business, but liability judgments often do.

- Make proper use of deductibles. Full coverage can be uneconomical because of the high cost of covering the "first dollar" of loss. Make the deductible an affordable amount.

- Review the insurance periodically. Renewing policies automatically increases the likelihood that management will fail to increase limits of liability where indicated or that possible rate reductions are not taken.

- Check the market occasionally to see that the insurance is being purchased for a reasonable price. Do not switch insurers each time a lower price is quoted, but keep aware of average costs for the amount and types of coverage required.

- Analyze insurance terms and provisions. When an owner attempts to save money by purchasing a cheaper policy, it sometimes is discovered that the specific hazard insured against is not adequately covered because of a technicality.

- Buy insurance in as large a unit as possible. Take advantage of the savings most insurers allow for large-unit policies, particularly for life insurance and many types of property insurance. Usually, the more property included in a single policy, the cheaper it is for the insurer to handle.

Summary

- Risk management does not mean risk avoidance. It implies that risk is assessed, measured, and reduced to the extent that it is economically feasible.

- The more common types of non-criminal business risks include fire, natural disasters, personal liabilities, economic downturns, business interruptions, and loss of key personnel.

- Insurance for fire, natural disasters, or personal liabilities are often good hedges against the risks involved, but programs designed to prevent hazards and problems from occurring are essential to minimizing these risks.

- The pharmacy owner can partly prepare for economic downturns, business interruptions, and the loss of key personnel by keeping alert to internal changes and those in the environment.
- The main types of criminal risks are burglary, robbery, shoplifting, credit card fraud, bad checks, false insurance eligibility cards, and employee theft.
- Protection against internal theft by employees often is neglected. Management must be aware of opportunities for theft and control areas within the pharmacy that would be more prone to internal theft, as well as carefully evaluate prospective employees.
- Most of the risks described in this chapter are insurable, and coverage should be considered for each.
- The most common types of insurance are fire and natural disaster, general liability and casualty, professional liability, workers' compensation and liability, fidelity and surety bonds, business interruptions, and life and key person insurance.
- Insurance should not be taken for trivial risk areas or for expensive total coverage that is unnecessary.
- In determining the amounts and types of insurance to buy, management should place special importance on areas that threaten the pharmacy's survival.
- In choosing an insurance company, the following should be evaluated: types of insurance offered, financial stability, ability to adapt coverage to the pharmacy's needs, premium costs, and willingness to pay benefits.
- Of equal importance to the stature of the insurance company is an agent who is fair, capable, and will work with the policyholder.

Questions for discussion

1 What are the non-criminal business risks?
2 Describe precautions that can be taken to protect the pharmacy from loss of key personnel.
3 List the criminal business risks.
4 What measures can be taken to prevent burglary losses?
5 What are the most common risks taken by the owner, and how can they be deterred?

6 List some standard precautions against internal theft.
7 What are the common clues to embezzlement?
8 Name some common types of business insurance.
9 What is the difference between a mutual and a stock company?
10 What must be taken into account when selecting an insurance company?

Self-test review

True/false statements

1 The key to risk reduction is making sure that some unexpected or uncontrollable circumstances cannot unilaterally destroy the business.
2 Fire insurance will fully cover losses due to fire.
3 Burglary is a common risk in most pharmacies.
4 Purchasing insurance is one of the best hedges against natural disasters.
5 Less than 2 percent of all employees are hardcore pilferers.
6 The key to protection against burglary is to make entry difficult and noisy.
7 Losses stemming from credit card fraud and bad checks often are the result of poor business practices by management.
8 Theft is the fraudulent appropriation of property by a person to whom it has been entrusted.
9 Fidelity bonds are used to protect a business from losses due to external theft.
10 Life insurance is important to individuals, but of little importance to small pharmacies.

Multiple choice questions

1 Which of the following is a non-criminal business risk?

(A) Business interruptions.
(B) Credit card fraud.
(C) Shoplifting.
(D) Employee theft.

2 The best deterrent to robbery is to have:

(A) Uncluttered windows.
(B) Little cash on hand.
(C) Ample lighting.
(D) Surveillance cameras.

3 Key person insurance is especially important in pharmacies which have a large number of:

(A) Unskilled employees.
(B) Highly technical employees.
(C) Highly paid employees.
(D) All of the above.

4 Which of the following is the most serious criminal risk faced by the pharmacy?

(A) Shoplifting.
(B) Burglary.
(C) Robbery.
(D) Employee theft.

5 Which of the following is a non-profit insurance company owned by policyholders?

(A) Mutual company.
(B) Stock company.
(C) Consolidated company.
(D) Conglomerated actuarial company.

Cases for Part II*

Short cases

Case II.1 Lockhardt's Medical Pharmacy

When Dr. Mark Kilgore purchased Lockhardt's Medical Pharmacy nearly six months ago, he did not realize how poorly it had been run. Although Lockhardt's had been a popular pharmacy in a complex of medical office buildings, Dr. Kilgore found that internal operations were in disarray. Patients were not being served promptly, and the quality of service was inconsistent. For the first few months, Dr. Kilgore tried to learn the business while not making any radical changes. Now that six months had passed and revenues were down nearly 15 percent, he believed that some actions were necessary before his investment was lost.

Located in a Midwestern town of approximately 55,000 people, Lockhardt's was the oldest of five independent and three chain pharmacies in the town. Three of the independent pharmacies were located within 2 miles of Lockhardt's. Over the years, the pharmacy had remained popular because of the personality of the owner, friendly service, and its location. Unlike other nearby pharmacies, there was a coffee shop adjacent to the pharmacy which had become a meeting place for town residents. This increased the exposure to and convenience of Lockhardt's.

With his outgoing personality, the original owner, Fred Lockhardt, took advantage of this location by taking time to chat with the patrons as they entered and ate in the coffee shop. Even the five employees,

who had worked an average of nearly 9 years at Lockhardt's, were encouraged to mingle with customers during their breaks and lunch periods.

During the 25 years that Mr. Lockhardt owned and managed the pharmacy, he became quite wealthy. Over the last 5 years, he began lowering prices and raising employee wages as a means of showing his appreciation for the loyalty his customers and employees had shown him. As a result, business grew even more. A year ago, however, Mr. Lockhardt decided to retire and sell the pharmacy to Dr. Kilgore, a relatively new resident in town who worked as an assistant manager of one of the chains.

Upon taking over, Dr. Kilgore indicated that he wanted to maintain the same image and atmosphere that Mr. Lockhardt had so successfully created. But he could not ignore the casual approach to operations. Most surprising to Dr. Kilgore was that employees set their own work schedules, had no predetermined operating procedures for dispensing prescriptions, and did not have job descriptions detailing what employees were supposed to do. In addition, two pharmacists often would sit and visit with patients, and at times give them discounts by not taking the co-payments on their prescriptions.

Dr. Kilgore's training in chain store management led him to believe that a more structured operation was necessary for long-term success. This perspective had caused two pharmacists and one technician to threaten to take jobs with a competitor. They complained that Dr. Kilgore said he wanted to maintain the same type of business, but then frequently criticized them for not serving customers more rapidly, and for spending too much time with others in the coffee shop. These employees also were receiving

*Names of the organizations, individuals, and locations of all cases are fictional. Any likeness to actual organizations and/or individuals is purely coincidental.

some complaints from customers that prices were rising and that the pharmacy did not have its traditional warm, friendly atmosphere.

Questions

1 Evaluate the approach Dr. Kilgore has taken to managing Lockhardt's since buying the pharmacy.

2 What actions must Dr. Kilgore take if he is to build Lockhardt's into a successful business?

Case II.2 Anderson's Pharmacy

After his pharmacy was burglarized for the third time in seven weeks, Jon Anderson decided it was time to reassess his risks and review his insurance. The last year had been a bad one for Mr. Anderson. He was burglarized five times, subject to one armed robbery, and caught an employee not ringing up a $70 payment for a private pay prescription.

Anderson's Pharmacy catered predominately to Medicaid patients. When Jon Anderson opened the pharmacy nearly 3 years ago, he knew that the site he selected was not in the best part of town, but the rent on his 5-year lease was relatively low and the landlord was agreeable to some leasehold improvements on a shared-cost basis. Believing that the deal was too good to pass up, Mr. Anderson accepted the fact that he faced greater risks than he would if he had located in another part of this southeastern city of 200,000 people.

Still, he did not believe that the pharmacy would be the target of much crime. The equipment and fixtures were not especially valuable, except for his computer and stereo system. And, as part of his leasehold improvement, he had installed a silent alarm system on the doors and the windows.

While the burglaries were more nuisances than costly losses, the recent armed robbery was another matter. Entering the pharmacy late in the afternoon, one robber held three customers at gunpoint while another took their wallets, jewelry, the cash receipts, and the new stereo—the old stereo had been stolen two weeks earlier.

Also of concern to Mr. Anderson was the incident of an employee's not running a purchase through the cash register. His customer told Mr. Anderson that the employee just took the cash and put it into the register without ringing up the sale. She thought this was strange and when she asked for a receipt, the employee indicated that the register was broken.

Although the monetary loss was not critical, he was wondering if that was the only time it had happened, especially since he left the employee alone on several occasions each week. Since he employed four other people, all of whom had access to the cash register, there always seemed to be opportunities for this to happen. While he believed that he treated his employees fairly, a degree of transience among non-pharmacists created some risk.

Given the history of problems in this location, Mr. Anderson was reluctant to buy more insurance. He was paying nearly $21,000 annually as a result of the claims he had submitted, and additional coverage would cost another $6,000 which would come directly from profits. Yet, he did not like the idea of protecting windows with bars since that would create a negative image for the pharmacy. Furthermore, to protect against robbery, he thought he might have to install security cameras.

Similarly, Mr. Anderson did not know how to protect himself from the employee problems he experienced. He could not be in the pharmacy every minute, and he wanted to make employees feel he trusted them.

Considering the business risks and insurance needs, Mr. Anderson wanted to balance the probable losses with the costs of protection. Even though most of the individual losses had been small, they added up to between $4,500 and $8,000 per year. He considered the total to be a considerable sum—too much for him to continue to absorb for the remaining 2 years of his lease.

Questions

1 How can Mr. Anderson determine the right balance between the risks of loss and the costs of insurance?

2 What steps could Mr. Anderson take to reduce his risks?

3 How should Mr. Anderson solve the problem of employees not accounting for all of their receipts?

Case II.3 G & J'S Pharmacy

After working for a large discount drug chain in the Midwest for nearly 15 years, Burt Schaffer and Jack

Grange decided to quit and open their own pharmacy. During the 4 years that it had been open, sales had nearly tripled while profits increased by about 50 percent.

G & J's Pharmacy was a 5,200 square foot pharmacy that catered primarily to upper-income groups. There were two other similar types of pharmacies in the town which sold comparable non-prescription products at about the same prices. However, G & J's was the only pharmacy to special order nearly any item a customer wanted, and to have at least one owner in the pharmacy from the time it opened (7 a.m.) until it closed (10 p.m.), 6 days a week.

Both Mr. Schaffer and Mr. Grange worked more than 50 hours per week in the pharmacy, spending much of that time dispensing prescriptions (45 percent), stocking shelves (30 percent), and just walking around and talking to patients (20 percent). They still hired a large number of employees for a pharmacy its size to ensure that attentive customer service was maintained. These policies of having the owners available to customers and plenty of support personnel to provide fast service were thought to be the primary factor in their success to date. With pharmacists' and non-pharmacists' wages and benefits growing, and not as much control over prescription prices, they expressed concerns about how they could keep expenses to a minimum and not have them totally deplete profits.

In reviewing their operations over the past 4 years, the owners felt they had to make some decisions that would significantly affect their future. First, Mr. Schaffer was getting tired of working so many hours and having little time for his family. He wanted to reduce his time in the pharmacy to 45 hours per week. Mr. Grange was not married, and did not seem to mind the long hours. These differences had caused some friction to develop between them in the past year.

Second, quite a few of the better customers had asked that the pharmacy begin to carry some food items. The requests centered mostly on a wider selection of natural food items in bulk. With the limited space available and the added costs of expanding, the owners knew that they had to be careful in adding lines. However, Mr. Schaffer was concerned that if they did not make these additions, they might lose some of their customers.

Third, the owner of one relatively small medical pharmacy located on the other side of town was preparing to retire, and had asked Mr. Schaffer and Mr. Grange if they were interested in buying him out. Although they had not discussed price, it appeared to the owners that a reasonable agreement could be reached in that regard. Of greater importance was whether they wanted to expand their operations. This other pharmacy was about one-fifth the size of G & J's, and focused much more heavily on dispensing prescriptions to indigent patients. Its hours were 9 a.m. to 7 p.m., and the current owner felt that he had to be there most of the time to watch over the pharmacy's compounding operations and the high costs of goods and labor.

At this time, the owners were beginning to evaluate each of these three issues. Although they did not want to make hasty decisions, they believed that they had to take some action on them soon.

Questions

1 How should the owners go about evaluating each of these issues?

2 How can the owners resolve their differences with respect to working hours?

3 What steps could they take to better plan pharmacy operations?

Major cases

Case II.4 Advanced Health Hospital

After completing their shift as staff pharmacists at Advanced Health Hospital (AHH), Virginia Dietrich, Traci Michelle, and Carrie Denise sat down in the employee lounge to discuss their futures. All three were classmates in pharmacy school and graduated at the top of their class. Having developed a strong friendship while in school, they decided to try to obtain positions together at AHH, a hospital well known for its innovative approaches to healthcare.

From its beginnings 14 years ago, AHH emphasized a team approach to medical care for its patients. Accordingly, most patients are assigned a team that consists of at least an internist, registered nurse, and pharmacist. Specialists were added to the team based on patient need. Jim Chambers, the CEO of AHH commented about the approach:

> Our approach is to ensure that we treat the entire patient with the best expertise available. For that reason, an internist always takes the

lead because we have found that even localized diseases have implications for other parts of the human body. We can get the best results, and sometimes at the lowest cost, by bringing together a team that jointly decide the best course of therapy. So, even if a family practice physician has one of her or his patients admitted to our hospital, we assign a team for that patient. Of course, we keep the admitting physician involved in the team as well. There is no one source for good ideas for maximizing patient care. That is why we use what we call "medical teams" to treat our patients.

Having worked for AHH for nearly 5 years, Virginia, Traci, and Carrie had served as consultant pharmacists on numerous teams. During their first year of employment, they worked primarily as staff pharmacists but spent some time with a variety of teams as observers. Once Mr. Chambers and the medical chief of staff agreed that they were ready to assume active roles as members of medical teams, they started splitting their time between dispensing prescriptions and participating as medical team members. As Virginia noted:

> When we graduated from pharmacy school, we saw what AHH was doing and all three of us felt this would be a great opportunity if we had the chance to work for this hospital. It would give us a tremendous amount of experience in the broader realm of patient care. And, because AHH is a prestigious hospital, it certainly would look good on our resumes. It is extremely difficult to get positions here, and the three of us were very fortunate.

Despite enjoying what they were doing at AHH, the three agreed that it was time to assess their futures and decide if there were other options which could enhance their careers. While they wanted to consider all opportunities, they also knew that they were going to remain in the area. All three had families and it would not be easy for their husbands and children to move to other cities. But, they also wanted to stay at the forefront of healthcare delivery and ideally wanted to work together if possible.

Based on this preliminary discussion, they identified several options that they felt had possibilities:

- continue working for AHH and try to move more into consultant positions

- leave AHH and start a "consultant pharmacist" practice and try to contract with various healthcare providers to provide advice on drug therapy that would enhance patient care and possibly reduce overall costs of healthcare
- purchase an independent pharmacy and try to bring some of the innovative techniques they learned at AHH to that practice setting by starting a health consulting component to the pharmacy's operations.

In reflecting on the options, Traci and Carrie commented jointly:

> The three of us really would like to remain tied in some way to AHH because it has been such a great experience. And, we could stay doing what we are doing for the next 30 years if it came down to it. But, we went to AHH because it was at the forefront and we like being ahead of the curve. We need to think about what role pharmacists will have in healthcare delivery over the next 10 years and position ourselves as best we can. If that means leaving AHH, then that's what we need to do.

Advanced Health Hospital

AHH is a large hospital located in a major city in the Midwest. It was started by a group of community leaders led by three retired physicians. Although retired, these physicians remained very active in local and national medical associations and felt they saw a need for the future of healthcare. They came up with an idea of forming a hospital that would be committed to a team approach for medical care. After finding a number of investors who shared their vision, they purchased a hospital in the outskirts of the city that had been struggling and named it Advanced Health to reflect their goal of being innovative. Mr. Chambers commented on the creation of AHH:

> The team approach really was not that new. Many hospitals and health systems bring teams together when they think it is necessary. And, they all talk about how well integrated their medical staff is in working together. But, the reality is that in most places, the physicians, nursing staff, and pharmacists are so busy they only consult with one another when they need to do so and have the time. In many hospitals, the communication between medical personnel is pretty limited.

What we have here is a proactive approach. Working together is required and the medical staff has gotten used to taking the time to talk to each other and share opinions concerning courses of treatment. So, it's really more of the extent to which the team approach is practiced on an on-going basis that separates us from many other hospitals. Consultation between these team members is not just encouraged, it is mandatory if anybody wants to practice here.

Over the years, AHH became well known for specialty care in three areas: cancer, cardiac, and diseases associated with aging. It was no coincidence that among the three retired physicians one was an oncologist, another was a heart surgeon, and the third was a specialist in internal medicine.

Occupancy of this 350-bed hospital was nearly always between 95 and 100 percent. It was fully accredited and had a strong residency program as well. Although it was not profitable in its first 2 years, AHH has shown a healthy profit ever since, and had adequate funds to keep the hospital and equipment up-to-date.

As AHH grew in recognition, it began receiving some of the more complex cases from other local hospitals and became the hospital of choice among some of the more high-profile members of the community. It also was a place where many of the top medical school graduates wanted to do their residencies, and where other healthcare professionals such as registered nurses and pharmacists wanted to work even though AHH pay scales were somewhat on the lower end.

Pharmacy services

The pharmacy staff consisted of 26.5 full-time equivalent pharmacists plus technicians and other staff needed to support pharmacy services functions. The number of pharmacists was thought to be somewhat larger than normally found in hospitals of this size. This was due to the time pharmacists spent as team members when they were not dispensing prescriptions.

In general, the allocation of pharmacists' time change based on the years of employment. First year pharmacists spend about 80 percent of their time dispensing prescriptions, 10 percent of their time assigned to medical teams as an observer, and 10 percent of their time on miscellaneous duties. For years 2 through 5, they spend about 70 percent of their time dispensing, 20 percent of their time as medical team members, and 10 percent of their time on miscellaneous duties. After 5 years, the percentage of time spent dispensing goes down about 1 percent to 2 percent per year and the time spent on medical teams goes up by that amount. Currently, the maximum amount of time a pharmacist can spend consulting is 40 percent and as little as 5 percent on miscellaneous duties.

Virginia commented on the staffing:

There are a lot of pharmacists working for AHH. This is because we spend increasing amounts of time working with medical team members so there needs to be more staff pharmacists dispensing prescriptions. While we all like working here, there is some sense that not everybody likes the time allocation schedule that AHH has established for pharmacists. Some of us would like to do more consulting as team members and others prefer to dispense more prescriptions and spend relatively little time consulting with physicians and nurses. But, our system does not allow for individual choice. No matter what you want, if you stay long enough you will be spending about 55 percent of your time dispensing and 40 percent as medical team members. I think it would be much better of AHH would group pharmacists according to what they want to do and then let them do it.

The city and surrounding area

The city and surrounding area within which AHH was located had a population of just over 950,000. Although AHH was originally situated on the outer edge of the city, much of the city's growth had been in the direction of AHH. As such, AHH found itself in a major suburban area. And with a reasonably good transportation system in the city, the hospital was accessible to both physicians and residents throughout the area.

Selected demographic characteristics of the population are presented in Table II.4.1. Although the city has been growing at the rate of about 0.8 percent per year, much of that has been in the suburbs. As Mr. Chambers noted:

Initially, the hospital that the investors purchased and made into AHH was really out in a remote part of town. I'm not sure why it was located there in the first place but the land must have been quite cheap. However, as the city grew, it moved out our direction. Either the original investors were true visionaries or incredibly lucky. Whatever the case, we are located in a better part of the region. Since we draw from all parts of the surrounding area, the location is not a major consideration other than the fact that the land value has more than tripled.

Healthcare community

When Virginia, Traci, and Carrie began assessing the opportunities for the future, they identified other hospitals and health systems and community pharmacies. They felt it was important to consider what options they had to stay with AHH, start a consulting company that could try to contact with the health systems and/or physician groups, or purchase an independent community pharmacy.

Health systems and hospitals in the community

Within the surrounding area, there were eight other hospitals operated by three separate health systems. These three systems had been in the community for a long time and each had a good reputation, especially for specific areas of medical care.

Faith Health System (FHS) was the smallest of the three health systems. It operated two hospitals in different geographic areas of the community. FHS was a faith-based not-for-profit health system that had a total of 400 hospital beds in its two facilities. While each hospital was somewhat small, this system was known for taking care of people with little or no private health insurance. Many of its patients were on the state's Medicaid program. FHS offered a full range of services at each of its hospitals, but did not have a strong reputation for any particular medical field such as cancer or cardiac care. Its occupancy was generally in the 85–95 percent range. Because it primarily catered to lower income patients, its compensation packages were lower than those of competing systems. The lower pay appeared to be one of the main reasons this system had a high turnover of hospital staff, including staff pharmacists. As Traci noted:

FHS is a good system because it takes patients that the other systems don't necessarily want. While there have been no major problems at their hospitals, the system is not known for being among the leading

Table II.4.1 Selected demographic characteristics of the city

Gender	
Male	445,900
Female	506,700
Total	952,600
Age	
5–19 years	173,200
20–44 years	253,400
45–64 years	279,600
65–74 years	78,900
75 years and over	62,200
Total	952,600
Education (population 25 and older)	
Less than 9th grade	6.4%
9th to 12th grade, no diploma	14.4%
High school graduate (includes equivalency)	35.9%
Some college, no degree	15.8%
Associate's degree	5.3%
Bachelor's degree	12.9%
Graduate or professional degree	9.1%
Employment status (population 16 and older)	
In labor force	59.0%
Civilian labor force	58.9%
Employed	51.8%
Unemployed	7.1%
Armed Forces	0.1%
Not in labor force	41.0%
Percent unemployed	12.10%
Occupation (population 16 and older)	
Management, professional, and related occupations	33.8%
Service occupations	21.3%
Sales and office occupations	26.3%
Farming, fishing, and forestry occupations	0.1%
Construction, extraction, maintenance, and repair occupations	6.6%
Production, transportation, and material moving occupations	11.8%
Household income	
Less than $25,000	31.8%
$25,000–$49,999	26.2%
$50,000–$74,999	17.3%
$75,000–$99,999	10.5%
$100,000–$149,999	9.1%
$150,000 or more	5.1%
Total	100.0%

places to receive medical care. It could really use some advanced approaches to medical care to improve its image in the community. The only concern is that I don't know whether FHS would be willing to consider a consulting service like we could offer. I guess, if it could help them retain staff or cut costs somehow, they might be interested.

Allied HealthCare (AHC) was a privately owned system. It had three hospitals in the area and a total of 900 beds. The overall occupancy rate ranged from 65 to 90 percent. Unlike FHS, it much preferred to take patients who had private insurance, and especially those with more generous contract terms. It was most well known for its cancer centers and birthing centers at all three hospitals. Two of its three hospitals were designated trauma centers for the region. While trauma units tend to be very costly to operate, the reimbursements for their services are quite high. Carrie commented on AHC:

> This system is probably the closest competitor to AHH. It is very profit oriented. Its patients tend to be more affluent, although it has to accept whoever comes through the doors of the emergency departments and trauma centers. I think this could be a good candidate for consulting services because if we can develop a model to show how our services could save the system money, or generate more revenues, AHC would likely give it some consideration.

The third system was Systems Healthcare (SH). Unlike the other two, SH was a health maintenance organization that served about 15 percent of the community. It had three hospitals with a total of 680 beds, and had an overall occupancy rate ranging between 75 percent and 95 percent. SH operated a capitated health plan and its members paid on a monthly basis for physician services, laboratory tests, and hospital services. Since it made more money if its members did not utilize its services, SH was heavily oriented to preventive care. And, while it sold its program on the concept of offering a full range of services, it contracted with the other two health systems and AHH for some specialty care, including both cancer and cardiac care. This was the way it kept its investment lower and overall costs down. Carrie commented on SH:

> SH is different. From everything I have heard, its members are quite satisfied with the services

they receive. Most medical care is under one roof so-to-speak, so the medical records of every member are available to any healthcare provider who works for SH and has authorization to access those records. So, it is possible for a wider range of service providers to know what is going on with a patient. The quantity of information that is available here is much greater than AHH, FHS, or AHC because SH has the records of physician visits, lab tests, prescriptions and anything else that goes on with the patient. How much of that information is used by the different care providers is the question. I know some people who work for SH and they say that there seldom is time for a provider to thoroughly review the medical records of each patient. So, my guess is that the information is not being utilized anywhere near the extent it could be.

Community pharmacies

A total of 198 community pharmacies were located in the city and surrounding area. Of the total, three national chains operated 79 of these. The other 119 pharmacies were independently owned and ranged in size from small medical shops to larger stores with extensive front-end merchandise.

Nearly half of the independent pharmacies (55) were small medical pharmacies. These focused primarily on dispensing prescriptions and tended to be located near medical office buildings and hospitals. A few were situated in older shopping centers, but most had some physical proximity to physician offices and hospitals.

The other independent pharmacies were larger in size and similar in nature to chain pharmacies. While prescriptions still accounted for the majority of their revenues, these pharmacies tended to be located in residential areas and business districts of the community. They all carried a reasonably broad array of front-end merchandise, but some focused more heavily on home healthcare products and durable medical equipment. These preferred to limit their non-prescription business to other healthcare lines rather than sell merchandise commonly found in mass merchandise stores.

Even before the three got together, Virginia had been looking at the opportunities associated with owning an independent pharmacy and summarized what she found:

If we wanted to start or buy a pharmacy, there are a lot of options we could consider. Since there always are pharmacies for sale, I am not sure it would be wise to just try to start another one from scratch. It probably would be best to buy either a small medical pharmacy or a larger one that is oriented to both prescriptions and home healthcare merchandise. Several of the ones for sale seem to be reasonably successful, but the owners want to retire. And, of course, there are a few that appear to be having serious financial difficulties. If we went this route, we could try to start a consulting business with patients, using something like a medication-therapy-management (MTM) approach. We could make this more attractive if we could show that we would be in consultation with the patients' physicians, assuming that was possible.

Future considerations

In considering the different options, Virginia, Traci, and Carrie pondered several possible courses of action:

- Develop a plan that would become a proposal for AHH that would allow staff pharmacists who wanted to be more involved in medical teams to do so and let those who preferred to focus more on dispensing remain in the pharmacy services department.
- Develop a plan to start a consulting company that could offer its services to AHH and/or one or more of the other health systems. This would entail helping these systems incorporate the expertise of staff pharmacists into the decisions that are made regarding patient care in the hospitals and upon discharge.
- Develop a plan to purchase an independent community pharmacy and augment its current prescription services with a consultation program for patients. This could include consulting on not only the medications customers take but also lifestyle issues such as diet and exercise. They thought there might be opportunities to partner with other organizations in the health field, such as nutrition stores, fitness centers, and weight loss centers.

As they concluded their meeting in the employee lounge, Virginia commented:

We have at least these three options and we should either select one and see where it takes us, or examine all three in more detail and then decide. If we want to be on the cutting edge, we have to decide what the edge will be and how we can take advantage of this for ourselves. I am not sure how any of these plans should be designed, but think that as a first step we should develop an outline of what should be contained in a plan and what key points we would want to make in order to "sell" the idea to either ourselves or someone else.

Possible discussion questions

1 What pharmacy services are most needed in the future by healthcare organizations?
2 What are the advantages and disadvantages of each option the three pharmacists are considering? Which would be best for the future?
3 What should be the structure of a business plan overall and for each option?
4 How should the three pharmacists go about developing business plans for each option?

Case II.5 Community Markets and Drugs

Community Markets and Drugs (CMD) is a chain of 27 combination supermarkets and drug stores located in the Northwest. It started nearly 25 years ago when a local grocery store owner and the owner of a pharmacy met on a golf course and began discussing their businesses. During the course of about 4 hours, they both realized that by joining their operations, expertise, and financial resources, they would be better able to compete in the marketplace.

Within about 18 months, they found a suitable location and moved their respective stores into a single space. Because both men were very involved in the community, they decided to name their new market and drug store "Community Markets and Drugs." Although they both lost the name value of their individual stores, they felt that this was a better foundation for future growth.

Over the course of 25 years, CMD grew to its current size and expanded to eight small- to medium-sized communities in two states. The founders of the chain had long ago retired and nobody in either family wanted to take charge of the company. Accordingly, the founders hired a president who reported to the CMD board of directors which was comprised of equal numbers of members of each of the founders' families.

Within the last year, the founders hired a new president to manage the company. The previous president had come up through the ranks of store operations, starting as a clerk and then moving into the role of buyer and then oversaw a portion of the chain in one state. When he decided to relocate to the east coast, the founders decided it was time to bring in someone from outside the company. Accordingly, they hired Betty Manyen to be the new president. Unlike her predecessor, Ms. Manyen had been a very successful manager of a club warehouse that sold a wide range of products and had a pharmacy unit.

One of Ms. Manyen's first steps was to request that the vice presidents of all CMD operating units develop a 2-year plan for their units. Her primary goal was to treat the various operating units as "profit centers" with each accountable for generating profits for the company. However, she added another twist to the request, and that was to incorporate into the plan a set of strategies for having each unit assist at least one other unit in generating sales and profits. As she noted:

> My background in large store retailing tells me that it is not only important for each unit within a store to be profitable, but for units to help each other be profitable. This way, the units cannot just work for their own good and not the good of the company as a whole. It also means that the managers of all units have to know something about the other units, including what works and does not work. This is a bit different from what CMD has done in the past, and it will be a little tricky at first to get plans that are more integrated, but I think it will really help CMD. If you think about it for club warehouse stores and mass merchandise stores, everything they do is designed to build overall store traffic and sales, not just for individual lines of merchandise, but for a wide variety of goods.

Van Kliver, the vice president of prescription department operations, was charged with developing the 2-year plan for pharmacy operations in the 27 stores. Ms. Manyen's request was for a plan for pharmacy operations overall and not for each individual store. Both Ms. Manyen and Mr. Kliver recognized that the overall plan would have to be adjusted because of the differences in markets within which each store operated. Those more specific plans would come later, but the initial step was to set some direction for each operating unit that would be profitable and help other operating units. As Van noted:

> I like the idea of doing this. It is not going to be easy because I will always be thinking about whether this will work in all stores or not, and most likely the answer will be "not in such-and-such store" but it will be interesting to put a plan in place overall and then tweak it to the needs of individual marketplaces.

The immediate goals Van established for himself were to:

- increase revenues and profits in the prescription departments
- strengthen the image of the prescription departments as being very patient oriented
- use the prescription departments to build total store revenues and profits
- identify at least one other operating unit within the stores to work closely with to jointly increase each unit's revenues and profits.

In reviewing these goals, Van commented:

> I think our prescription departments have done quite well over time, especially considering that our prices for prescription drugs are limited to what we received from private insurance contracts and the states' Medicaid programs. It is difficult to get higher margins out of prescriptions when you cannot raise prices. But, we need to find a way to do so and to do more with the non-prescription lines we oversee. I'm also not sure about partnering with another operating unit. As I said, I like the idea, but I'm not sure what would be the best unit for this.

Community Markets and Drugs

The founders of CMD believed that once you have a formula for success, apply that formula across all stores. Accordingly, all of the stores originally were as identical as possible in size, merchandise lines, organizational units, store layout and design, and advertising and pricing. The general idea was that a customer could go to any of the CMD stores and feel like they were "at home" in that the merchandise they were looking for would be found in the same place. The founders thought that this strategy would keep customers from switching patronage because it would be more painful to become oriented to another store where the merchandise could be in very different places.

In time, this concept gave way to less standardization. The previous president instituted changes in merchandise lines, store layout and design, and pricing based on where the stores were located, and the demographics and competition within the immediate marketplaces for the individual stores. As Ms. Manyen commented:

> One of the biggest contributions made by my predecessor was to start moving CMD to being more individualized to the community within which each store was located. It is somewhat ironic that the founders would want everything the same in each store they opened when they were so community oriented. For some reason, they felt that the benefits of standardization outweighed the benefits of adapting to individual marketplaces. While we are a good-sized company, I think the ability to adjust operations at each individual store is our greatest advantage over the types of retailers I worked with over the years.

As the chain grew in size at about the rate of one new store a year, care was taken to locate the stores in middle to upper income areas. This was done partly because the grocery stores in most areas were competing on a price basis and the founders were reluctant to enter markets in which price would be the main determinant of patronage. They felt that they were too small to purchase in the quantities needed to get discounts that could allow them to win price wars if they were to arise. Van commented on all of this:

> In some respects, the founders were ahead of their time. Because they did not want to compete strictly on price, it really helped the chain to grow and not be confronted directly by the growth of the mass merchandise stores and club warehouses that began offering more food products and having their own pharmacies. In the early days, people with more money did not go to those types of stores to anywhere near the extent they do now. Unfortunately, today nearly everybody goes to the mass merchandise stores

and club warehouses, irrespective of whether they are wealthy or not. But, during the growth years of the chain, this strategy was beneficial.

Because of this philosophy, all of the CMD stores were located in suburban areas of small and medium-sized cities and towns. Generally, these cities and towns had populations of 50,000–250,000 people.

Although there were some variations in the stores due to their locations, most were between 30,000 and 40,000 square feet in size, with the average being 38,780 square feet. Although the stores were of varying ages, they have been well maintained in structural appearance both on the outside and on the inside.

The number of individual items carried in an average store (i.e. stock-keeping units, or SKUs) was about 40,000, but this varied directly with store size. This was thought to be about the same as most competing stores of similar sizes. Average store revenue and expenses, and average store revenues by type of merchandise are shown in Tables II.5.1 and II.5.2.

An average store employed about 109.2 people on either a part-time or full-time basis. This number was thought to be somewhat higher than competing stores. As Ms. Manyen noted:

> Historically, CMD employed a greater number of people than an average competitor. The reason for this is to ensure that we keep service levels high. We know it is more costly, but if we are to be at higher price points, and if we are to attract a higher income clientele, we need to shower them with service. I am not sure if the tradeoff between higher payroll and higher prices is paying off for us, but that's the way it is.

The stores ran advertisements in the local newspapers on a weekly basis using one page within the food section. Typically, these would be on Wednesdays because that was the expanded food section day of the local newspapers. The advertisements would have some specials, most commonly on products for which the manufacturers gave promotional allowances. Normally, the specials would take about half of the page, leaving the other half for script explaining the reasons for purchasing items from selected departments of the store. These would be rotated between the meat department, produce, general merchandise (e.g. dry food and dry non-food), and the drug center. Ms. Manyen explained the advertising strategy:

Table II.5.1 Average store revenues and expenses for last 3 years

Average CMD store	Last year	Two years ago	Three years ago
Revenues	$12,698,405	$12,498,805	$12,502,498
Cost of goods sold	$9,104,756	$8,861,653	$8,689,236
Gross margin	$3,593,649	$3,637,152	$3,813,262
Operating expenses			
Payroll	$1,507,301	$1,474,859	$1,450,290
Employee benefits	$469,841	$449,957	$450,090
Property rental	$203,174	$187,482	$187,537
Depreciation and amortization	$177,778	$149,986	$175,035
Utilities	$190,476	$149,986	$125,025
Supplies	$101,587	$124,988	$112,522
Maintenance and repairs	$88,889	$87,492	$75,015
Taxes and licenses	$50,794	$49,995	$50,010
Insurance	$40,635	$38,746	$36,257
All other operating expenses	$546,031	$512,451	$487,597
Total	$3,376,506	$3,225,942	$3,149,379
Net profit margin before taxes	$217,143	$411,211	$663,883

Table II.5.2 Percentage of average store revenues by types of merchandise for last 3 years

Average CMD store	Last year (%)	Two years ago (%)	Three years ago (%)
Alcoholic beverages	3.2	4.0	4.2
Dry grocery (food)	25.7	26.1	27.6
Dry grocery (non-food)	5.5	6.1	7.2
Pharmacy, over-the-counter medications, health and beauty aids	8.9	9.3	10.2
Perishables	52.7	53.4	50.1
Meat, fish, poultry	10.8	11.5	11.7
Service deli	5.9	5.3	3.5
Self-service deli	0.8	0.8	0.6
Floral	1.0	0.6	0.5
Produce	8.9	11.0	11.4
Baked goods	3.8	3.9	3.2
In-store bakery	4.2	3.5	2.0
Dairy	10.0	9.8	10.1
Frozen foods	7.3	7.0	7.1
Other	4.0	1.1	0.8
Total	100.0	100.0	100.0

We are rethinking this entire approach to promotion, but in the past we mainly tried to just enhance our store's name exposure. We did not really push price specials because that is not how we have been competing. So, the past president didn't think it was worth using circular inserts that contained a lot of sale items in the newspaper. I know the other chains and some of the mass merchandisers advertise much more heavily than we do. I am not totally comfortable with the amount and style of our promotion, so I am open to business plans that include more proactive advertising if it can be done profitably.

Competition

The amount of competition CMD stores faced varied somewhat by geographic area. In general, however, each of the areas had at least two other supermarkets and various other specialty stores. While most of the competing supermarkets continued their long tradition of competing on the basis of price, both Ms. Manyen and Mr. Kliver have seen an increase in the number of higher end markets. Ms. Manyen noted:

The combination food and drug stores have not changed a lot over the last several years. No new ones have opened, and I don't anticipate there being a great many opening up in the next five years. There aren't that many good locations left and the only areas it makes sense is in new residential developments. But, these are going up slowly, so it will be a while.

What we have seen, however, is the entry of specialty food stores that really push the organic lines. This is especially significant in terms of their meat departments and produce. There is at least one of these stores in each of the eight communities we are located in; they are targeting a higher income clientele and pushing both freshness and quality. Their stores are considerably smaller than ours, and do not have pharmacies. I think they are playing on the theme that being smaller gives them better opportunities to buy better quality merchandise than the "big" chains. It may be working because sales of meats and produce in our stores have declined somewhat. My concern is that if people shop at these, they may take their prescription business to independent drug stores or chain drug stores because they will no longer find combinations of markets and drug stores more convenient.

Ms. Manyen thought the other major competitors were the mass merchandisers and club warehouses:

While the other supermarkets are competition for us, I am not particularly worried about them. We have been competing with them for a long time, and they tend to stay focused on pricing. So, they are not as big a problem because we don't even try to compete on price.

My bigger concern, aside from the specialty food stores, is the growth in numbers of mass merchandisers and club warehouses because they have both food and drug centers. In the old days, these stores were patronized mostly by lower income people. But, having worked with a club warehouse for many years, I know for a fact that affluent people shop at these stores too. With them carrying foods and drugs, they may make significant inroads to our business. And these organizations have the financial resources to invest heavily in advertising to make their stores successful.

The numbers of CMD stores and the number of competing outlets in each of the eight communities in which CMD is located are presented in Table II.5.3. None of the specialty food stores and only half of the other grocery stores have pharmacies. Furthermore, about one-third of the mass merchandise stores and all of the club warehouses have pharmacies.

CMD pharmacy department operations

Mr. Kliver had been vice president of drug center operations for CMD for the past 12 years. He had overseen the addition of six new stores and the remodeling of nine of the existing pharmacy departments. Van, a licensed pharmacist, had worked in numerous venues:

I have a long history of working in pharmacies. I initially started in a hospital setting and after about 5 years decided that I wanted to move more into the retail side. So, I went to work for a small independent community pharmacy located near a hospital. When the owner of that

Table II.5.3 Number of CMD stores and competing stores in each of the communities

Community	Population	CMD stores	Other grocery stores	Specialty food stores	Mass merchandise stores	Club warehouses
City A	245,000	5	9	2	3	2
City B	175,000	3	4	2	2	1
City C	168,000	3	4	1	2	1
City D	250,000	5	4	3	3	2
City E	55,000	1	5	0	1	1
City F	67,500	2	6	0	1	0
City G	128,500	3	9	1	2	1
City H	237,800	5	11	3	4	2
Total	1,326,800	27	52	12	18	10

pharmacy wanted to retire, he offered me the opportunity to purchase it from him. I thought about it for a short time, but opted to go to work for a national chain pharmacy. This gave me the chance to really learn management practices used in the bigger settings. I came to work here because the past president had worked for that chain and asked me to come join him.

Most of the pharmacy departments within the CMD stores were similar in nature. Each of the stores assigned one pharmacist to be both the lead pharmacist and manager of the pharmacy department. This person reported to both the store manager and to Mr. Kliver. Organizationally, the pharmacy department consisted of the prescription department, over-the-counter medications (OTCs), and health and beauty aids (HBAs).

Each prescription department employed between five and nine pharmacists on either a part-time or full-time basis. While the store hours were 7 a.m. to 11 p.m. seven days a week, the prescription department was open from 8 a.m. to 7 p.m. Monday through Friday, and 10 a.m. to 6 p.m. on Saturday. The prescription departments were closed on Sundays.

Prescriptions accounted for about 8.9 percent of store sales in the last year, declining from 10.2 percent 3 years ago. The various lines and the percents of sales of an average pharmacy department are presented in Table II.5.4. Mr. Kliver was somewhat concerned about the prescription department sales:

> Our prescription sales are not up to where they should be. I am not satisfied with them, and I know that Betty is troubled by the decline as well. We both think that it is due to more people shopping at mass merchandise stores and club warehouses and getting their prescriptions there while they are shopping. I am sure that people spend more time in those types of stores, so it is especially easy for them to have their prescription refill needs taken care of there as well.

Mr. Kliver wanted to have at least two pharmacists and one to two technicians working during the busier hours so patients would not have to wait long times for their prescriptions. As he commented:

> We have a long running battle in some stores. The store managers want the pharmacy department to take its time filling prescriptions

Table II.5.4 Percentage of sales of non-prescription merchandise in an average CMD store

Non-prescription categories	Last year (%)	Two years ago (%)	Three years ago (%)
Pain remedies	14.5	13.9	13.0
Shampoos and conditioners	13.9	15.4	15.9
Vitamins and nutritional supplements	9.8	9.9	10.8
Cold remedies	9.5	7.8	8.2
Toothpaste	8.9	9.5	10.2
Antacids	8.6	7.9	5.8
Lotions	8.0	8.4	9.2
Laxatives	7.6	6.8	6.6
Deodorants	7.2	8.2	8.5
Nutritional products	6.2	5.4	4.8
Sanitary napkins and adult incontinence	5.8	6.8	7.0
Total	100.0	100.0	100.0

so that the customer will wander through the store longer and purchase more. But, those customers then become mad at us for making them wait. This has been a major source of disagreement between some of the other vice presidents and myself. I know they want customers to stay in the stores longer, but making them wait reflects poorly on us. So, my view is that if we make them wait, they'll take their prescription business to other pharmacies, and their other purchases will go with them too. That includes about everything else we sell.

The patient mix for prescriptions was heavily weighted to those over 50 years of age. Mr. Kliver thought that about 40 percent of the patients getting prescriptions filled in CMD stores were aged 51 to 64, and another 25 percent were 65 or older. He also indicated that about 60 percent of the prescriptions were filled under private insurance plans, 20 percent by Medicare, 15 percent by the state's Medicaid program, and the remainder was cash customers.

Future plans

In reflecting on Ms. Manyen's request for a business plan for the pharmacy departments within the stores, Mr. Kliver identified several issues that he felt he needed to address:

- How to increase the volume of prescriptions filled in each pharmacy. What could be done to make the prescription department the primary destination of store customers?
- What other services could the prescription department offer either linked directly to prescriptions or to other products within the pharmacy department? Would it make sense to offer special consulting services related to prescriptions? Should the pharmacists spend more time in the OTC aisles talking to customers about pain and other medications and thereby bolster sales of those items? If so, how could he or she do this and still make money given that it would take time away from dispensing?
- What could be done to better link the pharmacy department to other departments within the stores. Which departments within the store would have the most attractive link to the pharmacy department in terms of providing better customer service and cross-selling. The other departments are shown in Table II.5.2.

Ms. Manyen had given each of the vice presidents a template for developing their business plans. She indicated that this was a draft and could be modified as needed, but was a starting point. The template had eight major categories:

- Situation analysis: What does and does not work?
- The future: What will pharmacies in the future look like and be doing?
- Goals: What can you achieve in the next 2 years? What cross-selling should there be with another organizational unit(s)?
- Target market: Who should we be targeting to maximize sales and profits?
- Operations: What changes should be made in operations to achieve the goals?
- Marketing: What new or different marketing activities need to be undertaken to achieve the goals?
- Human resources: What changes need to be made in staffing to achieve the goals?
- Finance: What will it cost to do what needs to be done, and how does that compare to what can be achieved?

Mr. Kliver began thinking about how to start the process of developing the plans:

I need to develop a plan very soon. I intend to start with the basics of what needs to be done overall, and then develop the detail after that. I'm not sure I want to use the template that Betty gave me, but it is a place to start. I talked this over with the vice president of store operations who oversees all of the other departments with the stores and we are going to try to find some common ground. Before this is all over, I am sure I will be one of the biggest buyers of our headache relief medicines. Good thing I get an employee discount!

Possible discussion questions

1 What are the main things that need to be done to increase the revenues and profits of Community Markets and Drugs?

2 What should be the contents of a business plan? Is the one proposed good? Why or why not?

3 What are the steps that should be undertaken to prepare a business plan along the lines suggested?

4 What would be good links for the pharmacy department? Is this is a good or bad idea? Why?

Case II.6 Agnes's Drugs

It was a dark and stormy night, and when Eric Senga got up at his usual time of 5:30 a.m., he looked out the window and saw what appeared to be nearly 18 inches of new snow. This has been a particularly brutal winter, and Mr. Senga wondered to himself: "What am I doing? It's 5:30 in the morning and I could be sleeping instead of worrying about how I'm going to get through all this snow, and wondering if anybody else will be crazy enough to go out in this weather and come into my pharmacy. I think I am getting too old for this."

Agnes's Drugs is an independent community pharmacy located in a relatively small mostly rural community in the eastern portion of the USA. Mr. Senga opened the pharmacy nearly 40 years ago, and the store had remained somewhat of a landmark in the town over time. Mr. Senga commented about the development of the pharmacy:

When I started this pharmacy, my parents loaned me about $5,000 to help me get going. They were very supportive. I wanted to show them how much I appreciated them, so I decided to name the pharmacy in both of their first names. But my father thought that would be awkward so he said that if this is what I wanted, I should name it after my mother.

My parents were quite active in the town and it proved to be a good idea to name the pharmacy as I did. I won't say that my pharmacy has become a local "hangout," but it was and to some extent still is one of the more frequently visited places downtown. Some of the businesses in the center of town changed hands, others have relocated to the eastern part of the town, and still others closed permanently. But, we are still here and doing reasonably well. When people talk about office locations and retail stores in the downtown area, they describe them in relation to where Agnes's Drugs is located. I guess that says something for what we have accomplished.

Although Mr. Senga had talked about retiring many times in the past, he was seriously considering his options at the current time and recently received inquiries about the availability of his pharmacy for sale. He just turned 72, and being very active, he celebrated his birthday by playing a round of golf, going for a 10 mile bicycle ride, and then swimming for an hour before attending a small party in his honor given by his wife and friends. He commented about the situation:

I used to be somewhat concerned about what I would do if I retired. But, as all my friends tell me, I have a lot of other interests and not that much time left to do everything. I guess it is time to really sit down and plan the future. I enjoy what I do, but there are some offers for the pharmacy that I need to consider seriously. These opportunities won't be here forever.

Both of our children are located in different parts of the state and neither wants to take over the business. I suggested to my wife that since she handles all of the accounting functions she should run the place for the next 40 years. That didn't go over very well. She said that sticking with me all these years was harder than what I do, and unfortunately, she's probably right about that.

Agnes's Drugs

Mr. Senga's pharmacy was located on a corner site on the main street in the downtown area. It was considered to be a prime location because it was at nearly the absolute center of downtown and close to all of the office and local government buildings. Everything else in the downtown area radiated out in both directions from this center point.

Agnes's Drugs had about 25,000 square feet of floor space, and the general layout of the pharmacy is presented in Figure II.6.1. Mr. Senga commented about his pharmacy:

I know I operate like an "old world" pharmacy, but that's how I like it and that seems to be what the people in this area prefer. I keep things simple and don't make a lot of changes in either the layout of the store or the types of merchandise I carry. After customers have been in this place once or twice, they become comfortable knowing what we carry and where things are located. It makes it simple for them and for me.

I realize that there have been and still are many other opportunities to grow the pharmacy. For example, we have not done much at all with durable medical equipment or home healthcare supplies. There might be decent profit margins in those lines, but the costs of carrying inventory and making those sales are higher than for other merchandise. Besides, some of the competing

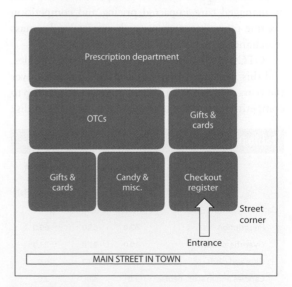

Figure II.6.1 Agnes's Drugs layout.

chains are focusing on these lines and able to purchase them at lower costs than I could. So, we rely on location and old-fashion customer service as our main attractions. We know most customers by name, offer free prescription delivery to where they live or work, and I sometimes even offer in-store credit to help people until they get their next paycheck. My employees cringe when I do give credit, but I really haven't had any abuse of this and bad debts amount to less than 2 percent of sales. I am giving some thought to starting to offer some medication therapy management for a fee, but haven't really given it serious consideration yet.

Organization

Mr. Senga organized the pharmacy into four departments: prescriptions, over-the-counter medications (OTCs), gifts and cards, and candies and miscellaneous goods.

Mr. Senga manages the overall store operations and the prescription department. His one full-time pharmacist dispenses prescriptions and is in charge of the OTC section. Another of his full-time staff employees is in charge of gifts and cards and candies and miscellaneous.

As shown in Table II.6.1, prescription sales accounted for more than 60 percent of total pharmacy sales over the last 3 years. It had been even higher in prior years, but declined as a percent of the total as managed care impacted pricing and competition became more intense as new pharmacies and a mass merchandise store came into the marketplace.

OTCs accounted for nearly 20 percent of sales, and this percentage also has declined somewhat over the years. Mr. Senga attributed this percentage drop to competition from the opening of a mass merchandise

store and a club warehouse store in the eastern portion of the town about 4 years ago.

Gifts and cards have grown in importance to total pharmacy sales in recent times. Mr. Senga explained this situation:

The percentage of sales coming from gifts and cards is somewhat misleading. It has become a considerably greater percentage partly because prescription and OTC sales have not increased much. So, as percentages erode for prescriptions and OTCs, something else has to increase.

> However, we have done a pretty good job with gifts and cards. One of my older employees retired 3 years ago and I hired a new person, Angela, who has taken a real interest in bringing in gift items. She started bringing in new stuff, and when I saw what she could do, I began sending her to regional gift shows to find types of merchandise to carry. Angela has done an amazing job with this. We now carry unique gifts that mass merchandise stores and the chain pharmacies don't want to stock because the volume potential is not adequate to fit their business models. But, the margins on these items are good for me.

The other department is candies and miscellaneous goods. Mr. Senga described this department:

In the past, this section just contained cheap candy, mostly attracting children of our customers. We also carried other items that just happened to come along. When I ordered merchandise from my primary wholesaler, if I saw something that I thought might sell, we would make a small purchase and put it in this section. It's close to the door and the checkout register, so it's in a high-traffic spot. About half of these sold pretty well, and, well, the other half didn't.

When Angela came into the store, she also took over this department. She replaced most of the cheap candy, "junk" as she called it, with more expensive candies that are unique and can be used as gifts. We still have some candy for the kids, but that is a small part of the stock. She finds this stuff when she goes to the buying shows, and we have done well with it.

She totally revamped what I called "miscellaneous" merchandise. She created a

Table II.6.1 Composition of sales for last 3 years			
	Last year (%)	Two years ago (%)	Three years ago (%)
Sales			
Prescription	62.0	65.0	69.0
Over-the-counter	19.0	21.0	23.0
Gifts and cards	12.0	10.0	6.0
Candies and miscellaneous	7.0	4.0	2.0
Total	100.0	100.0	100.0

small section for arts and crafts, with most of the merchandise being made by local residents and put into the store on consignment. We are doing very well on this since we keep half of the selling price and we have no inventory-carrying costs, just the use of space. The only problem we have had is that it is a bit awkward when one of our customers brings in pretty ugly or stupid stuff that they made and think it is museum-quality art. We then have to tell the person that it isn't suitable for our store. It's a little touchy, but we are dealing with it, and I don't think we have lost customers because we rejected their merchandise.

Operations

Agnes's Drugs is open six days a week. Store hours are 8 a.m. to 7 p.m. on Mondays through Fridays and 10 a.m. to 4 p.m. on Saturdays. The pharmacy is closed on Sundays.

Mr. Senga explained that most of the stores in the downtown area are open from 9 a.m. to 6 p.m., so he wanted to be open an hour earlier and an hour later to accommodate employees of those stores. He felt that they represented a very significant portion of his customer base.

The second largest group of customers was thought to be residents of the immediate area. They typically come in after work and on Saturdays. Mr. Senga thought that the employees in the office buildings represented the smallest group of customers. He felt that they mostly lived in the eastern part of the town and came into the downtown area only to go to work. They did most of their shopping and pharmacy purchase closer to their residences.

The pharmacy employed four people on a full-time basis and several more on a part-time basis. In addition to Mr. Senga, the prescription department had one full-time and two part-time pharmacists. It also had a full-time technician who worked in both the prescription department and in OTCs depending on customer volume and what needed to be done.

The full-time pharmacist has been employed by Mr. Senga for nearly 15 years and has become very popular with customers. On several occasions, he expressed an interest in either investing in the pharmacy or purchasing it outright if and when Mr. Senga retires. Nearly all of the other full-time and part-time staff, with the exception of Angela, have been employed for at least 8 years.

Mr. Senga commented about his staff:

I have been very fortunate to have a wonderful staff. They are like family and all try to help each other out. Some of these people are the children of former employees, so we have this generational thing going. This is one reason why I haven't retired or sold the pharmacy. They make it easy to work here, and I try to be a good employer. I was a little concerned when I hired Angela because she is so energetic, kind of like me, but she has fit in well.

I sometimes think that I could take more time off and the pharmacy would do just fine. However, I have seen other owners do this and it didn't work well for very long. I guess if you aren't there, things will deteriorate sooner or later. I've heard enough horror stories to know that I just couldn't take more days off. While I have great people, I would have to make some serious organizational changes to keep the place running like I want when I'm not here.

Financial statements

Overall revenues and expenses for the last 3 years are presented in Table II.6.2. Sales have grown in each of the years, but very slowly. Mr. Senga attributed this slow growth to several factors.

First, while the number of prescriptions dispensed has grown, the revenues per prescription have declined. This is due to reduced reimbursements from managed care and the increased use of generic drugs instead of brand name products. Accordingly, he felt that he is doing more volume but at lower sales per prescription.

Second, unit sales of OTCs also have grown each year, but this is more a function of the population growth in the town than increased revenues per customer. Mr. Senga also indicated that he had to lower prices because of the increased competition. With chain stores, a mass merchandiser, and a club warehouse in the town, Mr. Senga feels it is difficult to charge prices much higher than the competition. He already lost some customers to the competition and has adopted a "we will match any competitor's prices for over-the-counter medications." The result was to shrink profit margins on OTCs, and he was not sure whether the growth in total unit sales offset the decline in margins.

Table II.6.2 Revenues and expenses for last 3 years

	Last year	Two years ago	Three years ago
Dollar sales			
Sales	$3,370,061	$3,327,471	$3,289,444
Cost of goods sold	$2,494,765	$2,453,976	$2,399,255
Gross profit	$875,296	$873,494	$890,189
Operating expenses	$757,187	$774,440	$753,184
Net profit before taxes	$118,109	$99,054	$137,005
Percent of sales			
Sales	100.00%	100.00%	100.00%
Cost of goods sold	74.03%	73.75%	72.94%
Gross profit	25.97%	26.25%	27.06%
Operating expenses	22.47%	23.27%	22.90%
Net profit before taxes	3.50%	2.98%	4.16%

Costs of good in total and as a percent of sales also have grown over the years. Mr. Senga attributes this to rising costs and not being able to increase prices due to insurance contracts and competition.

Mr. Senga was most proud of being able to control operating costs. He trimmed some part-time staff hours and kept other expenses to a minimum. He even brought together a few downtown retailers to create an informal buying group for office supplies and other commonly purchased items. By purchasing jointly once per month, they were able to get quantity discounts from local and online suppliers. As Mr. Senga noted:

> I really tried to tighten up on our operating costs. We are pretty lean now and I am not sure there is much fat left to cut. Salaries are our biggest component of operating costs and they have grown considerably because most of our employees have stayed with us. New hires could be less expensive, but our "old timers" are good employees and the customers like them. This is a tough issue.
>
> I know that this informal group I started just brings in "nickels and dimes," but they do add up. All I have to do is get the orders from the other retailers by the 20th of the month and make the purchases from the suppliers in one shot. When the merchandise arrives at my store, the retailers pick it up and pay for the items they have ordered. I think we save at least 10–15 percent by doing this, and it doesn't take much of my time. It's pretty automatic now and since the retailers pay me when they take the

merchandise, I have their money for about 20 days before having to pay the suppliers.

Operating expenses also include a base salary of $50,000 per year to Mr. Senga. He then takes some or all of the profits as income, depending on his needs.

The balance sheet for Agnes's Drugs is presented in Table II.6.3. The note payable and long-term debt are owed to Mr. Senga for remodeling the pharmacy. Some of this took place 4 years ago and some about 6 years ago.

The town

Over the last 20 years, the town has grown from a population of about 15,000 to nearly 60,000. This growth rate of more than 7 percent per year was not expected to continue. However, town planners projected the growth to be approximately 3–5 percent per year over the next 10 years and then to flatten out. Part of the slower growth was due to desires of town managers to restrict population expansion and to keep too much open land from being developed.

Geographically, the town could be divided into three sections: downtown, eastern section, and western section. As previously indicated, Agnes's Drugs was located on a corner site on the main street in the downtown area. This area consisted mostly of business offices, local government offices, and retail stores. Although most sites were occupied, the 10,000 square foot site next to the pharmacy and the 20,000 square foot site next to that were vacant. Both sites were owned by the same person and had been unoccupied for quite some time.

Table II.6.3 Balance sheet for last year

	Last year
Assets	
Current assets	
Cash	$88,795
Trade receivables	$164,406
Inventory	$262,517
Other current	$9,330
Total current	$525,049
Fixed assets	$78,155
Total assets	$603,204
Liabilities	
Current liabilities	
Notes payable	$61,487
Trade payables	$215,810
Other current	$87,173
Total current	$364,470
Long-term debt	$154,363
Total liabilities	$518,833
Net worth	$84,372

Surrounding these downtown commercial sites were residential neighborhoods that had a mix of small lower income homes and large high-income residences with big yards. The larger residents were quite old and "stately" and were home to some of the town's elite, including retired and semi-retired business owners, and high government officials. Generally, the population in this area had grown slowly because of space limitations and more desirable upper- and middle-income areas to the east. Accordingly, the residents were mainly younger singles who worked in the offices and retail outlets, families with lower incomes, and older residents who were retired or semi-retired.

The fastest growing area of the town was to the east, accounting for about 75 percent of the population growth. It consisted primarily of upper- and middle-income residents and suburban style homes with relatively small backyards. Residents tended to be younger and middle-age families. The area also had several strip shopping centers and the town's only indoor mall. As such, the area consisted nearly entirely of residential and retail structures.

To the west of the downtown area was the third section. This area accounted for about 20 percent of the growth the town had experienced over the years. It consisted mostly of light industry, although there were some retail businesses to serve a relatively small lower-income housing area. Most of the housing was occupied by those who worked nearby. Residents tended to be mostly young singles and middle-aged families.

The competition

In addition to Agnes's Drugs, there were two national chain pharmacies, one local supermarket chain with pharmacies, and approximately 15 independent community pharmacies. Both national chains had one pharmacy located in the eastern section and one in the western section of the town. Neither national chain had a presence in the downtown area. These pharmacies focused on low prices and advertised heavily in the local newspaper and on television. One of the chains had been in the town for more than 20 years, and the other came to town nearly 4 years ago.

The local supermarket chain had four outlets and has been in the area for nearly 7 years. It had one location in the downtown area, two in the eastern area, and one in the western area. The chain competed on the basis of "quality at a fair price." It ran weekly specials in the local newspaper and advertised selectively on television. While it did not run specials for prescriptions, it nearly always included OTC medications in its advertisements.

Of the 15 independent community pharmacies in the town, Agnes's Drugs and three others were located in the downtown area. Two of those others were small in size and most of their revenues came from prescription sales. The other was somewhat smaller than Agnes's Drugs and was not considered by the residents of the area to be especially attractive. Seven of the other independent pharmacies were located in the eastern section of the town, and the others were in the west.

Mr. Senga commented on the competition:

> I'm not especially concerned about most of the other independent pharmacies, with the exception of one of them. Most have been here for quite some time and I don't think any of them has the name recognition or respect that we have.
>
> My only fear, however, is that the other larger independent in the downtown area will be taken over by a chain or the one independent pharmacy currently operating only in the eastern part of the town. This store is not doing

very well and would be ripe for a purchase if the owner was a little brighter and understood how much trouble he is in going forward. The only thing holding back a sale is that its location is not that great, it only has about 17,000 square feet, and it has not been remodeled for many years. So, it would not be overly attractive to a chain, but if the price were right, someone might try to fix it up. I really doubt that the current owner can hang on for too many years. He can't be that rich from that pharmacy's profits.

The national chain that came into the area about 4 years ago is very aggressive. I would expect it to add stores somewhere, especially given the growth the town has already experienced and will experience over the next 10 years. It really advertises low prices and is a tough competitor.

The supermarket chain also is a strong competitor. Fortunately for me, for some reason it hasn't really focused on its pharmacy operations. It is too busy selling produce and meats at this time. I have to believe that sooner or later, it will want to push its prescriptions. I'm not sure how much that will affect me because we have a pretty loyal customer base. But, if people can get their groceries and prescriptions with one-stop shopping, and do so at lower prices, I could have a problem. Since my pharmacy has a great location and is a central point in the downtown area, I think we are somewhat insulated from this chain. People just like to come into our place. Strangely, it seems like it's a social outing for them.

The future

As Mr. Senga stepped out of his car at 6:45 a.m. and into the cold, he started thinking again about the future. He quickly recounted several options he had.

One was to sell all or part of the pharmacy to his full-time pharmacist. This man had been a good employee over the years and wanted to have a pharmacy of his own someday. Mr. Senga was not sure how long he would stay if there was no opportunity to purchase Agnes's Drugs at some point. If he left, he might try to buy one of the other downtown pharmacies, open a new pharmacy in the downtown area, or open one in

either the east or west. The concern was that because this pharmacist was quite popular, he could take some of Mr. Senga's customers with him.

Another option was to talk to the national chain that had moved into the area within the last 4 years. Representatives of this chain had approached Mr. Senga about whether his pharmacy would be for sale, and they also talked to the owner of the vacant sites next to Agnes's Drugs. Mr. Senga did not believe that this chain would try to purchase both the 10,000 and 20,000 square foot sites and open a new chain right next door. However, he thought it might want both his and the 10,000 square foot site next to his and make a larger store. It might also want to purchase the other independent pharmacy, even though it only had 17,000 square feet.

A third option was to sell or merge with one of the independent pharmacies located in the eastern section of the town. One of the most successful owners also approached him about either selling out or joint venturing. This owner wanted a presence in more than just the east, and Mr. Senga believed she would prefer to have location in the downtown area. She started her pharmacy about 3 years ago and it was about the same size as Agnes's Drugs, but he thought it did about 20 percent more business than him. He was concerned that she might buy the other larger independent pharmacy downtown.

Finally, Mr. Senga thought about just keeping his pharmacy and continuing as he had over the last 3 years. Although the declines in prescriptions and OTCs troubled him, he still was making a good living and was his own boss. The only real problems with this option, he thought, were how long would things stay good, and how long could he enjoy getting up at 5:30 a.m. and trudging through the snow.

Possible discussion questions

1 How well has Mr. Senga operated his pharmacy over time?

2 What has Mr. Senga done well and what mistakes has he made with respect to planning for the future?

3 What information should he consider when planning for the future of the pharmacy and his personal future?

4 What options should he consider further, and how should he go about assessing each?

PART III

Accounting and financial management

6

Accounting and financial records

Learning objectives

The objectives of this chapter are to assist you to be able to explain:

- why records are kept for a pharmacy
- what are the basic books for recordkeeping
- what financial statements must be prepared
- how financial records are kept
- how financial records are maintained.

Key terms

Accounts payable ledger
Accounts receivable ledger
Balance sheet
Cash disbursements journal
Cash flow statement
Cash receipts journal
Double entry bookkeeping
General journal
General ledger
Income statement
Purchases journal
Records for external purposes
Records for internal purposes
Sales journal

There is an old saying in business: "If you sell your products below cost, you can't make it up by volume." Managers often look only at their revenues and the number of prescriptions dispensed as indicators of success or failure. "We had a good month" generally refers to the volume of prescriptions sold and, perhaps, non-prescription sales. What these owners and managers do not realize is that the key issue is how much profit they made. It may be that their cost of doing business was more than the sales volume.

Good financial records can determine this and resolve other issues (e.g. which activities were most profitable, where labor costs were too high) associated with developing a profitable business.

Owners must come to grips with the concept that profit is a function of revenues minus costs, and that costs need to be monitored just as do sales. Many owners do not know their cost of doing business, or whether they are making profits or incurring losses, and have no way of determining their exact current financial situation.

It is not uncommon to find "checkbook businesses"—businesses whose financial transactions are intermixed with the owner's personal checkbook. Business transactions conducted in this manner may become almost impossible to separate from personal transactions. A typical dilemma is: Was that $85.95 check to Staples for office supplies or for a wading pool for the kids?

Why keep records?

Many new pharmacy owners question why the lack of records is bad and why a personal checkbook cannot be used for business transactions. Since they own the pharmacy, who cares if expenses are all mixed together?

For one, the Internal Revenue Service (lRS) cares. Declaring a $85.95 wading pool as a business expense violates tax laws. IRS agents will want clearly detailed accounts of the activities of the pharmacy.

Regulatory agencies also care. There are a great many recordkeeping activities involved in accounting for money, purchases, and so forth. For example, hospital pharmacies are precluded from purchasing drugs for inpatient dispensing and then diverting them to their outpatient pharmacies. Maintaining records to demonstrate that this has not taken place is important.

Creditors and potential lenders care about the state of the records. They want to see how profitable the pharmacy is—without wading pools, underwear, and groceries.

Finally, management should care if the pharmacy is run properly. Records provide a visual and permanent basis for observing the operation of the pharmacy and are a management tool for sound decision-making.

Good records are needed for both internal and external purposes.[1] The types of books needed for internal management, however, might be different from those called for by outside creditors. It is not uncommon to find owners who maintain two sets of books. One highlights management decision areas, and another is for outside sources. While often thought to

be indicative of unscrupulous business, the use of two systems may instead signify sound management.

One example of this is the use of different approaches to valuing inventory. For tax purposes, it may be best to use a LIFO (last-in, first-out) method in which the value is based on the most recent acquisition costs of merchandise. This increases the cost of goods and reduces profit and its accompanying taxes. For internal use, however, the pharmacy may use a FIFO (first-in, first-out) method—using the actual acquisition costs at the time the merchandise was purchased. The key point is that the types of records needed by the IRS, lending institutions, and others may not be suitable for management decision-making.

Records for internal purposes

Sound business management relies not only on good executive judgment but also on high-quality and timely data with which judgments can be made. Internal records for these purposes typically center on keeping track of revenues and expenses.

Records on the generation of revenue by the pharmacy may include information on who made purchases, whether they purchased prescriptions or non-prescription merchandise, how much they purchased in both quantity and monetary terms, and when the purchases occurred. For a small pharmacy, this information can be used to identify more important customers and payers (e.g. Medicaid, private insurance) and their buying patterns. For example, knowing that a customer purchases a maintenance drug in 60-day supplies can be used to alert the pharmacy to send refill reminders at appropriate times. Similarly, some buyers may purchase prescriptions but not non-prescription merchandise. Knowing that a customer does this will help management determine whether the pharmacy carries the proper non-prescription merchandise.

With the following basic records, an accounting system can be created:[2]

- *Cash receipts journal*: This is used to record the cash that comes into the pharmacy.
- *Cash disbursements journal*: This is used to record the pharmacy's expenditures.
- *Sales journal*: This is used to record and summarize monthly revenues.

- *Purchases journal*: This is used to record purchases of prescription and non-prescription merchandise bought for dispensing and resale. In instances where manufacturer rebates are given for selected purchases, it is critical that these be highlighted both for internal and regulatory reporting purposes.
- *Inventory*: This is a record of the pharmacy's investment in merchandise and parts, which is needed for arriving at a true profit on financial statements and for income tax purposes.
- *Accounts receivable ledger*: This is used to record the balances that private patients, governmental agencies, insurance companies, and managed care contractors, insurers, and governmental agencies owe the pharmacy. This has become quite complicated because of the many different formulas used in managed care contracts to compute product reimbursements, dispensing fees, and incentives for generic substitutions, payments for cognitive services and intervention, etc.
- *Accounts payable ledger*: This is used to record what the pharmacy owes its suppliers and other creditors.

The mainstay of a sound internal recordkeeping system is the budget, which is described in Chapter 7. Since a budget essentially is a quantified planning and controlling device, it needs to be kept current and evaluated often. Is the sales volume where it should be? Is too much or too little being spent on inventory for the level of sales being generated? Are labor expenses too high for the number of prescriptions dispensed and the non-prescription merchandise sold?

These and other questions need to be answered if management is to achieve its goals. In addition, any "yes" answer to one or more of these questions must be followed up with "Why?" and "What is the impact?" Answers to the last two questions may not be contained in the financial records. Nevertheless, finding that something is amiss requires sound recordkeeping. From that point, the manager can take the necessary steps to correct the situation.

Records for external purposes

Records must be maintained to satisfy local, state, and federal agencies as well as customers and creditors. Depending on the type of pharmacy and its location, the amount of data required will vary. If for no other purpose, detailed records on revenues and expenses need to be maintained for the IRS and the state tax agency. However, there have been increasing requirements placed on pharmacies to maintain records relating to the amount and cost of their purchases, rebates provided by manufacturers, etc.

In addition to government requirements, creditors may well demand periodic reports on the financial position. Some commercial lending institutions, for example, want from their borrowers quarterly, semi-annual, or annual reports of income and assets and liabilities. For the pharmacy that requests a loan, these statements are mandatory not only for the current period but most likely for previous years.

Pharmacies that are incorporated will have to file a number of statements for tax and other purposes at both the federal and state levels. Complete financial disclosure is needed for chains whose stock is traded on the open market.

Recognition of what data are necessary and useful in this regard is important. Although in some instances the records needed for external purposes may differ substantially from those wanted for internal management, in most cases they can be blended to serve both purposes simultaneously. This eases the recordkeeping burden and expense.

Financial records

Many owners do not keep their own books. Instead, they hire a certified public accountant (CPA) or bookkeeping service to record and prepare their statements. Nevertheless, it is critical for management to understand the meaning of the reports they receive.

The financial records maintained in community and hospital settings, of course, will vary. Nevertheless, the desirable attributes of the recordkeeping process are quite similar.

Necessary attributes of an accounting system

Developing a set of financial records is the owner's responsibility. Only in this way is there any guarantee that the books will be understood and used in the process of managing. Therefore, the financial recordkeeping system must be geared, within limits, to the needs of the owner and other managers who use financial information.

While certain conventions in recordkeeping must be adhered to, the system itself can be fairly well tailored to individual needs. Most of the material presented in this chapter deals with standard approaches to bookkeeping systems.

A good recordkeeping process should serve management by being:

- simple to understand
- flexible and adaptable to changing needs
- inexpensive to maintain
- not excessively time-consuming to maintain
- handy and convenient to use for internal and external purposes.

For a bookkeeping system to be valuable, it should be as simple as possible. Otherwise, its use will be impaired and fade into obscurity. Sophisticated terminology can be replaced with more pedestrian language. "Owner's equity," for instance, may be changed to "owner's investment in the pharmacy." Buzzwords can take the place of more conventional terms if they aid in clarity and are referenced as to their true meaning. Generalized entries also can be broken down into their component parts so that the manager can readily see what each entry contains. "Prepaid expenses," for example, can be itemized on the balance sheet to show advance payments for insurance, advertising, and other expenses if this helps simplify the process and makes the reports more understandable and usable.

A second attribute of a good bookkeeping system is its flexibility and adaptability to change. As a pharmacy grows and expands its services, the types of entries in the financial records may have to be altered. This usually is handled by adding categories to account for new or different types of markets and goods and services sold. When setting up the system, consideration should be given to the capabilities for expanding with new facets of business.

A third attribute is that the system be relatively inexpensive to operate. Elaborate processes can cost more than good financial controls can save. It makes little sense to spend $1,000 to keep track of an expense category that only amounts to $700 annually.

Related to this is the fact that maintaining the records must not demand inordinate amounts of time. The system should work for the owner—the owner should not be working for the recordkeeping system. As the process begins to consume more and more

management time, maintaining and using the financial records becomes burdensome and more likely to be neglected.

Finally, financial records must be readily available to management for everyday use. They should be kept up to date on a monthly basis and stored in a place convenient for management. However, access to the records must be limited only to those who need the information to perform their duties.

Basic books for recordkeeping

When referring to financial records, most managers think only in terms of income statements and balance sheets. And it is erroneously assumed that these can be prepared easily from even the most rudimentary records, such as loose receipts and canceled checks.

Journals

Maintaining a modest set of books is a prerequisite for preparing useful statements for management purposes. The first step in establishing a sound recordkeeping system is to develop the necessary journals that will be used to record business transactions. From these, financial information can be transferred to appropriate ledgers that serve as a means of classifying each transaction into specified groups. Note that in double entry bookkeeping there must be offsetting entries for all transactions. Thus, for every debit amount there must be a corresponding credit amount. This serves to create a checks-and-balances system and reduces the likelihood of error. As shown in the figures that follow, the total of debits (DR) made in a transaction equals the total number of credits (CR).

The *general journal* essentially is a book within which some or all of the business activities can be recorded. Typically, this is done by the date, type of transaction, and the amount of money involved. An example of a general journal is presented in Figure 6.1.

In some instances, this journal can be the only one used. Normally, however, it serves as a catchall for transactions that are not appropriate for one of the other journals. The main reason for not using it alone is that it is more tedious and difficult to sort out the larger number of entries at later points. Since the entry must be made anyway, why not do the sorting at the same time? A number of specialized journals can be used to record and sort the transactions concurrently.

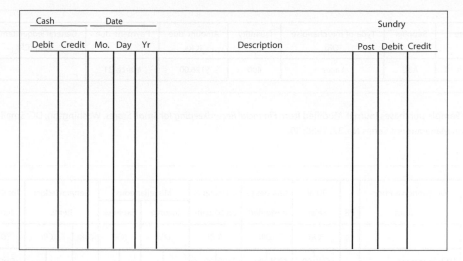

Figure 6.1 Sample general journal. From Gaedeke RM and Tootelian DH. *Small Business Management*, 3rd edn. Boston: Allyn and Bacon, 1991: 331. Used with permission.

The *purchases journal* is used to record credit purchases. Because cash payments for supplies will be recorded in a different journal, these credit transactions serve to identify the supplier, the merchandise bought, the amount owed, and when payment is due (Figure 6.2). At any time, management can tally the amount of money owed to suppliers and array the payment dates.

A *sales journal* is critical for companies that sell goods and services on credit—as nearly all do for third-party prescriptions. These journal entries essentially become the accounts receivable. The sales journal records the purchases, the date, the merchandise involved, and the amount due (Figure 6.3). A comparison of this and the purchases journal will provide a quick means of analyzing the differences between some of the anticipated cash inflow and outflow. Gross disparities will signify potential periods when cash will be plentiful and when it will be in short supply.

Payments to suppliers on a cash basis or payments on credits previously entered in the purchases journal are recorded in the *cash disbursements journal*. Other cash outlays also will be entered in this journal. Each transaction will be recorded in terms of to whom the payment was made, the amount owed, the date, any discounts taken, and the actual amount paid (Figure 6.4).

This journal is especially important in that all outflow of money from the pharmacy will pass through here. In many cases, the petty cash held in the cash register to handle the nickel-and-dime transactions is accounted for only as a total in the cash disbursements journal. As long as petty cash expenditures do not become excessive, they usually are not worth the effort for individual entry in the journal.

All cash sales and payments from credit customers previously entered in the sales journal are recorded in the *cash receipts journal*. Included here is information giving cash register totals and cash receipts from credit sales and from whom the cash was received (Figure 6.5).

This journal is highly important because it identifies cash sales and payables by credit customers. Comparisons of this journal with the sales journal also will reveal which customers pay their bills promptly and which do not. In addition, an examination of this journal with the cash disbursements journal will reasonably reflect the overall cash inflow and outflow. As described in following chapters, control of cash flow is critical to survival.

Ledgers

Once the transactions are recorded in the appropriate journals, they need to be posted to the ledger accounts. Ledgers provide a convenient way to systemize the financial activities and prepare them for use in the income statement and balance sheet. This is the function of the *general ledger*—to provide a handy mechanism for scrutinizing the pharmacy's financial

Date	Supplier	Type of merchandise (OR)	Quantity	Amount due (CR)	Payment due	General ledger items (OR) (CR)
March 10	ABC	Laces	400	$126.00	March 31	

Figure 6.2 Sample purchases journal. Modified from *Financial Recordkeeping for Small Stores*. Washington, DC: Small Business Administration Management Series No. 32. 1966: 30.

Date 19—		Description and/or account	PR	Total sales		Charges to customers		Collections on account		Miscellaneous				General ledger Items				Total cash deposit	
										Income		Expense							
				(CR)		(DR)		(CR)		(DR)		(CR)		(DR)		(CR)		(DR)	
Mar	23	Daily summary		$660	00	$225	00	$100	00									$544	00
		Refund on merchandise										$15	00						
		Cash short								$6	00								
Mar	23	Daily summary		$660	00	$225	00	$100	00									$562	00
		Refund on merchandise										$15	00						
		Cash short								$6	00								
		Exchange														$18	00		

Figure 6.3 Sample sales and cash receipts journal. From *Financial Recordkeeping for Small Stores*. Washington, DC, Small Business Administration Management Series No. 32. 1966: 18.

position. The *accounts receivable* and *accounts payable ledgers* are used to keep track of payments due and owed.

The accounts within the general ledger should roughly correspond to the accounts within the income statement, balance sheet, and other statements described later in this chapter. Entries made from the specified journals are recorded in debit and credit fashion and provide an easy way to total individual accounts and keep track of each aspect of the financial activities (Figure 6.6). From this ledger, most closing or final statements for internal and external purposes are derived.

Although sometimes contained within the general ledger, two accounts are often broken up for extra analysis and control. If the pharmacy buys from many suppliers and sells to many credit customers,

it is too cumbersome to keep all these within the general ledger. Consequently, accounts receivable and accounts payable ledgers (Figures 6.7 and 6.8) are used partly for convenience and partly for control purposes.

These ledgers help in examining how much is owed and who owes and is owed. If the pharmacy establishes credit limits for its private-pay customers or if credit limits are established by suppliers, these can be noted in the ledgers so that when the limits are approached, management will know.

Financial statements

While many types of statements could be constructed from journal and ledger entries, the three most important statements for internal and external use are the

Date 19—	Payee and/or account	Ch. no.	Amount of check (CR)	Merchandise purchases (DR)	Gross salaries (DR)	Payroll deductions Income tax (CR)	Soc. sec. (CR)	Miscellaneous Income (DR)	Expense (CR)	General ledger items (DR)	(CR)
	Miscellaneous entries—rent, merchandise, purchase, asset purchase, spoiled check, payroll										
Jul 1	John Smith—Rent	92	$200 00					$200 00			
14	ABC Company	93	$115 00	$115 00							
19	Z Company—Furn. & Fix.	94	$30 00							$30 00	
	VOID	95									
20	Payroll	96	$50 85		$58 50	$5 90	$1 75				

Figure 6.4 Sample cash disbursements, purchases, and expense journal. From *Financial Recordkeeping for Small Stores*. Washington, DC: Small Business Administration Management Series No. 32. 1966: 26, 27.

Date 19—	Description and/or account	PR	Total sales (CR)	Taxable sales (Memo)	Charges to customers (DR)	Collections on account (CR)	Sales tax (CR)	Miscellaneous Income (DR)	Expense (CR)	General ledger items (DR)	(CR)	Total cash deposit (DR)
Mar 23	Daily summary		$651 00	$300 00	$225 00	$100 00	$9 00					$544 00
	Refund on merchandise								$15 00			
	Cash short								$6 00			

Figure 6.5 Sample sales and cash receipts journal showing taxable sales and sales tax. From *Financial Recordkeeping for Small Stores*. Washington, DC: Small Business Administration Management Series No. 32, 1966: 120.

Posting from the sales and cash receipts journal

The total sales column and the summary of the miscellaneous income and expense items column in the *cash receipts journal* have already been posted to the profit and loss statement. The remaining column totals are posted to the *general ledger* as follows:

The charges to customers column is posted in the debit column of the accounts receivable account.

The collections on account total is posted in the credit column of the accounts receivable account.

The general ledger columns have already been summarized by accounts, Each net total, debit or credit, is posted in the proper column of the corresponding account in the *general ledger*.

The total cash deposit column is posted in the debit column of the cash in bank account.

Posting from the cash disbursements journal

The columns headed "Merchandise purchases," "Gross salaries." and "Miscellaneous income and expense items" in the *cash disbursement journal* have already been posted to the profit and loss statement. The other column totals are posted to the *general ledger* as follows:

The amount of check column is entered in the credit column of the cash in bank account.

Payroll deductions are entered in the credit columns of the corresponding accounts. The general ledger items, as in the *cash receipts journal,* have already been summarized by accounts. Each net total, debit or credit, is posted to the corresponding *general ledger* account.

Finishing touches in the journals and ledger

As in posting to the profit and loss statement, when each total is posted from the journals, a checkmark (*j*) should be made beside the column total in the journal to show that it has been posted. Entries in the *general ledger* should be dated as of the end of the month to which they apply. The posting reference in the *general ledger* (column headed "PR" or "Ref.") should be "CR" for the *cash receipts journal* or "CD" for the *cash disbursements journal*, followed by the number of the journal page from which the item was posted.

General ledger sheet

ACCOUNT:					NO.		
Date	Description	PR	Items posted		Balance	
			Debit	Credit	Debit	Credit

Figure 6.6 Journal and ledger posting. Modified from *Financial Recordkeeping for Small Stores*. Washington, DC: Small Business Administration Management Series No. 32. 1966: 63–64.

balance sheet, the income statement, and the cash flow statement. The use of these reports for management purposes provides an excellent picture of business activities in terms of assets and debt position, profits or losses, and how efficiently cash is being used.

The balance sheet

The balance sheet is a statement of the financial condition at a given point in time. Composed of three basic parts, the balance sheet keeps track of what the pharmacy owns, what it owes, and what the owner has invested in the pharmacy (Figure 6.9).

Entries and evaluations of balance sheet accounts are based on the conventional accounting equation:

$$\text{Assets} = \text{liabilities} + \text{net worth}$$

What this says is that anything owned by the pharmacy (assets) is either owed to creditors (liabilities) or to the owner (net worth).

Accounts receivable ledger: Customer's account

JOHN DOE

345 Sixth Street

Date		Item	Debit		Credit		Balance	
Sep	1	Balance					$47	62
	8	Sales check #195	$4	50			$52	12
	10	Received on account			$47	62	$4	50
	19	Sales check #231	$42	50			$47	00
	20	Sales check #243, return sale	$35	00			$12	00

Accounts receivable ledger: Control sheet

Accounts receivable control sheet

Date		Item	Debit		Credit		Balance	
Nov	1	Balance brought forward					$2,395	00
	1		$80	00			$2,475	00
	2		$230	00	$195	00	$2,510	00

Figure 6.7 Sample accounts receivable ledger. From *Financial Recordkeeping for Small Stores*. Washington, DC: Small Business Administration Management Series No. 32. 1966: 76, 78.

The assets can be divided into three conventional categories: current, fixed, and intangible. This is shown in the sample balance sheet presented in Figure 6.9. Assets are the income-producing agents of the pharmacy. They are obtained or purchased and then used in the sale of prescription and non-prescription products and services.

Some of the assets are more "liquid" than others, meaning that they can more quickly be turned into cash. These are called *current assets*, and generally are convertible into cash within 1 year. They typically include cash, accounts receivable, office supplies, inventory, and short-term investments (e.g. stocks, bonds). If the pharmacy has any long-term debt due to it

within a 1-year period, this will be transferred from fixed assets to current assets. Similarly, any prepaid expenses that will be used up within the year also should be part of the current assets. An insurance premium that is paid in advance is an example of a prepaid expense.

Fixed assets are assets that will not be used up within a 1-year period. The pharmacy computer, equipment for intravenous (IV) preparation, delivery vehicles, office equipment, buildings, and land are the most common types of fixed assets found. If the pharmacy holds any notes from borrowers that are not due within 1 year, they too are considered fixed assets. For fixed assets that are used up over the course of some

transactions in financial terms over a defined period of time. Although an income statement may only be developed at the end of a fiscal year, it is generally recommended that it be constructed monthly. By doing this on a monthly basis, it is easier for the owner to see how profitable the pharmacy is before it is too late to take any necessary corrective action.

Unlike the balance sheet, the income statement reports on all sales generated and expenses incurred over a specified time period. It is composed of two to three general parts, depending on the operations of the pharmacy: business income generated, business expenses incurred, and sometimes non-business-related income and expenses (Figure 6.10). For the pharmacy that has non-business-related assets that generate revenue (e.g. land or building rentals), it is wise to separate them from the purely business-related transactions. This provides a better method of appraising the operations on their own.

The income section of the income statement contains three important elements. The total revenues generated must be totaled from the sales and cash receipts journals. While many owners look at total revenues as the all-important measure of pharmacy activity, they are not.

The net sales are much more important because they reflect the true revenue generated. There are two common deductions from total sales that may be necessary. First, any merchandise returned or allowances given for defective goods or services or incorrect orders must be subtracted from total sales. Since money is returned or the buyer is not charged for the goods or services, it should not be counted as a part of sales. Second, any discounts offered to and taken by customers (e.g. employee discounts) should also be subtracted. If, for example, a 20 percent cash discount is given to an employee for a $100 purchase, the $100 would be recorded in total sales, and $20 subtracted out as a sales discount, leaving net sales of $80.

A common question relating modifications to total sales is: "Why count them in the first place?" In the cash discount example, why not simply record a sale of $80 instead of the manipulation of entering $100 less $20? The reason is that the amount of sales returns and allowances and sales discounts needs to be specified for management control purposes. Excessive returns and allowances may indicate bad products or services, while few discounts taken may signify a poor or ineffective discount policy. By highlighting these

in the income section, management can see the true picture of total and net sales.

Business expenses incurred by the pharmacy can be grouped into two categories: costs of goods sold and operating expenses. While it may seem cumbersome to separate these expenses, such a breakdown is important for management decision-making. Being able to identify the prescription and non-prescription costs of goods purchased, and the operating costs gives a better perspective on operations and trouble spots. This is described more fully in Chapter 7.

The costs of goods sold are shown by the formula:

Beginning inventory + purchases

    − ending inventory = costs of goods sold

Consequently, the costs of goods sold requires only an inventory check at the end of a fiscal period, and this also serves as the beginning inventory for the next fiscal period.

Pharmacies that serve home-health businesses or skilled nursing facility contracts may have more difficulty determining their costs of goods. The costs include the raw materials and direct labor involved in producing the solutions, unit-dose packages, etc., plus the overhead (e.g. supervisor wages) which can be directly attributed to the preparation of the products. The difficulty in determining the costs lies in deciding whether some cost should be part of overhead or a part of operating expenses. In general, costs obviously incurred in the preparation of products, and an estimated percentage of questionable direct costs are used for this computation.

Other costs incurred are considered operating expenses. These include such expenses as employee wages, promotion, supplies, depreciation, insurance, and taxes. Keeping track of these on an individual basis allows management to maintain closer control over expenses that could severely hurt profitability.

If the pharmacy generates income from sources not directly a part of its normal operations, these should be separated out for evaluation and control purposes. Examples include rental property, postal stations, lottery ticket sales, and sales of unrelated goods on a one-time basis. The reason for isolating these is that profits or losses on them may grossly distort the financial picture of the pharmacy as shown on the income statement. For instance, if the pharmacy is incurring losses on its prescription

Description of income statement terms

A. Net sales: The dollar amount of sales made during the year, excluding sales tax and any returns or allowances.

B. Cost of goods sold: The cost value of beginning physical inventory plus merchandise purchased during the year (including freight costs), less discounts received from suppliers, minus the ending physical inventory.

C. Gross profit (gross margin): The difference between net sales and cost of goods sold.

D. Operating expenses: Selling, administrative, and general overhead costs involved in store operations throughout the year.

E. Net profit before owner's withdrawal and income taxes: This is the figure on which the owner will pay income tax, and represents his or her compensation.

(Name of business)

INCOME STATEMENT

For the year ending December 31, 19_

OPERATING RATIOS

A. NET SALES

B. COST OF GOODS SOLD
    Inventory Jan. 1
    Purchases (net)
    Less inventory Dec. 31
    COST OF GOODS SOLD

C. GROSS PROFIT

D. OPERATING EXPENSES :
    Accounting and legal
    Advertising
    Bad debts
    Delivery costs
    Depreciation
    Employees' wages
    Entertainment and travel
    Insurance
    Interest
    Maintenance and repair
    Miscellaneous
    Rent
    Supplies
    Taxes and licenses
    Utilities and telephone
    Total expenses

E. NET PROFIT BEFORE OWNER'S
    WITHDRAWAL AND INCOME TAXES

Figure 6.10 Sample income statement. From *Financial Recordkeeping for Small Stores*. Washington, DC: Small Business Administration Management Series No. 32. 1966: 10.

and non-prescription business but making an overall profit on non-business activities, the owner could be lulled into the belief that the pharmacy is a success when in fact it is not.

Cash flow statement

Because cash is the most liquid asset, it is to some extent the lifeblood of the pharmacy. Consequently, the inflow and outflow of cash must be monitored on a continuous basis[3] (Figure 6.11).

While it is commonly thought that cash flow problems are most typical of companies with poor sales levels, this is not necessarily true. It is possible for a thriving pharmacy to experience cash flow troubles, especially if the vast majority of its prescriptions are dispensed under government and private third-party programs. Assume, for instance, that it takes 45 days to receive payment on prescription claims, but the pharmacy only has 30 days to pay its suppliers. Trying to match inflow and outflow will be very difficult because of the 15-day discrepancy in time. Nearly all third-party claims-processing programs have gone to

on-line processing. As a result, payments to pharmacies have been speeded up to the point where checks for payments can be received within 7–20 days, depending on when the claim is electronically transmitted.

The *cash flow statement*, sometimes called the sources and uses of cash statement, is mainly an internal statement used by management to keep track of cash flow over time. Like the income statement, it reflects a series of transactions over a period of usually three months.

Cash inflow to the pharmacy comes from cash sales, collections on accounts receivable, sale of assets, loans to the pharmacy, and additional investments made by the owner. Taken from the cash receipts journal, these represent the total amount of cash coming into the pharmacy for its use. When cash receipts are too low, additional cash must be obtained through either loans or the sale of some assets, or by delaying payments to creditors.

Payments of cash will be for merchandise and raw materials, operating expenses, repayment of debt, and

Cash flow statement for XYZ business for the year ended 31st of December 2010	$s
CASH FLOW FROM OPERATING ACTIVITIES:	
Cash receipts from customers	83,000
Cash paid to suppliers and employees	(56,000)
Cash generated from operations	27,000
Dividends received	250
Interest received	500
Interest paid	(500)
Tax paid	(2,450)
Net cash flow from operating activities	24,800
CASH FLOW FROM INVESTING ACTIVITIES	
Additions to equipment	(2,500)
Replacement of equipment	(7,000)
Proceeds from sale of equipment	500
Net cash flow from investing activities	(9,000)
CASH FLOW FROM FINANCING ACTIVITIES	
Proceeds from capital contributed	3,400
Proceeds from loan	16,000
Payment of loan	(5,400)
Net cash flow from financing activities	13,000
NET INCREASE/DECREASE IN CASH	28,800
Cash at the beginning of the period	2,430
Cash at the end of the period	31,230

Figure 6.11 Sample cash flow. Modified from Celender M. *Accounting Basics for Students*. e-book, accessible at www. accounting-basics-for-students.com/index.html.

withdrawals of funds by the owner. All of these need to be reflected in the cash flow statement since they act as a cash drain on the pharmacy.

As shown in Figure 6.12, the cash receipts and disbursements need to be reconciled to show increases or deficiencies of cash. Every pharmacy needs some cash on hand to provide a cushion between the timing of inflow and outflow. How large this balance must be depends on the level of sales activity and the disparity between collection and payment periods.

If cash excesses exist over a prolonged time period, management should consider using all or part of the excess to purchase more inventory or to buy something else the owner finds potentially profitable. Otherwise, the excess cash should be invested in some highly liquid short-term securities that will pay interest on the money.

If cash deficiencies exist, management is faced with a potentially serious problem. Creditors must be stalled, money borrowed, or assets sold for cash. While none of these alternatives is desirable, at least the manager will be able to recognize the oncoming problem and deal with it accordingly. This is prefer-

able to being faced with a crisis and having to borrow or sell on unfavorable terms, or damaging credit relations with suppliers.

How to keep records

Being able to have good data available for management decision-making depends on how well and how accurately the information is recorded in the journals and ledgers. Sloppy and haphazard entries usually result in inaccurate and out-of-date information.[4]

Recording information

Letting invoices and receipt vouchers sit in a drawer is one way of getting the books confused. As noted earlier, the accounting equation necessitates the use of a double entry form of recordkeeping. If payment for $100 was received from Insurance Company A, an entry would have to be made in the cash receipts journal to show the extra $100 in cash. Under the double entry system, another entry would have to be

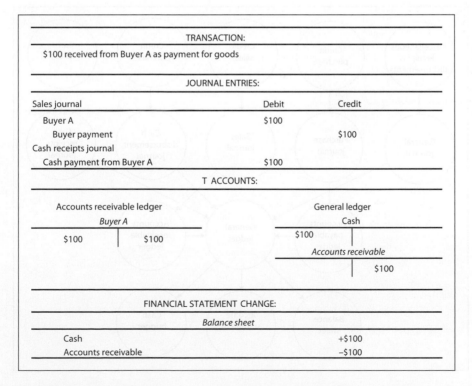

Figure 6.12 Flow of bookkeeping entries. From Gaedeke RM and Tootelian DH. *Small Business Management*, 3rd edn. Boston: Allyn and Bacon, 1991: 346. Used with permission.

made to show that Insurance Company A paid off what it owed.

In order to show this more clearly, T accounts often are used in the ledgers. On the left side are the debits and on the right the credits. Debits reflect the assets of the pharmacy, while credits reflect liabilities and the owner's net worth. In the previous example, then, the payment of $100 from Insurance Company A would look like that shown in Figure 6.12. This process must be followed for each transaction. The basic flow of entries is shown in Figure 6.13.

Beginning with cash receipts, daily sales on a cash basis are first recorded as a debit in the cash receipts journal to reflect the increase of, say, $200 in cash. This will then be transferred to the cash accounts in the general ledger. When preparing income statements and balance sheets at a later time, this $200 will be shown as part of the sales in the income statement and will be partially offset by the costs of merchandise sold. Assuming, for illustrative purposes, the costs are $150, the excess $50 will be profit. In the balance sheet, the cash account will be increased by $200,

while the inventory will decrease by $150 since the goods were taken from inventory and sold. The final entry will be a $50 increase in the owner's net worth because this is profit that belongs to the owner. These entries in the cash flow statement will be as a source of funds (Figure 6.14).

Cash purchases are handled in a similar way. Here, any purchase of materials, assuming $150 from the previous example, to be used in or by the pharmacy is first recorded in the cash disbursements journal. This in turn is transferred to the general ledger as a decrease in cash and increase in inventory.

From the general ledger, the income statement would show the increase of $150 in costs of goods sold. Entries in the cash flow statement would be a use of cash. The income statement would show the increase of $150 in costs of goods sold as the partial offset to the $200 sale. Similarly, the purchase would serve to decrease the inventory by $150, as shown in Figure 6.15. The net result of these transactions in cash is a $50 increase in cash and a $50 increase in net worth.

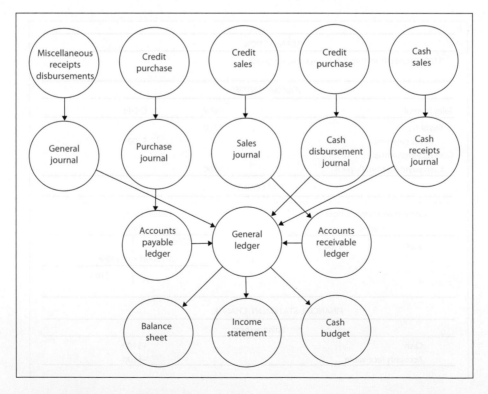

Figure 6.13 Accounting flow of transactions. From Gaedeke RM and Tootelian DH. *Small Business Management*, 3rd edn. Boston: Allyn and Bacon, 1991: 347. Used with permission.

TRANSACTION:

Cash sale of $200

JOURNAL ENTRY:

Cash receipts journal: +$200

T ACCOUNTS:

General ledger:

Cash	Inventory
+$200	−$200

FINANCIAL STATEMENT CHANGE:

Income statement:

Sales		$200
Cost of goods sold	$150	
Profit		$50

Balance sheet

Assets		Liabilities and owner's capital	
Cash	+$200		
Inventory	−$150	Owner's capital	+$50
	+$50		+$50

Figure 6.14 Cash sale transaction. From *Financial Recordkeeping for Small Stores*. Washington, DC: Small Business Administration Management Series No. 32. 1966: 70, 71.

TRANSACTION:

Cash purchase of $150

JOURNAL ENTRY:

Cash payments journal: +$150

T ACCOUNTS:

General ledger:

Cash	Inventory
$150	$150

FINANCIAL STATEMENT CHANGE:

Balance sheet

Assets		Liabilities and owner's capital
Cash	−$150	
Inventory	+$150	

Figure 6.15 Cash purchase transaction. From *Financial Recordkeeping for Small Stores*. Washington, DC: Small Business Administration Management Series No. 32. 1966: 70, 71.

The process of recording is slightly different for credit purchases and sales. A credit sale, for example $300, is recorded in the sales journal to reflect the $300 due from Insurance Company B. This in turn is recorded as a debit in Insurance Company B's account in the accounts receivable ledger and as an increase of $300 in the total accounts receivable in the general ledger. At the time the financial statements are prepared, the credit sale of $300 will be reported like any other unless the owner wishes to separate cash and credit sales in this statement. The only exception is in the balance sheet, where the $300 will be in accounts receivable instead of the cash account, as shown in Figure 6.16.

When Insurance Company B pays off the debt, an entry will be made in the sales journal (these transactions are in parentheses, shown in Figure 6.16) and offsetting credits made in the accounts receivable ledger and general ledger. The balance sheet also will change to show the increase in cash of $300 and the corresponding decrease in accounts receivable. The

payment of the $300 will be entered into the cash receipts journal and posted to the general ledger as a $300 increase in cash. Reflection of this will be made in the cash flow statement.

Credit purchases are recorded in much the same way as credit sales. A credit purchase of $200 in goods from Supplier A would first be posted to the purchase journal and then to the accounts payable ledger. The general ledger will show an increase in total amounts payable of $200 in goods for sale. When the merchandise is sold, it will be an addition to costs of goods sold like that shown in the income statement. If the merchandise is not paid for or sold before the financial statements are prepared, it will be recorded in the balance sheet as $200 in accounts payable and $200 in inventories (Figure 6.17).

When the pharmacy pays off Supplier A, an entry will be made in the purchase journal (see Figure 6.17; all payment transactions are in parentheses). This will be transferred to the accounts payable ledger as a debit and to the general ledger as a debit to accounts

---

TRANSACTION:

Credit purchase of $200

JOURNAL ENTRIES:

Sales journal

Buyer B	−$300
(Payment	+$300)
Cash receipts journal	+$300

T ACCOUNTS:

Accounts receivable ledger:

Buyer B

+ $300	($300)

General ledger

Accounts receivable		*Inventory*		*Cash*	
$300	($300)		$300		($300)

FINANCIAL STATEMENT CHANGES:

Income statement

Sales	$300
Cost of goods sold	$200
Profit	$100

Balance sheet

Assets		*Liabilities and owner's capital*	
Cash	$300		
Inventory	($200)		
		Owner's capital	$100
	+$100		+$100

Figure 6.16 Credit purchase transaction. Modified from *Financial Recordkeeping for Small Stores*. Washington, DC: Small Business Administration Management Series No. 32. 1966: 71, 72.

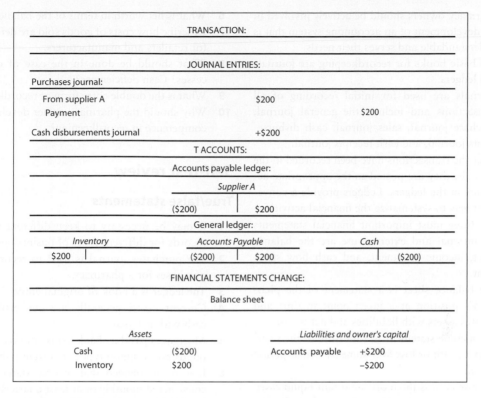

Figure 6.17 Purchase of merchandise. Modified from *Financial Recordkeeping for Small Stores*. Washington, DC: Small Business Administration Management Series No. 32. 1966: 75.

payable and a credit to cash. Again, if the merchandise is sold it will be shown in the income statement. If not, the reduction in cash and accounts payable will be indicated on the balance sheet.

Any payment will be posted to the cash disbursements journal, which in turn shows changes in cash in the cash flow statement. The last type of entry concerns miscellaneous receipts and disbursements, which are first recorded in the general journal and then posted to the general ledger. From here, the entries will be made to the relevant financial statements.

Maintaining the books

The fact that the bookkeeping must be done does not necessarily mean that each transaction must be recorded as it occurs. Normally, entries are made daily, twice weekly, or weekly, depending on the volume and the needs of the owner.

One point of concern in this process is separation of the recordkeeping functions from paying the bills and handling incoming cash. Giving these responsibilities to one person makes the pharmacy highly vulnerable to employee embezzlement. For example, a fictitious supplier may be paid for merchandise never received and which eventually is "lost." The fictitious supplier could be the employee or an accomplice.

Many owners cannot or prefer not to do the bookkeeping themselves, nor do they want it done by employees. Hiring someone else can provide a solution to this dilemma. There are several outside sources of recordkeeping available.[5] Public accountants, CPAs, and bookkeeping services can provide guidance in setting up the system, and can maintain the books on an ongoing basis.

Summary

- Records should be kept for internal and external reasons, as a permanent and visual basis for observing operations, and for keeping records for IRS purposes and for creditors.

- Pharmacy owners should be actively involved in the development of an accounting system that is understandable and serves their needs.
- The basic books for recordkeeping are journals and ledgers.
- Journals are used for initial recording of all transactions and include the general journal, purchase journal, sales journal, cash disbursements journal, and cash receipts journal.
- After the transactions have been recorded in the journals, they are posted to the appropriate accounts in the ledgers. Ledgers provide a convenient way to systematize the financial activities.
- The three most important financial statements for internal and external use are the balance sheet, income statement, and cash flow statement.
- The balance sheet is a statement of the pharmacy's position at a given point in time and equates assets with liabilities and net worth.
- The income statement is a measure of the pharmacy's profit or loss over some particular period of time.
- Because cash is the most important liquid asset, it is important that the inflow and outflow of cash be monitored on a continuous basis. This is the object of the cash flow statement.
- In recording transactions, it should be done systematically utilizing the proper double entry accounting procedures to ensure continued accuracy of all accounts.
- The activities of recording entries, paying bills, and receiving cash should be separate functions, because of the possibility of embezzlement if left to one person.
- There are several outside sources of recordkeeping available, including public accountants and CPAs, and bookkeeping services.

Questions for discussion

1 Why should a pharmacy keep records?
2 What are the uses of financial records for internal purposes? For external purposes?
3 What are the characteristics of a financial recordkeeping system for the pharmacy?
4 Distinguish between a journal and a ledger.
5 Differentiate current, fixed, and intangible assets.

6 What is net worth in terms of the balance sheet?
7 Describe how costs of goods sold are determined for retailers and manufacturers.
8 What should be done in the case of cash excesses? Cash deficiencies?
9 What is the double entry form of recordkeeping?
10 Why should the pharmacy owner develop some competence in recordkeeping?

Self-test review

True/false statements

1 It may be necessary to keep different types of records for different types of business purposes.
2 The purchases journal is used to record credit purchases for a pharmacy.
3 The ledger is a book of original entry.
4 Current assets generally are convertible into cash within 1 year.
5 Mortgages payable, bank loans, and redeemable bonds are common types of current liabilities.
6 It is recommended that income statements be constructed monthly or at least quarterly.
7 Operating expenses are not directly attributable to the production or sale of goods.
8 The accounting equation necessitates the use of a single entry form of recordkeeping.
9 A transaction that increases the amount of assets or net worth is called a credit.
10 It tends to be advantageous to have the same person receive purchased goods, pay the bills, and receive incoming cash.

Multiple choice questions

1 Which of the following is used to record cash sales?

(A) Sales journal.
(B) Purchases journal.
(C) Cash receipts journal.
(D) Cash disbursements journal.

2 A financial statement that is a report on financial conditions at one particular moment is:

(A) A balance sheet.
(B) An income statement.
(C) A cash flow statement.
(D) A capital expenditure statement.

3 Assets that are not used up within a year and are not easily converted into cash are:

(A) Current assets.

(B) Fixed assets.

(C) Intangible assets.

(D) Prepaid expenses.

4 A financial statement that reports financial conditions over a period of time is:

(A) A balance sheet.

(B) An income statement.

(C) A cash flow statement.

(D) A capital expenditure statement.

5 Which of the following is a debit?

(A) An increase in assets.

(B) An increase in liabilities.

(C) An increase in net worth.

(D) None of the above.

References

1. Ragan RC. *Financial Recordkeeping for Small Stores*, Management Series No. 32 Washington, DC: Small Business Administration, 1966.
2. Cooper IM. *Accounting Services for Small Service Firms*, Management Aid No. 1.010 Washington, DC: Small Business Administration, 1982.
3. Cash flow/cash management. *Small Business Reporter*. San Francisco: Bank of America NT& SA, 1985: 2.
4. Understanding financial statements. *Small Business Reporter*. San Francisco: Bank of America NT& SA, 1980: 1.
5. Establishing an accounting practice. *Small Business Reporter*. San Francisco: Bank of America NT& SA, 1985: 1.

7

Use of accounting and financial records

Learning objectives

The objectives of this chapter are to assist you to be able to explain:

- what budgets are and what they are supposed to do
- how budgets can be used for control purposes
- how ratio analyses can be used to evaluate a pharmacy's financial condition
- what value there is to financial audits
- the types of taxes the pharmacy must pay.

Key terms

Accounts receivable and payable budget
Average collection period
Budget
Capital budget
Cash budget
Current ratio

Federal taxes
Financial audit
Master budget
Performance review
Ratio analyses
Sales budget
Sales expense budget
State taxes

Keeping good financial records ensures that pertinent information is available for internal and external use. For outside purposes, an accurate set of accounting records is essential for meeting tax obligations and creditor requirements. From an internal perspective, financial records can be used to help establish operating budgets for future time periods, evaluate the pharmacy's current financial condition, and control some of the more critical problem areas (e.g. cash flow discrepancies).

Budgeting

One of the most important management tasks is to decide where the pharmacy should be heading and how it should get there. An integral part of this process is to develop budgets which serve to direct activities.

Nature and purpose of the budget

A budget is a quantified business plan. Although it is commonly referred to as a single entity, in fact the owner and manager may develop several budgets to cover various aspects of the operations. Cash budgets and sales expense budgets can help provide an important degree of management control.

The budgeting process provides a mechanism through which management can design activities and attach dollar costs and expected revenues to their implementation. This serves to better define the details of the plan and highlight financial trouble spots where costs are too high and where profits will be too low.

While preparing budgets can be a very helpful management tool, there are drawbacks to the process. It can be a time-consuming and arduous task in that it deals with an unknown future. For example, a manager who wants to increase dollar sales may decide that extra advertising is necessary. After determining how much the pharmacy should spend, he or she may suddenly be faced with increased media rates that go beyond the budget. Similarly, forecasting costs of goods sold can be difficult simply because of uncertainties surrounding price increases by manufacturers and the introduction of new and expensive drugs (e.g. high-tech drugs).

Too many owners and managers do not realize that a budget can and should be revised periodically to meet changing internal and external conditions. As long as each change receives a thorough investigation,

the purpose of budgeting is attained. Developed from financial records and tempered by forecasts of the future, the budget provides the mechanism to direct the financial reserves toward achieving the pharmacy's goals.

While budgets need not be developed to cover every facet of the business, they should include all activities that are important—whether because of their high cost or because they are troublesome to operations. Owners and managers usually will develop a master budget and component budgets.

The master budget is an overall financial plan that looks similar to the income statement and balance sheet. This is typically developed for a 1-year period to show anticipated profits or losses and the financial position of the pharmacy. It can serve as a summary of the other expected activities over the relevant time period. An example is shown in Figure 7.1.

Essentially, there are two methods for preparing master budgets. One involves developing an overall budget and then breaking it down into components on a monthly or quarterly basis. This is known as the "breakdown" method. The other approach is to prepare the component budgets on a monthly basis and combine them into the master budget. This is known as the "buildup" method. While either approach can be effective, many managers prefer the buildup method because it is easier to account for seasonal or periodic fluctuations, and because it is simpler to plan for 1 month than to plan for a full year.

Component budgets

The details of the master budget are contained in a series of component budgets. Depending on the nature of the business and the need for budgetary control, there can be as many as six components focusing on all of the critical financial aspects of operations.

Sales budget

The sales budget is used to forecast sales of each department along one or more dimensions (Figure 7.2). For example, if a chain operates in several geographical areas, the sales budget may be itemized by product and territory. On the other hand, in a hospital, the budget may be broken down by products or therapeutic categories. The sales budget provides the basis

	Department				
	A	B	C	D	Total
Sales	$___	$___	$___	$___	$___
Cost of goods	$___	$___	$___	$___	$___
Gross margin	$___	$___	$___	$___	$___
Operating expenses					
Accounting and legal	$___	$___	$___	$___	$___
Advertising	$___	$___	$___	$___	$___
Bad debts	$___	$___	$___	$___	$___
Delivery	$___	$___	$___	$___	$___
Depreciation	$___	$___	$___	$___	$___
Employee wages	$___	$___	$___	$___	$___
Entertainment and travel	$___	$___	$___	$___	$___
Insurance	$___	$___	$___	$___	$___
Interest	$___	$___	$___	$___	$___
Maintenance and repair	$___	$___	$___	$___	$___
Management salaries	$___	$___	$___	$___	$___
Rent	$___	$___	$___	$___	$___
Supplies	$___	$___	$___	$___	$___
Taxes and licenses	$___	$___	$___	$___	$___
Telephone	$___	$___	$___	$___	$___
Utilities	$___	$___	$___	$___	$___
Miscellaneous	$___	$___	$___	$___	$___
Total	$___	$___	$___	$___	$___
Net profit before taxes	$___	$___	$___	$___	$___
Assets					
Current assets					
Cash	$___	$___	$___	$___	$___
Accounts receivable	$___	$___	$___	$___	$___
Inventory	$___	$___	$___	$___	$___
Securities	$___	$___	$___	$___	$___
Prepaid expenses	$___	$___	$___	$___	$___
Other	$___	$___	$___	$___	$___
Total	$___	$___	$___	$___	$___
Fixed assets					
Automobiles	$___	$___	$___	$___	$___
Equipment	$___	$___	$___	$___	$___
Fixtures	$___	$___	$___	$___	$___
Other	$___	$___	$___	$___	$___
Total	$___	$___	$___	$___	$___
Total assets	$___	$___	$___	$___	$___
Liabilities					
Current liabilities					
Accounts payable	$___	$___	$___	$___	$___
Notes payable	$___	$___	$___	$___	$___
Taxes payable	$___	$___	$___	$___	$___
Wages payable	$___	$___	$___	$___	$___
Other	$___	$___	$___	$___	$___
Total	$___	$___	$___	$___	$___
Long-term liabilities					
Notes payable	$___	$___	$___	$___	$___
Other	$___	$___	$___	$___	$___
Total	$___	$___	$___	$___	$___
Total liabilities	$___	$___	$___	$___	$___
Net worth	$___	$___	$___	$___	$___

Figure 7.1 Master budget. Modified from Gaedeke RM and Tootelian DH. *Small Business Management*, 3rd edn. Boston: Allyn and Bacon, 1991: 356. Used with permission.

	Product group			
	One	Two	Three	Total
Sales department				
Prescriptions	$ _____	$ _____	$ _____	$ _____
Over-the-counter drugs	$ _____	$ _____	$ _____	$ _____
Cosmetics	$ _____	$ _____	$ _____	$ _____
Durable medical equipment	$ _____	$ _____	$ _____	$ _____
Home health	$ _____	$ _____	$ _____	$ _____
Gifts	$ _____	$ _____	$ _____	$ _____
Cards	$ _____	$ _____	$ _____	$ _____
Magazines	$ _____	$ _____	$ _____	$ _____
Other	$ _____	$ _____	$ _____	$ _____
Total	$ _____	$ _____	$ _____	$ _____

Figure 7.2   Sales budget.

for other component budgets since all activities are contingent on selling products or services.

To develop a sales budget, the manager needs to identify the departments and forecast what the sales will be for each. If the pharmacy sells only prescriptions, this can be easy. For example, if the pharmacy sold 40,000 prescriptions in the past year, and if the growth rates in prescriptions dispensed from the preceding years averaged 5 percent, the manager may project sales for the next year to be 42,000 (40,000 × 1.05). In addition, if these sales had not experienced much seasonal fluctuation, the monthly estimate would be 3500 (42,000/12).

Similar approaches can be used if management decides to forecast for whole departments, such as prescriptions, over-the-counter medications, cosmetics, gifts and cards, and durable medical equipment. This also can work for chains that break down sales by territory. In this case, management can estimate territory sales growth based on past trends or information from pharmacies in each area. From this, the historical mix of sales can be determined from past records to get an indication of expected sales by product or product line. For instance, assume territory 1 has a forecasted sales volume of 40 million. If pharmacy A historically has accounted for 25 percent of sales, management can estimate its sales to be 10 million (40 × 0.25).

Sales expense budget

A pharmacy must keep its revenues and costs of selling in some reasonable proportion. Spending

$200,000 to sell $150,000 in merchandise will always be a losing proposition. Meshing the desired sales level with the anticipated costs is a necessary step in successful financial management. This serves not only to allocate funds, but provides the mechanism for assuring that selling costs do not get out of hand.

The sales expense budget should be itemized by salespersons' salaries, anticipated commissions, delivery costs, travel expenses for nurses engaged in home healthcare, advertising, sales promotion, and other selling expenses (Figure 7.3). This can be done either on a yearly basis and then reduced to a monthly one, or vice versa. From the sales budget, estimates will have to be made as to the level of expenditure needed to generate such sales. Here again past financial data can provide some rough guidelines.

To prepare the sales expense budget, management needs to specify and list all expense items involved in the sale of prescription and non-prescription goods and services. Dollar projections can be based on such elements as historical trends and salesforce estimates.

Production budget

Many managers do not think in terms of a "production" budget. However, in many settings "production" does occur. Prescriptions are filled in a production manner, home intravenous (IV) solutions are produced, as are unit doses, and so forth. Determining what processes, including labor and material, are

	Area				
	North	South	East	West	Total
Air travel	$ _____	$ _____	$ _____	$ _____	$ _____
Automobile	$ _____	$ _____	$ _____	$ _____	$ _____
Commissions	$ _____	$ _____	$ _____	$ _____	$ _____
Entertainment	$ _____	$ _____	$ _____	$ _____	$ _____
Hotel	$ _____	$ _____	$ _____	$ _____	$ _____
Promotional material	$ _____	$ _____	$ _____	$ _____	$ _____
Salaries	$ _____	$ _____	$ _____	$ _____	$ _____
Supplies	$ _____	$ _____	$ _____	$ _____	$ _____
Telephone	$ _____	$ _____	$ _____	$ _____	$ _____
Other	$ _____	$ _____	$ _____	$ _____	$ _____
Total	$ _____	$ _____	$ _____	$ _____	$ _____

Figure 7.3 Sales expenses budget.

involved in producing goods, such as home IV solutions and unit dose supplies, is important to any pharmacy engaged in home healthcare. For a small home healthcare business, with little room for financial error, it is vital that accurate cost estimates be made of production activities.

Developing a production budget begins with the sales forecast so the amount of goods to be produced can be estimated. Then the manager will decide how many pharmacists, technicians, nurses, and other employees are needed in the dispensing process and how much in the way of prescription drugs must be ordered. Care must be taken to consider any anticipated increases in prices from suppliers, and any labor or union negotiations that may affect labor costs within the relevant period.

Accounts receivable and payable budget

Since nearly all pharmacies sell on a credit basis, developing an accounts receivable and payable budget is important (Figure 7.4). Receivables can be projected based on historical accounts of the time involved in collecting from established payers. If the pharmacy has dealt with particular suppliers and plans to continue doing so, the terms they offer for payment are known for estimating payables.

The timing of receivables and payables should be estimated as closely as possible in order to pinpoint

future trouble spots in the cash flow. While it is difficult at best to schedule these inflows and outflows, projected excesses or shortages of cash can be planned for in advance.

Cash flow budget

The cash flow budget should be developed by all managers (see Figure 7.5). To some extent it follows closely the receivables and payables budget just described. This particular budget should be prepared on at least a monthly basis and the composite made into a yearly budget.

While many of the items contained in the cash budget will be determined from other budgets, it is necessary to synthesize them into a single one that clearly shows the movement of cash into and out of the pharmacy. Not only will this account for the normal receipts and expenditures, it also will include any cash used to purchase capital goods such as computers and new fixtures.

Monthly evaluations of this budget allow management to pinpoint times when cash balances may be too low and necessitate short-term lending or the sale of some asset(s). In addition, periods when cash is overabundant highlight opportunities for increasing expenditures for promotion, purchasing added inventory, or making short-term investments.

Accounts receivable budget

Customer/Payor	Age (days) Under 30	30 – 45	46 – 60	Over 60	Total
A	$____	$____	$____	$____	$____
B	$____	$____	$____	$____	$____
C	$____	$____	$____	$____	$____
D	$____	$____	$____	$____	$____
E	$____	$____	$____	$____	$____
F	$____	$____	$____	$____	$____
Other	$____	$____	$____	$____	$____
Total	$____	$____	$____	$____	$____

Accounts payable budget

Creditor/Supplier	Age (days) Under 30	30 – 45	46 – 60	Over 60	Total
A	$____	$____	$____	$____	$____
B	$____	$____	$____	$____	$____
C	$____	$____	$____	$____	$____
D	$____	$____	$____	$____	$____
E	$____	$____	$____	$____	$____
F	$____	$____	$____	$____	$____
Other	$____	$____	$____	$____	$____
Total	$____	$____	$____	$____	$____

Figure 7.4 Accounts receivable and accounts payable budgets. Modified from Gaedeke RM and Tootelian DH. *Small Business Management*, 3rd edn. Boston: Allyn and Bacon, 1991: 360. Used with permission.

Capital budget

Purchases of capital goods typically require large outlays of money, and should be planned for well in advance. By developing a capital budget, the owner will be better able to identify how much money will be needed and when it will have to be spent. Sound financial management requires that the necessary funds be saved or borrowed on the most advantageous terms.

While management may not be making capital purchases in each fiscal year, it is important that any anticipated expenditures be itemized in the capital budget. Accordingly, this budget may be developed for a 1- to 3-year period (Figure 7.6). The budget itself may be a simple listing of needed equipment, buildings, land, and so on, along with the anticipated cost of the purchase, and timing will be planned in advance.

Flexible budgets

Because the future is uncertain, it is difficult for management to precisely project sales, expenses, and costs of capital purchases. When these variables prove to be higher or lower than expected, budgets lose their meaning as a planning and control device. Few managers will turn away customers simply because their purchases will cause sales to exceed projections.

To be most effective, therefore, "flexible" budgets should be prepared to compensate for possible errors in forecasting. In this way, they can be adjusted to changing internal and market conditions and still give direction to achieving the owner's goals.

For example, if actual sales exceed projections by 10 percent, it would be unrealistic to expect the costs of goods and some operating expenses to remain within the original budget. If the owner were to try to keep costs to budgeted amounts, it might stunt

CASH FLOW BUDGET
(for three months, ending March 31, 20___)

	January		February		March	
EXPECTED CASH RECEIPTS	Budget	Actual	Budget	Actual	Budget	Actual
1. Cash sales						
2. Collections on accounts receivable						
3. Other income						
4. Total cash receipts						
EXPECTED CASH PAYMENTS						
5. Inventory						
6. Payroll						
7. Other factory expenses (including maintenance)						
8. Advertising						
9. Selling expense						
10. Administrative expense (including salary of owner-manager)						
11. New equipment						
12. Other payments (taxes, including estimated income tax; repayment of loans; interest; etc.)						
13. Total cash payments						
14. EXPECTED CASH BALANCE at beginning of month						
15. Cash increase or decrease (item 4 minus item 13)						
16. Expected cash balance at end of month (item 14 plus item 15)						
17. Desired working cash balance						
18. Short-term loans needed (item 17 minus item 16, if item 17 is larger)						
19. Cash available for dividends, capital cash expenditures, and/or short-term investments (item 16 minus item 17, if item 16 is larger than item 17)						
CAPITAL CASH						
20. Cash available (item 19 after deducting dividends, etc.)						
21. Desired capital cash (item 11, new plant equipment)						
22. Long-term loans needed (item 21 less item 20, if item 21 is larger than item 20)						

Figure 7.5 Cash flow budget. From Feller JH. *Is Your Cash Supply Adequate?* Management Series No. 174. Washington, DC: Small Business Administration, 1990: 4.

	Department				
	A	B	C	D	Total
Automobiles	$ ---------	$ ---------	$ ---------	$ ---------	$ ---------
Equipment	$ ---------	$ ---------	$ ---------	$ ---------	$ ---------
Fixtures	$ ---------	$ ---------	$ ---------	$ ---------	$ ---------
Other	$ ---------	$ ---------	$ ---------	$ ---------	$ ---------
Total	$ ---------	$ ---------	$ ---------	$ ---------	$ ---------

Figure 7.6 Capital budget. Modified from Gaedeke RM and Tootelian DH. *Small Business Management*, 3rd edn. Boston: Allyn and Bacon, 1991: 362. Used with permission.

growth or reduce the quality of the merchandise or services.

To overcome this problem, costs of goods and operating expenses should be estimated based on several different volumes of sales. Thus, if sales rose faster than anticipated, additional funds would be allocated to satisfy the higher costs. An example of a flexible budget is shown in Figure 7.7.

Flexible budgets are particularly important as biotech and other highly expensive drugs become more prominent in drug therapy. To the extent that the pharmacy stocks and dispenses these products, its purchases will increase significantly. Having budgets that take these into account allows the manager to maintain some semblance of budgetary control over costs of goods. In this instance, possible variances in costs of goods resulting from the purchase of expensive drug products can be planned for and monitored.

Budgetary control

In addition to serving as a mechanism for defining and refining plans, the budget can be an effective control device. Since most component budgets are prepared for each month as well as for the entire fiscal year, they measure progress toward established objectives. To be an effective tool for control, any budgetary device must satisfy certain requirements:

- The budget must represent a realistic set of goals. Idealistic budgetary figures can be detrimental, since management may spend considerable time and money trying to achieve the impossible.

- The budget needs to be flexible if it is to be effective. Conditions both internal and external to the pharmacy may change and require modifications to the budgets. While budgets should not be subject to arbitrary revision, neither should they be considered unchangeable. Budget revisions should be rigorously questioned to ascertain whether the modification is really necessary and what caused it (e.g. an inaccurate forecast of sales or an error in identifying an important variable).

- The master budget must have component budgets that focus on factors important to operations. Excluding key factors from the budgetary process destroys the potential value of a control process.

- The budgets must provide a relatively inexpensive and quick reporting mechanism. A control device that costs as much or more than the amount to be saved is counterproductive. Similarly, a reporting mechanism that is slow is of little value.

	Budget	+5%	+10%	−5%	−10%
Sales	$_____	$_____	$_____	$_____	$_____
Costs of goods	$_____	$_____	$_____	$_____	$_____
Gross margin	$_____	$_____	$_____	$_____	$_____
Operating expenses					
Accounting and legal	$_____	$_____	$_____	$_____	$_____
Advertising	$_____	$_____	$_____	$_____	$_____
Bad debts	$_____	$_____	$_____	$_____	$_____
Delivery	$_____	$_____	$_____	$_____	$_____
Depreciation	$_____	$_____	$_____	$_____	$_____
Employee wages	$_____	$_____	$_____	$_____	$_____
Entertainment and travel	$_____	$_____	$_____	$_____	$_____
Insurance	$_____	$_____	$_____	$_____	$_____
Interest	$_____	$_____	$_____	$_____	$_____
Maintenance and repair	$_____	$_____	$_____	$_____	$_____
Management salaries	$_____	$_____	$_____	$_____	$_____
Rent	$_____	$_____	$_____	$_____	$_____
Supplies	$_____	$_____	$_____	$_____	$_____
Taxes and licenses	$_____	$_____	$_____	$_____	$_____
Telephone	$_____	$_____	$_____	$_____	$_____
Utilities	$_____	$_____	$_____	$_____	$_____
Miscellaneous	$_____	$_____	$_____	$_____	$_____
Total	$_____	$_____	$_____	$_____	$_____
Net profit before taxes	$_____	$_____	$_____	$_____	$_____

Figure 7.7 Flexible budget. Modified from Gaedeke RM and Tootelian DH. *Small Business Management*, 3rd edn. Boston: Allyn and Bacon, 1991: 365. Used with permission.

- For maximum effectiveness, all budgets should be clearly described to those affected, and their support for its achievement should be encouraged. The owner must recognize that budgets by their very nature are viewed as restrictive and thereby adversely affect people. By having employee pharmacists and perhaps other personnel help in the preparation of budgets, they become personally involved in their creation and more supportive of them.

Evaluating financial conditions

Management must critically evaluate past performance just as it must prepare for future business activity. Performance reviews are a basic step in future planning both in terms of determining the pharmacy's existing position as well as trying to learn from previous actions and events.

Nature of performance review

Certainly one way to evaluate operations is to compare budgeted revenues and expenses with the actual results. By simply making each budget a two-column entry, one for projected and one for actual sales, cost of goods, and operating expenses, any significant differentials can be observed. This is illustrated in Figure 7.8. Since the budget should represent the financial goals, under- or overachievement can be monitored and analyzed to discover why the disparity occurred.

In much the same manner, the owner can compare income statements and balance sheets of the last period with those for the most recent period. This will allow for a more enlightening view because it compares current operations with those of previous periods.

For example, if sales have remained relatively stable over a few fiscal years, but operating costs have been increasing, it is an indication that cost controls are not being exercised. Gradual increases in inventories, bad debts, and long-term debt might not be of great concern at any given point, but such trends over time may be indicative of serious problems.

Some managers like to graph changes of certain parts of their financial statements in an effort to

	Department			
	Prescription		Over-the-counter drugs	
	Actual	Budget	Actual	Budget
Sales	$ _____	$ _____	$ _____	$ _____
Cost of goods	$ _____	$ _____	$ _____	$ _____
Gross margin	$ _____	$ _____	$ _____	$ _____
Operating expenses	$ _____	$ _____	$ _____	$ _____
Accounting and legal	$ _____	$ _____	$ _____	$ _____
Advertising	$ _____	$ _____	$ _____	$ _____
Bad debts	$ _____	$ _____	$ _____	$ _____
Delivery	$ _____	$ _____	$ _____	$ _____
Depreciation	$ _____	$ _____	$ _____	$ _____
Employee wages	$ _____	$ _____	$ _____	$ _____
Entertainment and travel	$ _____	$ _____	$ _____	$ _____
Insurance	$ _____	$ _____	$ _____	$ _____
Interest	$ _____	$ _____	$ _____	$ _____
Maintenance and repair	$ _____	$ _____	$ _____	$ _____
Management salaries	$ _____	$ _____	$ _____	$ _____
Rent	$ _____	$ _____	$ _____	$ _____
Supplies	$ _____	$ _____	$ _____	$ _____
Taxes and licenses	$ _____	$ _____	$ _____	$ _____
Telephone	$ _____	$ _____	$ _____	$ _____
Utilities	$ _____	$ _____	$ _____	$ _____
Miscellaneous	$ _____	$ _____	$ _____	$ _____
Total	$ _____	$ _____	$ _____	$ _____
Net profit before taxes	$ _____	$ _____	$ _____	$ _____

Figure 7.8 Comparative budget: actual to budget. Modified from Gaedeke RM and Tootelian DH. *Small Business Management*, 3rd edn. Boston: Allyn and Bacon, 1991: 365. Used with permission.

money sooner. Another approach is to vigorously pursue insurance claims. Generally, the longer the payment is outstanding, the greater the probability that it will never be paid.

Fixed assets to net worth

Another measure of liquidity is the relationship between the pharmacy's fixed assets and net worth. The net worth is the true measure of what the owner actually owns in the pharmacy. The ratio is:

Fixed assets/net worth

Total liabilities to net worth

A standard measure of who owns what is the debt-to-equity ratio, computed by the formula:

Total liabilities/net worth

This is an overall appraisal of the debt structure. As this ratio approaches 100 percent, it means that creditors have nearly as much interest in the pharmacy as does the owner. A high ratio may be indicative of heavy debt or the lack of much equity by the owner. In either case, future borrowing may be restricted since the creditors already have a heavy investment in the pharmacy.

Current liabilities to net worth

This is another measure comparing what is owned to what is owed creditors. The greater this ratio, the less sound the owner's value in the pharmacy. Short-term creditors can quickly deplete some of the ownership's net worth if current assets have to be sold at large discounts to meet obligations. The ratio is:

Current liabilities/net worth

When the ratio exceeds 80 percent, it may indicate that the owner is relying too heavily on short-term debt to finance operations.

Total liabilities to total assets

One of the better measures of the safety of creditor claims against the pharmacy is the debt-to-assets ratio:

Total liabilities/total assets

It is a measure of the security of the debt, based on what assets the pharmacy has to sell should it need to do so. As this ratio approaches 100 percent, creditors

will become more concerned because there will be an insufficient value in assets to cover the debt.

Times-interest-earned ratio

One of the most important ratios affecting the pharmacy's ability to borrow is the times-interest-earned (TIE) ratio. This is given by the formula:

(Net profit before tax + interest expense)/

interest expense

This ratio measures the pharmacy's ability to meet its interest obligations out of profits. The importance of this ratio lies in the desire of creditors to be repaid their loans without the pharmacy having to obtain more debt. As a general rule, this ratio should be at least 5 : 1, and preferably 10 : 1. At these levels, the pharmacy should be able to meet its interest obligations out of profits and not have to rely on additional infusions of capital.

Costs of goods to inventory

Just as accounts receivable can be out of control, so too can inventory levels. Holding excess inventory is a common and serious financial problem. Too much inventory ties up funds that could be used for other purposes. Also, merchandise can become obsolete and thus unsaleable. For these reasons, it is important for the pharmacist to be aware of manufacturer and wholesaler policies concerning the return of unused inventory. In some instances, it is possible to reduce the amount of inventory by returning merchandise. However, the conditions under which this is possible vary by supplier.

On the other hand, too little inventory can mean that the pharmacy is losing sales because of stock-outs or an insufficient variety of lines. Or the pharmacy may not be taking advantage of quantity purchase discounts.

A delicate balance must be maintained. This is done by monitoring the turnover of inventory—the number of times the inventory is sold over the course of the year. The ratio is:

Costs of goods/average inventory

The result is the number of times inventory is bought and sold. If, for example, the turnover is 12 times (e.g. costs of goods = \$2,400,000 and average inventory = \$200,000), it means that the average inventory was bought and sold 12 times, or approximately every month.

While this is an important area for control, the formula does have a major flaw if not interpreted properly. In the example above, it would appear that the inventory is being bought and sold with very good speed. Accordingly, management may assume that inventory is not a problem. However, the inventory figure is the average, and not for each product line. It is quite likely, in fact, that some merchandise is turning over too slowly (suggesting that too much inventory is being held), while other merchandise is turning over too quickly (evidence of an inventory deficiency). Because these two factors can balance each other out, the problem may never be discovered if this ratio is the only evaluation made of inventory levels.

Net sales to total assets

Just as inventory should be turning over with reasonable speed, so should total assets. Since assets generate sales volume, this ratio measures the extent to which assets are being sold. The computational formula is:

Net sales/total assets

The result is the number of times total assets are converted into sales. If the number is low, it indicates that the money invested is not being put to good use. If it is too high, it may mean that the pharmacy does not have the assets to take advantage of its sales potential.

Net profit to net sales

Many owners equate a high level of sales with success. A statement often made with considerable pride is: "My pharmacy just passed the million dollar sales level." But, a large sales volume is not necessarily indicative of high levels of profitability. Many pharmacies could sell a million dollars' worth of merchandise if they spent $2 million on promotion and sold their products well below cost. However, that strategy is likely to cause business failure.

One mark of business success is dollar profit in relation to dollar sales. The ratio for this is:

Net profit/net sales

This measure will provide a clear indication of what income is to be derived from the sale of prescription and non-prescription goods and services.

If this ratio is too low, it may be indicative of higher-than-necessary costs of operations. This may be due to high costs of goods in relation to what prices the manager can charge for prescriptions, or to operating expenses that are too high.

Net profit to net worth

The most critical test of the pharmacy's success is measured by the formula:

Net profit/net worth

This ratio shows how much money is being earned on the owner's investment. Sometimes called the return on investment (ROI), it should be at least as high as the amount that could be earned by purchasing a government bond, or placing the net worth into a savings account in a bank. If, for example, this ratio were to be 6 percent (e.g., net profits = $4,800 and net worth = $80,000) the owner might be better off financially by selling the business, taking the net worth (or whatever could be obtained for the pharmacy), and placing it in a time deposit that earns 8–10 percent. Not only will the $80,000 be more secure, but it will be more profitable.

Net profit to total assets

A somewhat different measure of profitability is given by the formula:

Net profit/total assets

Instead of measuring profits on the owner's investment with ROI, this ratio measures the profits being generated on the funds supplied by both the owner and creditors. This ratio is sometimes called the return on assets (ROA), and is of greater concern to creditors than the ROI formula.

Use of ratios and their limitations

The calculations of ratios provide a more objective approach to assessing the financial condition of the pharmacy. Comparing the operating ratios over time provides a chronological basis for evaluation. This is very useful in monitoring progress in succeeding periods. Increases or decreases in the current ratio, for example, can be watched to ensure that adequate liquidity is being maintained or achieved.

In addition, ratio analyses can be used to make comparisons between the pharmacy and others within the industry. Dun & Bradstreet and Robert Morris

As in the case of employee income tax withholding, the owner must deduct the social security taxes from employee wages and forward them to the government on a quarterly basis. The only significant difference between social security and employee income tax withholding is that the owner also must pay social security taxes. Certain remitting requirements vary by the size of the business, and in some cases prepayment deposits are required. Owners should check applicable regulations with their accountants, bankers, or IRS agent.

Unemployment taxes

If there are employees, the pharmacy may be liable for federal unemployment taxes depending on the amount of wages paid in a calendar quarter or if an employee was hired for at least some part of 1 day in 20 or more calendar weeks (not necessarily consecutive). In many cases, quarterly deposits must be made and all closing payments for a calendar year paid by January 31 of the following year. Federal liability is partially reduced by state unemployment taxes.

Excise taxes

Depending on the type of products the pharmacy sells, payment of federal excise taxes also may be required. For example, alcoholic beverages sold in a pharmacy are subject to excise taxes. Quarterly reports and in some cases monthly prepayment deposits are required. Owners should check with their local IRS office to determine if they must pay excise taxes, and how reporting and payment should be made.

State taxes

In addition to federal taxes, the pharmacy may have to pay state taxes. These vary according to the location of the pharmacy, but the most common types are income, unemployment, and sales taxes.

Income taxes

In states that impose income taxes, the pharmacy will generally have to pay taxes in a manner similar to that outlined for federal income taxes. In addition, the owner may have to withhold taxes on the wages earned by employees. State income tax rates vary considerably from state to state.

Unemployment taxes

While all states have unemployment taxes, the specifics on filing, charges, and qualifications vary significantly. According to the Small Business Administration, unemployment taxes often are based on the taxable wage base of a quarter. The unemployment experience of the individual business and the unemployment experience of the state in which the business is located determine the rate of tax charged.

Sales taxes

Many states impose sales taxes on all or some retail transactions, and some local governments add a percentage to the tax to finance various civic projects. When sales taxes are used, the pharmacy is required to collect the taxes on the transactions and remit the funds to the state. While the pharmacy does not pay the tax, it is fully responsible for its collection. Therefore, accurate records must be kept for verification purposes.

Summary

- The budgeting process provides a mechanism through which management can lay out the planned activities and attach dollar costs and revenues to their implementation and results.
- There are essentially two methods by which budgets can be prepared—breakdown and buildup—each of which utilizes the same basic process for looking at the past and present to predict the future.
- The primary budget is the master budget, and it contains the projections of several component budgets, including the sales, sales expense, production, accounts receivable and payable, cash, and capital budgets.
- Budgets can be used as effective control devices. To be effective for control, the budget must contain realistic goals, be flexible, have components covering all operational factors, be relatively inexpensive, offer quick reporting, and be clearly described to those affected.
- The budget can be useful for evaluating operations by comparing budgeted revenues and expenses with actual results.
- The use of business ratios as a means of financial evaluation can range from a cursory glance at a few key ratios to close scrutiny of many ratios.

- In using ratios, comparisons can be made with past ratios of the pharmacy, industry averages, or both.
- Independent audits can benefit the pharmacy in two key areas: discovering internal fraud and embezzlement, and spotting problems overlooked by management.
- Financial reports are very important for meeting the pharmacy's tax obligations.
- Federal taxes include income, social security, unemployment, and excise taxes. State taxes include income, unemployment, and sales taxes.

Questions for discussion

1 What are the disadvantages of budgeting?
2 What is wrong with the question "How can I budget when things change so quickly?"
3 Differentiate between the two methods used to prepare budgets.
4 What is necessary in preparing the sales expense budget?
5 Explain the value of historical data for internal statements of budgets.
6 Name two types of comparisons using financial statements or budgets.
7 Differentiate between the current ratio and the acid test ratio.
8 Which ratio is an overall appraisal of the debt structure?
9 What does the ratio of net profit to net worth describe?
10 What kinds of ratio comparisons can be made?

Self-test review

True/False Statements

1 In preparing a sales budget, management should make as detailed an estimate of anticipated sales as possible.
2 All pharmacy owners should develop accounts receivable and accounts payable budgets.
3 In comparing past financial conditions with present ones, a stable growth pattern is most desirable.
4 When the current ratio is too low, it may mean that the pharmacy is holding too much in current assets.

5 The acid test ratio is a measure of the pharmacy's ability to borrow.
6 The average collection period for a small pharmacy will always be less than the average payable period.
7 The ratio of net sales to net worth is called the return on investment.
8 Comparisons of ratios with industry averages are the only means of evaluating how well the pharmacy is doing.
9 A financial audit is a method for protecting the pharmacy from embezzlement.
10 Generally, pharmacies must pay their federal income tax in quarterly installments.

Multiple choice questions

1 Which of the following is the preferred method of budget preparation?

(A) Developing an overall budget only.
(B) Developing monthly component budgets only.
(C) Developing an overall budget and then breaking it down into monthly component budgets.
(D) Developing monthly component budgets and then building them into an overall budget.

2 The sales expense budget should not include:

(A) Salespersons' salaries.
(B) Raw materials.
(C) Cost of goods.
(D) Advertising and other promotion.

3 Which of the following is not a measure of liquidity?

(A) Current ratio.
(B) Acid test ratio.
(C) Average collection period.
(D) Total liabilities to net worth.

4 The most critical test of the pharmacy's success is measured by:

(A) Net sales to net worth.
(B) Net profit to net worth.
(C) Net profit to net sales.
(D) None of the above.

5 Which of the following is a key benefit of an audit?

(A) It protects the pharmacy from internal fraud.

(B) It protects the firm from external fraud.

(C) It satisfies the IRS.

(D) None of the above.

References

1. Tootelian DH and Gaedeke RM. *Small Business Management: Operations and Profiles*, Glenview, IL: Scott Foresman & Co, 1984.

2. Radics SP. *Steps in Meeting Your Tax Obligations, Marketers Aid No. 142*, Washington, DC: Small Business Administration, 1982.

Cases for Part III*

Short cases

Case III.1 Gaines & Wilder Pharmacies, Inc.

After working together in a large hospital inpatient pharmacy for 8 years and a relatively small chain for the past 2 years, Dr. Jack Gaines and Dr. Jerry Wilder decided to go into business for themselves. Although neither had much business experience, Dr. Gaines and Dr. Wilder thought they could avoid many of the mistakes they had witnessed in independent pharmacies. So, they each used some funds they had individually saved up and purchased two pharmacies that were for sale. They agreed to each manage one pharmacy but consolidate operations to the extent that it made sense.

Because both had some experience with home healthcare and durable medical equipment, they decided to focus their efforts on prescriptions and these two non-prescription areas rather than on lines such as cosmetics, gifts and cards, and other products. While they thought home healthcare was a little speculative in light of changing reimbursement programs being considered under Medicaid, with an aging population they felt that it had good growth potential for the long term.

Recent managed care contracts were not especially profitable, but it appeared that some opportunities to be paid for greater involvement in managing patients' drug therapies were becoming more possible. Thus, they assumed that they would have more stable revenue patterns even if they were on a smaller

scale and that prescriptions, home healthcare, and durable medical equipment would be the future.

Dr. Gaines and Dr. Wilder agreed that it was essential to maintain good financial records. Their previous employer had been lax in recordkeeping and suffered because of it. The chain had not monitored the inflow and outflow of cash, and did not watch expenses closely. As a result, the company had financial problems that eventually forced them to close nearly one third of their stores.

Determined not to suffer the same fate, Dr. Gaines and Dr. Wilder wanted to have the best recordkeeping system possible. To ensure that everything was done properly, Dr. Gaines wanted to hire an accountant to set up and maintain the records. He was especially concerned because corporations were required to file special reports and forms.

Dr. Wilder, however, thought it would be best to set up and maintain the records themselves. He argued that the cost of having an accountant, approximately $1,250 per month, was more than they needed to spend. More important, Dr. Wilder felt that if they learned how to do the recordkeeping and were forced to do this on a regular basis, they would gain a better understanding of G & W Pharmacies' financial position. He thought that if they turned it over to an accountant they would begin to devote less and less time to this aspect of the business.

To resolve this difference of opinion, Dr. Gaines agreed to let Dr. Wilder explore further the possibilities of their doing the recordkeeping for the business. Since neither had much experience in this area, Dr. Wilder decided to determine what type of recordkeeping system would be best for the corporation. After that was done, he thought they could better

*Names of the organizations, individuals, and locations of all cases are fictional. Any likeness to actual organizations and/or individuals is purely coincidental.

decide whether to do the recordkeeping themselves or turn it over to an accountant.

Both agreed that nearly all of their prescription revenue would be under government and private third-party programs, and that keeping track of claims for services was critical to success. They also planned to purchase and then rent durable medical equipment, such as walkers, wheelchairs, and hospital beds. This would require some monitoring of rental payments.

Dr. Wilder knew that there would be payables and receivables as well as cash payments in advance. Accordingly, he thought that an extensive set of records would be necessary in order to watch cash, receivables, payables, and profits.

Questions

1 What types of books will Dr. Wilder need in order to establish a recordkeeping system for G & W Pharmacies, Inc.?

2 Evaluate the differing views of Dr. Gaines and Dr. Wilder concerning recordkeeping, setup, and maintenance.

Case III.2 Palm Pharmacy

John Scand, owner of Palm Pharmacy, had just finished reviewing his financial statements for the first half of the current fiscal year. Sales have increased nearly 7 percent over the same period last year, but profits have risen by only 0.3 percent (see Tables III.2.1 and III.2.2). Despite the higher sales volume, the pharmacy had been having problems with cash. There never seemed to be enough money available to pay the bills on time.

On several occasions, Dr. Scand had to forego cash discounts and even be late in paying his suppliers. He knew that this situation must be corrected so that his suppliers would not put him on a cash-only basis, or stop selling to Palm Pharmacy altogether. He already lost some negotiating power with his primary wholesaler because of the cash issues. Currently, he had only 15 days to pay vendors.

Palm Pharmacy was a relatively large community-oriented pharmacy located in the southwest. Of its approximately 4,500 square feet of floor space, nearly 3,400 of it was devoted to the sale of front-end merchandise: over-the-counter drugs, cosmetics, greeting cards, photography equipment and supplies, and

Table III.2.1 Palm Pharmacy's condensed income statements for the last 2 years

	Last year	Two years ago
Net sales		
Prescriptions	$953,022	$1,036,332
Front-end merchandise	$1,609,478	$1,489,668
Total	$2,562,500	$2,526,000
Cost of goods	$1,693,300	$1,690,883
Gross margin	$869,200	$835,117
Operating expenses		
Owner's salary	$184,044	$168,080
Employee wages	$360,344	$361,132
Rent	$123,000	$121,017
Utilities	$35,989	$32,656
Delivery	$14,578	$9,124
Advertising	$34,622	$19,689
Bad bebts	$12,300	$8,644
Interest expense	$9,567	$9,605
All other	$59,678	$68,673
Total	$834,122	$798,619
Net profit before taxes	$35,078	$36,497

gifts. The other 1,100 square feet were used for the prescription department, which accounted for 48 percent of total sales.

During the first 7 years, the pharmacy's sales and profits grew slowly but progressively. There was little competition in the immediate area, and Dr. Scand had most of the business for himself.

One year ago, however, two discount chain drugstores moved nearby, and from that point on, sales stagnated and profits declined. Consequently, at the beginning of the current year, Dr. Scand decided to compete more aggressively with the chain stores by reducing prices on front-end merchandise by 10–15 percent, and reducing prices on private-pay prescription drugs where possible. He even began accepting all insurance plans that he could, despite some not offering much profit potential. He also began offering some customers in-store credit, free delivery and advertised heavily in the local newspaper. He felt the in-store credit was needed, although it was taking about 45 days to collect the money. He also had some billing issues with third-party contracts and a considerable number of claims were being held in suspense for anywhere from 30 to 60 days.

Table III.2.2 Palm Pharmacy balance sheet for last year

Assets	
Current assets	
Cash	$12,560
Accounts receivable	$98,640
Inventory	$450,500
Other	$4,400
Total	$566,100
Fixed assets	
Fixtures and equipment	$82,560
Total	$82,560
Total assets	$648,660
Liabilities	
Current liabilities	
Accounts payable	$382,800
Notes payable	$35,040
Total	$417,840
Long-term liabilities	
Notes payable	$100,800
Total	$100,800
Total liabilities	$518,640
Net worth	$130,020

Even though this strategy has been successful, Dr. Scand was not happy with the resulting cash flow problems. Furthermore, he was not sure that the pharmacy's overall performance was what it should be since profits have not grown much. He thought that part of his cash problems and lack of profit growth were due to the price. Yet, he was not certain that this was the sole cause.

As he looked over the financial statements for the past 2 years, he realized that he did not know just what the pharmacy's financial position was or how well it was doing compared to other pharmacies. He wondered if it was important to evaluate the performance of the pharmacy, and how that would help him to make a decent profit and help with his cash flow problems.

Questions

1 Evaluate Dr. Scand's questioning of the importance of making financial analyses. Does he really need to evaluate the financial performance of the pharmacy? Why?

2 Evaluate the financial position of Palm Pharmacy. How good or bad is its financial position?

3 What problems are there with how Dr. Scand is conducting business?

Case III.3 Garvey's Markets

After being an employee–pharmacist for nearly 10 years in a major drug chain located in the Northeast, Kerry Jones took a position as a manager of the pharmacy department of a supermarket chain. Unlike most of the other pharmacies in the supermarket chain, this one needed considerable updating. Although management of the supermarket chain had considered renovations for some time, the past prescription department manager of this supermarket had not assessed how much money would be needed, where the funds would come from, or what would be gained by a renovation of this store.

Dr. Jones had an extensive background in business because his father was a pharmacist in both independent and chain pharmacy settings. As a result, he was continually exposed to various aspects of the business while he was growing up. In addition, even before entering pharmacy school, his father helped him get a job in a large mass merchandise store, and he learned much about how large companies operate.

After graduating from pharmacy school, his skills led him to work for a drug manufacturer for a short time, and he then decided to go to work for the most successful chain pharmacy in this city of nearly 300,000 people. Loyalty to the chain, coupled with the security of employment, kept him from making his career move earlier.

Before taking this position, several drug wholesalers expressed an interest in working with him should he open his own pharmacy, and offered to help finance his beginning inventory. And one hospital wanted to enter into a partnership for an outpatient pharmacy and stated that it would supply much of the needed capital.

In planning for the renovation of the prescription department, Dr. Jones assembled as much of the pertinent cost information he could find in the time available. He believed the most important factors in getting the renovation approved were the cost and how long it would take to recover the "investment" in this department by the supermarket chain.

Dr. Jones was confident that he could create and offer high-quality pharmacy services if he could get

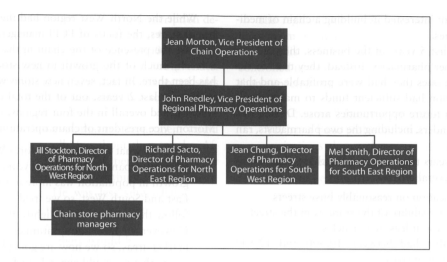

Figure III.4.1 Organizational chart for Full Care Pharmacies, Inc.

The front-end departments were responsible for the following:

- household supplies
- food and beverages (non-alcoholic)
- alcoholic beverages
- cosmetics
- gifts and cards
- personal care products
- general merchandise.

The North West region

The population base for the North West region was nearly 650,000 people, and spanned two of the four states. The population had been growing at a rate of about 0.9 percent annually for the last 3 years. Selected demographics for the region are presented in Table III.4.1.

Overall, the size of this region was about comparable to that of the North East, and only slightly less than in either of the South regions. Each of the four regions was somewhat different in terms of demographic composition. Residents of the North West tended to be somewhat younger and have lower incomes than those in the North East and South East.

The South West region had a demographic profile much the same as the North West. Top management of FCPI had, from time to time, considered merging the two regions to reduce expenses, but the distances between all of the pharmacy locations was considered too great to make this workable from an operating control perspective.

Much of the North West region consisted of smaller cities and towns. There were only three relatively larger cities in the region, each with a population base of approximately 150,000 to 165,000 people. These three cities accounted for about 75 percent of the total population base, and eight of the nineteen pharmacies in the region were located in these cities.

Despite the relatively low incomes compared to two of the other regions, the North West was considered by top management to be the most stable and have good prospects for growth. Ms. Stockton commented:

> We know that more than 50 percent of our population base is under 35 years of age, and that means that incomes will be somewhat lower than if we had an older population. In fact, nearly 70 percent of the residents of this region have incomes of less than $50,000 a year, and nearly half have no college education. This suggests to me that residents will be a bit more price sensitive because they have to stretch their dollars more, and as a result probably are going to shop at the mass merchandise stores and club warehouses for much of their non-prescription needs.

> However, the cost of housing is far less than exists in the North East and South East, so I think we can expect to see growth in the population as people decide they want to own a home and the only way to do so is to move into our region. And, the people who already live

Table III.4.1 Selected demographics of North West region

Annual population growth over past 3 years	0.93%
Gender	649,888
Male	310,478
Female	339,410
Age distribution	
Under 20 years	187,039
20–35 years	156,255
35–54 years	172,556
55–64 years	61,534
65–74 years	34,561
75–84 years	26,583
85 years and over	11,360
Household income	
Less than $25,000	115,691
$25,000–$49,999	72,714
$50,000–$74,999	39,471
$75,000–$99,999	20,289
$100,000–$149,999	14,129
$150,000–$199,999	4,311
$200,000 or more	3,650
Household sizes	
Number of households	270,256
Average household size	2.28
Average family size	3.14
Education of population 25 years and over	403,316
Less than 9th grade	26,938
9th–12th grade, no diploma	55,021
High school graduate (includes equivalency)	119,030
Some college, no degree	75,110
Associate's degree	33,661
Bachelor's degree	53,604
Graduate or professional degree	39,953
Vehicles available	270,256
No vehicles available	72,970
1 vehicle available	116,944
2 vehicles available	62,683
3 or more vehicles available	17,658
Home value	
Less than $50,000	28,351
$50,000–$99,999	57,284
$100,000–$149,999	14,907
$150,000–$199,999	5,969
$200,000–$299,999	4,507
$300,000–$499,999	3,381
$500,000–$999,999	1,957
$1,000,000 or more	373
Number of homes	116,729

here could not afford to relocate to the North East or South East, so they are pretty much permanent residents. This gives us some additional stability to our population base.

FCPI Pharmacies in the North West region

Of the 19 pharmacies located in the North West region, eight were more than 15 years old and four were more than 5 years old. When FCPI began to look for growth in the region, it added two new stores two years ago and five in the last year. Sonny Reedley commented on the growth:

> Historically, our plan was to grow slowly in each region. But, that certainly has not happened in the North West. We didn't do much there for many years, preferring to spend more resources on what management considered faster growth areas. But, as that slowed down, and we realized how under-represented we were in the North West, we got busy. The addition of five stores within the last year was something we have never done in the history of the company. In the past, we were lucky to add that many stores across all regions in two years.

While there was some variation in pharmacy departments based on their size and specific location, they were quite similar overall. Each sold over-the-counter medications (e.g. pain relievers, cold and flu medications, laxatives, antacids), health and beauty aids other than cosmetics and skincare products (e.g. vitamins and minerals, diet aids, woundcare products), and home healthcare products.

The great majority of revenues in each of the stores were generated from prescription sales. Because of the relatively low incomes of residents of the region, between 15 and 25 percent of the prescriptions dispensed were under the state's Medicaid program, and nearly all others were covered under other insurance. Cash sales in prescriptions were rare.

All of the pharmacies utilized both pharmacists and technicians to the extent allowed by state law. In addition, all encouraged patient consultations irrespective of whether the prescription was a new one or a refill. And, pharmacists were encouraged to step away from the prescription area whenever possible to take a more proactive role in advising customers on over-the-counter medications, health and beauty aids, and especially home healthcare products. Ms. Stockton commented about the prescription areas:

> We really try to have our staff pharmacists talk to patients. We feel this is important from a healthcare perspective and it is a good business practice. While some of our competitors offer advising services, it is more hit-and-miss compared to ours. Of course, we are somewhat limited in what we can do from a cost standpoint because pharmacist time is precious.

North West region financial statements and budgeting for the pharmacy departments

Condensed financial statements for an average pharmacy department in the North West region are presented in Tables III.4.2 and III.4.3. Each pharmacy department was responsible for its own operating expenses except for advertising, legal and accounting, taxes and licenses, and interest expense. These were

centralized at the regional level and allocated to each pharmacy based on its sales.

For example, Ms. Stockton, the North West regional director for front-end, and Mr. Reedley would work together to set an advertising budget for the entire region so that FCPI could obtain some economies of scale in advertising. Then, the costs would be allocated to each pharmacy department based on its sales as a percent of the total sales for the region. Legal and accounting services were centralized and allocated in the same manner. Taxes and licenses and interest expenses were simply accumulated and allocated evenly among the pharmacy departments and front-end departments in the region.

All other operating expenses were set by Ms. Stockton in consultation with the individual pharmacy department managers and approved by Mr. Reedley, and ultimately by Ms. Morton. As shown in Tables III.4.4 through III.4.6, the pharmacy departments were responsible for entertainment and travel, which included developing good relations with

Table III.4.2 Condensed financial statement for typical chain pharmacy department in North West region

	Last year	Two years ago	Three years ago
Revenues			
Prescriptions	$6,042,398	$5,660,221	$5,312,686
Over-the-counter medicines	$835,904	$726,799	$722,763
Health and beauty aids	$392,364	$477,191	$464,310
Home healthcare products	$510,073	$420,431	$395,316
Other	$66,532	$56,760	$54,748
Total	$7,847,270	$7,341,402	$6,949,823
Costs of goods sold	$5,642,368	$5,212,266	$4,794,752
Gross margin	$2,204,902	$2,129,136	$2,155,071
Operating expenses			
Salaries and wages	$962,714	$894,843	$870,300
Entertainment and travel	$24,829	$23,360	$24,127
Advertising	$17,511	$18,031	$17,470
Maintenance and repairs	$4,221	$3,843	$5,299
Office supplies	$7,381	$8,294	$6,667
Legal and accounting	$8,000	$8,000	$8,000
Rent	$344,417	$322,214	$305,028
Taxes and licenses	$174,994	$163,713	$159,887
Interest expense	$141,251	$123,879	$127,623
Depreciation and amortization	$106,414	$103,910	$105,882
Miscellaneous	$175,266	$207,071	$238,166
Total	$1,966,997	$1,877,159	$1,868,449
Net profit before taxes	$237,905	$251,976	$286,623

Table III.4.3 Condensed financial statement for typical chain pharmacy department in North West region as percent of revenues

	Last year	Two years ago	Three years ago
Revenues			
Prescriptions	77.00%	77.10%	76.44%
Over-the-counter medicines	10.65%	9.90%	10.40%
Health and beauty aids	5.00%	6.50%	6.68%
Home healthcare products	6.50%	5.73%	5.69%
Other	0.85%	0.77%	0.79%
Total	100.00%	100.00%	100.00%
Costs of goods sold	71.90%	71.00%	68.99%
Gross margin	28.10%	29.00%	31.01%
Operating expenses			
Salaries and wages	12.27%	12.19%	12.52%
Entertainment and travel	0.32%	0.32%	0.35%
Advertising	0.22%	0.25%	0.25%
Maintenance and repairs	0.05%	0.05%	0.08%
Office supplies	0.09%	0.11%	0.10%
Legal and accounting	0.10%	0.11%	0.12%
Rent	4.39%	4.39%	4.39%
Taxes and licenses	2.23%	2.23%	2.30%
Interest expense	1.80%	1.69%	1.84%
Depreciation and amortization	1.36%	1.42%	1.52%
Miscellaneous	2.23%	2.82%	3.43%
Total	25.07%	25.57%	26.88%
Net profit before taxes	3.03%	3.43%	4.12%

physicians, maintaining and repairing all fixtures and equipment, and other expenses associated with their operations.

Next year's budget

In starting to prepare the flexible budget for next year, Ms. Stockton began looking at the total sales for the chain over the last 3 years. These are presented in Tables III.4.5 and III.4.6. She knew that she had to estimate pharmacy department sales for the region and then try to allocate costs based on those revenues. At this time, two new stores were being planned for the coming year, and Mr. Reedley provided some information that he thought might be helpful in her deliberations. These are presented in Table III.4.7.

In assessing the budgeting process, Ms. Stockton commented:

> I'm not sure whether I should start by evaluating the trends in sales and then allocate

costs or try to estimate the trends in costs as well. I probably should do both and see what I get. I know that Ms. Morton wants to see revenues grow somewhere between 3.5 percent and 5.0 percent, and for profits to go up as well. So, I will have to figure how much I need to spend to generate the sales growth, and at the same time keep costs under control so that I can increase the profits. She also wants to see the flexible budgets, and that means deciding what happens if my revenue projections are 5.0 percent higher or 5.0 percent lower than what I am planning for the coming year.

Possible discussion questions

1 What are the advantages and disadvantages of using a flexible budget like the one being requested?

2 What should the expected revenues be for Full Care Pharmacies?

South Store. The South Store was located on the corner of a busy intersection. The store was the largest of the five and had above average total sales. The surrounding area was well maintained even though nearly all of the commercial buildings and residences were over 30 years old. The area immediately around the supermarket was among the oldest in the community in terms of both homes and residents. Competition for groceries and medications was not considered overly intense because there was limited space in which to place other stores. While there were three supermarkets in the area, only one had a pharmacy. And, even though there were several community chain and non-chain pharmacies, few competed aggressively on the basis of price. U-Save Markets was considered the only true discount supermarket in the community.

The pharmacy departments in each store also are quite similar in size and layout. Each contains a prescription area and immediately adjacent to these are the shelves for over-the-counter medications. Due to space limitations, there is no separate space for patient counseling, so this activity is conducted at the far end of the prescription counter to provide as much privacy as possible.

On the average, each pharmacy had two registered pharmacists working a shift along with one technician. The department also had two clerks working to transact sales, assist customers, and stock the OTC shelves. Staffing was highest in the Central Store because of the greater volume of OTC sales, and because the pharmacy manager of that store indicated that customers demanded more attention for both prescription and OTC products.

The assessment

As Ms. Poland prepared to make her assessment of each pharmacy, she generated both the prescription

activity of each store and the financial statements for the last year. Presented in Table III.6.2 is the prescription activity, and Tables III.6.3 and III.6.4 contain the profit and loss statements for each pharmacy for the last year.

In reviewing the profit and loss statements, she made a note that advertising and legal and accounting expenses were allocated to each store overall. The other operating expenses were incurred by each store. The "Miscellaneous" expenses included mostly allocated costs for such things as insurance, the salaries and benefits of the officers of the company (e.g. president, vice presidents), and taxes and licenses. Ms. Poland did not feel she had control over most of these costs.

Mr. Golder did not use central purchasing for the five supermarkets, preferring instead to negotiate buying agreements with selected vendors and allowing the store managers to purchase directly. However, what the stores carried was limited to an "Approved list" that was established by Ms. Poland and Mr. Reberg. Store managers could not purchase anything that was not on the Approved list" unless authorized to do so by one of the vice presidents. Mr. Golder felt that this approach to purchasing gave more authority, within limits, to store managers, and avoided the overhead associated with central purchasing.

As she prepared to begin the assessment, Ms. Poland commented:

> Irv did not give me any particular format to use for making the assessment of pharmacy operations in each store, so I am not sure exactly how I want to proceed. I know he is going to want me to closely analyze the profit and loss statement alone and in relation to the prescription activity. I also think I should view all of this in terms of the separate communities within which our supermarkets are located. But, it still comes down to the financials in

Table III.6.2 Prescription activity of each market					
	Central	**East**	**West**	**North**	**South**
Number of prescriptions per year	38,069	40,379	32,733	38,388	39,698
Average price per prescription	$66.90	$71.53	$84.40	$68.23	$82.84
Prescription mix					
Cash	3.5%	9.8%	12.8%	4.1%	8.1%
Medicaid	18.1%	11.2%	7.2%	17.6%	15.4%
Other third party	78.4%	79.0%	80.0%	78.3%	76.5%
Total	100.0%	100.0%	100.0%	100.0%	100.0%

Table III.6.3 Last year's profit and loss statements for each market

	Central store	East store	West store	North store	South store
Revenues					
Prescriptions	$2,546,810	$2,888,298	$2,762,692	$2,619,191	$3,288,580
Over-the-counter medicines	$744,790	$525,119	$494,507	$575,991	$354,889
Total	$3,291,601	$3,413,417	$3,257,200	$3,195,182	$3,643,469
Costs of goods sold					
Prescriptions	$1,887,441	$2,156,240	$2,040,000	$2,060,753	$2,646,159
Over-the-counter medicines	$437,192	$352,355	$328,648	$348,841	$193,132
Total	$2,324,633	$2,508,595	$2,368,648	$2,409,594	$2,839,291
Gross margin					
Prescriptions	$659,369	$732,057	$722,693	$558,438	$642,421
Over-the-counter medicines	$307,598	$172,764	$165,859	$227,150	$161,757
Total	$966,968	$904,821	$888,552	$785,588	$804,178
Operating expenses					
Salaries, wages, and benefits	$493,241	$449,138	$437,988	$439,751	$463,861
Advertising	$15,349	$15,248	$15,197	$12,264	$11,527
Maintenance and repairs	$16,848	$35,985	$30,706	$18,495	$19,198
Office supplies	$6,470	$7,014	$5,799	$4,449	$5,386
Legal and accounting	$7,012	$6,765	$6,959	$6,872	$6,899
Rent	$128,075	$100,213	$108,436	$104,024	$100,982
Depreciation and amortization	$93,276	$87,873	$82,104	$70,328	$90,128
Miscellaneous	$144,299	$112,474	$130,118	$101,445	$100,476
Total	$904,571	$814,711	$817,307	$757,627	$798,457
Net profit before taxes	$62,397	$90,110	$71,245	$27,961	$5,721

Table III.6.4 Last year's profit and loss statements for each market as percent of total revenues

	Central store	East store	West store	North store	South store
Revenues					
Prescriptions	77.4%	84.6%	84.8%	82.0%	90.3%
Over-the-counter medicines	22.6%	15.4%	15.2%	18.0%	9.7%
Total	100.0%	100.0%	100.0%	100.0%	100.0%
Costs of goods sold					
Prescriptions	57.3%	63.2%	62.6%	64.5%	72.6%
Over-the-counter medicines	13.3%	10.3%	10.1%	10.9%	5.3%
Total	70.6%	73.5%	72.7%	75.4%	77.9%
Gross margin					
Prescriptions	20.0%	21.4%	22.2%	17.5%	17.6%
Over-the-counter medicines	9.3%	5.1%	5.1%	7.1%	4.4%
Total	29.4%	26.5%	27.3%	24.6%	22.1%
Operating expenses					
Salaries, wages, and benefits	15.0%	13.2%	13.4%	13.8%	12.7%
Advertising	0.5%	0.4%	0.5%	0.4%	0.3%
Maintenance and repairs	0.5%	1.1%	0.9%	0.6%	0.5%
Office supplies	0.2%	0.2%	0.2%	0.1%	0.1%
Legal and accounting	0.2%	0.2%	0.2%	0.2%	0.2%
Rent	3.9%	2.9%	3.3%	3.3%	2.8%
Depreciation and amortization	2.8%	2.6%	2.5%	2.2%	2.5%
Miscellaneous	4.4%	3.3%	4.0%	3.2%	2.8%
Total	27.5%	23.9%	25.1%	23.7%	21.9%
Net profit before taxes	1.9%	2.6%	2.2%	0.9%	0.2%

terms of what the pharmacies have done in the past and what they will do in the future.

Possible discussion questions

1 What process should be used to make the assessment? What format should be used to report the findings of the assessment?

2 How well did each pharmacy perform financially in the last year? What were the good and bad financial indicators of each? In what areas do the pharmacies need to improve?

3 What should be expected of each pharmacy in the next year? Three years?

4 What should Ms. Poland recommend for each of the five pharmacies?

PART IV

Marketing strategies

8

Prescription product and service strategies

Learning objectives

The objectives of this chapter are to assist you to be able to explain:

- the role of prescription product and service strategies in community and institutional settings
- how managers make decisions concerning the purchase of full vs. basic and specialty lines
- what prescription and non-prescription consultations can be offered, and how they should be provided
- the essentials of developing a fee-based consulting service
- why and how pharmacists should consult with prescribers.

Key terms

Basic product lines
Drug formularies
Drug interaction
Drug utilization review
Fee-for-service consulting
Full product line

Intervention
Non-prescription consultation
Patient monitoring
Pharmacy services
Prescriber consultations
Prescription medication consultations
Prescription product mix
Specialty products

Historically, the profits of most pharmacies have been made or lost within the prescription department. Prescription merchandise and related healthcare services have generated the majority of sales. Of course, they also have accounted for the greatest percentage of total costs.

Even though some of the issues of what prescription inventory to carry and what services to offer seem fairly routine, careful decisions are essential to a well-managed and successful pharmacy. Usually, prescription products are not what distinguish one pharmacy from another. However, the manner in which prescriptions are dispensed and services offered has a major impact on the pharmacy's ability to attract patients, generate prescriber referrals, and control costs.

The role of product and service strategies

Some owners and managers fail to see the importance of developing a well-defined and coordinated set of product and service strategies. They do not appreciate how product and service strategies must be in place before management can finalize any other elements of its marketing mix.

The relative importance of products and services

When people think of what a pharmacy offers, they tend to think of products—prescriptions, over-the-counter drugs, and, in past years, sodas. However, the needs of consumers are very complex, and most patients do not patronize a pharmacy just to buy "things."

Physical products are not as important to consumers as is often thought. Consumers buy benefits, not products. The services that go with the products can be as critical as the product, and frequently even more so. This certainly is the case for consultations accompanying all new prescriptions and for many refills. The physical products are of little value if patients do not know how to use them, or if they use them improperly. Management must examine the needs of its target customers closely to determine what they really need.

The professional services provided to ensure that prescription medications are taken properly make consultation services at least as important as the physical products dispensed. In addition, the range and quality of services offered can very effectively distinguish the pharmacy from its competitors. Since products are standardized, they are directly comparable. Services, however, cannot be so readily duplicated. For example, if consulting services are exceptionally good owing to the pharmacist's knowledge, ability to communicate, ability to gain rapport with the patient, and so forth, the pharmacy may have a major advantage over its competition. The types and quality of service available to customers can be a major component of the pharmacy's overall marketing program.

How products and services interrelate with other marketing strategies

Many marketing experts consider the product and service strategies of a business to form the hub around which all other strategies revolve. As such, prescription and non-prescription products and services are key elements in the overall marketing mix, and dictate much of what is done with respect to pricing, distribution, and promotion.

The dependence of other marketing strategies on products and services can readily be seen. The pharmacy's pricing structure will be governed partly by the quality of merchandise carried, the services offered, management's ability to purchase merchandise on favorable terms, pharmacists' ability to dispense generic as well as brand-name prescription drugs, and management's ability to maintain control over the level of inventory.

What is promoted about the pharmacy will be based partly on the merchandise carried and the services offered. This is a natural relationship since products and services are designed to satisfy the needs of customers, and what is promoted about the pharmacy must focus on the benefits it provides.

Special considerations in institutional settings

Prescription product and service strategies have an even more prominent role in institutional settings since there are very few opportunities to sell non-prescription merchandise. From a purchasing and inventory control perspective, it is somewhat easier to establish order points and quantities owing to the somewhat stable pattern of usage and because of the relatively low costs of many prescription drugs purchased for institutional use.

Stability of demand comes from the fact that the pharmacy is dealing with a known group of prescribers who are affiliated with the institution, and a known maximum occupancy rate. The low cost of drugs makes it possible to stock greater inventory without incurring excessive carrying costs.

Perhaps the greatest uncertainty for strategy development concerns what services the pharmacy can and should offer. The needs of patients have to be balanced with those of physicians and other medical staff with whom the pharmacist works closely. In many instances, there is less freedom in developing a set of services since they can infringe upon the "territorial rights" of other healthcare professionals.

Establishing a prescription product mix

There are many decisions to be made in terms of the prescription product mix. They include what basic lines to stock, what non-standard lines in which to specialize, and how full a line of prescription merchandise to carry.

Full vs. basic product lines

A preliminary factor in making product line decisions is whether the pharmacy needs to maintain what would be considered a full line of prescription drugs. In some practice settings, the demand for medications will be quite varied and the pharmacist will not be able to delay dispensing a prescription. In these instances, a wide range of prescription drug inventory will be needed. The list given in Figure 8.1 can assist in identifying those categories in which the pharmacy should maintain at least some level of inventory.

In general, however, keeping a full line "just in case someone needs something" is not recommended. Full lines should only be maintained in situations where it is necessary to do so. Too much money and space can be tied up in inventory, and problems of dated merchandise can become serious. In most cases, it is better to pick and choose the drug categories to keep in inventory, and rely on special orders for the rest.

Providing good patient services by having prescription inventory on hand must be balanced against the need to keep investment in inventory to acceptable levels. Attempting to stock everything for everybody can lead to financial ruin.

Therefore, management usually will opt for a basic product line. Prescription drugs that the pharmacist wants to stock either because they are used extensively or because they are occasionally needed for patients of important prescribers are known as "basic product lines." The main consideration in deciding what to include is whether a drug is prescribed in sufficient volume to make it worth stocking. In some instances, however, a few drugs that are infrequently called for must be stocked because the prescribers are important to the pharmacy.

The simplest way to determine the basic product line is to review past purchases to identify those drugs that were used extensively. From this, management most likely will be able to identify the relatively small number of drugs that account for the majority of the pharmacy's dispensing.

This can be evaluated based on past purchases, patient profiles (refills), lists of drugs most often prescribed, and lists of the pharmacy's main prescribers. Try to identify 30–50 drugs that are dispensed most frequently, and determine how much inventory of those drugs to maintain. In addition, review the profiles of patients and prescribers being served to determine what other drugs might be dispensed with reasonable frequency, and the quantities to keep in stock to achieve acceptable levels of turnover.

One factor that helps the manager maintain some degree of control over the basic product mix is the drug formulary. These lists of prior approved medications are used in both governmental and private healthcare plans. The primary use for formularies is to limit the range of products that can be dispensed to patients under Medicare, Medicaid, and private insurance plans. While these lists can be rather large, the manager can begin to at least identify the types of products that are most likely to be prescribed.

Perhaps the most important consideration in establishing a mix of prescription drugs is to review patient files to determine the number of refills coming due and the quantities of those drugs to be dispensed. Knowing the characteristics of the pharmacy's patient base is critical to determining product lines.

In addition, most wholesalers provide pharmacies with monthly summaries of purchases. These serve as

	Demand			
	Heavy	Medium	Light	None
Antihistamines				
Anti-infective				
Amebicides				
Anthelmintics				
Antibiotics				
Antituberculotics				
Antivirals				
Antimalarials				
Sulfonamides				
Sulfones				
Antitreponemals				
Trichomonacidals				
Antineoplastics				
Anticholinergics				
Sympathomimetics				
Sympatholytics				
Skeletal muscles relaxants				
Autonomic nervous system				
Parasympathomimetics				
Blood derivatives; bloodformation, coagulation				
Antianemics				
Coagulants, anticoagulants				
Hemorrheologic agents				
Thrombolytics				
Cardiovascular drugs				
Cardiac depressants, cardiotonics				
Antilipemics				
Hypotensives				
Sclerosing agents				
Central nervous system				
General anesthetics				
Analgesics, antipyretics				
Opiate antagonists				
Anticonvulsants				
Psychotherapeutic				
Respiratory, cerebral				
Anxiolytics, sedatives, hypnotics				
Contraceptives				
Dental agents				
Diagnostics				
Adrenocortical insufficiency				
Amyloidosis				
Blood volume supporters, expanders				
Brucellosis				
Cardiac output determination diagnostic aids				
Antidiabetics				
Diphtheria				
Drug hypersensitivity				
Gallbladder function				
Potassium absorption				
Liver function				
Mumps				
Myasthenia				
Thyroid hormones, inhibitors				
Pancreas				
Pituitary				
Radioactive agents				
Scarlet fever				
Diaphoretics				
Trichinosis				
Urine, feces				
Disinfectants				
Electrolytes				
Acid-base balance				
Acidifiers				
Alkalizers				

Figure 8.1 Categories of prescription and non-prescription drugs and pharmaceutical products *(continued)*.

good guidelines to what is and is not selling within the pharmacy.

Finally, management should identify the most frequent prescribers and define the types of drugs they

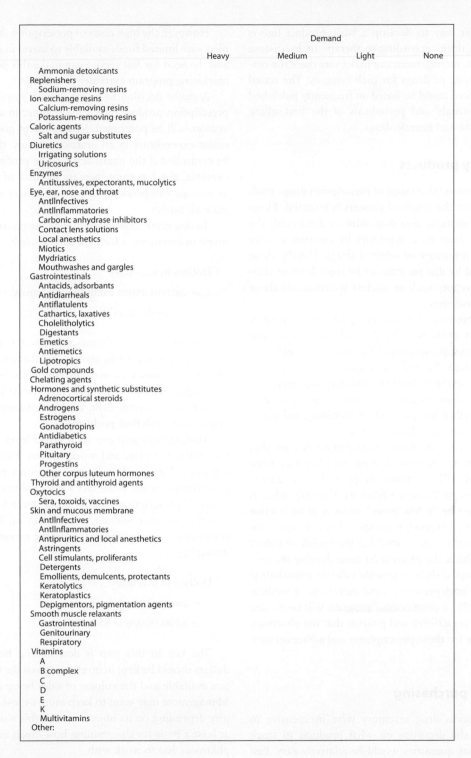

	Demand		
Heavy	Medium	Light	None

Ammonia detoxicants
Replenishers
  Sodium-removing resins
Ion exchange resins
  Calcium-removing resins
  Potassium-removing resins
Caloric agents
  Salt and sugar substitutes
Diuretics
  Irrigating solutions
  Uricosurics
Enzymes
  Antitussives, expectorants, mucolytics
Eye, ear, nose and throat
  AntiInfectives
  AntiInflammatories
  Carbonic anhydrase inhibitors
  Contact lens solutions
  Local anesthetics
  Miotics
  Mydriatics
  Mouthwashes and gargles
Gastrointestinals
  Antacids, adsorbants
  Antidiarrheals
  Antiflatulents
  Cathartics, laxatives
  Cholelitholytics
  Digestants
  Emetics
  Antiemetics
  Lipotropics
Gold compounds
Chelating agents
Hormones and synthetic substitutes
  Adrenocortical steroids
  Androgens
  Estrogens
  Gonadotropins
  Antidiabetics
  Parathyroid
  Pituitary
  Progestins
  Other corpus luteum hormones
Thyroid and antithyroid agents
Oxytocics
  Sera, toxoids, vaccines
Skin and mucous membrane
  AntiInfectives
  AntiInflammatories
  Antipruritics and local anesthetics
  Astringents
  Cell stimulants, proliferants
  Detergents
  Emollients, demulcents, protectants
  Keratolytics
  Keratoplastics
  Depigmentors, pigmentation agents
Smooth muscle relaxants
  Gastrointestinal
  Genitourinary
  Respiratory
Vitamins
  A
  B complex
  C
  D
  E
  K
  Multivitamins
Other:

Figure 8.1 *(continued)*.

are most likely to prescribe. Being attentive to the prescriber list and new prescribers who are working

within the market area is important to maintaining an appropriate inventory of prescription drugs.

Another way to develop a basic product line is to classify drugs according to therapy or by disease state. Then, management can make sure there is a reasonable range of drugs for each category. The actual drugs stocked could be based on frequently published lists in journals and periodicals of the best-selling brand-name and generic drugs.

Specialty products

Having a reasonable range of prescription drugs available to meet the needs of patients is essential. However, management also may want to distinguish the pharmacy from its competitors by carrying a more extensive inventory of selected drugs. Usually these are defined by disease state, or by some form of therapeutic category such as nuclear pharmaceuticals or biotech medicines.

The objective of maintaining a greater inventory of specialty drugs is to build the pharmacy's identification among prescribers as the source for particular types of drugs. To make this successful, pharmacists must develop the technical knowledge associated with dispensing these medications so that they can assist both prescriber and patient in determining and maintaining appropriate drug therapy.

Several considerations are important to a decision to establish specialty lines. First, the pharmacy must carry what will be viewed by prescribers as an exhaustive list of those medications. Carrying what is perceived to be "a few more" items is of little value to prescribers. Second, there should be adequate market potential to make stocking the added inventory feasible. Third, the pharmacist must develop the necessary technical skills to provide valuable consultation services to both prescribers and users of these medications. Finally, a promotional program will be needed to inform prescribers and patients that the pharmacy is the place for these prescriptions and advice on their use.

Product purchasing

If prescription drug inventory were inexpensive to purchase, the decisions on what products to stock and in what quantities would be relatively easy. Past purchase records, patient profiles, and numerous published lists of drugs most commonly prescribed provide many clues as to what to stock and what to emphasize with respect to prescription products.

However, the high costs of prescription drugs coupled with limited funds available to invest in inventory and the need for fast service can make this part of the marketing program extremely important.

A major decision to be made with respect to the prescription product mix is the manner in which inventory will be purchased. Since costs of goods are a major expenditure in all practice settings, they must be controlled if the pharmacy is to be profitable. For example, a 4.5 percent increase in costs of goods in an average independently owned pharmacy will eliminate all profits.

To determine how much money the pharmacy can invest in inventory, a formula can be used:

Dollars in inventory
= current assets excluding inventory
− current liabilities

Normally, if the pharmacy keeps the excess of current assets (e.g. cash, savings, accounts receivable, prepaid expenses, etc.) over current liabilities (e.g. accounts payable, payroll payable, taxes payable, current portion of long-term debt, etc.) in inventory, it can avoid many cash flow problems.

Management also can set a target level of inventory turns per year, and work its way backward to determine how much to keep in inventory to accomplish this given the pharmacy's sales volume. For example, if prescription costs of goods were $300,000, and management wanted to maintain an inventory turnover rate of six times per year, the inventory level would be:

Dollars in inventory
= costs of goods/turns per year
= $300,000/6 = $50,000

The key to this step is determining how many dollars should be kept in inventory given the total dollars available and the volume of sales being achieved. Management may want to keep more or less in inventory depending on its objectives, but this will provide at least a basis for determining how much money the pharmacy has to work with.

There are a number of ways to keep costs of goods under control through effective purchasing. Typically, this is accomplished by taking appropriate discounts when they can be profitable, and controlling the dollar value of prescription and non-prescription inventory.

Taking advantage of supplier terms is important to reducing costs of goods. Quantity discounts, discounts for early payment, forward dating, etc., offer opportunities to minimize unit costs. The dangers of many such "deals," however, often outweigh the benefits derived. Quantity purchases will reduce unit costs and the possibility of being out of stock on key merchandise.

However, they also increase the pharmacy's investment in inventory and the risks associated with merchandise dating, damage and obsolescence. Furthermore, the actual discount on quantity purchases is directly dependent on the time it takes to sell the excess inventory.

Cash discounts can be an excellent way to reduce costs and still keep control over the total dollars invested in inventory. However, this discount can place strains on pharmacies with limited cash reserves. Forward dating reduces the need for cash and does not increase the investment in inventory. Nevertheless, the merchandise still must be sold within a reasonable amount of time to make it profitable. With prescription inventory, the pharmacy cannot run "sales" to rid itself of excess inventory as it can with non-prescription merchandise. While it may try to sell some excess inventory to other pharmacies that may need the drug products, this is not always possible or easy to do.

Maintaining an adequate supply of goods while minimizing the investment in inventory is a difficult process at best. Yet, it is essential if the pharmacy is to provide a high level of patient service and keep the pharmacy's financial position sound.

Deciding on pharmacy services

Perhaps the greatest opportunity offered for a pharmacy to distinguish itself from its competitors, and for individual pharmacists to distinguish themselves in institutional and community settings, is in the area of services. The types of services that are offered, and the manner in which they are made available are critical to successfully penetrating any market or gaining the attention of hospital administrators.

Of particular importance is patient counseling. Many people do not self-medicate, and will seek the advice of healthcare professionals who make themselves available. Furthermore, they may adjust their lives to their drugs rather than fit their drugs into their lives. Eventually, this proves to be too burdensome, and compliance declines. And, of course, they are susceptible to adverse drug reactions.

Pharmacists who not only make themselves available, but who also take the initiative to offer information—rather than just respond to questions—will be much more likely to effectively penetrate a market. Individual, face-to-face counseling certainly is the preferred method for disseminating information. This serves to create a professional relationship with the patient that can last indefinitely. It is the only means available for specialized or critical questions that arise.

A good selection of prescription merchandise is of little value if it is not complemented by appropriate pharmacy services. Pharmacy services, like prescription inventory, however, must be carefully developed. Both are expensive, but unlike prescription drugs, pharmacy services are more difficult to charge for since patients are not accustomed to being billed for them directly.

Consequently, management must be cautious in deciding what services to offer. While some services have to be made available to patients and prescribers, they should be oriented to improving therapeutic outcome, quality of patient care, convenience of care, and other desired benefits. Furthermore, all services should serve to increase pharmacy profits either directly or indirectly. Some of the more common services are shown in Figure 8.2.

Management needs to determine what services patients and prescribers want from the pharmacy. From the patient files in the pharmacy, the manager can assess what needs the pharmacy should try to satisfy. Management also should examine what services competing pharmacies are offering, and try to find some services that they are not providing or not providing well. Care should be taken to identify possible services that prescribers may want to have offered to their patients (e.g. consultations, monitoring drug compliance). And the pharmacist will have to direct particular attention to needs for patient or prescriber consultations and patient monitoring.

The manager then must try to estimate the costs of these services to determine if the pharmacy can afford to offer them. Furthermore, management, in conjunction with staff pharmacists, should identify two or three services which they think may appeal

	Value to patient				
	High	Medium	Low	Yes	No
Blood pressure monitoring					
Compounding					
Credit card acceptance					
Delivery					
Dispensing prescriptions requiring TARs					
Drug interaction evaluation					
Emergency prescription dispensing					
Non-prescription consultations					
Participation in third-party programs					
Patient consultations					
Drug compliance monitoring					
Patient information sheets					
Patient profile records					
Patient tax records					
Pharmacy credit program					
Prescriber consultations					
Unit dose dispensing					

Figure 8.2 Common pharmacy services.

most to patients and prescribers. These can be emphasized in contacts with patients and prescribers, and be the focus of the pharmacy's promotional strategies.

Prescription drug consultations

Certainly one of the most important services a pharmacy can offer is patient consultations for prescription drugs. It is critical that patients understand the nature of their drug therapies (e.g. what the drug does, possible side-effects) and how the drug should be administered.

Making consultations available and encouraging patients to discuss their prescription drugs are two distinct phenomena. While most pharmacies offer consultations, many only provide the service when patients request assistance. To make consultations a focal point of a marketing program, management must take an active approach to educating patients about the value of the service and how they can use it to their benefit. Many patients do not fully appreciate what information their pharmacists can provide and how consultations can lead to improved therapeutic results.

There are several key elements to making patient consultations an effective professional and marketing service. A quality service that will distinguish the pharmacy from its competitors requires the proper physical environment, pharmacists skilled in communicating with patients about their drugs, time to

provide the necessary information, and supporting written materials as appropriate.

By their very nature, prescription departments are not designed for effective pharmacist–patient interaction. In most instances, the pharmacist is physically removed from the patient by several feet, and a counter or other physical barrier (e.g. glass partition, bars). Often, the pharmacist's work area is elevated so that he or she looks down on the patient. And relatively few pharmacies have private areas set aside for confidential discussions that are free from interruption.

To provide good consultation service, the patient must be comfortable and secure in the surroundings. Space must be allocated to provide a more desirable environment for one-to-one discussions that may be sensitive in nature. Many people like to talk about their medical problems, but they prefer to decide this themselves rather than have it decided for them by other parties, and in front of strangers.

This concern also applies in hospital settings where privacy is more difficult because of the immobility of patients and the use of multi-bed rooms. Any element of privacy and confidentiality that can be created will enhance the consultation process.

In addition to having an environment that is conducive to consultations, pharmacists must be able to communicate with patients. It is important for pharmacists to remember that patients do not have a technical understanding of drugs and may not be in an emotional state ready to absorb the information the pharmacist wants and needs to convey.

To communicate effectively with patients, there are several general rules pharmacists need to consider:

- Establish credibility as quickly as possible by demonstrating an understanding of the symptoms, causes, and treatment of the condition for which the drug has been prescribed. Ideally, the pharmacist should have a good idea of what the prescriber told the patient, and be able to repeat some of that to illustrate consistency of knowledge with the patient's physician.
- Inform the patient early in the consultation of the value of discussing his or her condition and medication. Focus on the benefits received by the patient from the consultation process, and repeat this at least once during the conversation.
- Avoid the use of technical terms as far as possible. Use terms that the patient is likely to have heard before, so long as they are professionally appropriate.
- Ask the patient questions early in the consultation. This will encourage the patient to become more involved in the process and can lead to an atmosphere conducive to learning.
- Use props to explain complex processes. It is difficult for people to visualize things they have not seen or heard before.
- Watch for physical cues that indicate the patient does not understand what is being said. Furrowed eyebrows, erratic hand or facial movements, etc., all signal that there are barriers to the flow of information.
- Test the patient discreetly on his or her understanding of what is being said. Ask the patient to repeat the key points being made, or reemphasize them several times if necessary.
- Give the patient an opportunity to talk and ask questions. Avoid appearing to be in a hurry or very busy, even if that is the case.
- Smile and use other friendly gestures that put the patient at ease. Discuss the nature of the patient's condition, but avoid scaring the patient unless there is a special medical reason for doing so.
- Avoid interruptions to the consultation. Allocate sufficient time to the process to assure that the necessary information is conveyed. The patient should not feel rushed. However, be careful not

to extend the discussion too long so that it loses its value to the patient, and becomes too costly to the pharmacy.

Fee-based prescription consultations and medication therapy management

Most often, consultation services to patients, physicians, and nurses need not be especially time-consuming. A few well-directed questions or statements (e.g. When and how are you taking your medication? Have you noticed any changes in how you feel since beginning to take this medication?) can be an effective service strategy.

The key to making consultations successful, however, is to make them proactive rather than reactive. Initiate the dialogue rather than wait for questions from the patient. All too often, patients do not know what to ask, and have little understanding of what types of counseling the pharmacist can provide. The pharmacist's time and associated expenses with brief consultations must be considered a cost of doing business in this market that may not be recoverable in the short term.

Brief discussions with patients are essential to reaching this market, but that time is difficult to charge for. Consumers in general expect to be able to ask questions about products they are purchasing without being charged additional fees.

A fee-based consulting service can be developed when it involves more intense discussions of drug therapy, equipment use, etc. The pharmacist must educate patients to recognize extensive counseling as a valuable commodity. Only then will they be willing to pay for such services. Essentials of developing a fee-based consulting service for prescription drugs are presented in Table 8.1.

Non-prescription consultations

The basics of good pharmacist–patient consultations are the same for prescription and non-prescription merchandise. However, discussing the purchase and use of non-prescription merchandise is at times somewhat more difficult. Patients have, or think they have, a better understanding of non-prescription than prescription products, and the pharmacist's credibility as a source of expertise is less established for

Table 8.1 Developing a fee-based consulting service

Tips for building an appreciation for the value of services

1.	Offer services, rather than responding to questions
2.	Focus on providing information that the patient does not expect you to possess
3.	Show the importance of the pharmacist's role in overall healthcare (e.g. relationship with physicians)
4.	Have a patient consulting area and use it to discuss medications other than just prescriptions being dispensed
5.	Isolate key information needs by type of prescription and be sure to convey that information periodically
6.	Isolate key information needs by type of non-prescription products and be sure to convey that information to patients who are examining those items
7.	Train staff to encourage patients to look for opportunities to suggest that patients talk to the pharmacist, and for opportunities to suggest that the pharmacist talk to the patient

Tips for initiating a consulting program

1.	Initially, develop a consulting program that is either individualized to patients, or "theme" consulting services for specific medical problems (e.g. arthritis)
2.	Consider linking counseling to special services, such as blood pressure monitoring and cholesterol measurements. Fees for conducting these tests prepare patients for paying for pharmacists' services independent of prescriptions
3.	Consider establishing on a quarterly or semi-annual basis a "seniors' club" that provides patient counseling about their overall use of drugs
4.	Consider offering group counseling by medical problem
5.	Establish times for meeting with patients, usually for 10–15 minutes in duration
6.	Promote the benefits of a consulting service through direct mail, the media, or both. This should be separate and distinct from brief consultations following dispensing
7.	Have handouts available at the pharmacy counter that explain what the consulting program does and why it is beneficial to patients
8.	Set fees low initially to begin orienting patients to paying for more extensive counseling

Adapted from Tootelian DH. Marketing to the mature population, Part 2. *American Pharmacy*, February 1991: 58.

over-the-counter (OTC) drugs and sundries (e.g. hand lotions, sunscreens).

Patients also have choices and discretion in purchasing, which they do not have with prescriptions they bring into the pharmacy. In addition, if the pharmacy is to take an active role in non-prescription counseling, its pharmacists must go to the patients rather than wait for them to come to the prescription counter.

If conducted properly, consultations for non-prescription merchandise can be a very significant competitive advantage. Because many pharmacists do not offer assistance in the purchase of OTC drugs and sundries, those that do can build greater community recognition and closer customer rapport.

While the "rules" of consultations for prescription drugs generally apply here as well, there are some slight differences:

- Establishing credibility with non-prescription items may be more difficult in instances where the pharmacist does not know the customer well. Some people only recognize the pharmacist's knowledge of prescription drugs and have not thought about his or her expertise in terms of other products.

- While it may not be appropriate to use a private area for non-prescription consultations, be sensitive to desires for confidentiality and privacy. To the extent possible, come out from behind the prescription counter to meet the patient at the point where the product choices are available.

- Be careful to avoid appearing to recommend only higher priced products even if they are more effective. Present the customer with a set of options that accurately reflect the cost-benefit choices to be made.

- Be sure to determine the customer's needs before recommending any product. Do not respond to questions about product usage without determining if the customer has correctly diagnosed the medical need.
- Once sure that the customer has the right product to satisfy his or her need, do not be afraid to ask for the sale. Good service extends to seeing that the customer leaves the pharmacy with the appropriate product.

Patient monitoring

Pharmacists can monitor the healthcare of their patients in a number of ways. Some of the more common types of monitoring include maintaining patient profiles, prescription intervention, evaluating potential drug interactions, monitoring side-effects, drug utilization review, and taking blood pressures.

One of the most important areas for pharmacy services is monitoring compliance with drug therapy. This can be accomplished in several ways. By reviewing patient profiles on at least a monthly basis, the pharmacist can identify instances where refills are not being requested. In cases where patients have not used their medications within the expected time frame, the pharmacist can become actively involved with the patient and prescriber to ensure better compliance.

Increasingly, too, pharmacists are being asked by managed care programs to intervene in healthcare by not dispensing prescriptions they believe to be erroneous or otherwise not in the best interests of the patient. While this can create some awkward situations for the pharmacist in developing good relations with prescribers, it has become a critical safeguard at the point of sale.

Evaluating potential drug interactions, monitoring side-effects, taking blood pressures, and other healthcare services have been parts of pharmacy services for some time. Since pharmacists are directly and conveniently accessible to patients, these services can be used to build closer relations with both patients and prescribers.

If pharmacists are to monitor the health of patients, they must explain what they are doing and why and how the services are beneficial. All too often, pharmacists have services such as these available,

but fail to use them to build or maintain patronage. Make sure that patients are aware of these services and encouraged to use them when appropriate. While the services may be somewhat time-consuming and expensive, they can be important in building and maintaining patient–prescriber relations.

Prescriber consultations

Everybody benefits when pharmacists can develop close working relationships with prescribers. These services can involve consulting on specific drug therapy for particular patients, discussing the general implications of new drugs that have recently been approved for use, monitoring patient compliance with the drug regimen, monitoring the appropriateness of prescription drugs and dosages, explaining changes in drug utilization resulting from conversions from prescription to OTC status, etc.

As in the case with all other types of services, these have to be made known to the people involved. Management must convey to prescribers a willingness for pharmacists to provide information and assist in attending to the medication needs of patients. The focus must be on the benefits prescribers and their patients receive, not on the benefits to the pharmacy from increased business.

In describing this service to patients, management should indicate that their services are designed to increase the quality of healthcare. The presentation should be conducted in a manner that appears to support rather than infringe upon prescriber–patient relationships.

Other services in community settings

A number of services are commonly offered in non-institutional practice settings that can be beneficial to patients and valuable in the development of the pharmacy's marketing program. Any services offered, however, should either be useful to good patient care or capable of generating sufficient revenue to recover their costs and contribute to pharmacy profits.

Some of the services to consider are listed below, along with policy questions that have to be resolved. Among the more common services are:

- *Emergency prescription service*: Being available to patients on a 24-hour basis is an attractive service, but one that should be evaluated carefully. Who will dispense the prescriptions? Is this service available for refills on maintenance drugs as well as for acute care prescriptions? Will it be available 365 days per year? Will there be extra charges for this service, and if so, what will be the fee?

- *Delivery*: Most pharmacies offer this service either with their own personnel or through an independent service. What will be the territorial boundaries for delivery? Will there be a minimum dollar order necessary to obtain delivery? Will deliveries be made for non-prescription merchandise only? What charges, if any, will there be for delivery? At what time(s) of day will deliveries be made?
- *Tax and insurance records*: Many pharmacies offer prescription records for tax and insurance purposes. Who will maintain the records? Which patients will be given these records?
- *Internal credit*: One of the most difficult services to evaluate in terms of the costs and benefits to pharmacy is an internal credit program. While it can be attractive in a marketing program, an internal credit program tends to be costly to administer and difficult to control. How much total credit can the pharmacy afford to offer? To whom will credit be made available? What will be the credit limits available to individual customers? What billing system will be used? What, if any, service charges will be assessed for late payments?

Service considerations in institutional settings

Many of the services offered in institutional settings are similar to those provided in community practices. These include patient and prescriber consultations, patient monitoring, drug interaction evaluations, intervention, drug utilization review, and developing patient information sheets. However, there also are some other services to consider.

One service offered in some institutions is admission and discharge interviews with the patient. This service allows the pharmacist to gain a better understanding of the patient's medical history, and develop a relationship that might otherwise be difficult to establish. The results of these interviews may also provide physicians with further information useful in creating an appropriate drug regimen for the patient. Exit interviews are especially important for ensuring that the patient understands the nature of the drug therapy and how the medication is to be taken.

Some institutions have the pharmacist make rounds with the physician. In this way, closer ties can be created between pharmacist, prescriber, and patient. It also provides added assurance that medications will not be incorrectly prescribed since the pharmacist will have a more complete medical history of the patient and his or her current status. The difficulty in implementing this service is determining what role the pharmacist is to play in this process.

A service available in many institutions is consultations with other healthcare professional staff, including nurses, dieticians, and respiratory care therapists. Pharmacy services are quite valuable in building more cohesive healthcare teams, but are difficult to establish. Territorial conflicts as well as time pressures create problems in making this a workable service. To be effective, clear lines of authority and responsibility must be established for each healthcare professional in order to minimize possible conflicts. The task of the pharmacist is to show how these types of consultations can help the other healthcare professionals do their jobs more effectively, improve patient care, and reduce the costs of healthcare for the institution.

Summary

- Even though some of the issues of what prescription inventory to carry and what services to offer seem fairly routine, careful decisions are essential to a well-managed and successful pharmacy.
- Physical products are not as important to consumers as is often thought. Consumers buy benefits, not products.
- Many marketing experts consider the product and service strategies of a business to form the hub around which all other strategies revolve.
- Prescription product and service strategies have an even more prominent role in institutional settings since there are very few opportunities to sell non-prescription merchandise.
- There are many decisions to be made in terms of the prescription product mix. They include

what basic lines to stock, the non-standard lines in which to specialize, and how full a line of prescription merchandise to carry.

- Perhaps the most important consideration in establishing a mix of prescription drugs is to review patient files to determine the number of refills coming due and the quantities of those drugs to be dispensed.
- Management may want to distinguish the pharmacy from the competition by carrying a more extensive inventory of selected drugs. Usually these are defined by disease state, or by some form of therapeutic category such as nuclear pharmaceuticals or biotech medicines.
- There are a number of ways to keep costs of goods under control through effective purchasing. Typically, this is accomplished by taking appropriate discounts when they can be profitable, and controlling the dollar value of prescription and non-prescription inventory.
- A good selection of prescription merchandise is of little value if it is not complemented by appropriate pharmacy services. The manager, however, must try to estimate the costs of various services to determine if the pharmacy can afford to offer them.
- To provide good consultation service, the patient must be comfortable and secure in the surroundings.
- The key to making consultations successful, however, is to make them proactive rather than reactive.
- A fee-based consulting service can be developed when this involves more intense discussions of drug therapy, equipment use, and other services that offer opportunities for establishing a fee schedule. The pharmacist must see to it that patients recognize extensive counseling as a valuable commodity.
- Pharmacists can monitor the healthcare of their patients in a number of ways. Some of the more common types of monitoring include maintaining patient profiles, prescription intervention, evaluating potential drug interactions, monitoring side-effects, drug utilization review, and taking blood pressures.
- Counseling on the use of non-prescription merchandise is somewhat more difficult. Patients have, or think they have, a better understanding of non-prescription products, and the pharmacist's credibility as a source of expertise is less established for OTC medications and sundries.
- Everybody benefits when pharmacists can develop close working relationships with prescribers.

Questions for discussion

1 How can a pharmacy manager determine the relative importance of prescription products and services in a particular setting?
2 In what ways do products and services interrelate with other marketing strategies?
3 How do product and service strategies differ between community and institutional settings?
4 What considerations are necessary in deciding between carrying a full vs. a basic line of prescription drugs?
5 How can specialty products serve to distinguish one pharmacy from another?
6 What are the key ingredients to successful prescription drug consultations?
7 How can a pharmacy begin to establish a fee-based consulting service for prescription drugs? For non-prescription medications and sundries?
8 Why is patient monitoring becoming so important a part of a pharmacy's services?
9 Why are prescriber consultations so important? How can they be developed?
10 What other, non-traditional, services can be offered in community settings? In institutional settings?

Self-test review

True/false statements

1 Prescription merchandise and related healthcare services generate the majority of sales, but also account for the greatest percentage of costs.
2 Consumers buy products.
3 Since prescription products are somewhat standardized, consumers can make direct comparisons among pharmacies.

4 Many marketing experts believe that promotional strategies form the hub around which all other business strategies revolve.

5 Prescription products and services have a less prominent role in institutional settings than in community settings.

6 The simplest way to determine the basic product line is to call all possible prescribers in the market area.

7 Full lines of prescription drugs should be maintained at all times within every pharmacy.

8 If conducted properly, consultations for non-prescription merchandise can provide a very significant advantage to a community pharmacy.

9 A fee-based consulting service can be developed when it involves more intense discussions of drug therapy, equipment use, and so on.

10 It is unusual for pharmacists in institutional settings to make rounds with physicians.

Multiple choice questions

1 Products that are stocked either because they are used extensively or because they are occasionally needed for patients of important prescribers are known as:

(A) Full-line products.
(B) Specialty products.
(C) Basic-line products.
(D) Conversion products.

2 Nuclear pharmaceuticals ordinarily would be one type of which of the following types of products?

(A) Full-line products.
(B) Specialty products.
(C) Basic-line products.
(D) Conversion products.

3 Which of the following would not be a general rule of communication as it applies to counseling patients on prescription drugs?

(A) Establish credibility as quickly as possible.
(B) Inform the patient early in the consultation of the value of discussing his or her condition and drug.
(C) Use technical terms as much as possible in order to establish a professional atmosphere.
(D) Use props to explain complex processes.

4 Which of the following is not true as it applies to counseling patients on non-prescription drugs?

(A) Establishing credibility may be more difficult than it is for prescription drugs.
(B) Be careful to avoid appearing to be recommending only higher-priced merchandise.
(C) Determine the customer's needs before recommending any product.
(D) Do not ask for the sale because it will appear to be unprofessional.

5 Which of the following is not a common service offered in community pharmacy settings?

(A) Emergency prescription service.
(B) Delivery.
(C) Tax and insurance records.
(D) All of the above are commonly offered services.

Acknowledgments

Sections of this chapter have been adapted from *Developing and Implementing Your Marketing Plan*, vol 2. Sacramento, CA: California Pharmacists Association & G.D. Searle, 1991: 48–64.

Portions of this section were adapted from Tootelian DH. Marketing to the mature population, Part 2. *American Pharmacy*, February 1991: 53–58.

9

Pharmacy location, layout, and merchandising

Learning objectives

The objectives of this chapter are to assist you to be able to explain:

- the advantages and disadvantages of store layout arrangements
- criteria for allocating space and determining space productivity
- where to locate departments within pharmacies
- guidelines to follow in arranging individual items within departments
- factors to consider in displaying merchandise.

Key terms

Cross-selling
Free-flow layout
Grid layout
Impulse products
Inventory turnover
Merchandise density
Merchandising
Planogram
Point-of-purchase displays
Store layout

The physical environment of a pharmacy is a major factor influencing its success. The layout and ambience of the pharmacy, the services it provides, and its display of merchandise and allocation of space to merchandise categories are all integral to profitable pharmacy operations.

Successful pharmacies create a store atmosphere that is pleasing and conducive to shopping. The pharmacy's atmosphere is the psychological effect or feeling (i.e. the image) created by the physical characteristics of the pharmacy.

Physical characteristics of the pharmacy that are used to develop an image and draw customers consist of several elements, including the exterior design, the interior design, the store layout, and merchandise presentation.

All pharmacies depend, in varying degree, on walk-in customers, and the decision to enter a pharmacy depends partly on a customer's impression of its exterior. The uniqueness of the storefront and the creative use of entrances, display windows, and distinctive outdoor signs can help create a favorable pharmacy image.

Once the customer is in the pharmacy, there are numerous elements that affect his or her perceptions of it. The general interior elements that serve as stimuli and attention attractors of customers to a store include: fixtures, lighting, flooring, colors, scents and sounds, temperature, width of aisles, cleanliness, modernization, merchandise assortment, display of prices, and personnel.

The importance of deciding where to locate a pharmacy and what advantages to offer customers vis-à-vis competitors can hardly be overstated. It is often said that the three secrets to success in a pharmacy's operation are: location, location, and location. Although this may be exaggerated, the importance of location in the pharmacy's overall marketing strategy is critical. To a large extent, the location determines the type and number of customers the pharmacy will attract. Good locations provide ready access to large numbers of targeted customers and prescription buying power.

Selecting a location

One of the principal reasons for the success of a new pharmacy is good site location. Despite this, locations are too often selected in an unscientific manner. It is the relatively lasting effect of the location decision that makes it so important. Because the location decision represents a long-term fixed investment, the disadvantages of a poor location may be difficult to overcome. Once the pharmacy is established, it is costly and perhaps impractical to move. If the initial choice of location is especially poor, the pharmacy may never be able to get off the ground, irrespective of what other advantages the pharmacy might offer vis-à-vis competitors.

Sometimes pharmacies suffer because they are just outside the flow of traffic, not quite visible from the street, or "one block away from success." A prime location is one of the strongest competitive edges a pharmacy can have. Finding a prime location, however, is no small task. Chain store pharmacies spend thousands of dollars on market surveys before entering a market area. Community pharmacy owners should imitate them insofar as careful community and site evaluations are concerned.

Underestimating the importance of a carefully selected location can be the first and final mistake for the fledgling pharmacy. The prospect of low rents and attractive leaseholds can lure the uninitiated into a trap, crushing what might become a profitable business.

Several sources of information are available for an accurate and complete evaluation of a prospective location. Helpful data can be obtained from the following:

A *trading area* is a geographic area containing the customers of a particular firm for specific goods or services. A trading area can be divided into three zones of influence:

- The *primary trading area* encompasses roughly 55–70 percent of a pharmacy's customers. It is the area closest to the pharmacy and possesses the highest density of customers to population and per capita sales.
- The *secondary trading area* contains an additional 15–25 percent of a pharmacy's customers. It is located outside the primary trading area, and customers are widely dispersed.
- The *tertiary (fringe) trading area* includes all the remaining customers, and they are more widely dispersed. It consists of customers who patronize the pharmacy for reasons not related to its proximity.

Choosing a location within a community

Where to locate within a community—whether in a central business district, a solo location, or a shopping center—is determined by the relative importance of front-end merchandise, the class of patron desired, accessibility and convenience for customers, the adjacent stores, and the neighborhood. In short, different pharmacies have different location requirements.

Downtown business district

A central or downtown business district is common to every community. In large communities, the central business district might contain several pharmacies, and hundreds of retail outlets and office buildings. Although declining in relative importance for most retailers and service firms, the downtown of large cities has become increasingly important as a center of administrative, financial, and professional services. Other attractions of many downtown areas include the proximity of hotels, convention facilities, and cultural events. Downtown pharmacies cater largely to downtown workers, downtown apartment occupants, regional shoppers, tourists, and other occasional visitors.

Solo location

Some pharmacies may want to locate in a solo or free-standing location. Freestanding locations on heavily traveled streets have several advantages, including:

- the lack of close competition
- low rent
- more space for parking and expansion
- greater flexibility in store hours.

The most successful pharmacies in such locations are those with strong patronage loyalty.

Shopping centers

Shopping centers are a geographic cluster of retail stores. These stores collectively offer a variety of goods and services designed to serve the needs of customers within the trading area of the center. Shopping centers—notably malls—provide a convenient location, free parking facilities, uniform operating hours, and special events to create an overall retailing environment to attract shoppers. For many pharmacy owners, however, the terms of lease contracts and uniform operating hours are distinct disadvantages.

Types of planned shopping centers

There are three common types of shopping centers, distinguished by the size and type of stores: neighborhood shopping centers, community shopping centers, and regional shopping centers.

Neighborhood shopping center

The neighborhood shopping center typically consists of 5–15 stores with an emphasis on convenience goods, and a trading area of about 5 minutes driving time from the center. It is designed to serve fewer than

20,000 people. The major store—and the prime traffic generator in the center—is typically a supermarket. The other stores in the center, which may include a pharmacy or drugstore, hardware store, bakery, and beauty shop, offer convenience goods and services. The most common form of neighborhood shopping centers are the unplanned "strip" centers.

Community shopping center

A community shopping center usually consists of 15–50 stores with an emphasis on both convenience and shopping goods, and a trading area of about 10–20 minutes driving time from the center. The dominant store is generally a department store, such as Macy's, J.C. Penney, or Sears.

Community shopping centers serve between 20,000 and 100,000 people. Unlike the neighborhood center, a community shopping center is carefully planned and coordinated. It is likely to have several major annual events to generate publicity and attract shoppers.

Regional shopping center

A regional shopping center is designed to serve from 100,000 to 1 million or more customers who can be expected to drive 30 minutes and beyond to reach it. A regional complex often has three or more major department stores in addition to over 100 stores carrying shopping and specialty goods. However, a number of stores also carry convenience goods.

New regional centers are almost exclusively closed malls with walkways. They are managed as a unit and sponsor numerous special events to attract shoppers. Today they account for more than 40 percent of total retail sales, providing people not only with goods and services but also with eating facilities, nightlife, and a place to socialize.

Factors to consider in the shopping center choice

Whether or not a pharmacist can get into a particular shopping center depends on the market and management. A small shopping center may need only one pharmacy, for example, while a regional center may expect enough business for more than one pharmacy or drugstore. The management aspect is simple: developers and owners of shopping centers look for successful retailers.

In finding tenants whose line of goods will meet the needs of the desired market, the developer–owner first signs on a prestige merchant as the lead tenant. Then the developer selects other types of stores that will complement one another. In this way, a tenant mix is created that offers a varied array of merchandise. Thus, the center's competitive strength is bolstered against other centers as well as supplying the market area's needs.

To finance a center, the developer needs major leases from companies with strong credit ratings. The developer's own lenders favor tenant rosters that include the triple-A ratings of national chains. However, local merchants and pharmacists with good business records and proven understanding of local markets have a good chance of being considered by a shopping center developer.

Retail compatibility

For a small pharmacy in its first year of operation, with limited funds for advertising and promotion, retail compatibility can be the most important factor in the survival of the pharmacy. Will the pharmacy be located next to businesses that will generate traffic? Or will it be located near businesses that may clash?

With the advent of the super mall and regional shopping center, shopping goods and convenience goods outlets may be found coexisting easily under the same roof. In this situation, it is still important for a store to be located in a section of the shopping complex that will not clash with what it is selling and in fact will be conducive to sales. For example, a pet store should not be located immediately adjacent to a restaurant, dress shop, or salon. A drugstore should be near places like department stores, theaters, restaurants—in short, any place where lines of patrons may form, giving potential customers several minutes to look in the drugstore's display windows. The department store has become less important than it used to be. Today, specialty merchants are very important in developing a shopping center in the suburbs without a department store. But, department stores advertise heavily; they bring name recognition to a center; and they bring customer loyalty.

Rental and lease arrangements

Most shopping center leases are negotiated. Rental payments are usually arranged in one of two ways: either a flat monthly rate or a percentage-of-sales sum involving a base amount or percentage of gross monthly sales, or both. Flat monthly rents stay the same from month to month, allowing owners to project operating budgets more easily. Frequently a flat rental lease contains an escalator clause, which adjusts the rent upward over a period of time.

Under a percentage-of-sales agreement, which is typically between 5 and 7 percent of gross sales, rent is generally based on the square-footage of the store and its sales volume. The percentage payments depend primarily on the sales volume expected and what the landlord will provide in the way of physical facilities.

Percentage-of-sales agreements are normal for stores located within a shopping center. It is also common that these agreements are in addition to a regular flat monthly fee. In signing such agreements, the operator might request an "exclusivity clause" to prevent other shops in the center from selling the same type of merchandise. Increasingly, however, such clauses have been ruled to be in violation of the antitrust laws.

Before signing a lease arrangement, an attorney should review the contract. This is essential for anyone who wants a clear understanding of lease clauses covering non-rent charges, escalation clauses, subleasing, and renewal options. Non-rent charges, for instance, are normally made in planned shopping centers where all tenants share costs for services, such as maintenance and security guards.

Other experts should also be consulted to check the condition of the heating, plumbing, and air-conditioning equipment. An insurance agent should be contacted to determine the amount of insurance needed to cover both liability and property damage claims if the lease agreement does not provide them.

Store layout

Store layout involves planning the internal arrangement of departments and allocating the amount of space for each department. Whether consciously planned or not, the pharmacy's layout design evokes certain feelings that influence consumer behaviors within the store, including:

- shopping in the store with enjoyment
- spending time browsing and exploring the store's merchandise
- spending more money, perhaps, than originally planned
- returning to the store.

The pharmacy manager should recognize the psychological effects of the store layout on customer buying behavior. It has been suggested that:

> A subtle dimension of in-store customer shopping behavior is the environment of the space itself. Retail space, i.e. the proximate environment that surrounds the retail shopper, is never neutral. The retail store is a bundle of cues, messages, and suggestions which communicate to shoppers. Retail store designers, planners, and merchandisers shape space, but that space in turn affects and shapes customer behavior. The retail store ... does create moods, activates intentions, and generally affects customer reactions.[1]

In short, the store layout should create a pleasant atmosphere, encourage customer traffic, and utilize store space productively.

Layout arrangement

The layout of the pharmacy and the use of in-store fixtures should be designed to direct traffic around the store to increase sales. The objective is to have the customer visit as many areas of the pharmacy as possible, notably those having high gross margin front-end merchandise.

There are basically two types of layout: grid and free-flow or open plan. In a grid layout, all the counters and fixtures are at right-angles to one another so that merchandise is displayed in straight, parallel lines. This type of layout is typically used in drugstores. Figure 9.1 shows a grid layout for a store without cross-aisles, while Figure 9.2 shows a grid layout with cross-aisles. Note how these layouts move the customer past a wide assortment of front-end merchandise, thus ensuring maximum travel time in the store and maximum product exposure.

In addition to the advantage of front-end merchandise exposure, the grid arrangement lends itself more readily to inventory control, simplified security, utilization of all available floor space, ease of cleaning, the possibility of self-service, and customer familiarity.

The free-flow layout groups merchandise and fixtures into patterns that allow an unstructured flow of customer traffic. Many of the fixtures are irregularly shaped, such as circles, arches, and triangles.

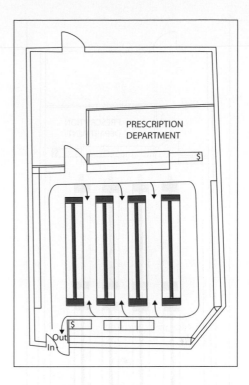

Figure 9.1 Grid layout without cross-aisles. The arrows show the traffic flow pattern. This traffic flow ensures maximum travel time in the store and maximum product exposure.

The free-flow layout is often used in gift stores and specialty stores to let customers move in any direction and wander freely, thus encouraging browsing and impulse purchasing. Compared to grid layouts, free-flow layout arrangements are more costly and use space less efficiently. On the other hand, they have greater visual appeal and flexibility.

Allocation of space

Store space is a scarce and costly commodity. Allocating more space for one particular line of merchandise inevitably reduces the allocation for another. It is the task of the pharmacy manager, therefore, to allocate store space efficiently in order to attain the highest possible sales volume at the lowest possible cost. Specifically, high-performance results can be achieved using the following means:[2]

- Ensure maximum space utilization, with all selling areas activated and all "dead" areas and wasted space eliminated.

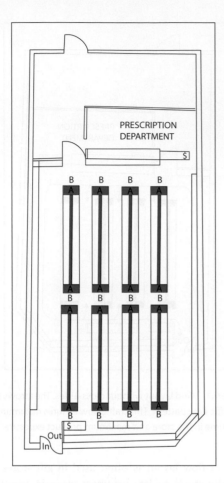

Figure 9.2 Grid layout with cross-aisles. An exceptionally deep store needs cross-aisles. Promotional displays—e.g. end displays (A) and floorstands (B)—should be placed in various locations.

- Eliminate losses and wasteful practices, including merchandise lost through theft and breakage.
- Departmentalize merchandise, as advocated in publications such as *Drug Topics* and *American Druggist*. Space is allocated on the basis of departmental profitability and merchandise relationships. Additional customer purchases are encouraged by obtaining maximum merchandise exposure and traffic flow through strategic placement of departments, fixtures, and aisles.
- Provide customer convenience and comfort through lighting, decor, and interior climate control.
- Reduce costs through efficient utilization of personnel and simplified building maintenance.

These principles must be applied in reference to other considerations discussed in previous chapters. For example, the needs and wants of the clientele should determine the basic mix of front-end merchandise carried and the arrangement of individual products within departments.

Furthermore, the space management techniques utilized influence the image and atmosphere desired by the pharmacy. Different types of pharmacies require different space utilization techniques. For example, a clinic or prescription pharmacy provides little, if any, front-end merchandise, whereas the traditional community pharmacy typically devotes significantly more space to the front-end section than to the prescription department.

Management can perform space allocation in one of several ways, including industry averages by type of merchandise and the sales-per-square-foot method.

Industry averages

Pharmacy managers can use the national average percentage of selling space that a particular merchandise line (e.g. health and beauty aids, "drugs" or "home remedies," such as analgesics, antacids or vitamins, greeting cards, gifts, and so forth) occupies in specific merchandise space allocation.

Sales per square foot

The pharmacy manager can determine the amount of space a department needs by relating the planned total sales for that department to its expected sales per square foot. Sales per square foot of selling space equals net sales divided by square feet of selling space. This formula shows how much in annual net sales dollars the pharmacy generates for each square foot of selling space.

To determine the amount of space a department requires, the pharmacy manager has to estimate planned sales and expected sales per square foot. Assume that the planned annual sales for health and beauty aids in a community pharmacy with total annual sales under $400,000 is $80,000. If the national average sales per square foot for this department in this type of pharmacy is $150, then management would allocate 533 square feet to the department.

In other words:

$$\text{Required space (sq. ft)} = \frac{\text{planned sales}}{\text{expected sales per sq. ft}}$$

$$= \frac{\$80,000}{\$150/\text{ft}} = 533 \text{ sq. ft}$$

The major advantage of this method is its simplicity. Nevertheless, pharmacy managers must apply it with care. The method assumes that it is possible to estimate both planned sales and expected sales per square foot accurately. Even a well-established pharmacy should be cautious in estimating space productivity. Although past performance and trade associations provide a basis for estimating future performance, pharmacies must adjust past data for anticipated future conditions.

General inflation affects dollar sales per square foot, boosting sales volume even while unit sales hold constant. The pharmacy manager must also consider how well the department utilized its space in previous years. If it allocated space inefficiently in the past, productivity could improve in the future.[3]

Space productivity

Irrespective of what method is employed to allocate space to merchandise, the pharmacy manager must continually strive to increase the efficiency of the expensive space. Each square foot must produce as much sales productivity as possible throughout the year.

Two primary determinants of space productivity are inventory turnover and merchandise density. Inventory turnover is the number of times average inventory is sold during a specified time period (usually 1 year). Turnover management is important to retail space productivity because space is required to merchandise and store inventory, and the higher the inventory turnover, the less space is required. Merchandise density reflects how densely inventory has been put into the limited space available (i.e. the inventory investment per square foot). The greater the merchandise density, the greater the space productivity.

The gross-margin-per-square-foot-of-selling-space method can also be used to evaluate space productivity. This simple measure reflects how many gross margin dollars (net sales less cost of goods sold) a pharmacy generates for each square foot of selling space. High-ticket items may result in more sales

than lower priced merchandise, yet the ratio of gross margin to square feet may be smaller for high-priced items.

As illustrated below, three calculations are involved in assessing space utilization by the gross-margin-per-square-foot-of-selling-space method. Sales per square foot less cost of merchandise sold per square foot equals the gross margin. With such calculations, departments of varying sizes selling different assortments of merchandise can be compared. Gross margin per square foot of selling space can show management which departments are doing well, which are not, which might be improved if changed, and which can be reduced in space allocation.

$$\frac{\text{Total sales}}{\text{Total sq. ft}} = \text{Sales/sq. ft of selling space}$$

$$\frac{\text{Cost of merchandise sold}}{\text{Total sq. ft}} = \text{cost of merchandise}$$
$$\text{sold/sq. ft of selling space}$$

$$\text{Sales/sq. ft of selling space} - \text{cost of merchandise}$$
$$\text{sold/sq. ft of selling space}$$
$$= \text{gross margin/sq. ft of selling space}$$

An example is shown in Table 9.1.

Locating departments

After allocating space to each department, the pharmacy manager must decide on the locations for the departments within the pharmacy. At a minimum, location of the various departments should reflect the impact of the following factors:

● *Traffic flow and value of space*: Because some locations attract more customer traffic than others, merchandise displayed in the high-value

Table 9.1 Example of calculations for gross margin per square foot of selling space

	Department A	Department B
Sales	$25,000.00	$35,000.00
Cost of merchandise sold	$15,000.00	$20,000.00
Selling space	300 ft^2	400 ft^2
Sales/ft^2 of selling space	$83.33	$87.50
Cost of merchandise sold/ft^2 selling space	$50.00	$50.00
Gross margin/ft^2 selling space	$33.33	$37.50

locations has more potential to generate sales owing to its greater exposure to traffic flow.

- *Merchandise characteristics*: The characteristics of merchandise also influence where it should be located. Impulse products, for example, should be located in high-traffic areas for maximum customer exposure. Impulse products are convenience products that are bought on the spur of the moment, without advance planning or serious consideration at the time, and often by the stimulus of point-of-sale promotion or observation. The prescription department is usually located in the rear of the pharmacy. This location maximizes traffic flow since the prescription department is the major demand department in most pharmacies.

- *Merchandise compatibility*: Since customers frequently shop for more than one item at a time, related departments should be near each other in order to facilitate cross-selling. Cross-selling is the process of selling across departments to facilitate larger transactions and to make it more convenient for customers to furnish themselves with accessories. A common arrangement of departments that facilitates cross-selling is: cosmetics, toiletries, health and beauty aids, proprietary and over-the-counter (OTC) products. Opposite these departments on the same aisle are found related merchandise (e.g. hair care, feminine hygiene, dental care products, etc.). This type of arrangement provides for a logical transition from one front-end merchandise category or department to the next.

- *Seasonal considerations*: Pharmacies should plan department locations that can be adapted to seasonal sales patterns. For example, toys might be placed next to a department whose sales peak in summer (e.g. sun block lotions, insect repellent, etc.). In fall and winter when toy sales are high, the toy department can then be expanded by allocating some of the space from other departments whose sales fall during winter.

Arrangement of individual products

After deciding on the department locations, individual products must then be arranged within departments. A number of guidelines may be followed in the arrangement of individual items, for example:

- The most salable and profitable items and brands occupy the most prominent locations within the department. Products may be arranged by package size, price, color, or brand, customer interest, or any combination of these.

- Eye-level positions can significantly affect sales. Moving an item from the bottom shelf to an eye-level shelf could increase sales by 50 percent or more.

It is also important to recognize that a high percentage of sales can be generated outside a product's own department. Indeed, the pharmacy manager should place certain fast-moving, high-profit items outside their own departments (i.e. on an out-of-department display in the store). Guidelines to follow when selecting the best out-of-department location for a specialized display include:

- An entirely new product will benefit most from a location in the mainstream of the traffic flow.

- A standard, well-established item will probably sell best if placed next to a related type of merchandise.

- A small impulse purchase item should be positioned as closely as possible to the checkout stand.

It is a demonstrated fact that displays generate extra sales, regardless of the existence of or absence of special prices.

Planograms

To ensure proper shelf positions in all their outlets, pharmacy chains use planograms to control the location of each item. A planogram shows in a detailed schematic plan the amount of space allocated to, and the arrangement of, each item within a department.[3] A planogram produced from a wide range of current market information will enable the pharmacy to give high-margin items eye-level shelf positioning where they will influence the buying decisions of impulse shoppers.

The design of planograms for chain drugstores is undertaken by the corporate merchandising department at the chain's headquarters and sent to the managers of all outlets. Since the planogram specifies in detail the relative shelf position of each item and the number of items to stock, it ensures standardization of merchandise and display across the chain's outlets, which helps to project a consistent image.

Every marketing variable, from an individual store's consumer profile to national buying trends by category, can be included in a space analysis computation to produce an on-target planogram for any situation. Few pharmacies, however, have all the resources necessary—the sophisticated equipment and software, a highly skilled space management staff, a full complement of product movement databases—to develop their own planograms. Community pharmacies can take advantage of the merchandising programs offered by wholesalers and independent consultants.

Maximum sales turnover can be achieved by customizing a product planogram to a pharmacy's exact department or section and fixture size. These points are critical to providing the highest turnover, gross sales, and net profits, leading to the best return on investment possible.

Merchandise presentation

Every pharmacy has a merchandising program. For many pharmacies it is the result of unplanned evolution. Other pharmacies formulate a comprehensive merchandise program developed in response to the needs of customers and conditions in the marketplace.

The concept of merchandising has historically been defined in many ways. To the retailer, merchandising means "the planning involved in marketing the right merchandise at the right place at the right time in the right quantities at the right price." Effective merchandising requires the retailer to be able to plan product purchases, manage inventory, and develop a merchandising program involving product assortment, pricing, promotion, and display management, among others.

To the pharmacy manager, the term merchandising should mean "a combination of techniques for positioning, arranging, and promoting a product within a store so that the consumer is motivated to buy it as he or she shops." In short, merchandising is visual selling. Products that are not properly merchandised will not sell to their full potential.

When properly designed, visual merchandising techniques encourage customers to spend more time in the pharmacy, exposing them to more merchandise items. As its overall objective, visual merchandising is designed to convert those who pass by an item from mere browsers to actual buyers.

Numerous visual merchandising aids are supplied by manufacturers and wholesalers to support in-department merchandising. Such aids include display cartons designed to fold out into a self-contained display; "shelf talkers," which are printed cards designed to be positioned on the shelf under the product; and price signs, which might compare the pharmacy's special selling price with the pharmacy's normal retail price, the pharmacy's selling price with the manufacturer's suggested price, or the pharmacy's private label price with the national brand price.

Point-of-purchase displays

Merchandising a product outside its own department typically involves the use of point-of-purchase fixtures and displays. Point-of-purchase displays are interior displays that provide consumers with information, add to store atmosphere, and serve a substantial promotional role. The characteristics of a good display are:

- The display should gain the attention and interest of shoppers. It should be able to catch the eye through use of color and design.
- The display should be pleasing to the eye and appropriately placed in the store.
- The display should convey the image the pharmacy wants to project.
- The display should present a simple message that the shopper can quickly receive and understand.
- The display should be clean and neat, but not so neat that customers do not want to take products from the display for fear of messing up the arrangement.

The importance of displays can hardly be overemphasized. Counter, floor stand, dump, end-cap, and floors tack displays create buying excitement and generate extra sales, regardless of whether or not the prices of the items on display are special prices.

Choosing items to display

The selection of merchandise to display should be guided by a number of factors:

- *New merchandise*: Displays effectively announce the arrival of new brands and merchandise, as well as trial-size products in the store.

- *In-season merchandise*: Merchandise in displays should reflect seasonal changes (e.g. cough and cold remedies during winter months and tanning and sunburn products during the summer months).
- *Special events merchandise*: Displayed merchandise should be coordinated with special events (e.g. Mother's Day, Father's Day, Valentine's Day, Thanksgiving Day, etc.).
- *Popularity of merchandise*: Popular items, such as vitamins, gifts, candies, and cards, are excellent for display because they tend to attract attention and sell easily.
- *Profitability of items*: High-margin items should be displayed to justify their location at a premium space.
- *Promotional tie-ins*: Displays should call attention to special sales and remind the customer of a product he or she has seen advertised and wants to try.
- *Potential for impulse purchases*: Items that are bought on the spur of the moment, without advance planning or serious consideration at the time, are excellent candidates for display.

Another effective way to increase impulse sales and create new selling space at the same time is by using J-hooks and cricket clips. They are great for impulse sales at the checkout stands, on end caps, hanging from tag molding, and at other strategic locations.

Irrespective of what items are displayed, it is important to remember that merchandising a product outside its own department should not affect in-department inventory. The normal shelf inventory should remain the same at all times because removing merchandise from the regular location can actually hurt sales. This is because the majority of regular customers will continue to look for the product in its "customary" location.

Summary

- The pharmacy's layout design has significant effects on customer buying behavior.
- The most common type of layout arrangement in a pharmacy is the grid layout.
- Grid layouts are less costly and more space-effective than free-flow layout arrangements.
- The main objective in allocating space is to obtain the highest possible sales volume at the lowest possible cost.

- Efficient use of store space can be achieved by eliminating "dead" areas and wasteful practices, departmentalizing merchandise, obtaining maximum merchandise exposure and traffic flow, and by providing customer convenience.
- Space can be allocated by using industry average by type of merchandise or through the sales-per-square-foot method.
- Using the sales-per-square-foot method requires estimating planned sales and expected sales.
- Two primary determinants of space productivity are inventory turnover and merchandise density.
- The location of departments within a store should reflect traffic flow and value of space, merchandise characteristics, merchandise compatibility, and seasonal considerations.
- The arrangement of individual items within departments can be accomplished through planograms.
- Planogramming programs are available from wholesale distributors and independent consultants.
- Merchandising programs should be planned in accordance with the needs of customers and conditions in the marketplace.
- Merchandising is basically visual selling.
- Visual merchandising techniques encourage customers to spend more time in the pharmacy, thereby exposing them to more merchandise items.
- Merchandising products outside their own departments involves the use of point-of-purchase fixtures and displays.
- Displays can create buying excitement and generate extra sales, regardless of whether or not the prices are "specials."
- Merchandise that should be displayed includes new merchandise, in-season merchandise, special events merchandise, popular merchandise, profitable merchandise, promotional merchandise, and merchandise purchased on impulse.
- Merchandising products outside their own department should not affect in-department inventory.

Questions for discussion

1 What physical characteristics of a pharmacy influence its image and customer draw?

2 What psychological effects of a pharmacy layout may influence customer buying behavior?

3 What are the advantages and disadvantages of grid layouts and free-flow layout arrangements?

4 How can high performance of space allocation be achieved?

5 Where can data relating to national average percentages of selling space allotted to individual merchandise lines be obtained?

6 What are the requirements for allocating department space on the basis of sales per square foot?

7 What calculations are required in assessing space utilization by the gross-margin-per-square-foot-of-selling-space method?

8 What factors influence the specific location of departments within a pharmacy?

9 What guidelines should be followed in arranging individual items within departments?

10 Why is the planogram a useful tool for locating items within departments?

11 How can planogramming maximize department sales?

12 What is the underlying objective of visual merchandising?

13 What are some commonly employed visual merchandising aids?

14 What are the characteristics of effective point-of-purchase displays?

15 What factors should be considered when choosing items to display?

Self-test review

True/false statements

1 The layout of a pharmacy should be designed so that customer traffic flow is minimized.

2 The grid layout is typically used in community pharmacies, whereas the free-flow layout is commonly used in chain drugstores.

3 High-performance space allocation results can be achieved through the departmentalization of merchandise.

4 Space management techniques utilized rarely influence the image and atmosphere of a pharmacy.

5 The major disadvantage of using the sales-per-square-foot space allocation method is its complexity.

6 High-ticket items always result in more sales and a higher gross margin than lower priced merchandise.

7 A high percentage of sales can be generated outside a product's own department.

8 Planograms can be used to plan the amount of space allocated to each item within a department.

9 The essence of merchandising is visual selling.

10 When merchandising a product outside its own department, one should reduce the normal shelf inventory.

Multiple choice questions

1 Which of the following is not an advantage of a grid layout?

(A) Simplified security.
(B) Customer familiarity.
(C) Visual appeal and flexibility.
(D) Maximum utilization of floor space.

2 Primary determinants of space productivity include:

(A) Inventory turnover.
(B) Inventory value.
(C) Merchandise density.
(D) A and C.

3 The location of departments within a pharmacy should reflect:

(A) Traffic flow and value of space.
(B) Merchandise characteristics.
(C) Merchandise compatibility.
(D) All of the above.

4 Which of the following types of merchandise should not be selected for display purposes?

(A) New merchandise.
(B) Special events merchandise.
(C) Low-margin merchandise.
(D) Seasonal merchandise.

5 Compared to _____ layouts, _____ layout arrangements are more costly and use space less efficiently

(A) Free-flow, grid.
(B) Merchandise, store.
(C) Store, merchandise.
(D) Grid, free-flow.

References

1. Markin RJ, Lillis CM, Narayana CL. Social psychological significance of store space. *Journal of Retailing*, Spring, 1982: 56.

2. Baldwin HJ. Space management, in *Effective Pharmacy Management*. 3rd edn. Kansas City: Marion Laboratories, 1986: 85.

3. Ghosh G. *Retail Management*, Chicago: Dryden Press, 1990: 473–474, 476.

10

Pricing procedures and credit policies

Learning objectives

The objectives of this chapter are to assist you to be able to explain:

- common pricing objectives for pharmacy management
- fundamentals in cost-oriented and demand-oriented pricing
- pricing front-end merchandise
- prescription pricing and professional fees
- credit practices and ways to reduce bad debts.

Key terms

Cost-plus approach
Marginal cost
Marginal revenue
Markdowns
Markups
Price ceiling
Price elasticity
Target pricing
Target return on investment

One of the most critical and complex decisions a pharmacy owner has to make relates to pricing prescriptions, over-the-counter drugs, and front-end merchandise. Price is a key element in operations because it relates directly to the generation of total revenue and affects the pharmacy's profits. Pricing decisions are complex because many dimensions need to be considered.

Prices affect a pharmacy's profits [(prices × quantities sold) − total costs] which are the lifeblood of long-term survival. Price influences profits in several ways. It influences the quantities sold as well as total cost through its impact on quantities sold. If consumers perceive a price to be too high, they may patronize competing pharmacies, leading to a loss of sales and profits. If prices are too low, sales may increase, but profits may also decline.

The complexity of pricing can be seen in the way consumers perceive a product's price. Relatively high prices may symbolize superior quality and prestige. Relatively low prices, on the other hand, may be perceived as inferior quality by some patrons and as a bargain by others. That is why pricing requires more than technical expertise. It requires creative judgment of who consumers are, why they patronize certain pharmacies, and how they make their buying decisions. It calls for understanding what value consumers place on the benefits they receive by patronizing a particular pharmacy.

Fundamental pricing considerations

There is no ideal set of pricing formulas because many factors have to be considered. Pricing procedures must take into account a pharmacy's mix of prescriptions, goals and objectives, costs, demand characteristics, competition, and legal considerations. A well-designed pricing strategy takes these factors into account and improves profitability without a negative impact on competitive position. The strategy must be unique to the pharmacy.

Because there is no ideal set of pricing formulas, many hours of evaluation and analysis are required to determine the proper pricing strategy for a pharmacy. The traditional pricing formulas used by independent pharmacies are extremely vulnerable to the above-mentioned factors. Indications are that many pharmacies tend to overreact to the competition and often price too competitively.

Recognizing the importance and complexity of pricing, drug wholesalers provide expertise, the tools, and the time to assist pharmacy managers in their pricing programs. The benefit of designing a pricing strategy is its uniqueness to a particular pharmacy and sensitivity to the pharmacy's ongoing needs. In turn, the pharmacy owner will benefit with an enhanced price image, a strengthened competitive position, and most important, increased profit margins.

Pricing objectives

Pricing objectives are goals that describe what the pharmacy wants to achieve through its pricing ef-forts. While such objectives vary from pharmacy to pharmacy, they can be classified into profitability objectives, volume objectives, meeting-the-competition objectives, and image objectives. Because of the many areas involved, pharmacy managers often use multiple pricing objectives. The ultimate objective, of course, is to set prices which will allow the pharmacy to operate profitably.

Profitability objectives

In classic economic theory, the most appropriate pricing objective is to maximize profits. This requires identifying the point at which the addition to total revenue is just balanced by the increase in total cost. The manager needs to determine the marginal cost of selling one additional unit and the net change in total revenue (i.e. the marginal revenue that results from the sale). While this is theoretically sound, in practice it is difficult at best to measure and achieve the balance between marginal revenue and marginal cost. That is why a more practical profitability objective is to achieve a target return on investment.

Target return on investment or target pricing is determined by adding a desired rate of return on investment (or sales) to total cost (i.e. the variable costs and fixed expenses). Most pricing objectives based on rate of return on investment (ROI) are achieved through trial and error because not all cost and revenue data needed to project the ROI are available when prices are set.

Volume objectives

Volume objectives are typically designed to maximize sales or control a portion of the market for a pharmacy. When a pharmacy seeks to maximize sales, the goal is to sell as much as possible within some profit constraints. This is based on the belief that it is wise to expand sales as long as total profits do not drop below a minimum acceptable return.

Rather than seeking to maximize sales, a pharmacy's specific goal may be either to maintain its share of a particular market or to increase its share. One advantage of this approach is that the objective is more clearly defined, and allows the manager to more precisely establish prices that will accomplish the objective.

Meeting-the-competition objectives

Some pharmacy managers are more concerned with meeting competitors' prices than with profitability or volume objectives. The result of this objective is to nullify price as a marketing variable and to focus instead on non-price competition.

It is true that setting prices on the basis of what competitors charge is much less difficult than profitability and volume objectives. However, because every pharmacy has different fixed and variable costs, meeting competitors' prices should be made judiciously on a product-by-product basis. Community pharmacies, for example, would find it ruinous in the long run if they tried to match the prices of chain pharmacies.

Image objectives

Image objectives are unrelated to either profitability or sales volume objectives. Instead, they involve setting prices to develop or maintain a particular positioning strategy for the pharmacy.

Positioning is the customer's perception of the pharmacy and prices are often the single most important factor influencing how the pharmacy is actually positioned. Low markup prices suggest a discount-oriented pharmacy with little or no patient–pharmacist contact. Pharmacies featuring traditional or above-market prices tend to suggest more professionalism.

Pricing methods

There are numerous ways to set prices for both prescription and non-prescription products. These are described below. Importantly, there is no one right way to price products. However, consideration needs to be given to costs, consumer sensitivity to price, and the competition.

Cost-oriented pricing

Cost-oriented pricing is the most common method for setting prices because it is simple and easy to apply. In its simplest form, the cost-plus approach means that the selling price for an item is equal to the cost plus a desired profit. Costs provide a floor below which prices cannot go in the long run, while profits provide the necessary return on investment.

Using cost-oriented pricing methods requires understanding the various costs the pharmacy incurs.

This is not as simple as it might appear, however, because several types of costs may have to be considered. Furthermore, as the volume of output or purchases changes, not all costs behave the same. The following costs may need to be determined when prices are based on cost: total cost, total fixed costs, total variable costs, average total costs, average fixed costs, average variable costs, and marginal costs. The variable costs are the actual costs of procuring and selling a product (e.g. drug items or front-end merchandise). These costs vary directly with sales levels. They include inventory costs, labor, and other expenses that can be directly attributed to the particular item.

Fixed costs are those expenses that do not vary with the number of units sold, and will be incurred whether anything is sold or not. Depreciation on buildings and equipment, utilities, insurance, administrative salaries, and other expenses are part of the pharmacy's fixed costs.

While cost-oriented approaches have the advantage of simplicity, they can be criticized for two basic reasons. First, they give little or no consideration to demand factors. Second, they fail to reflect competition adequately.

Demand-oriented pricing

Even if a pharmacy manager determines prices solely on cost, consumer demand cannot be ignored. Prices based solely on cost may be seriously limiting because consumers may not be willing or able to pay the price demanded. Or consumers may be both willing and able to pay more than the price being asked.

Fundamental to demand-oriented pricing is an understanding of the concept of price elasticity. Price elasticity of demand is a measure of consumers' price sensitivity. It is formally defined as the percentage change in quantity demanded relative to a given percentage change in price.

Elasticity of demand is influenced by many factors. If a product or service has close substitutes, demand for it is said to be elastic. This means that a cut in price increases the quantity sold enough that total revenue is increased. Demand is inelastic when a cut in price yields such a small increase in quantity sold that total revenue decreases.

Estimating elasticity of demand for a product or service is difficult at best. Some of the factors that need to be considered are availability of substitutes, urgency of need, and customer satisfaction derived from the product. Indeed, the price a consumer is willing to pay may be largely a function of the perceived quality of the item.

Price ceiling

Determining the price ceiling is usually difficult. Economic, market, competitive, customer, and other factors will influence it. Two approaches can be used to determine price ceiling: hit-or-miss and market research.

The *hit-or-miss* approach is essentially a gamble that consumers will accept the price set initially. One principle should always be kept in mind when using this approach: It is easier to lower prices than to raise them. Lowering the price from a high margin is much more acceptable to consumers than finding that the price was too low and having to raise the price.

The *market research* approach offers the benefit of not having to risk finding out whether consumers will accept the item. But usually this requires the use of outside experts and this can be costly. The principle to remember is that most items are bought on the basis of perceived value in the minds of the buyer and not on the basis of what it costs the pharmacy.

Competitor-oriented pricing

Regardless of the pricing method used, a pharmacy cannot ignore prices charged by competitors, nor how competitors will react to price changes initiated by others. If competitors offer quantity discounts, for example, and are successful in inducing consumers to purchase in larger quantities, other pharmacies may be forced to follow suit. Similarly, competition may influence what pharmacies have to offer with respect to price specials or discounts (e.g. senior citizen discounts).

Competitor-oriented pricing must consider such factors as:

- location of competitors
- size of competitors
- services provided by competitors
- type of products sold by competitors
- cost structure of competitors
- historical reaction of competitors to price changes.

These factors help determine whether a pharmacy's selling prices should be at the same level as

those of competitors ("going rate pricing"), below competition, or above competition. A price below (or above) competition may be justified due to lower fixed or variable costs, and the pharmacy's image in the community.

In these times of discount selling, community pharmacies and small, independent drugstore chains are unable to meet the prices of deep-discount drugstore operations. Powerful operators of deep-discount chains such as Walmart Stores depend on selling massive volumes of merchandise at cut rates. Unlike most pharmacies and drugstores, these discounters specialize in getting great deals on certain merchandise, which they turn around and offer to customers at super low prices. They provide customers with dazzling deals on pharmaceuticals, health and beauty aids, non-perishable groceries, and household items. Under these conditions, community pharmacies and small, independent drugstore chains should compete on a non-price basis (i.e. offer personalized service).

Legal considerations

Generally speaking, a pharmacy can charge whatever it wants to charge—even "outrageously high" prices—but there are some legal restrictions. For example, antitrust legislation prohibits price fixing. This occurs when competitors get together and agree on what prices to charge.

The temptation to fix prices by collusion is at times almost irresistible, especially when rising costs put a squeeze on profits. Although community pharmacies may not feel as threatened by government action against price fixing as chain pharmacies, they can also be targets of investigation. Firms convicted of price fixing face stiff monetary penalties and the persons responsible may get jail terms.

Prescription drug pricing

Prescription drug pricing is of concern not only to a pharmacy but also to the public. It is of concern to a pharmacy because prescription department sales have expanded steadily over the past two decades. The public concern with prescription drug prices is based on the relationship between trusting the pharmacist as a professional person to provide the necessary advice and the correct drug, and trusting him or her to charge a reasonable price. If there is lack of trust with respect to price, the pharmacist will lose the professional trust, and vice versa. It is important, therefore, to use a dispensing fee that is both competitive and defensible.

In reality, many prescription drug prices are set by managed care programs, and the pharmacy has little choice but to accept the reimbursement rates set by the public and private insurers or not fill those prescriptions. However, because they comprise such a high percentage of total prescription volume, averaging somewhere around 90 percent of all prescriptions, discretion over pricing is limited to the approximately 10 percent of cash sales.[1]

To develop a customized pricing strategy for cash prescription sales, therefore, the pharmacy manager needs to determine which drugs will comprise the "hot" list of highest volume drugs primarily in terms of number of scripts and total dollars which are marked up less because of patients' sensitivity to price (10–12 items), the competitive list (about 35–45 items), the in-between list, the non-competitive list and the generic list.

After rating each drug, selling prices can be chosen at various cost break-even points depending upon the quantity to be sold. By checking the prices of local competitors, and reviewing the pharmacy's price strategy, a selling price can be determined using one of the pricing methods described earlier in this chapter.

Professional fees

The cost of dispensing prescriptions has to be included in the price of prescription drugs. In other words, the pharmacy manager has to determine what charge to levy for professional services. In general, the amount of the professional fee is based on the premise that flat fees are more appropriate than fees based on the amount of time spent with individual patients.

In its simplest form, a professional fee policy establishes the use of a single charge that is added to the cost of an item to determine the price. In theory, the fee would include all of the costs incurred in providing prescription services. Low-cost items, therefore, will yield a greater profit margin than high-cost items, but the dollar return is the same for every item.

The basis of fee computation must consider three factors: (1) the cost of the ingredient and the container; (2) the cost incurred in dispensing the prescription; and (3) the profit necessary to sustain the practice. The major problem in considering these factors is determining the cost of dispensing.

The cost of dispensing should be determined by conducting a departmental cost analysis which assigns direct costs and allocates indirect costs through the use of formulas or ratios. For example, RE Abrams suggested the following formula:

$$\frac{(AE - PS)\left(\frac{RS}{TS}\right) + PS}{TR} + NP = PF$$

where AE is all expenses, PS is proprietor's salary, RS is prescription sales, TS is total sales, TR is total number of prescriptions dispensed, NP is desired net profit, and PF is professional fee.

While there are several such formulas or "cost-of-dispensing models" available, none is a panacea for prescription pricing.

Pricing front-end merchandise

Pharmacy managers frequently use the following approaches to setting prices on merchandise:

- using prices suggested or required by vendors or franchisers
- meeting competitors' prices, regardless of cost or profit factors
- recognizing and using prices that consumers expect to pay for certain merchandise
- applying a traditional percentage markup to the cost
- generating cost, expense, and profit data and then applying them pro rata to units on a break-even basis
- using the contribution margin, which covers the cost of goods plus variable expenses, as a minimum price.

All of these approaches are cost-oriented (i.e. they use a pricing policy that is based on markup or markdown). It is essential, therefore, for the pharmacy manager to understand the nature of markups and markdowns and how they are determined.

Markup calculations

A markup is an addition to the cost of a product to reach a selling price. For example, if a pharmacy buys a drug for $5 and sells it for $10, the markup is $5.

Markups are usually expressed as percentages. Although many pharmacy owners consider markup a percentage of the selling price, retailing authorities point out that figuring markup on the cost price is easier and less confusing in everyday pricing. The important thing to remember is that when markup is figured on the selling price, a different markup percentage must be used than when figuring the markup on the cost price. Otherwise the anticipated margin will not be attained.

Markup on price is the difference between the cost of goods and the selling price, expressed as a percentage of the selling price. An example is:

$$\frac{\text{Selling price} - \text{cost}}{\text{Selling price}} = \frac{\$10 - \$5}{\$10}$$
$$= 50\% \text{ markup on selling price}$$

Markup on selling price, or margin, corresponds to the gross profit figure on a profit-and-loss statement. It is the margin available to cover the costs of selling and to provide a profit.

Markup on cost is also the difference between the cost of goods and the selling price but is expressed as a percentage of cost. An example is:

$$\frac{\text{Selling price} - \text{cost}}{\text{Cost}} = \frac{\$10 - \$5}{\$5}$$
$$= 100\% \text{ markup on cost}$$

In dollar terms, margin and markup figures are the same, but when put in terms of percentage the figures are different. Some pharmacies fail to make an expected profit because the owner or manager makes the wrong assumption that the percentages of margin and markup on cost are the same.

Easy conversion of margin to markup percentages can be made by using conversion tables as shortcuts. Table 10.1 represents a typical comparison of margins and markups. Thus, to achieve a profit margin of 25 percent on an item, the cost markup is 33.3 percent. To achieve a profit margin of 33.3 percent on an item, the cost markup would have to be 50 percent.

To use this table, find the margin or gross profit percentage in the left-hand column. Multiply the cost of the item by the corresponding percentage in the right-hand, or markup, column. The result added to the cost gives the correct selling price.

Markdown calculations

Markdowns are reductions in the original price set on a product. For example, if a pharmacy sells some aspirin for $2.49 instead of $2.99, the markdown percentage is figured as follows:

Markdown percentage
= markdown/net sales price
= $0.50/$2.49 = 20.1%

The markdown percentage is calculated on the basis of the new selling price, not the original asking price. Markdowns are necessary when customers do not buy at the initial offering prices. They are commonly applied to seasonal, dated, and overstocked merchandise.

Credit policies

Buying goods and services on credit has become an accepted part of everyday living in the USA. "Buy now, pay later" allows consumers to buy what they want when they want it and to pay for it from future earnings. This widespread availability and use of retail credit in the nation's economic system helps maintain a balance between production, distribution, and consumption of goods and services. In short, credit sales are an indispensable part of business today. Few, if any, pharmacies sell on a cash-only basis.

Credit is indispensable not only for pharmacies but also for almost every other business. But the common offering of credit poses several problems. One must decide (1) whether to offer credit, (2) what type of credit to offer, and (3) how to reduce bad debts. Like any powerful marketing tool, credit must be managed.

Types of retail credit

Retail credit can be offered in various forms, including 30-day charge accounts and bank credit cards.

Through the *30-day charge accounts* or ordinary open account, customers usually arrange for credit service on a short-term basis of 30 days. Customers with this type of account can charge merchandise in almost any amount. This type of credit requires that payment be made in full within 30 days after the billing date. The customer generally does not pay any

Table 10.1 Markup table

Margin percent of selling price	Markup percent of cost	Margin percent of selling price	Markup percent of cost
4.8	5.0	25.0	33.3
5.0	5.3	26.0	35.0
6.0	6.4	27.0	37.0
7.0	7.5	27.3	37.5
8.0	8.7	28.0	39.0
9.0	10.0	28.5	40.0
10.0	11.1	29.0	40.9
10.7	12.0	30.0	42.9
11.0	12.4	31.0	45.0
11.1	12.5	32.0	47.1
12.0	13.6	33.3	50.0
12.5	14.3	34.0	51.5
13.0	15.0	35.0	53.9
14.0	16.3	35.5	55.0
15.0	17.7	36.0	56.3
16.0	19.1	37.0	58.8
16.7	20.0	37.5	60.0
17.0	20.5	38.0	61.3
17.5	21.2	39.0	64.0
18.0	22.0	39.5	65.5
18.5	22.7	40.0	66.7
19.0	23.5	41.0	70.0
20.0	25.0	42.0	72.4
21.0	26.6	42.8	75.0
22.0	28.2	44.4	80.0
22.5	29.0	46.1	85.0
23.0	29.9	47.5	90.0
23.1	30.0	48.7	95.0
24.0	31.6	50.0	100.0

This table shows what the markup on cost must be to give the desired margin of selling price.

interest for this credit privilege. When payment is not made on time, a small penalty is often charged.

Under the *revolving credit account*, a customer agrees to pay a fixed amount in equal monthly payments. Unlike the open account in which there is usually no interest payment, the revolving credit account involves an interest charge levied against the unpaid balance. If the customer pays off the entire balance at the end of the billing period, no interest charge is made.

Bank credit cards have had a dramatic effect on the various categories of consumer credit. Visa, MasterCard, Discover, and American Express are four universally known and accepted credit card programs. Today these cards are even accepted in some grocery stores and fast-food outlets. Customers are allowed to charge goods and services at any participating firm up to a predetermined ceiling. Purchases are then billed through the local bank or through the issuer of the credit card.

The popularity of bank credit cards is widespread among pharmacies. In return for paying a percentage of charged sales (usually 2–6 percent) to the bank or issuing agency, participating pharmacies receive immediate repayment and are relieved of credit investigation, billing, bookkeeping, and collection. Because it is seldom practical to open store charge accounts when the average sales ticket runs from about $10 to $20, credit card sales are commonly the only type of credit extended.

Extending credit

In the past, it was rare to find community pharmacies that did not extend credit. However, with the expanding role of credit cards, most community pharmacies do not offer private credit to customers. A pharmacy owner's decision to extend credit depends on a number of factors. The decision is often based on what competitors are doing. For some independent community pharmacies, it may be necessary to have a private credit program to attract and retain customers.

Providing retail credit requires considerably more cash than is necessary in a cash-and-carry business. The cost of merchandise, not to mention the profit, is not returned to the credit retailer for the term of the credit, and that means that the pharmacy must finance customer purchases and assume the risk of non-payment.

The extension of credit has disadvantages, especially if the customer fails to repay on time or in full. When collections begin to fall off on accounts receivable, capital reserves must be drawn on in order to continue in business. Attempts to recover unpaid accounts through professional collectors may help, if made in time. Unfortunately, as the accounts receivable age, chances for collection decline rapidly. Because of these disadvantages, credit experts often advise that small retailers should not extend credit except through bank credit cards.

It is common practice to write off a percentage of sales to bad debts. In most businesses, the write-off or charge-off rate runs from 0.5 percent on low-profit transactions to 5.0 percent on high-profit sales and services. But a business does not have to accept excessive losses as part of doing business. When the charge-off rate exceeds 5 percent, it is not only possible but also necessary to find ways to improve controls over bad debt losses.

A clear understanding of payment terms is the most neglected requirement when extending credit. Then, assuming there is regular billing, most credit users will pay as agreed. A certain number will pay after a mild reminder. Some will have had changed circumstances, such as unexpected illness or loss of a job. But after a regular follow-up, they will voluntarily give good reason for non-payment, promise future payment, and then fulfill their promise.

Because risk is a part of the extension of credit, there will be unpaid accounts even when collection procedures have been followed. A certain percentage of these bad debts can be recovered, and it is important to identify this type of account. There is more to identifying potential bad debts than merely considering the age of the account.

Potential bad debts should be identified early so that they can be kept to a minimum and have the best chance of recovery. Action at this point in the credit collection process is important. It may mean the difference between recovery or loss. Normally, the more time debtors get, the less they pay.

Summary

- Price is a key element in operations because it relates directly to the generation of total revenue and affects the pharmacy's profits.
- Numerous factors have to be considered in pricing, including the mix of prescriptions, goals and objectives, costs, demand, competition, and legal considerations.
- Pricing objectives can be classified into profitability, volume, meeting-the-competition, and image objectives.
- Profitability objectives include maximization of profits and target return on investment.
- Cost-oriented pricing is the most commonly used method for setting prices.
- Demand-oriented pricing requires an understanding of price elasticity.
- Competitor-oriented pricing cannot be ignored by any pharmacy.
- Antitrust legislation prohibits price fixing.
- The impact of third-party plans has caused independent pharmacies to alter their way of doing business.
- Pricing front-end merchandise is usually based on a cost-plus approach.

- Markup is an addition to the cost of a product to reach a selling price. It can be computed as a percentage of sales or cost.
- Markdowns are reductions in the original price set on a product.
- Prescription pricing has to consider the relationship between trusting the pharmacist as a professional person and trusting him or her to charge a reasonable price.
- A method of setting prices for prescription drugs is based on dispensing frequency.
- Many prescription drug prices are set by managed care programs.
- A professional fee policy established the use of a single charge that is added to the cost of an item.
- Several formulas or "cost-of-dispensing models" are available, although none is a panacea for prescription pricing.
- Credit sales are not as important today as they were in the past due to the increased use of credit cards.
- Retail credit may take several forms, including 30-day charge accounts and bank credit cards.
- The extension of credit often depends on competitors, but the most important factor is that some consumers demand and expect it.
- By providing credit, a pharmacy needs more cash and runs the risk of late payments and lack of full payment.
- Firms often write off a percentage of sales to bad debts.
- It is important to identify bad debts early and to act quickly to minimize these losses.

Questions for discussion

1 Why is pricing one of the most critical and complex decisions a pharmacy manager has to make?
2 What are four basic pricing objectives?
3 What is the difference between profit maximization and target return on investment pricing?
4 What factors need to be considered in using a cost-plus pricing approach?
5 What is the meaning of price elasticity and how can it be estimated?

6 Why is competitor-oriented pricing important to every pharmacy?
7 What factors should be considered in competitor-oriented pricing?
8 How are markups and markdowns calculated?
9 Why is prescription pricing of concern to both pharmacy managers and the public?
10 What does a professional fee policy establish?
11 What factors must be considered in fee computation?
12 Why are credit sales an indispensable part of business today?
13 What are the most important requirements when extending credit?
14 What steps should be taken after the first sign of delinquency?
15 When should a manager look for help in collecting bad debts?

Self-test review

True/false statements

1 Pharmacy managers typically use a single pricing objective.
2 Most pricing methods are versions of the cost-plus approach.
3 Price elasticity of demand is a measure of competitors' price sensitivity.
4 Markup on cost is the difference between the cost of goods and the selling price expressed as a percentage of the selling price.
5 Prescription drug pricing is of concern only to a pharmacy manager.
6 A professional fee policy establishes the use of a single charge that is added to the cost of an item to determine price.
7 There is no one best "cost-of-dispensing model" that fits the needs of every pharmacy.
8 The primary reason for extending credit is because competitors offer it.
9 A clear understanding of payment terms is the most neglected requirement when extending credit.
10 Using a professional collector is the only hope of obtaining payment from a delinquent debtor.

Multiple choice questions

1 Which of the following must be considered in making price decisions?

(A) Cost.

(B) Customer demand.

(C) Prices of competitors.

(D) All of the above.

2 Target pricing is consistent with:

(A) Volume objectives.

(B) Profitability objectives.

(C) Competition objectives.

(D) None of the above.

3 If an item costs $10 and sells for $15, the markup on cost is:

(A) 33.3 percent.

(B) 50 percent.

(C) 100 percent.

(D) None of the above.

4 Which of the following is the most important reason for offering credit?

(A) Competitors are offering credit.

(B) The type of transaction requires credit.

(C) Some customers demand and expect it.

(D) To increase profits.

5 To help reduce bad debts, the pharmacy manager should:

(A) Follow up on non-payment as soon as it occurs.

(B) Send debts to a collection agency as soon as they are past due.

(C) Just absorb the loss as part of the cost of doing business.

(D) Stop selling to the customer as soon as the credit is past due.

References

1. National Association of Drug Stores (NACDS) Foundation. *The Chain Pharmacy Economic Profile*, NACDS Foundation, 2007: 75.

11

Promotion and personal selling

Learning objectives

The objectives of this chapter are to assist you to be able to explain:

- what is involved in creating an advertising campaign
- major methods used in deciding the size of the advertising budget
- how to measure advertising results
- the nature and objectives of sales promotion
- what is involved in creative personal selling.

Key terms

Advertising
Affordable method
Competitive-parity method
Cooperative advertising
Cost-per-thousand (CPM)
Frequency
Objective-and-task method
Percentage-of-sales method
Personal selling
Promotion
Reach
Sales promotion

The importance of promotion and personal selling in pharmacy management must be understood if the pharmacy manager expects to succeed financially. In today's ongoing battle for the consumer's attention, no pharmacy can rely on word-of-mouth communication alone (i.e. the process by which people express their opinions and pharmacy-related experiences to one another). Without sustained positive word-of-mouth communication, it is difficult at best for a company to succeed.

Promotion is any form of communication used to inform, persuade, and remind people about a pharmacy's goods, services, image, ideas, community involvement, or impact on society. The three most

His city's newspaper is published evenings and Sunday

1. Set a sales goal

Department	Sales Goal	% of Goal
....	$ ______	______ %
....	$ ______	______ %
....	$ ______	______ %
....	$ ______	______ %
....	$ ______	______ %
....	$ ______	______ %
....	$ ______	______ %
....	$ ______	______ %
....	$ ______	______ %
Totals	$ ______	______ %

2. Decide how much advertising

______________________ % of sales
______________________ dollars
______________________ rate
______________________ linage

3. Decide what to promote

Write in percent of month's sales which each department contributes. Allot percent of month's advertising on an equivalent basis. Calculate the linage for each department.

Department	% of Sales	% of Adver tising	Linage
....	______	______	______
....	______	______	______
....	______	______	______
....	______	______	______
....	______	______	______
....	______	______	______
....	______	______	______
....	______	______	______
....	______	______	______
Total	100%	100%	______

4. Fill in this day-by-day schedule

Sunday	Monday	Tuesday	Wednesday	Thursday	Friday	Saturday
1	2	3	4	5	6	7
8	9	10	11	12	13	14
15	16	17	18	19	20	21
22	23	24	25	26	27	28
29	30	31				

Figure 11.2 Sample worksheet representing one retailer's approach to scheduling. From Gaedeke RM and Tootelian DH. *Small Business Management*, 3rd edn. Boston: Allyn and Bacon, 1991: 418. Used with permission.

weekend, or next week.[3] An example of such decision-triggering advertising is an ad that promotes regularly priced merchandise with immediate appeal. Other examples are ads that use price appeals in combination with clearance sales, special purchases, seasonal items, and "family of items" purchases.

Such advertising should be checked for results daily or at the end of one week from appearance. Because all advertising has some carryover effect, it is a good idea to check also at the end of two weeks from advertising runs, three weeks from runs, and so on to ensure that no opportunity for using profit-making messages is lost. In weighing the results of immediate response advertisements, the following devices are useful:

- *Count coupons brought in*: Usually redeemed coupons represent sales of the product. When the coupons represent requests for additional information or contact with a pharmacist, were enough leads obtained to pay for the ad? If the coupon is dated—and it should be—the number of returns for the first, second, and third weeks can be determined.

- *Requests by phone or letter referring to the ad*: A "hidden offer" can cause people to call or write (e.g. inclusion in the middle of the ad of a statement that on request the product or additional information will be supplied). Results should be checked over a one-week through 6- to 12-month period because this type of ad may have considerable carryover effect.

- *Testing ads*: Prepare two different ads and run them on the same day. Identify the ads, in the message or with a coded coupon, so it can be determined which is more effective. Ask customers to bring in the coupon or to use a special phrase. Run two broadcast ads at different times or on different stations on the same day with different "discount phrases." Ask a newspaper to give a "split run" (i.e. print ad A in part of its press run and ad B in the rest of the run). Count the responses to each ad.

- *Sales made of particular items*: If the ad is on a bargain or limited-time offer, consider that sales at the end of one week, two weeks, three weeks, and four weeks came from the ad. It may be desirable to determine how many sales came from in-store displays and personal selling.

Testing image advertising

Image advertising is advertising used to keep a pharmacy's name and merchandise before the target market.[3] Some people think of this type as image-building advertising. With it, people are reminded week after week about regular merchandise or services or told about new or special services or policies. Such advertising should create in the minds of customers the image a pharmacy wants them to have about the pharmacy, its merchandise, its service, and its policies.

To some degree, all advertising should be image advertising. It is a reputation-builder for the business.

Image advertising is more difficult to measure than immediate response advertising because a specific sale cannot always be attributed to it. Sales are usually created long after the ad has appeared. For example, an ad or a series of ads that announces the exclusive franchise for a particular brand start to pay off when customers who want that brand only and ask no questions about competing brands begin to come in.

Because image advertising is spread out over an extended period of time, measurement of results is difficult and not very accurate. Some image advertising, such as a series of ads about the brands the store carries, can be measured at the end of one month from the appearance of the ads or at the end of the campaign.

One approach is to make comparisons on a weekly basis. If an ad is run each week, for example, at the end of the first week after the ad appears or is broadcast, one should compare that week's sales with sales for the same week a year ago. At the end of the second week, one should compare sales with those at the end of the first week as well as with the figures for a year ago.

At the end of the third week, 1 month, 3 months, 6 months, and 12 months from the running of the ad, one should repeat the process even though additional ads may have appeared or been aired in the meantime. For each of these ads, one should make the same type of comparison. The momentum of all of the ads, as well as the results of a single ad, will thus be measured.

Sales promotion

Sales promotion has become a popular promotional tool for pharmacies. As stated earlier in this chapter, sales promotion is designed to provide an incentive to the target market. The range of sales promotion methods is large—coupons, free product samples, cents-off promotions, premiums, sweepstakes, in-store demonstrations, point-of-purchase displays, frequent purchase programs, and many others.

There are several reasons underlying the increased spending for sales promotion. Primarily, however, it is because results can easily be measured and they accomplish specific objectives.

Objectives of sales promotion

Sales promotion objectives are commonly intended to increase short-term sales or help build long-term market share. The objective may be to entice consumers to try a new product or service, lure customers away from competing pharmacies, get customers to load up on products, stimulate product usage, or hold and reward loyal customers.

up the sale to make certain that the services promised were fulfilled. The follow-up fosters repeat business and can provide leads to new prospects.

Attributes of a creative salesperson in community and inpatient settings

In addition to having personnel who understand and apply the creative selling process, a pharmacy should try to have salespeople who possess the attributes that make them more effective in their jobs. These attributes, which can be grouped into mental and physical categories, merit further discussion.

It is important to note that in building relations with physicians, and in building relationships in hospital settings, the pharmacist should always be the person doing the "selling." This role cannot be assigned to technicians or pharmacy clerks because the level of trust will nearly always be between the pharmacist and these audiences.

Judgment

Common sense, maturity, intelligence—these and other terms are used interchangeably with judgment. A salesperson knows that it does not pay to argue with a customer. The salesperson also knows that the firm should never be "cut" in front of the customers. These situations reflect the use of good judgment on the part of the employee. Please note that the term maturity is sometimes used in place of judgment but that it is not necessarily a function of age. Many older people do not use good judgment while some young employees will have a high level of common sense.

Tact

If an employee has a keen sense of what to say and do, many problems can be overcome before they are created. Many employees give little thought to the effect of their actions. A child playing with toys in a pharmacy is told bluntly to "quit playing with the toys and go find your mother," while the mother is standing behind the salesperson. Was a confrontation with the child necessary? No. Could it have been handled differently? Yes. How do child and mother feel about the pharmacy? The feeling is not good. This salesperson lacked the ability to know what to do and say in order to maintain good customer relations. Be tactful.

Attitude

A good salesperson will have a positive attitude toward customers, merchandise, services, and the pharmacy. A good attitude means that an employee is willing to accept suggestions, to learn and apply the steps in the creative selling process, and not be afraid of work. A salesperson with a bad attitude can create unnecessary problems. A bad attitude is contagious. If an employee is otherwise competent, the manager should work with this employee to develop a positive attitude. Positive attitudes can result in sales.

Improving personal selling in community settings

Developing a program for improving creative selling skills in non-pharmacist salespeople is the essence of building an effective personal selling effort. A framework for such a program should consist of the following basic elements:

- selecting people who are suitable for particular sales positions
- providing regular and frequent training
- devising an appropriate compensation plan.

If a pharmacy is willing to develop a program based on these three elements, a more effective and rewarding selling program should emerge.

Selection

Finding good salespeople is a problem for most pharmacies. There is little disagreement over how hard it is to find good people, especially today in light of the shrinking labor pool. What too many pharmacy managers fail to realize is that much of the problem is of their own making because they do not define clearly what they mean by a "good" salesperson. They do not specify what qualities they want in the salesperson they are seeking. It is no wonder, then, that they are not satisfied with many of the people they hire.

An effective way to help avoid this problem is to use job specifications. This device has been used successfully for many years by large firms, and it can be used with equal effectiveness by small firms. A job specification is basically a written statement, typically no longer than one or two paragraphs, delineating the requirements for a particular job. The value of writing a job specification is that it forces the pharmacy to be more explicit about what the job requires and thereby provides a guide for appraising the abilities of prospective employees. Many salespeople can do an excellent selling job on low-unit-value merchandise but have trouble closing sales on the big-ticket items. Job specifications help avoid such problems.

Training

When the word "training" is mentioned, too many managers typically associate it with the formalized programs conducted by chain pharmacies. However, sales training by a neighborhood pharmacy does not have to be a formal and structured program. Any conscious effort the owner–manager makes aimed at improving the basic skills needed for effective selling is a form of sales training.

Compensation

There is no one best way of compensating salespeople. Compensation plans depend on the type of product sold, the position of the salesperson (training or post-training), and common practices in the industry. There is, however, a general principle that should be observed in any type of compensation plan: compensation should be closely linked to performance.

The key to gaining a real understanding of the principle and being able to apply it to a compensation plan is in how performance is defined. Performance does not necessarily mean simply sales volume. While the importance of sales volume cannot be overemphasized, other factors, such as providing information to customers, creating goodwill for the pharmacy through friendly and courteous service, and a willingness to help out with non-selling tasks, are also important and should be rewarded. Failure to recognize these other aspects of performance is a mistake too many managers make. They tend to reward salespeople who make the most sales and neglect others who have acceptable sales volumes but do a better job in the other aspects of performance. Of course, if a salesperson does well in non-selling work and not in sales, this weakness must be dealt with through increased sales training.

Thus, if salespeople are doing a good job regardless of the volume they produce, they should be praised. For example, a retailer developed an ingenious approach using repeat business as a reflection of customer goodwill. This retailer developed an increasing schedule of commissions for sales to the same customer. This encouraged salespeople to treat customers right so that they would come back and ask for them by name.

Summary

- The three most widely used methods of promotion are advertising, sales promotion, and personal selling.
- There is no magic formula for successful advertising.
- Success in advertising involves critical planning, implementation, and evaluation of programs. Through analyzing the advertising target's needs, specific advertising objectives can be developed, and from these objectives a determination of the appropriate budget should be made.
- Advertising budgets are commonly decided through the use of the percentage-of-sales, competitive-parity, objective-and-task, and affordable methods.
- Advertising effectiveness involves not only the budget but also the message—when, where, and how it is communicated.
- The best advertising medium is limited by the type of message to be transmitted and, most important, by the target market—the audience—to be reached.
- Timing of advertising involves adjusting plans over seasons, months, weeks, and even days.
- Cooperative advertising is a sharing of advertising costs by retailers and manufacturers.
- Measuring advertising effectiveness is not easily accomplished because all the elements of the marketing mix affect sales, not just advertising. Measurements by advertising agencies involve pretests and posttests.
- Immediate response advertising can be determined by measuring the number of coupons returned, the number of requests made, the test results of two different ads run on the same day, the sales of advertised products, or store traffic generated by an ad.
- Measuring image advertising results requires making comparisons over regular time intervals, such as on a weekly basis.
- Advertising regulations exist at the federal, state, and local level.

- Sales promotion tools are used to increase short-term sales or to help build long-term market share.
- Personal selling holds certain advantages for the small firm. It is easier and less costly for a neighborhood pharmacy to compete on the basis of a strong personal sales program than on the basis of front-end merchandise assortments, advertising, or price.
- The personal selling process consists of the following steps: prospecting, the pre-approach, the approach, the sales presentation, overcoming objections, closing the sale, and post-sale follow-up.
- Effective personal selling involves knowing everything there is to know about the product or service and being able to convince customers that the product or service fulfills their needs.
- Attributes of a creative salesperson include judgment, tact, attitude, and physical characteristics.
- A program for developing good salespeople should consist of selecting people suitable for the particular sales program, providing regular and frequent training, and devising an appropriate compensation plan.

Questions for discussion

1 The three most widely used methods of promotion are advertising, sales promotion, and personal selling. What is the meaning of each of these promotion tools?

2 Why is there no magic formula for successful advertising?

3 In creating an advertising program, what areas should be evaluated?

4 Why is it important to state advertising objectives clearly and in measurable terms?

5 What are the four methods that can be used in determining advertising budgets and what are the weaknesses of each?

6 Where can an advertiser get help in preparing advertising messages and meeting copy requirements?

7 How do "reach" and "frequency" influence advertising media selection?

8 What are two types of cooperative advertising available to pharmacies?

9 Why is advertising effectiveness difficult to measure?

10 What is image advertising and how can it be measured?

11 How can a neighborhood pharmacy gain a competitive edge by emphasizing the role of personal selling and developing a good personal sales program?

12 What are the steps in the selling process?

13 What are the attributes of a creative salesperson?

14 Under what conditions are the physical attributes of a salesperson important?

15 What are the three basic elements for improving personal selling?

Self-test review

True/false statements

1 A pharmacy benefiting from positive word-of-mouth communication does not have to advertise.

2 The first step in developing an advertising campaign is to identify the advertising target.

3 The most defensible method used in setting the advertising budget is the affordable method.

4 Advertising expenditures should be viewed as a necessary part of the marketing strategy.

5 The cost-per-thousand (CPM) formula can be used to compare prices for media time and space.

6 Cooperative advertising is a program in which advertising costs are shared between manufacturers and the media.

7 Testing image advertising effectiveness is less difficult than testing immediate response advertising effectiveness.

8 A primary reason for the increased emphasis on sales promotion is because the results are easily measured.

9 Emphasis on personal selling by chain pharmacies has closed the gap that neighborhood pharmacies used to fill.

10 A skilled salesperson welcomes objections because they provide feedback about where additional sales emphasis is needed.

Multiple choice questions

1 Which of the following should be the first step in developing an effective advertising campaign?

(A) Establishing the budget.

(B) Choosing the media.

(C) Choosing the message

(D) None of the above.

2 Which of the following advertising budget methods treat advertising as a "luxury?"

(A) Competitive-parity method.

(B) Percentage-of-sales method.

(C) Affordable method.

(D) Objective-and-task method.

3 Which of the following is the most important consideration in selecting the advertising medium?

(A) The advertising objective.

(B) Requirements of the message.

(C) Cost of the medium.

(D) Customers' media habits.

4 Which of the following attributes is the most important for a creative salesperson?

(A) Judgment.

(B) Taste.

(C) Attitude.

(D) None of the above.

5 The sales process can be broken down into the following stages: (1) prospecting, (2) the approach, (3) handling objections, (4) the sales presentation, (5) the preapproach, (6) closing the sale, and (7) postsale follow-up. Which of the following is the order in which these stages should be carried out?

(A) (1), (5), (2), (6), (4), (3), (7).

(B) (1), (4), (5), (3), (2), (6), (7).

(C) (1), (5), (4), (2), (3), (7), (6).

(D) (1), (5), (2), (4), (3), (6), (7).

References

1. Leo Troy. *Almanac of Business and Industrial Financial Ratios*, 2011 edn. Chicago, IL: CCH Group, 2011.
2. What you provide in your drugstore is your last ad. *Drug Topics*, Oct 8, 1990: 19.
3. Small Business Administration. *Do You Know the Results of Your Advertising*? Management Aid No. 4.0202. Washington, DC: Small Business Administration, 1982: 2–4.

Cases for Part IV*

Short cases

Case IV.1 Gold Country Community Hospital inpatient pharmacy

Ginny Bradford, director of pharmacy at Gold Country Community Hospital, was in the process of developing a marketing plan for the hospital's inpatient pharmacy. One of Ms. Bradford's top priorities for the next year was to increase the stature of the pharmacy within the healthcare delivery system.

In particular, Ms. Bradford wanted to have her staff pharmacists more involved in patient care. She felt that by being more involved, the pharmacy would have greater opportunities to make a contribution—and a better chance to obtain a reasonable share of the hospital's limited budget.

Gold Country Community Hospital was a 250-bed acute care hospital located in a medium-sized Midwestern city. While the hospital had been well-established in its particular market area, competition had increased dramatically. Several other hospitals in the city had opened urgent care centers and outpatient surgery centers nearby, and a major health maintenance organization built a hospital within 3 miles of Gold Country.

One consequence of the more intense competition was a loss of several physician groups. Two decided to affiliate with one of Gold Country's primary competitors, and another group of ten physicians went to work for the health maintenance organization. As a result, hospital admissions declined by 15 percent.

In view of these events, the hospital's administrator, David Valencia, was especially sensitive to keeping physicians who admitted patients. He instructed all departments to take steps to ensure that the hospital's staff worked closely with the physicians and tried to accommodate their needs quickly and efficiently.

In developing her marketing plan, Ms. Bradford wanted to bring her pharmacists into greater contact with the physicians to advise them on drug therapy. Over the years, she had noticed many occasions where physicians prescribed wrong medications or drugs that were not the most appropriate for patient care. She felt that if pharmacists worked more closely with physicians, patient care would improve and the lengths of stay would decline.

After discussing her thoughts with the staff pharmacists, she was convinced that most were eager to take on the added responsibilities. They indicated a willingness to become involved even if they were not immediately provided with greater compensation.

The reception to her general plan, however, was not as well received by physicians and the hospital's nursing staff. Some physicians considered this to be an intrusion into their roles as primary care providers. And, some of the nurses stated that they thought that Ms. Bradford was trying to "invade their turf" by going directly to physicians. Several physicians and nurses also indicated that they had a good knowledge of prescription drugs, and did not believe that pharmacists could add much.

Although a few physicians and nurses encouraged Ms. Bradford to develop a prescription drug consulting service for them, it was apparent that the need and value of this was not universally recognized. Even Mr. Valencia expressed reservations because the

---

*Names of the organizations, individuals, and locations of all cases are fictional. Any likeness to actual organizations and/or individuals is purely coincidental.

service might increase the operating costs of the pharmacy.

Despite the less-than-enthusiastic response to her informal discussions, Ms. Bradford decided to proceed and develop the program. Because resources, particularly pharmacists' time, would be limited, she felt that any plan had to be quickly recognized and appreciated by at least some physicians and nurses. From that base, she could expand the service to others. The problem, however, was to find a way to do this.

Questions

1 Evaluate Ms. Bradford's rationale that a consultative service for physicians and nurses would improve the stature of the pharmacy within the hospital.
2 What steps should Ms. Bradford take to begin this service?
3 What other services, if any, could the pharmacy offer?

Case IV.2 Dayton Pharmacy

Buzz and Sally Dayton own and operate Dayton Pharmacy. They met while they were in pharmacy school nearly 18 years ago, married, and decided to open a community pharmacy. Since both were pharmacists, they felt that they could share the workload and provide a more personalized service than was currently available in the area.

From a profit perspective, Dayton Pharmacy is a financial success. The trading area surrounding the pharmacy contains a large number of senior citizen apartments, convalescent homes, and nursing homes. There are two other pharmacies in the area. One is an old established neighborhood pharmacy and the other is a small regional drugstore.

The size of the market where Dayton Pharmacy located remained stable until a year ago. Since then, there has been a significant increase in population in the area. New arrivals are largely singles who are attracted to the relatively low housing costs in the area. As a result of these new arrivals, Dayton Pharmacy and the other established pharmacies are beginning to feel the effects of aggressive competition from three chain pharmacies located in other parts of the city.

The chain pharmacies are offering weekly specials on front-end merchandise and aggressively advertise the services of their prescription department.

The largest chain advertises "Super low Prescription Prices." Each newspaper advertisement includes the following statements in bold print:

- Superior service from pharmacists who care about you!
- Ask about our special service on new or transferred prescriptions.
- We honor most insurance plans!
- Telephone us today with your health questions.
- Open every day.

To respond to this competition, the Daytons are considering the possibility of lowering their prices on selected front-end merchandise, namely, fine gift items and cosmetics. In addition, they are thinking about opening on Sundays, as they currently are open Monday through Friday from 10 a.m. to 7 p.m. and 10 a.m. to 5 p.m. on Saturday. And, they are considering offering seniors a 10 percent discount on all private pay prescriptions and front-end merchandise.

Although they are worried about the effects of lower prices on their carefully cultivated image, they believe that there is little choice but to become more price-competitive with the chain pharmacies. This is especially troublesome if they stay open longer because their operating costs will increase by about 4 percent. They wondered if offering a "frequent customer" program and giving discounts after ten purchases would be useful, but this would also increase their costs.

After reviewing their financial statement with their accountant (Table IV.2.1), the Daytons are led to believe that they can lower prices on fine gift items by as much as 20 percent and on cosmetics by up to 25 percent. Still, they are not sure whether to make any price changes or not.

Questions

1 Should Dayton Pharmacy be alarmed about the aggressiveness of the chain pharmacies?
2 Should Dayton Pharmacy make any changes in its price policy? If so, what should be changed and by how much?
3 How much more does Dayton Pharmacy have to sell if it lowers its prices just to remain the same as currently?

Table IV.2.1 Condensed gross margins for last 2 years

	Last year		Two years ago	
Profit and loss statement				
Revenues				
Prescriptions	$1,398,450	68.9%	$1,399,500	70.1%
Over-the-counter medicines	$279,580	13.8%	$289,420	14.5%
Cosmetics	$198,500	9.8%	$176,880	8.9%
Gift items	$154,000	7.6%	$129,800	6.5%
Total	$2,030,530	100.0%	$1,995,600	100.0%
Costs of goods sold				
Prescriptions	$1,090,791	78.0%	$1,035,630	74.0%
Over-the-counter medicines	$69,895	25.0%	$78,143	27.0%
Cosmetics	$99,250	50.0%	$88,440	50.0%
Gift items	$115,500	75.0%	$84,370	65.0%
Total	$1,375,436	67.7%	$1,286,583	64.5%
Gross margin				
Prescriptions	$307,659	22.0%	$363,870	26.0%
Over-the-counter medicines	$209,685	75.0%	$211,277	73.0%
Cosmetics	$99,250	50.0%	$88,440	50.0%
Gift items	$38,500	25.0%	$45,430	35.0%
Total	$655,094	32.3%	$709,017	35.5%

Case IV.3 Knoll Pharmacies

Knoll Pharmacies is a chain of seven medical pharmacies primarily located in medical office buildings in the western USA. Annual sales averaged about $2.7 million, and all of the pharmacies were reasonably similar in revenues, ranging between $2.4 million and $3.2 million. Profits for individual pharmacies varied somewhat based on the patient mix and the variations in prescription drugs dispensed and the volume of non-prescription merchandise sold. All pharmacies, however, carried the same non-prescription merchandise.

The chain traditionally allocated an amount equivalent to 0.5 percent of sales to advertise its products and services in local newspapers and on radio. This amount was based on forecasted sales and then the advertising budget was set.

About 80 percent of the total advertising budget was used for media which was exclusively newspaper and radio advertising. The other 20 percent was considered to be promotional dollars and distributed equally to each of the seven pharmacies to use how

it deemed best. Some pharmacy managers would purchase handout items such as magnetic stickers to give to patients, others would sponsor children's activities (e.g. soccer teams), and still others would print brochures and flyers.

Dick Knoll, owner of Knoll Pharmacies, was concerned about how effective this expenditure for advertising was in generating sales and profits. He was not sure about either the media advertising in the newspapers and radio or the promotional dollars spent by individual pharmacy managers. Considering that he spent about $141,750 for advertising of some sort, he felt that it definitely was time to start reviewing how the dollars were spent and what he got for the money.

One of Mr. Knoll's new store managers, Darrell Young, believed that the pharmacy he manages could get much more for the media advertising dollars spent by Knoll Pharmacies in the community. When he realized that the objective of 10 percent annual sales growth volume was not being met, he analyzed the costs and results of the advertising program and made a number of recommendations.

Mr. Young learned that although the media portion of the advertising expenditures was divided about evenly among the newspaper and three radio stations, inquiries generated as a result of the morning newspaper outnumbered inquiries generated by each of the other media by more than 2 to 1. So he recommended that Knoll Pharmacies increased the advertising in the morning paper and stopped advertising in the other media altogether. In the process, media expenses could be reduced by about 20 percent, and that additional money could be used by individual pharmacies as part of their promotional budgets. Neither Mr. Young nor Mr. Knoll had any idea as to how effective the individual pharmacy promotional dollars were in generating sales and profits.

New advertisements had stopped stressing price and quality exclusively, and have begun to emphasize personalized counseling services offered by Knoll Pharmacies. By carefully charting sales over a six-month period, Mr. Young discovered that the products advertised have shown inconsistent sales volume increases, while more and more time seems to be spent on free counseling services.

In addition, Knoll Pharmacies' advertising efforts have seldom taken advantage of cooperative advertising programs. Under a cooperative advertising program, the pharmacy pays 50 percent of the advertising costs, provided the advertised items are featured in conjunction with manufacturers' advertising campaigns. Mr. Young recommended that Knoll Pharmacies use cooperative advertising, even though it might mean adding product lines that the pharmacies have not carried before.

Questions

1 What are the strengths and weaknesses of the current approach taken with respect to the advertising budget using media advertising and promotional spending by individual pharmacies?

2 How sound is Mr. Young's new advertising program?

3 Should Knoll Pharmacies become more involved with cooperative advertising programs even if it means having to carry more non-prescription merchandise lines? What are the implications of doing so?

Major cases

Case IV.4 Johnson Medical Pharmacy

Rob Johnson, owner of Johnson Medical Pharmacy, had just walked out of his medical pharmacy for the evening. It was nearly midnight and had been a long day. After closing the pharmacy at 7 p.m., he had just finished taking inventory of the "front-end" (i.e. over-the-counter medications, greeting cards, and gifts and candy). In quickly looking over the number of items on the shelves and the amount of money he had tied up in inventory, he was more certain than ever that he needed to make some changes in his pharmacy:

> I really think it is time to make some adjustments to what I am doing here. My prescription sales are growing, but I'm selling virtually nothing in the front-end. With the rent I am paying, this space is not producing much in the way of revenues and profits. It's been this way for some time, and I have held off making changes partly because of the work involved, but mostly because I am not sure what to do differently. But, seeing how much "stuff" I have and how low I have to set prices just to get rid of it is getting to me. Some of the OTCs and candy are close to going out of date, and if I wait much longer, I'll be able to sell the gift items as antiques!

He made a promise to himself that he would immediately start to take a serious look at making some big changes in his pharmacy to better serve his patients and the physicians in the medical office building, and to improve his pharmacy's financial performance.

Downtown Medical Plaza

Johnson Medical Pharmacy was located in a medical office building in a large city in the southwest. Downtown Medical Plaza was situated approximately four blocks from a hospital that was on the border of what would be considered the city's downtown area. Most of the downtown area consisted of office buildings and high-rise apartments and condominiums. This was the only hospital that could be considered a "downtown" hospital in the city. The other four hospitals in the area were located in what would be considered the city's suburbs.

The medical office building was one of three similarly sized complexes designed specifically to accommodate physicians who had privileges at the hospital. Downtown Medical Plaza was the largest of the three complexes, but the furthest away from the hospital. Although all three medical office buildings had good reputations, the physicians at the Plaza were considered among the best in the entire city. Their patient bases include residents in the immediate area as well as from the suburban areas. A list of the physician tenants of the Plaza is presented in Table IV.4.1.

Dr. Johnson moved into the Plaza approximately 3 years ago when a small physician group moved out of the space. Although the landlord preferred to rent the space to another medical group, she was pressured by the other physicians to seek a pharmacy for the building. Dr. Johnson commented on the move:

> The landlord was not especially enthused about putting a retail business in the Plaza. She felt any store would be less stable than a group of physicians. But, the space was really not large enough for a growing medical practice. Unfortunately, it is a little too big for my pharmacy, but there was no way she was going to let me take less space or sublet a portion of the space to someone else. She made it very clear when I took the ten year lease that it was an all-or-nothing deal.

Despite having more space than he wanted, Dr. Johnson considered it a good opportunity to move from his corner store in the suburbs to a much more prestigious location. Having more than 40 physicians located in the building also was an attraction. And, there were approximately 70 other physicians located within about six blocks of his pharmacy. Only one of the three other medical office buildings had a pharmacy. Dr. Johnson commented on his location:

> When this opportunity came up, I moved pretty quickly. The downtown area has several other medical pharmacies, but only four chain drugstores. The spaces available are a little too small for most chain operations, so I don't think the competition is as intense in that regard. The one other medical pharmacy located in a medical office building has been there for a long time. But, that office building is the smallest of the three, and I really think that the owner of the pharmacy is content to just

make a decent living and is not looking to build the business to any great extent.

Johnson Medical Pharmacy

Johnson Medical Pharmacy was situated on the ground floor of the Plaza and just across from the elevator. Its hours of operation were Monday through Friday from 8:30 a.m. to 7:00 p.m. It was closed on Saturdays and Sundays because very few physicians had office hours on the weekends. However, Dr. Johnson told a few physicians that if they came in to see a patient and that person needed a medication right away, he would come in and fill the prescription. He indicated that this happens only about four to six times a year.

The pharmacy had approximately 1,900 square feet of space, with about 1,200 square feet being used for the prescription area. Gifts and candy consumed about 300 square feet, greeting cards had 225 square feet, and over-the-counter medications (OTCs) had 175 square feet. The general layout of Johnson Medical Pharmacy is shown in Figure IV.4.1.

The largest amount of space in the front-end was devoted to gifts and candy. Originally, Dr. Johnson thought that gifts would be good because two medical groups in the Plaza were a pediatrician group and an ob/gyn group. Accordingly, he purchased lines of gifts for children and newborns. However, in the last year, both groups moved out to the suburbs to be closer to another hospital system in the area. Their space was quickly filled with several other physician groups that specialized more on medical issues associated with aging. Dr. Johnson has not changed the mix of gift items in response to this change in physician composition in the Plaza:

> We really took a hit when the two medical groups left the building. Our gift sales, while never spectacular, dropped to about a third of what it had been. Initially, I thought that the older patients who are coming into this medical building might want gifts and candy for their grandchildren, but that has not been the case. And I doubt that we make more than 10–20 percent on most gifts these days.

Greeting cards consumed the next largest amount of space. While sales of greeting cards were not especially high, Dr. Johnson indicted that the gross margins on cards was good. He noted:

Table IV.4.2 Last year's condensed profit and loss statement for Johnson Medical Pharmacy

	Dollars	Percent of total revenue
Revenues		
Prescriptions	$2,711,250	95.8%
Over-the-counter medicines	$70,550	2.5%
Cards	$28,500	1.0%
Gifts and candy	$17,850	0.6%
Miscellaneous	$3,000	0.1%
Total	$2,831,150	100.0%
Costs of goods sold	$2,236,609	79.0%
Gross margin	$594,542	21.0%
Operating expenses	$449,042	15.9%
Net profit before taxes	$145,500	5.1%

that the great majority of our business and that of the physicians in the Plaza either live or work in the downtown area. So, I send candy on Valentine's Day and Thanksgiving to convey the message of love and thanks. I stay away from the holidays linked to religion because some of the physicians don't celebrate those.

The future of the front-end

When reviewing his sales and inventory levels, and the clientele he had, Dr. Johnson began thinking it might be time to change from selling some products to offering more services. In particular, he looked at the demographics of the immediate area within which his pharmacy was located and found that it had a large senior population, with 37 percent being 65 or older, and nearly 9 percent being 85 or older.

Selected demographic characteristics of the residents of the downtown area are presented in Table IV.4.3. When reviewing this data, three facts stood out to him:

- There is a large senior population in the downtown area. He assumed that the physicians in the Plaza primarily served this group, although probably 10–20 percent came from the suburbs and worked downtown.
- Over half of the downtown residents are not Caucasian. There are large Hispanic and Asian American populations in the area, and many primarily speak languages other than English. He knew that a reasonably large number of his patients were Hispanic and Asian American,

and that there were times when it was difficult to communicate with them about their medications. But he did not realize that these populations were so large.

- More than 20 percent of the residents of the downtown area were widowed, and it was likely that they lived alone. He assumed it was likely that a large percent of those who were not married or were separated or divorced also lived alone, but it appeared obvious that a sizable percent of the downtown residents lived by themselves and therefore had to take care of themselves.

Based on all of this, he thought it might be possible to start a consulting service for seniors, and use some of the current space for this. While he did not want to call it a "gerontology consulting service," he thought that since the average senior took 3.8 prescription medications on a daily basis, and given that seniors had considerable problems with their medications, it might be something he could market to the downtown residents as well as to the patients of physicians in the Plaza.

Dr. Johnson ran a report of the prescriptions dispensed by his pharmacy to see what medications were commonly taken. This report is presented in Table IV.4.4. He thought this might be useful in trying to design a service for people 65 and older.

As he sat down to start fulfilling the promise he made to himself, he thought it best to develop a marketing plan for a Senior Medication Counseling Program:

Table IV.4.3 Selected demographic characteristics of population in market area

	Number	Percent
Population by gender		
Male	26,896	45%
Female	32,899	55%
Total population	59,795	100.0%
Population by age		
Under 20	7,837	13.1%
20–34	8,043	13.5%
35–54	12,568	21.0%
55–64	9,289	15.5%
65–74	9,317	15.6%
75–84	7,448	12.5%
85 and over	5,293	8.9%
Total	59,795	100.0%
Population by ethnicity		
Caucasian	28,505	47.7%
Hispanic	14,777	24.7%
Asian American	9,868	16.5%
African American	4,443	7.4%
American Indian and Alaska Native	139	0.2%
Other/multiple ethnicity	2,063	3.5%
Total	59,795	100.0%
Main language spoken by population 20 years and older		
English only	29,506	60.3%
Spanish	7,493	15.3%
Asian and Pacific Islander languages	7,735	15.8%
Other Indo-European languages	3,923	8.0%
Other languages	301	0.6%
Total	48,958	100.0%
Household characteristics		
Average household size	2.11	
Average family size	2.85	

(continued)

I have been so involved in day-to-day activities there never has been enough time to just step back and see what else I could do. I think the market is large enough and has the money to spend on a consulting service if I can show them how they can do better with their

medications and live more healthy lifestyles. But, I have to charge for this because I will need to hire another pharmacist to dispense the prescriptions while I do the consulting.

My problem is that I need to design the consulting service, deciding specifically what to

Table IV.4.3 *(continued)*

	Number	Percent
Marital status of population 20 years and older		
Never married	7,653	15.9%
Now married, except separated	24,101	50.1%
Widowed	9,849	20.5%
Divorced/separated	6,458	13.4%
Total	48,061	100.0%
Educational attainment of population 25 years and over		
Less than 9th grade	1,950	4.2%
9th to 12th grade, no diploma	4,074	8.7%
High school graduate (includes equivalency)	16,002	34.1%
Some college, no degree	9,550	20.4%
Associate's degree	4,174	8.9%
Bachelor's degree	7,837	16.7%
Graduate or professional degree	3,282	7.0%
Total	46,870	100.0%
Household income		
Less than $25,000	7,229	25.5%
$25,000–$49,999	8,587	30.3%
$50,000–$74,999	4,941	17.4%
$75,000–$99,999	2,928	10.3%
$100,000–$149,999	2,077	7.3%
$150,000–$199,999	1,499	5.3%
$200,000 or more	1,079	3.8%
Total	28,339	100.0%

offer. Then, I have to figure out how to market it to patients in a way that shows value to them so they will pay some price for the service not just once but on an on-going basis. I am not going to try to get insurance companies to pay for this. The hassle is not worth that effort, at least not yet. I may also want to market this service through the physicians in the Plaza. But I also have to be careful not to infringe on what they do. Some may not want me to take possible business away from them, and that could be serious.

In thinking of all this, I now realize why I haven't done it before. There are a lot of loose ends that have to be linked together to make this work. I won't mind spending money on some type of marketing effort, but I'm not sure what that would entail.

Possible discussion questions

1 What are the major problems with the current products offered by Johnson Medical Pharmacy? How could those be resolved?

2 What should be the contents of the Senior Medication Counseling Program?

3 How should the Senior Medication Counseling Program be marketed to residents of the downtown area? To current patients of Johnson Medical Pharmacy?

4 How should the Senior Medication Counseling Program be marketed to physicians located in the Downtown Medical Plaza?

Table IV.4.4 Prescription drug activity

Number of prescriptions	45,000	
Number of prescriptions taken by average senior	3.8	
	Number Rx	Percent
Drug category		
Vascular agents	7,900	17.6%
Analgesics	4,500	10.0%
Anti-arthritics	4,200	9.3%
Psychotherapeutic drugs	4,000	8.9%
Anti-hyperlipidemic agents	3,800	8.4%
Anti-infectives	3,500	7.8%
Diabetes therapy	2,100	4.7%
Gastrointestinal	2,100	4.7%
Respiratory therapy	2,000	4.4%
Sedatives	1,900	4.2%
Genitourinary	1,800	4.0%
Neurological disorders	1,500	3.3%
Diuretics	1,200	2.7%
Other	4,500	10.0%
Total	45,000	100.0%

Case IV.5 Wang's Drugs

David Wang, general manager of Wang's Drugs, was in the process of reviewing the operations of the pharmacy chain he managed. A number of changes had taken place within the last year, and he was not sure that the methods he had been using to keep control over the pharmacies were still appropriate. Reflecting on the recent developments, he noted:

This is a family-owned business, and my father, my uncle, and two of my brothers wanted to expand our market area and the number of pharmacies we had. Although some of them are active at this time in the healthcare business, they are my elders and I had little choice but to accept their wishes. In the last year, we have grown much faster than I would have liked, but it was their decision. In our family, tradition and age carry considerable weight when it comes to making business decisions.

In any event, we now have two more pharmacies, and I need to reassess our business methods. Because of the big discount pharmacy chains, supermarket chains with pharmacies, and mass merchandisers with pharmacies moving into our area, we decided to compete more on a price basis than ever before. That was a tough decision for our family to make. Historically, we have stayed away from price competition, preferring to offer superior quality and service, and expecting our customers to pay a little extra for that. Now, with the lower prices, we have to watch our pharmacies' costs more closely as well as the prices and services offered by our competitors. This means more work and greater possibility of error. With the margins we are operating on now, a small increase in costs or a mistake in pricing too low will wipe out our profits. On the other hand, if we price even a little too high, we can be left behind by the big chains and discounters.

History of Wang's Drugs

Wang's Drugs is a chain of 14 pharmacies located in a large city in the northeastern USA. David Wang is the third of four sons of Mr. Ming (Mike) Wang, a

Chinese immigrant who came to the USA in the early 1980s. After becoming a pharmacist and working in pharmacies for several years, Mike Wang started his own pharmacy and 2 years later formed a partnership with his brother, Henry, when the latter came to the USA. Henry Wang also was a licensed pharmacist but had not practiced in years, working instead in the banking industry.

By the late 1990s, the Wang brothers owned six pharmacies. Mike Wang took over the management of the pharmacies and Henry Wang was the chief financial officer of the chain. Although not all of the children of the two founders became active in the business, several sons and cousins eventually took over facets of the operation. Mike Wang remained the president of the corporation and Henry Wang continued to serve as its vice president and treasurer.

As more family members became involved in the business, decisions were made to expand the scope of the pharmacies to include more over-the-counter medications and some specialty items. Over the years, the company branched out even more to include not only 14 pharmacies but also seven specialty food outlets. The most significant growth in the pharmacy section, however, came last year with the addition of two new pharmacies. Historically, the family had never approved the addition of more than one pharmacy in 2 years.

Organization

Each of the 14 pharmacies had a manager who was responsible for the overall store operations, including hiring of personnel, maintaining desired levels of sales and inventories, and preparing accounting reports. In addition, there were three departments within each individual pharmacy: prescription department, OTC and other health products department, and specialty food and other products department. One person in each department was designated as the "manager" and given approximately 5.0 percent more pay than the next highest-paid employee in the department for the added responsibilities. Sales by pharmacy are presented in Table IV.5.1.

Directly managing the operations of the 14 pharmacies were two supervisors who each oversaw seven pharmacies. Company policy was that the supervisors would visit each of their seven pharmacies on a daily basis, collect and review sales reports for the previous day, and check the general operations of the pharmacy. This included discussing operations with clerks and getting feedback from customers, monitoring inventory levels, evaluating pharmacy maintenance and general layout, and resolving any disputes between the manager and employees.

Mr. David Wang's primary responsibilities included monitoring the supervisors by discussing pharmacy activities with them at the end of each day, resolving any problems they could not handle, dealing with suppliers, setting prices, analyzing sales and profits, and planning in general.

Centralized purchasing guidelines for the pharmacies were handled by three purchasing agents (PAs) along the lines organized in each pharmacy: prescription drug PA, OTC and health products PA, and specialty food and other products PA. The prescription drug PA would help each pharmacy establish inventory levels, and negotiate terms with primary and secondary wholesalers and some manufacturers directly. On a daily basis, managers of each pharmacy would order prescription drugs directly from a primary or secondary wholesaler based on usage. The two supervisors did not get involved in prescription drug purchases or inventory control over these products.

Over-the-counter and other health products and specialty food and other products were purchased centrally by the other two PAs. These PAs would work with the supervisors to determine what lines to carry, inventory levels, optimal purchase orders, and other aspects of purchasing and inventory control. When there were disputes between the PAs, supervisors, and/or individual pharmacy managers—typically regarding lines to carry or the amount of inventory to keep on hand—David Wang would intercede to resolve the problems.

The market

Because Wang's Drugs were in virtually all areas of the city, the target markets and competitive conditions varied considerably from pharmacy to pharmacy. In general, however, the older pharmacies tended to be in lower income areas where there were greater percentages of young families and senior citizens. Commonly, these were situated close to the center of the city, which had become somewhat depressed. Most of the newer pharmacies were located along the outer edges of the city, in areas primarily populated by middle-income families.

Table IV.5.1 Total sales by pharmacy

Pharmacy[a]	Last year	Two years ago	Three years ago
1	$2,767,000	$2,404,000	$2,246,500
2	$2,293,000	$2,054,500	$1,903,000
3	$2,120,500	$1,957,000	$1,951,500
4	$1,937,500	$2,218,000	$2,409,000
5	$2,528,500	$2,198,500	$1,897,000
6	$3,048,500	$2,368,000	$2,381,500
7	$2,309,500	$1,937,500	$1,916,500
8	$2,552,500	$2,245,000	$1,918,000
9	$2,584,000	$2,227,000	$2,081,500
10	$2,251,200	$2,100,500	$1,985,000
11	$2,271,000	$1,883,500	$1,673,500
12	$1,865,000	$1,760,500	
13	$1,733,500		
14	$1,659,000		

[a] From oldest (1) to newest (14).

Just as the types of customers varied greatly, so did the competition faced by individual pharmacies. David Wang felt that pharmacies located closer to the center of the city did not confront the same quality of competition that faced those in the outer areas. He commented:

> The pharmacies in the center of town compete mostly with small independent pharmacies and two small and very old chains. Even though our pharmacies are old, they have been well-maintained or remodeled, and typically are bigger than those of the downtown chains. We can compete very well here.

Mr. Wang believed that the intensity and quality of competition were considerably greater in the outlying areas, where 65 percent of Wang's pharmacies were located. New, large, discount pharmacy chains, supermarket chains, and mass merchandisers with pharmacies had entered these areas and competed aggressively for market position. As David Wang noted:

> Our board of directors felt that we were being hurt badly in this market since the national discount pharmacy chains, mass merchandisers, and supermarket chains have used price as a competitive weapon. They have consistently

undercut our prices, even during our weekly advertised specials. The board was afraid that as customers became more price sensitive we would lose out, and be viewed as a high-priced pharmacy chain. Eventually, this could hurt us in the inner-city areas as well.

In addition to two national discount pharmacy chain stores, two supermarket chains, and two mass merchandise chains with pharmacies located in the city, there were three local pharmacy chains. One chain was larger than Wang's Drugs with 17 outlets, but was considered to offer below-average prescription service and low-quality non-prescription products. The other local chains had six and eight pharmacies, respectively, and were somewhat more aggressive. Their size, however, made it difficult for them to compete on a price basis because of their more limited purchasing power. In addition, both had small pharmacies and very limited amounts of non-prescription products compared to what was offered in most Wang's Drugs pharmacies. According to David Wang:

> We offer excellent quality products and services. We try to give the most attentive and friendly service possible. These are areas where we can really outshine the competition.

Pharmacy operations

Of great concern to Mr. Wang from a competitive standpoint were inventory for the non-prescription products and labor costs for each pharmacy's prescription department. He considered these to be the most critical aspects of internal pharmacy operations. Accordingly, he tried to maintain close control over each pharmacy's non-prescription drug inventory levels and labor costs. Without this control, he did not believe that Wang's Drugs could compete with the larger chains.

Based on the size of each pharmacy and its sales history, Mr. Wang set a general range of prescription and non-prescription inventory for the pharmacy and tried to keep it at or below that level. More leeway was given for the prescription drug inventory since this was directly ordered at the end of each day based on sales.

Non-prescription inventory was controlled on the basis of dollars in inventory rather than the number of units. He felt that he did not care much about the quantity of inventory; it was the dollars committed that were important from a cost-control perspective.

With central non-prescription ordering, Wang's Drugs had a warehouse from which its own truck distributed to the individual pharmacies. Mr. Wang thought that this was both good and bad. While the process made it somewhat easier to purchase in larger quantities, and therefore at lower prices, Wang's Drugs had only one truck available for deliveries. Although the routing of deliveries had been determined by Mr. Wang, it had not been changed for several years.

As new pharmacies were added to the chain, they were pieced into the existing routing system. As a result, there were occasional stock-outs which required special deliveries during the off-hours. This was especially costly, averaging $400 per special delivery for both labor and truck expense. However, Mr. Wang was not sure whether an entirely new routing plan would be any more effective and felt that it might even be counterproductive:

> If we start changing our deliveries, we mess up the cycles that every pharmacy has come to rely upon. I don't want to confuse people. I'd rather spend the extra $400, even if this happens twice a week as it often does.

The other aspect of internal operations that was of great concern to Mr. Wang was the cost of labor. Each pharmacy department employed four licensed pharmacists operating in two shifts (i.e. two from 8 a.m. to 4 p.m. and two from 1 p.m. to 9 p.m.), two technicians, and two clerks (i.e. one with each shift of pharmacists). The amount of money paid for labor occasionally bothered Mr. Wang:

> I know that the quality of our employees is crucial to the success of Wang's Drugs. We have always emphasized quality products and friendly service. But it still hurts me to see how much money we have to pay in wages, especially for unproductive time.

To control the costs of labor, Mr. Wang had repeatedly asked the supervisors to watch for opportunities to reduce the number of employees or the number of hours employees worked in the pharmacy departments. He emphasized the use of part-time employees as a way to schedule personnel more precisely around peak periods:

> I tried to get the pharmacy managers to use more part-time employees and schedule them only during the busy periods. But they complain that the problems encountered in using these people outweigh the benefits in cost savings. Since we do not have any manager-types in pharmacies other than the actual pharmacists, they don't want the added burdens of closely supervising their employees. But that's part of their jobs. That's what I pay the managers to do. They tell me that we cannot offer quality products and friendly service, and get by with a little less labor at the same time. I think they are just avoiding the issue.

Marketing

The marketing practices used by Wang's Drugs centered primarily on local newspaper advertising, point-of-purchase displays, and various pricing techniques. Until recently, the greatest attention went to weekly newspaper advertising. Like most other pharmacies in the city, Wang's Drugs ran weekly sales, and promoted them in two-page advertisements in the local newspaper. To get full use of the newspaper advertising, small portions of space were subcontracted to other family members who owned the specialty food stores. This joint advertising had been a policy of the board of directors because they wanted to keep the family together.

Newspaper advertising, however, was rather drastically reduced once the decision was made by the board to compete on more of a price basis. They felt that the advertisements were too expensive, and did not convey a desirable image for Wang's Drugs.

Instead of full-page advertising, therefore, Mr. Wang decided to use small ads, approximately one-eighth page, to remind customers that Wang's Drugs had "made across-the-board price reductions." In addition, leaflets in the form of "door hangers" explaining the new pricing program for select non-prescription merchandise were distributed in particular geographic areas as an inducement to customers to come into the pharmacy. Mr. Wang felt that since the board would not authorize newspaper advertising as it had in the past, the leaflets would be the best way to reach customers in the immediate geographic area surrounding each pharmacy.

Complementing the limited advertising efforts, Mr. Wang planned to devote more attention to in-pharmacy promotions. As he noted:

> I spend about 25 percent of my time visiting the pharmacies, stocking and remerchandising the shelves. This is one part of the business that I really enjoy. It gives me a chance to be a little creative with each pharmacy. Adjusting displays here and there can make a big difference in terms of sales. This is something that the chains usually don't do, and the discount warehouses cannot do. It also gives me an opportunity to talk to the customer and determine if they are getting good service from our employees. In the last year, I fired three employees who customers said were discourteous. That will not happen in one of my pharmacies.

Although he did not agree with the board's decision regarding this change in price and promotion strategies, he resigned himself to its implementation:

> I still do not like the idea of price reductions because we have always emphasized quality and service. I'm not sure we can continue to provide the same quality non-prescription products and services over the long term as we are going to have to compete aggressively on a price basis. I'm not even sure that customers believe that

we offer lower prices. Besides, we now have to continually monitor the prices being charged by our competitors. This has put greater pressure on our pharmacy managers and supervisors. The added responsibility will sooner or later take its toll on them. We may have to add more supervisors or a managerial level below that of the pharmacy manager. Either way, this will be an added cost that we must account for while simultaneously reducing prices. I only hope that we can increase sales volume enough to cover this. Our early returns seem to indicate that this strategy may be successful, but it's too early to tell. It may just be a novelty at this point.

To test the results of the price changes, Mr. Wang took a sample of non-prescription merchandise and set different prices on the goods in each of five pharmacies he considered to have similar customers. In monitoring prices and quantities demanded over a relatively brief period of time, Mr. Wang prepared the chart shown in Table IV.5.2. Pharmacy A was used for control purposes, so no changes were made in its merchandise prices.

Prices in Pharmacy B were discounted in the same manner as that used in the original change to a discount strategy. In Pharmacy C, the prices of some over-the-counter medications and health and beauty aids were lowered, while the prices of specialty foods were raised. Just the opposite strategy was employed in Pharmacy D. Finally, Pharmacy E used a mixture of higher and lower prices. Although Mr. Wang realized that his merchandise sample was not truly representative of all non-prescription product lines carried, he believed that it presented a reasonable facsimile of market conditions. Presented in Table IV.5.3 are sample products and the quantities sold of each at their respective prices.

Finance

Nearly all of the financial matters relating to Wang Brothers, Inc., were managed by Henry Wang. On a daily basis, he was responsible for monitoring the corporation's cash balance and ensuring that all excess funds were properly invested. Although separate records were kept for each pharmacy, all of the funds were pooled into a central account. In this way, funds could be diverted from one activity to another with

Table IV.5.2 Price comparisons for a sample of front-end merchandise

	Wang's old price	Wang's new price	National chain	Local chain	Discount warehouse
Over-the-counter medications					
Pain relief products	100%	99%	96%	91%	98%
Cold and flu products	100%	91%	94%	102%	90%
Eye care products	100%	91%	97%	92%	90%
Dental care products	100%	96%	95%	93%	89%
Wound care products	100%	95%	95%	95%	86%
Health and beauty aids					
Toothpastes	100%	97%	102%	100%	99%
Hand lotions	100%	100%	103%	98%	100%
High-end cosmetics	100%	92%	94%	92%	89%
Low-end cosmetics	100%	92%	94%	92%	89%
Deodorants	100%	85%	101%	93%	90%
Shampoos and conditioners	100%	90%	95%	85%	85%
Specialty foods					
Candies and cookies	100%	93%	92%	90%	91%
Spices and seasonings	100%	94%	93%	90%	91%
Bottled salad dressings	100%	87%	93%	96%	90%
Canned vegetables	100%	90%	97%	97%	88%
Canned meat products	100%	89%	103%	100%	90%
Beverages	100%	89%	102%	100%	86%

Henry Wang's approval. And it was believed that the corporation as a whole was in a better position than any one individual pharmacy to secure favorable terms. Condensed profit and loss statements are presented in Table IV.5.4.

Future

In reflecting on the future, David Wang was wondering how the expansion and changes in pricing strategy might affect the pharmacies. Both of the supervisors recommended that the prices set for Wang's Drugs be reduced even further, possibly 2–3 percent more, to gain a better advantage over the chains. This added to David Wang's existing concern about the wisdom of the change in price strategy instituted by the board. He felt that if he had to continually modify pharmacy prices, his present management processes would also have to be changed in order for the markets

to maintain a competitive edge in pricing over the long term.

Possible discussion questions

1 How well positioned is Wang's Drugs in the marketplace? Why is it well positioned or not well positioned, and what could be done to improve its position?

2 What are the advantages and disadvantages of the pricing strategy being used by Wang's Drugs? Is it a good or bad strategy? Why?

3 What should be done to evaluate the pricing tests that were conducted? What can be inferred from the results?

4 What other marketing strategies need to be taken along with the pricing strategy Wang's Drugs is using?

Table IV.5.3 Sample prices and quantities sold

	Pharmacy A	Pharmacy B	Pharmacy C	Pharmacy D	Pharmacy E
Price					
Over-the-counter medications					
Pain relief product	$3.99	$3.95	$3.79	$4.29	$4.09
Cold and flu product	$4.59	$4.48	$4.29	$4.89	$4.75
Health and beauty aids					
Toothpaste	$1.19	$1.14	$1.22	$0.78	$0.93
Hand lotion	$2.64	$2.47	$2.79	$2.32	$2.94
Specialty foods					
Cookies	$1.26	$1.17	$1.25	$1.07	$1.32
Seasoning	$2.14	$2.04	$1.74	$1.83	$2.17
Bottled salad dressing	$2.78	$2.74	$2.71	$2.59	$2.83
Quantity sold					
Over-the-counter medications					
Pain relief products	1,400	1,450	1,700	1,100	1,050
Cold and flu products	2,800	3,300	4,100	2,100	2,700
Health and beauty aids					
Toothpastes	500	510	440	750	600
Hand lotions	625	815	600	1,150	500
Specialty foods					
Candies and cookies	110	165	110	185	95
Spices and seasonings	230	240	410	330	220
Bottled salad dressings	285	315	330	510	270

Table IV.5.4 Condensed financial statements for Wang's Drugs for last 3 years

	Last year	Two years ago	Three years ago
Sales			
Prescription drugs	$19,381,000	$16,265,500	$14,761,000
OTC and health products	$7,819,500	$7,293,500	$7,272,700
Specialty foods and other products	$4,720,200	$1,795,000	$329,300
Total	$31,920,700	$25,354,000	$22,363,000
Cost of sales	$22,663,697	$17,722,446	$15,095,025
Gross profit	$9,257,003	$7,631,554	$7,267,975
Expenses			
Salaries and wages	$7,341,761	$5,704,650	$4,472,600
All other	$1,518,209	$1,613,934	$2,512,106
Total	$8,859,970	$7,318,584	$6,984,706
Net profit before taxes	$397,033	$312,970	$283,269

Case IV.6 Northwest Drugs, Inc.

Jennifer Stern, manager of Northwest Drugs, was reading a newspaper article about the grand opening of Kings Drugs, a regional chain of drugstores that had recently opened a store in town. In this relatively small town in the northwestern USA, the addition of a new store was big news and she felt it clearly meant that there would be more intense competition. After reading the article, she commented:

> This is just my luck. I take over our family's pharmacy and right away another one pops up. I think this means several things for us. First, it is hard to know how much of an impact it will have on our store, but I am sure it will hurt, at least at first as people go see what Kings has to offer. Second, it means that we will need to position our store carefully to distinguish us from Kings as well as the medical pharmacies in the area. Third, we need to intensify our marketing efforts. We have been somewhat lax in promoting ourselves, and I'm not sure if that contributed to Kings' decision to open a store here. Anyway, just my luck.

Based on what she read—that Kings Drugs had been happy with its opening—Dr. Stern was convinced that the chain planned to become more aggressive in its marketing efforts than Northwest Drugs has been in the past. While the town has grown in population over the last ten years, she also thought that competition for sales was becoming more intense. A new chain supermarket had opened in the last year, and there were rumors that a national mass merchandiser might come to town as well. Although neither the supermarket nor the mass merchandiser had pharmacies, their entry into the local market could impact non-prescription sales. As she noted:

> For many years, this was a sleepy little community from a business standpoint. Everybody knows everybody and we didn't feel like we had to do much other than open our doors and be nice to customers. But as our town has grown, it has attracted more regional and national companies who probably view the community as a growth opportunity. They probably also have noticed that none of the stores in town, including the two grocery stores and ours, did much to build our businesses. So they may think that they can market their stores much better than we could. I know that I would think the same if I were them. What scares me is that when the chain grocery store came into town, it really hurt the three local grocery stores even though the chain was

slightly higher in price. Maybe people in this town just want something new. And if that is the case, it does not bode well for us unless we become more active and aggressive ourselves.

Northwest Drugs

Northwest Drugs had been a fixture in this small town for more than 30 years. Dr. Stern's father purchased the pharmacy from a long-time resident of the community and built it from a very small corner drugstore with fountain beverage service into a large community pharmacy that carried a rather broad array of merchandise.

As the store evolved, it became as much a convenience store as a pharmacy. While prescription sales account for nearly 75 percent of total revenues at the current time, there were years in the past that non-prescription sales surpassed prescription sales. This changed somewhat dramatically as more grocery stores opened in town and took more of the food and household goods sales. With the decline in non-prescription sales, Dr. Stern's father concentrated more on the prescription side of the pharmacy and built volume by cultivating relations with physicians. Being well-known and respected in the community, Dr. Stern's father was able to build prescription sales.

However, the owners of several medical pharmacies in the area also became more intent on building good relations with physicians. They had somewhat of an advantage because three of the five pharmacies were located inside or very near medical office buildings. This gave them more opportunities to personally communicate with local physicians. The other two medical pharmacies, Town Drugs and Forest Pharmacy, were located on the main street of the town and were thought by Dr. Stern to be more important competitors to Northwest Drugs for prescription sales.

Dr. Stern summarized the evolution of Northwest Drugs:

> We pretty much had this community all to ourselves for many years. We were the main pharmacy, and we carried what at the time seemed like a good array of convenience items so we also were like a corner convenience store for those items. There really wasn't much competition, and even with some other pharmacies, there was enough for everybody.

So, we didn't make much of an effort to advertise or do any real marketing.

Now, however, the marketplace has changed. We have had a lot of people move into town over the last few years and that has brought other stores. I don't think we are the center of the universe like we were in the past. Newer townspeople are not loyal to us, and even the old timers like to try something different. I know we don't have an image problem. It's more likely that we just don't have much of an image at all.

Northwest Drugs was situated on the corner of the busiest intersection of the town. For the size of the town, it was a large store with approximately 13,000 square feet of space. It also had parking for about 20 cars in the lot that Dr. Stern's father had purchased. Although the building was quite old, the pharmacy was well maintained and had been renovated every 7–10 years. The last renovation was 2 years ago.

Dr. Stern took over as manager of Northwest Drugs nearly 2 years ago. After graduating from a major pharmacy school in the northeast, she first went to work for a chain pharmacy in that area. Starting as a staff pharmacist, she quickly moved up to become a pharmacy department manager and then store manager. After 5 years, she was transferred to one of the chain's largest stores in the northeast and managed that store for nearly 4 years.

With 9 years of experience, and nearly 7 of those as a store manager, the family decided it was time for the father to retire and have Dr. Stern come back to the area and take over Northwest Drugs. Dr. Stern commented about the shift from working for a regional chain to managing Northwest Drugs:

It was somewhat of a "culture shock" when I returned. While Northwest Drugs has done very well, I came from an organization that believed in heavy advertising and had the money to extensively promote. It worked well because when they ran newspaper advertisements that reached a wide geographic area, it was ok because we had stores in nearly everywhere. The organization had a plan for how they wanted the chain to be positioned relative to the competition, knew the demographics of the areas they served and pinpointed their target markets.

When I came here, my father was doing virtually no advertising. I am sure he felt that everybody in town was or should have been his customer. And in some respects that was the case. He was a very good businessman, but he didn't need to do much in the way of marketing. Now he knows the environment has changed and I think that is why he wanted to have me take over.

Northwest Drugs has a reasonably broad selection of merchandise. However, prescriptions, over-the-counter medications (OTCs), packaged foods, and greeting cards account for nearly 90 percent of total sales. All of the other lines account for less than 2 percent of total revenues each. A copy of last year's condensed profit and loss statement is presented in Table IV.6.1. This shows what lines are carried in Northwest Drugs as well as overall revenues and expenses.

Northwest Drugs was considered a good community pharmacy by town residents. The local newspaper conducted an image survey of all retailers in the town. Selected results of that survey are presented in Table IV.6.2. Dr. Stern generally agreed that the findings of the survey were accurate. Her only disagreement was that the ratings for advertising might not be right because Northwest Drugs did so little promotion. She knew that the prices charged at Northwest Drugs were somewhat higher than those of other stores, but she attributed that to the fact that historically there was little competition and the store typically carried better quality merchandise than found elsewhere.

Characteristics of town residents

Although the town was relatively small, with more than 29,300 residents, it had grown appreciably over the last few years. Just 5 years ago, the town had a population of 24,000. This meant that the town had grown at a rate of about 4.1 percent per year. Dr. Stern commented on the growth in population:

The town has grown in recent years well above what would be expected for the state as a whole. I think that people want to get back to the small town atmosphere and there have been jobs primarily in farming. Some of the crops farmers in the area have planted have done quite well, and farmland has started to stretch out geographically. In addition, we have a

Table IV.6.1 Condensed profit and loss statement for last year for Northwest Drugs, Inc.

	Dollars	Percent of revenues
Revenues		
Prescriptions	$4,359,700	74.9%
Over-the-counter medications	$612,700	10.5%
Packaged foods	$127,100	2.2%
Greeting cards	$125,100	2.1%
Dental care	$110,300	1.9%
Wound care	$89,500	1.5%
Paper products	$87,800	1.5%
Eye care	$78,100	1.3%
Beverages	$65,200	1.1%
Candy	$45,500	0.8%
Dairy products	$30,000	0.5%
Cleaning supplies	$23,000	0.4%
Electronics	$15,100	0.3%
Toys and games	$14,500	0.2%
Miscellaneous	$38,800	0.7%
Total	$5,822,400	100.0%
Costs of goods sold		
Prescriptions	$3,376,692	77.5%
All other	$832,276	56.9%
Total	$4,208,969	72.3%
Gross margin		
Prescriptions	$983,008	16.9%
All other	$630,424	10.8%
Total	$1,613,431	27.7%
Operating expenses		
Salaries, wages, and benefits	$825,400	14.2%
Advertising	$9,000	0.2%
Entertainment	$16,500	0.3%
Signage/posters/miscellaneous marketing	$12,000	0.2%
All other	$605,900	10.4%
Total	$1,468,800	25.2%
Net profit before taxes	$144,631	2.5%

larger city about 10 miles from us, and some people like our town better than that one so they commute to work. I don't expect to see this much growth continuing, but we should continue to grow even if it is at a much slower pace.

Dr. Stern assembled some demographic data on the population, as presented in Table IV.6.3. She also gathered some percentages related to housing just in case she decided to use more door hangers (i.e. fliers that are hung on front door knobs) or direct mail advertising.

Table IV.6.2 Selected results of newspaper survey

Attribute	Northwest Drugs	All other retailers
Recognized the store name	89.0%	78.0%
Shopped in the store in last month	25.0%	31.0%
Shopped in the store in last 6 months	37.0%	42.0%
Image of store:		
Convenient location		
Very good/good	72.0%	68.0%
Poor/very poor	28.0%	32.0%
Range of merchandise offered		
Very good/good	65.0%	80.0%
Poor/very poor	35.0%	20.0%
Quality of merchandise		
Very good/good	71.0%	58.0%
Poor/very poor	29.0%	42.0%
Speed of service		
Very good/good	89.0%	45.0%
Poor/very poor	11.0%	55.0%
Helpfulness of store employees		
Very good/good	91.0%	51.0%
Poor/very poor	9.0%	49.0%
Knowledgeable store employees		
Very good/good	85.0%	38.0%
Poor/very poor	15.0%	62.0%
Reasonableness of prices charged		
Very good/good	24.0%	59.0%
Poor/very poor	76.0%	41.0%
Value for prices charged		
Very good/good	35.0%	61.0%
Poor/very poor	65.0%	39.0%
Store cleanliness		
Very good/good	54.0%	68.0%
Poor/very poor	46.0%	32.0%
Quality of advertising		
Very good/good	21.0%	76.0%
Poor/very poor	79.0%	24.0%
Match between advertising message and reality		
Very good/good	55.0%	45.0%
Poor/very poor	45.0%	55.0%

(*continued*)

Table IV.6.2 (*continued*)

Attribute	Northwest Drugs	All other retailers
Community supporter		
Very good/good	50.0%	38.0%
Poor/very poor	50.0%	62.0%
Would shop at store again	81.0%	63.0%
Would recommend store to a friend	70.0%	61.0%

Table IV.6.3 Selected demographics of town

	Number	Percent
Population by gender		
Male	14,484	49.4%
Female	14,851	50.6%
Total	29,335	100.0%
Population by age		
Under 10	4,967	16.9%
10–19	5,011	17.1%
20–34	5,589	19.1%
35–54	7,274	24.8%
55–64	2,270	7.7%
65–74	979	3.3%
75 and older	3,245	11.1%
Total	29,335	100.0%
18 years and over		
Male	10,243	49.9%
Female	10,302	50.1%
Total	20,545	100.0%
65 years and over		
Male	1,286	30.4%
Female	2,938	69.6%
Total	4,224	100.0%
Employment of population 16 years and over		
Total	21,455	
Not in labor force	9,215	43.0%
Civilian labor force	12,240	57.0%
Employed	11,214	91.6%
Unemployed	1,025	8.4%
Employment type of population 16 years and older		
Management/professional	2,557	22.8%
Service	1,959	17.5%

(*continued*)

Table IV.6.3 (*continued*)

	Number	Percent
Sales	1,618	14.4%
Farming	2,378	21.2%
Construction	722	6.4%
Other	1,980	17.7%
Total	11,214	100.0%
Household income		
Less than $25,000	2,027	27.2%
$25,000–$49,999	2,109	28.3%
$50,000–$74,999	1,550	20.8%
$75,000–$99,999	851	11.4%
$100,000–$149,999	698	9.4%
$150,000 or more	218	2.9%
Total	7,454	100.0%
Population in households		
Householder	7,454	26.7%
Spouse	4,097	14.7%
Child	10,298	36.9%
Other relatives	4,603	16.5%
Non-relatives	991	3.6%
Unmarried partner	443	1.6%
Total	27,885	100.0%
Marital status of population 15 and older		
Never married	6,894	31.5%
Now married, except separated	10,903	49.8%
Separated	427	2.0%
Widowed	2,203	10.1%
Divorced	1,455	6.6%
Total	21,882	100.0%
Population 3 years and over enrolled in school		
Nursery school, preschool	307	3.6%
Kindergarten	563	6.7%
Elementary school (grades 1–8)	3,561	42.2%
High school (grades 9–12)	2,184	25.9%
College or graduate school	1,828	21.7%
Total	8,443	100.0%
Education of population 25 years and over		
Less than 9th grade	4,718	26.6%

(*continued*)

Table IV.6.3 *(continued)*

	Number	Percent
9th to 12th grade, no diploma	1,994	11.2%
High school graduate (includes equivalency)	3,257	18.3%
Some college, no degree	3,449	19.4%
Associate's degree	1,606	9.0%
Bachelor's degree	2,031	11.4%
Graduate or professional degree	710	4.0%
Total	17,765	100.0%
Housing occupancy		
Occupied housing units		95.4%
Vacant housing units		4.6%
Total		100.0%
Average household size of owner-occupied unit		3.53
Average household size of renter-occupied unit		3.92
Housing units		
1-unit, detached		73.1%
1-unit, attached		1.6%
2 units		1.9%
3 or 4 units		7.3%
5–9 units		5.6%
10–19 units		4.4%
20 or more units		2.8%
Mobile home		3.3%
Total		100.0%
Years in current residence		
Moved in within last year		16.0%
Moved in 2–3 years ago		30.0%
Moved in 4–10 years ago		25.5%
Moved in 11–20 years ago		16.2%
Moved in more than 20 years ago		12.3%
Total		100.0%
Home value		
Less than $100,000		8.9%
$100,000–$199,999		26.3%
$200,000–$299,999		36.0%
$300,000–$499,999		26.9%
$500,000–$999,999		0.9%
$1,000,000 or more		1.0%
Total		100.0%

She felt that it will be important in the future to identify groups of residents that the pharmacy should try to attract as customers. Overall, she felt that her customer base was somewhat older than the average population. While some of these people were more financially secure, they did not represent the majority of the townspeople, and certainly not the newer and younger residents. One challenge she thought she had was to find ways to position Northwest Drugs to continue to attract her current customer base while also attracting new customers who had different demographic characteristics. She noted:

> I don't want to lose the customers we have. They have been good customers over the years and tend to be among the more affluent people in town. Consequently, we have been able to stock higher quality merchandise and charge relatively high prices because they are not as price sensitive. But the growth in the town is not this demographic. They are younger and have less income. So, we may need to have somewhat lower quality merchandise and charge lower prices, or take lower profit margins and hope that the volume makes up for that loss in margin.

The competition

Northwest Drugs had competition in several retail areas. Until Kings Drugs opened, there were no other large community pharmacies in the town. When Kings Drugs opened, it became the largest in terms of square footage with nearly 15,000 square feet of space.

Northwest Drugs was considerably larger than the medical pharmacies. Of the five medical pharmacies in the town, only two were considered direct competitors for prescriptions. Both Town Drugs and Forest Pharmacy had good locations and their owners also were well known in town. One owner, in fact, had served on the city council several years ago, and both owners were active in the community from time to time. Neither, however, had the community stature that Dr. Stern's father had, especially among residents who had lived in the town for more than 10 years.

Dr. Stern spent considerable time assessing these competitors. First, she found out their store hours and then tried to determine what they offered in terms of prescription services and merchandise car-

ried. The results of this effort are presented in Table IV.6.4.

She realized, however, that the manager of Kings Drugs and the owners of the two medical pharmacies could make changes to all facets of their operations if they wanted to do so. Dr. Stern thought that it would be easier for the owners of the medical pharmacies to make adjustments than it would for the manager of Kings Drugs:

> Kings Drugs is part of a regional chain of about 40 stores. One of the advantages chains have is their ability to gain economies by standardizing as much as they can. I learned that when I managed stores for a larger chain. So making adjustments to fit this town will be harder for Kings. The owners of Town Drugs and Forest Pharmacy could make changes instantly, but they have relatively small pharmacies and cannot stock the merchandise we do. Besides, I am not sure they really compete with us other than for the prescription business.

Dr. Stern also tried to summarize the marketing activities used by the competition. Because Kings Drugs was so new, she could only estimate what it would do based on what its other stores had done in different communities. However, her background told her that Kings' management, like the chain she had worked for previously, would use a "formula" for marketing the store and building its recognition level and image in the community. This summary is presented in Table IV.6.5.

The future

In contemplating the future, Dr. Stern was uncertain about whom to target as key customers for the future and how to go about attracting them. She was willing to make adjustments and knew her father would support such action so long as it made sense and she developed a complete set of marketing strategies. One of her concerns was how to build for the future without alienating the pharmacy's current customer base. As she indicated:

> There is one thing I know for sure. That is, we need to be more aggressive with our marketing effort. We need to identify groups of people we want as customers, be sure to offer the pharmacy services and carry the non-prescription merchandise they want, price

Table IV.6.4 Comparisons with other pharmacies in town

	Northwest Drugs	Kings Drugs	Town Drugs	Forest Pharmacy
Store hours				
Days open	Everyday	Everyday	Mon–Fri	Mon–Sat
Hours Monday through Friday	9 a.m.–7 p.m.	9 a.m.–9 p.m.	9 a.m.–6 p.m.	9:30 a.m.–6 p.m.
Hours Saturday	9 a.m.–6 p.m.	9 a.m.–9 p.m.		10 a.m.–2 p.m.
Hours Sunday	11 a.m.–5 p.m.	9 a.m.–6 p.m.		
Prescription services				
Automatic refills	Yes		Yes	
Refill notification	Yes			
After-hours prescription services	Yes		Yes	Yes
Delivery	Yes	Yes		Yes
Compounding			Yes	Yes
Unit packaging			Yes	
Patient counseling	Yes	Yes	Yes	Yes
Merchandise carried				
Over-the-counter medications	Yes	Yes	Yes	Yes
Packaged foods	Yes	Yes		
Greeting cards	Yes	Yes	Yes	Yes
Dental care	Yes	Yes	Yes	Yes
Wound care	Yes	Yes	Yes	Yes
Paper products	Yes	Yes		
Eye care	Yes	Yes	Yes	Yes
Beverages	Yes	Yes		
Candy	Yes	Yes		Yes
Dairy products	Yes	Yes		
Cleaning supplies	Yes			
Electronics	Yes			
Toys and games	Yes			
Gifts		Yes	Yes	
Home health supplies				Yes
Durable medical equipment				Yes
Apparel		Yes		
School supplies		Yes		
Office supplies		Yes		
Sporting goods		Yes		

everything so they feel it has value and still gives us good profits, and promote whatever we do like crazy. The problem I am having is trying to figure out how to attract new customers which tend to be the newer residents of the town who are younger and less affluent while not losing the good customers we have now. I guess another option is to just keep the older and wealthier residents and try to sell them more or raise prices, but neither of these would be easy. The other dilemma is whether to focus our efforts more on the prescription services or

Table IV.6.5 Marketing activities by pharmacies in town

	Northwest Drugs	Kings Drugs	Town Drugs	Forest Pharmacy
Advertising				
Newspaper	Occasional	Yes		
Radio				
Television		Yes		
Door hangers	Occasional			
Direct mail	Yes	Yes	Yes	Yes
Billboards		Yes		
Brochures			Yes	Yes
Community sponsorships				
Senior events		Yes	Yes	Yes
Children's events				
Health fairs		Yes	Yes	Yes
General entertainment events	Occasional	Yes		
Physician contact				
Personal contact	Yes		Yes	Yes
Direct mail		Yes	Yes	Yes
Miscellaneous				
Point-of-purchase displays	Yes	Yes	Yes	
In-store signage	Yes	Yes	Yes	
Exterior signage	Yes	Yes		Yes
Primary promotional messages				
Everyday low price	Yes	Yes		
Weekly price specials		Yes		
High-quality products			Yes	Yes
Wide range of products	Yes	Yes		
Wide range of services		Yes		
Specific product promotion		Yes		Yes
Specific service promotion			Yes	Yes
Convenience	Yes	Yes	Yes	Yes
Location	Yes	Yes	Yes	Yes

on the other merchandise we carry. If we do the latter, we could risk losing our image as a pharmacy. But, if we focus on the prescriptions alone, I am not sure there is much growth potential over time. This is not going to be easy.

Possible discussion questions

1 How does the competition compare to Northwest Drugs in terms of what they offer? What changes, if any, should Northwest Drugs make relative to the competition?

2 Based on the demographics of the town, who should Northwest Drugs target as future customers?

3 How should Northwest Drugs position itself relative to the competition in terms of the prescription services it offers, nonprescription merchandise it sells, and prices it charges?

4 How should Northwest Drugs promote itself to the target market? What methods should it use, and what message(s) should it convey?

PART V

Organization and staffing the pharmacy

12

Organizing and staffing the pharmacy

Learning objectives

The objectives of this chapter are to assist you to be able to explain:

- the various organizational principles
- the different forms of organization and methods for organizing a pharmacy
- how to plan workforce requirements and develop job descriptions
- the process used to recruit personnel
- the process for selecting an applicant to work for the pharmacy.

Key terms

Application for employment
Delegation of authority
Delegation of work
Employee recruitment
Employment tests
Informal organization
Job description
Line-and-staff organization
Line organization
Occupational Safety and Health Act Organization
Parity of authority and responsibility
Scalar chain
Span of control
Temporary help
Unity of command
Unity of direction

No matter how large or small the pharmacy, it must be organized in some manner. Whether the organization is formal or informal, activities and people should be defined in terms of what is to be done and who is to do each task.

The need for organization

Many sole proprietors view organizing as a waste of time. A typical comment is: "Why should I develop an organizational chart? There are only three people here—me and two employees. We all know what we are supposed to do, and I'm the boss." There is some merit to this perspective—at least until an important task is left unattended to and creates a crisis for the pharmacy.[1]

The nature and importance of organization

The term "organization" often is misused. It is frequently used in the context of being synonymous with the pharmacy itself. Properly defined, however, organization refers to the designated structure of the activities, processes, and people who make up the business. Even in the smallest venture, many marketing, finance, accounting, and personnel activities must be defined and assigned to one or more persons. While the owner may know all the management functions,

some will surely be forgotten or bypassed in the hustle and bustle of daily activity.

As a result, bills may not be paid, supplies may not be ordered with sufficient lead time, or claims processing or payments reconciled. Accordingly, management will spend increasing amounts of time fighting unnecessary fires. Having a good organization will help reduce these types of problems.[2]

All employees need to know specifically what they are supposed to do, what they are responsible for, who they are to report to, and who is to report to them. An ambiguous work environment will result in unperformed tasks and breed frustration and uncertainty about the future. In a pharmacy where most employees can influence its survival and success, this is of paramount importance.

In large chain pharmacies, organizational structure is essential, yet it can insulate top management from lower level employees. Even in small pharmacies, this type of contact can be critical to keeping attuned to all facets of operations and maintaining employee morale.

Organizational principles and practices

Just as there is no one right way to manage, so too there is no one right way to organize. Each business is unique, and will reflect the interests and personality of the owner and the type of industry and environmental setting in which it is involved. However, there are some general principles of organization that can be applied to most businesses.[3]

Division of work

Except in the case of the pharmacist who owns and operates the business alone, work activities must be divided among employees in some logical manner. Early concepts of work division implied a narrowly defined job for each employee. Modern views, however, suggest that while the work should be divided, it should not be so specialized that the employee cannot see the end result of the work effort. Consequently, many businesses are moving to job enrichment in an attempt to expand the job vertically and make the task large enough so the employee can see the value of his or her labor. For example, in a hospital pharmacy, filling prescriptions can become unrewarding if the pharmacist does not have opportunities to consult with patients or physicians about appropriate drug therapy. Being involved in more of the healthcare delivery system is important to long-term job satisfaction.

Parity of authority and responsibility

Employees should have authority for assuring the proper completion of activities they are asked to perform. Workers who are given authority over some functions also should be held responsible for them.

Unity of command

Within any business that has more than one employee, a chain of command must be established, and every worker needs to be supervised by one and only one superior. Many large chain and hospital pharmacies have lines of authority that are unclear, and employees receive orders from several people at once—store managers, pharmacy managers, physicians, hospital administrators, etc.

Unity of direction

Each employee should have a clear understanding of, and a willingness to work for, the goals of the business. Without this unified effort, the pharmacy's efforts are likely to become fragmented and work in several directions at once. An example of this is the case of a chain pharmacy that has no clear direction as to whether it is to be a pharmacy first and foremost, or a mass merchandiser.

Scalar chain

In any organizational structure, ultimate authority rests at the top and flows downward. Scopes of and limits to authority and responsibility must be well delineated on paper as well as in the minds and actions of employers and employees. This is especially true in hospitals where there potentially can be many "bosses"—hospital administrators, physicians serving as chiefs of staff, etc.

Span of control

The principle of span of control states that there are only so many employees a manager can effectively supervise.[4] A general rule of thumb is that at lower levels managers can oversee between 8 and 20 employees, while at upper levels the number is reduced to between 4 and 8. The reason for the lesser number at higher levels is that there is a greater amount of communication needed to operate the pharmacy.

Key factors affecting the span are:

- employee training
- employee communications
- extent of planning
- use of assistance.

If the owner wants to relinquish some decision-making authority, it is necessary to prepare a comprehensive training program, develop an effective line of communication between personnel at all levels, and between management and non-management employees.

Delegation of authority

While responsibility for decisions cannot be passed on, authority to make them can be vested with others. Delegation of authority, however, often is not accomplished within smaller pharmacies. Owners, having gone into business to become bosses, and after developing and nurturing their pharmacies, tend to be unwilling to share control with many others. Even in those companies where delegation has occurred, owners frequently centralize authority during times of crisis or when they do not feel that their employees are performing as they should.

In terms of the formal organization, lack of delegation is typified by a flat pyramid as opposed to a tall one (Figure 12.1). Pharmacy owners tend to use more decentralized organizations when they feel comfortable that employees want, and are able to, make decisions, and when the nature of the environment, as in large chain settings, is such that it is better for decisions to be made close to the scene.

Formalizing the organizational structure

Whether in a community or hospital setting, developing the proper structure involves a two-step process. First, management identifies a relatively standard organizational design that most closely fits the pharmacy's needs. Then this design is molded to coincide with the unique desires of the owner or the hospital's administrator or board of trustees.

Formal organizational structures

A variety of pre-established organizational models are available to management. While somewhat standardized, they serve as a basis for customizing a structure

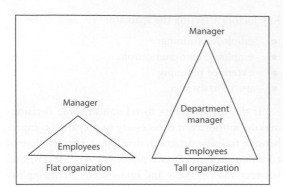

Figure 12.1 Flat and tall organizational structures. Modified from Gaedeke RM and Tootelian DH. *Small Business Management*, 3rd edn. Boston: Allyn and Bacon, 1991: 297.

to meet the preferences of the owner and the goals of the pharmacy.

In many smaller community and hospital pharmacies, management may think it unnecessary to have a formal organizational structure. However, this is not the case. It is essential that everybody within the pharmacy understands his or her position, reporting relationships, and tasks to be performed. Formal organizations help to ensure that this happens.

Line organization

The most common method for organizing a pharmacy is on the basis of line authority. Under this concept,

all personnel are involved in some facet of the preparation and sale of the pharmacy's prescription and non-prescription merchandise, and managers have the right to demand compliance from their subordinates.

A line organization approach, as illustrated in Figure 12.2A is found mostly in small pharmacies that employ relatively few people—typically three to eight. This method is the most effective and efficient in a small pharmacy. As the pharmacy grows and becomes involved in more complex and specialized matters (e.g. tax and financial issues, centralized purchasing), however, this structure does not allow for the inflow of the expertise needed to deal with these considerations.

Line-and-staff organizations

To compensate for the lack of needed specialists within a line organization, a line-and-staff structure evolved. This form of organization, illustrated in Figure 12.2B, is the most common for larger pharmacies that have experienced a degree of success and growth. The key benefit to this approach is that line management still is held responsible for the operations of the business, but now they are assisted by technical specialists who have expertise in some of the finer points of business.

Problems with this form of organization center on violations of the principle of unity of command.

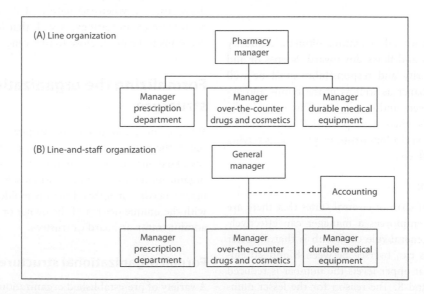

Figure 12.2 Line and line-and-staff organizations. From Gaedeke RM and Tootelian DH. *Small Business Management*, 3rd edn. Boston: Allyn and Bacon, 1991: 298.

Non-management employees often find themselves being given direction by both line and staff personnel.

A common example of this is between a hospital or chain's chief financial officer and the manager of the pharmacy. Both may try to dictate policy concerning cost control, cash flow management, etc., so the employee–pharmacist may get conflicting directives. The most effective way to control this problem is to give line managers (i.e. the pharmacy manager) absolute authority, and use staff members (i.e. the accountant) as advisers to line management only.

The informal organization

Despite almost every attempt to the contrary, an informal organization will develop within both large and small pharmacies. Since organizations are based on people, natural and spontaneous human interaction can drastically influence the effectiveness of formal structures. Consequently, informal leader–follower relationships develop which will not necessarily conform to those prescribed or desired by management.

The leader position often is the result of a non-job-related skill. The strongest physically, the best tennis player, the most personable, or the best-looking may be the informal leader.

Informal organizations can strengthen the cohesiveness within the pharmacy and increase the chances of goal achievement for all. The only time severe action should be taken against the informal organization is when its goals become counterproductive. In most instances, however, the informal group will neither help nor hinder operations to any significant extent.

Methods of organizing the pharmacy

Given some hierarchy in the business, employees and their work need to be grouped in some manner. Then, a manager should be assigned to oversee their functioning. The basic process of organizing follows a series of seven steps:

1 Define the goals of the pharmacy.
2 Identify and define each task to be completed.
3 Group related tasks into jobs that can be assigned to an employee(s).
4 Group the jobs into units that are related in some manner (e.g. skills needed, a facet of the pharmacy's operations).

5 Assign a manager to each unit and provide the manager with the necessary authority and responsibility to complete the jobs within the unit.
6 Arrange these units relative to one another, both horizontally and vertically (e.g. establish who reports to whom).
7 Establish a control system for measuring the progress and achievements of each group.

One of the most common difficulties found among managers with respect to organizing is their uncertainty about how to group jobs and their collective units. On what basis should job activities be joined? There is no one right answer. It depends on the type of healthcare services provided through the pharmacy and the personal preferences of management.

Organization by time

One of the easiest methods for organizing a homogeneous group of employees is on the basis of their working hours. If, as shown in Figure 12.3A, the pharmacy operates day and evening shifts, workers and managers can be assigned to each shift. An example would be a hospital inpatient pharmacy. This logical and convenient approach often is overlooked because of its simplicity. A danger of this method lies in trying to establish too many organizational units and increasing the costs of managing. For example, stores that are open from 10 a.m. to 7 p.m. may not need to have more than one organizational unit.

Organization by number

A homogeneous group of employees (e.g. pharmacists, technicians) that is too large to be effectively supervised by one person can be grouped on the basis of numbers. As illustrated in Figure 12.3B, the management of 20 pharmacists can be separated into two groups of nearly equal size. A disadvantage of this approach is that employees may become isolated from one another and not share information on patient care, physician services, etc.

Organization by function

Organizing by function applies to situations where there is considerable diversity in jobs and the skills required to perform them satisfactorily. As shown

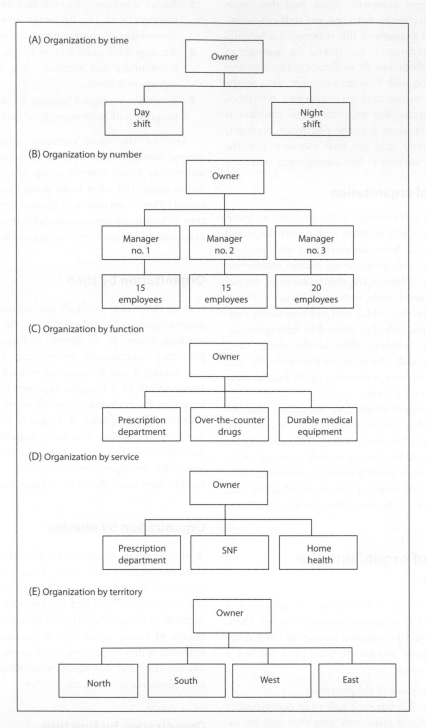

Figure 12.3 Methods of organizing the small business. SNF, skilled nursing facility. Adapted from Gaedeke RM and Tootelian DH. *Small Business Management*, 3rd edn. Boston: Allyn and Bacon, 1991: 300, 301.

in the example of a large independent pharmacy in Figure 12.3C, the services can be divided between pharmacists, non-pharmacist personnel, and a manager placed in charge of each unit. The commonality of tasks is not only a logical method of division but also serves to strengthen the work group and provide a means for sharing expertise. The danger of this approach is that the work units may become too specialized and incur higher administrative costs.

Organization by service

In some cases, management may find it expedient to organize on the basis of different services offered (Figure 12.3D). This is especially beneficial when dealing with highly complex products that require great amounts of technical knowledge, such as ostomy supplies, durable medical equipment, and cosmetics. The key advantage of this approach is that the pharmacy can be organized along profit centers, in which each service is held accountable for the costs it incurs and the revenue and profits it generates. The disadvantage lies in ensuring that all of the organizational units are coordinated to work together for the good of the pharmacy and share the limited financial and personnel resources available.

Organization by territory

For chain organizations that have pharmacies scattered over broad geographic areas, it is sometimes best to organize by territory (Figure 12.3E). Each territory can be a separate, autonomous unit that will respond to the specific needs of the market area being served. The primary advantage to this is that coordinated efforts between geographic areas in terms of achieving economies in purchasing and maintaining consistency build a corporate identity.

Organization by a combination of methods

Because each pharmacy's organizational structure will be unique, none of the methods described may prove satisfactory. Instead, it may be best to organize using a combination of methods. This is illustrated in Figure 12.4. While the structure should be kept as simple as possible, in some instances several organizational approaches may be needed to meet the needs of the pharmacy.

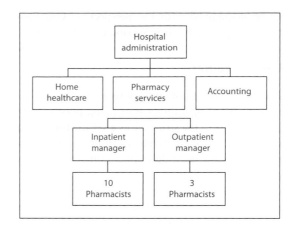

Figure 12.4 Combination of methods of organizing the small business.

Evaluating the organizational structure

Just as goals and plans must be continually monitored and adjusted to changing internal and environmental conditions, so too should the organizational structure. One of the primary advantages of smaller pharmacies is their flexibility to adapt to changing environmental conditions. Does it still suit the owner's needs and desires? Is it still appropriate for the market conditions within which the pharmacy operates? How well do employees and their capabilities match the structure?

Organizational changes are a necessary part of business life for pharmacies that are growing and reacting to market conditions.

When to evaluate

Evaluation of the organizational structure should be a continuous process, especially for large pharmacies and those experiencing rapid growth or decline. The manager must be alert to organizational units that are not operating effectively since their performances may be due to antiquated structures. However, care also should be taken to keep changes to a minimum to avoid creating unnecessary disturbances to operations.

For most pharmacies, a yearly in-depth organizational appraisal is sufficient. An evaluation can be made along with the normal evaluation of sales and expenses, profitability, and market share. When conducted in this manner, the proper role of the structure the employer needs a mechanism to provide at least a basic sketch of the person and his or her background and qualifications. The easiest method of doing this is to have the applicant complete an application form. Although there is some variation among application forms, nearly all contain questions pertaining to personal information, personal references, educational background, work history, and space for the employer–interviewer's comments.

Personal information typically requested from the applicant includes name, address, telephone number, social security number, and physical characteristics that are important to performing the job. The application cannot ask questions pertaining to sex, age, race, and other matters that may be deemed to be discriminatory.

Most application forms request the names, addresses, and telephone numbers of people who will supply additional information on the applicant or vouch for the person's moral character or qualifications. While these should be checked, they cannot be given too much weight unless the references are of known stature. Since most persons will list only people who will provide good recommendations, these cannot be taken as definitive measures.

A listing of the applicant's educational background is useful for two reasons. First, it is a measure of the person's professional qualifications. The second reason for asking for educational background is to be able to trace the person's movements since high school. This helps create a total perspective on the applicant. Frequent changes in colleges, for example, may be indicative of a wandering nature, immaturity, or a less-than-brilliant mind. Employment laws preclude asking for dates of attendance or the year in which the person graduated.

For reasons similar to those of educational background, the applicant's work history should be traced. How far back depends on the wants of the hirer. Some employers want a listing of every full- and part-time job ever held. Others want only the last two or three positions. The types of positions held and the reasons for leaving are important to the screening process.

On receiving the completed application form, the employer should examine the information and note any pertinent data. Questions for future interviews also should be noted.

Administering personal interviews

For applicants who appear to be qualified based on the application form, a personal interview is essential. This allows the employer to ask more questions, clarify existing ones noted on the application form, and simply gain a better general impression of the person. In addition, it provides an opportunity for the applicant to ask questions and decide whether he or she wants to work for the pharmacy.

Since interviews are hardly conducive to a relaxing and casual chat, the employer must try to make applicants feel at ease so they can speak freely. Based on the applicant's answers and questions, the employer should be in a better position to appraise his or her qualifications. Sample questions to include in the interview are shown in Table 12.2.

Checking the applicant's past

Verifying the applicant's statements on the application form as well as from the personal interview is critical. Any serious errors or omissions may indicate that the person is undesirable. This includes a check on personal references, and previous schools and employers.

The value of personal references has been called into question by many employers since court rulings in the 1980s made reference checks available to the applicant, and thereby can open up the possibility of lawsuits in the instance of unfavorable comments. Because of this, many people will not provide written statements. In such cases, personal telephone calls or visits are preferable. The employer should be on the lookout for vague recommendations and anything else that is less than a glowing endorsement.

Administering employment tests

There are essentially two types of tests that can be used in the screening process. One is a job proficiency examination in which the applicant is given an opportunity to demonstrate occupational skills. Demonstrations of ability to compound prescriptions, consult with patients, etc., can be used for pharmacists. For non-pharmacists, the tests may relate to bookkeeping, typing, computer use, etc.

The second type of test includes a series of psychologically related examinations. These include aptitude, personality, and vocational interest tests. They

Table 12.2 Information to obtain about potential employees

Questions to ask applicants	Why are you applying here?
	Why should this pharmacy hire you?
	With respect to employment, what do you want to be doing 5 years from now?
	What do you know about this pharmacy?
	What are your greatest strengths? Weaknesses?
	Why are your leaving your present job?
	With respect to your employment, what accomplishment are you most proud of?
What to watch for	Several jobs in a short period of time.
	Formal education and grades received
	Career and personal goals
	Health problems that could restrict ability to perform job
	Reasons for leaving present job
	Ability to get along with people with diverse personalities
	Communication skills
	Knowledge of the job
	Energy level
	Appearance
	Willingness to perform menial tasks
	Priorities between work and play
	Maturity

Modified from Gaedeke RM and Tootelian DH. *Small Business Management*, 3rd edn. Boston: Allyn and Bacon, 1991: 318. Used with permission.

can be administered by the employer, but are most often handled by a paid professional who will both administer and interpret the test. Because of the complexity of interpretation and the cost, employers tend to use psychological tests only for top managers in especially critical positions.

Requiring a physical examination

A medical history may be required for employee medical insurance or workers' compensation. To some extent, too, the employer then is protected from being charged for injuries occurring prior to coming to work for the pharmacy. Because employers usually pay for physical examinations, they tend to be provided only for a person likely to be hired.

Making a selection

Selection of an applicant should be the culmination of an intensive search and screening process, and based on the objective data collected and intuitive judgment. Throughout this procedure, the employer must be using a process of elimination (i.e. each step in the

process should result in fewer and fewer applicants still under consideration), and trying to sell the applicants on the benefits of coming to work for the pharmacy.

Eventually, some decision must be made. If one applicant is selected, procedures should be established to inform the others and present the pharmacy in the best light while maintaining the dignity of those not selected. Names of applicants who were not hired may be retained in a file for future consideration.

The employer may decide that none of the applicants suits the pharmacy's particular needs. Selecting the best of a group of undesirable applicants is rarely a good decision. Instead, the process of searching and screening should be reviewed and repeated if no procedural flaws are discovered. Temporary help may be used as an interim measure.

Using temporary and part-time help

Another aspect of workforce planning, and an important concern in the overall staffing process, is the possible use of temporary help. In some instances, it may be preferable to use temporary people on a very

Table 13.3 *(continued)*

	Bereavement
	Jury duty
	Clean-up allowance
	Supplemental unemployment
	Guaranteed annual wage
	Relief break
Employee services	Employee meals
	Social and recreational programs
	Legal services
	Christmas bonus
	Employee suggestion program
	Membership in professional trade associations
	Travel clubs
	Credit unions
	Discount purchases
	Credit cards
	Income tax services
	Preretirement counseling
	Relocation expenses
	Food services
	Work–study programs
	Scholarships for dependent children
	Matched donations—universities and colleges
	Preretirement planning

Modified from Hanna JB. *Managing Employee Benefits*. Management Aid No. 5.008. Washington, DC: Small Business Administration, 1980: 7.

while too high a wage may drain the pharmacy of its profits. The most pressing questions faced by employers are:

- What wage levels should be established?
- To what extent should wages be aligned in- and between management and non-management personnel?
- What benefits should be provided, and how should the costs of these benefits be allocated between the employer and the employees?

Establishing wage levels

To some extent, wage decisions have already been decided by the Fair Labor Standards Act of 1938 and its subsequent revisions, including one in 2009. This statute was enacted at the federal level to eliminate the sweatshops in certain industries in large cities which exploited home workers and allowed employers to treat them as independent contractors and thereby escape employment laws that precluded payment of very low wages and no benefits. In addition, many states have established their own regulations regarding wage rates, work hours, overtime pay, and wage discrimination. The employer should check with the Wage and Hour Division of the US Department of Labor to see if the pharmacy falls within the provisions of this law.

In general, most employers can expect to pay at least the federal minimum wage to hourly workers for a 40-hour workweek. Overtime pay may be at least one and a half times an employee's regular rate of pay for all hours worked over 40 in a workweek. Furthermore, the employer should adhere to the "equal pay for equal work" rule and be especially careful in the administration of wages, hours, and working conditions for child labor.

Although the federal minimum wage serves as a guideline, it is common to pay well above the rate or provide additional forms of compensation, as shown in Table 13.4.

Straight salary

The straight salary approach to establishing wages is the most common. Its simplicity and ease of administration are attractive advantages to the pharmacy owner. Although it can be used for management and non-management personnel alike, it is more frequently used for managers and employee–pharmacists. Overall, salary levels for managers will depend on the:

- size of the pharmacy
- geographical location of the pharmacy
- responsibilities of the job
- growth potential of the pharmacy
- pay method and whether bonuses are paid.

The level of pay must be reasonably close to salaries paid to others in comparable positions. For employee–pharmacists, comparisons should be made with what other pharmacies are paying. For non-pharmacists, evaluations will have to be made of other pharmacies and other types of businesses in

Table 13.4 Pharmacies and drugstores employment and wage estimates

Employment estimate	Wage estimates		
	Median hourly	Mean hourly	Mean annual
716,820	$12.42	$19.78	$41,140

From US Department of Labor Bureau of Labor Statistics, May 2010 National Industry-Specific Occupational Employment and Wage Estimates.

which the person could be employed. Although the employer may elect to offer a bit more or less than competitors, gross differences may either waste funds or make it difficult to attract competent people. Of course, salary levels vary widely depending on the geographical area. The cost of living is a critical factor in that high-cost areas usually necessitate higher pay levels. Consequently, the salary offered someone in Phoenix may be considerably less than what is offered in New York City.

While the salary level must be reasonably close, it should not be more than the pharmacy can afford or more than what is commensurate with the duties of the job. Establishing the salary should include a process of examining what comparable people are making and what the pharmacy can afford to pay. Competitive salary data can be obtained from local or national reports and surveys as well as the employer's contacts within the profession and community. Even a look through the help wanted section of the local newspaper can be useful, especially for non-pharmacist personnel. Pharmacy resources can be examined from the pharmacy's financial statements, with different salary levels inserted into projected income statements to see how much impact they have on the pharmacy's profitability.

Once competitive wages have been researched, and the pharmacy's ability to pay has been determined, the employer can begin to design a salary structure. In general, a system of salary ranges is most effective. The Small Business Administration suggests a variety of ranges for upper-, middle-, and lower-level managers[4] (Figure 13.1). Typically, the competitive salary is in about the middle of the range. Lower salaries tend to be reserved for training periods or less critical personnel, while higher salaries are provided to outstanding personnel. Salaries should be reviewed at least once a year to see if they remain in line.

Bonuses based on pharmacy profits frequently are used in small pharmacies that cannot afford large salaries. By developing a bonus system for employees, higher overall incomes can be obtained if the pharmacy prospers.

A bonus system, however, should be tied to profits and apply only to those persons who directly or indirectly (e.g. staff personnel) affect profits. In addition, the salary plus bonus usually is higher than a straight salary offered by a competitor. If, for example, a chain pharmacy can only afford to pay a manager $90,000 while managers for competitors are offered $95,000, the potential bonus should be at least $5,000, and more likely between $7,000 and $10,000. Not only does this protect the pharmacy from excessive salaries, it also serves to motivate the manager to better levels of performance.

Hourly wage

Most employees in non-management positions are paid an hourly wage. This is due partly to tradition and partly to the fact that some people are affiliated with labor unions. Hourly wages provide a relatively easy way to pay employees for their efforts, especially when their performance cannot be directly related to product and service sales.

These rates are usually set on the basis of those offered by competitors, with the same stipulation relating to geographical location and affordability described for straight salaries. When dealing with labor unions, the pharmacy owner will have to reckon not only with competitive rates but also with the pharmacy's profitability. If the pharmacy is quite profitable, the union may use this as an argument for paying higher-than-competitive wages. In addition to union issues, management will have to contend with federally established minimum wages, overtime pay, and other matters. Despite these potential problems, the hourly wage offers flexibility in paying for the time spent working. Since many pharmacies use this

5. Hanna JB. *Managing Employee Benefits, Management Aid No. 5.008*, Washington, DC: Small Business Administration, 1980.
6. Metcalf WO. *Health Maintenance Programs for Small Business, Management Aid No. 16*, Washington, DC: Small Business Administration, 1964.

7. Universal insurance recommended. *California Hospitals*, May/June, 1989: 7–10.
8. Patient data may reshape health care. *Wall Street Journal*, April 17, 1989: B-1.
9. ESOPs: Are they good for you?. *Business Week*, May 15, 1989: 116–124.

14

Personnel relations

Learning objectives

The objectives of this chapter are to assist you to be able to explain:

- how employers can mesh employee and pharmacy goals
- how employee motivation and morale can be improved within the pharmacy
- the role of organizational communication within the pharmacy
- how employers can discipline or dismiss employees
- the role of employee performance appraisals in the pharmacy.

Key terms

Autocratic leadership style
Democratic leadership style
Employee grievances
Employee morale
Employee performance appraisals
Goal congruence
Leadership style
Maintenance factors
Management by objectives
Motivation factors

Organizational communication
Production vs. personnel orientation
Union–management relations

One of the most valued of all assets in any business is one that does not appear on the balance sheet—the pharmacy's employees. The quality and loyalty of personnel often make the difference between a pharmacy's success or failure.[1] Employees who can be trusted and relied on not only ease many of the burdens placed on the employer but also increase the pharmacy's productivity and opportunity for profitability.

In the early 1800s, Robert Owen, manufacturer and social reformer, discussed the need to foster good employee relations. After noting that a manufacturer must maintain the enterprise's "innate" machinery by keeping it clean, well-oiled, and in good repair, Owen posed a significant question: If the owner should take such good care of innate machinery, shouldn't the same be done for the human machines? Owen argued that these machines were certainly more complex than the metal ones and they needed at least as much care and feeding.

Managing the workforce

Modern management recognizes the need to foster good employee relations. Simply hiring people is no guarantee that they will contribute much to the pharmacy. Even training cannot assure high levels of employee productivity. Concerted efforts must be made to provide a work environment conducive to success (Table 14.1). This involves cultivating morale, developing appropriate leadership styles, making a continuous effort to motivate employees to do their best, and constructively evaluating their performance.

Unfortunately, many pharmacy owners, and especially those who open their own stores, prove to be poor managers. The very desire to be involved in all aspects of operations makes it difficult for them to allow others to play a role in the pharmacy's success. Too many managers leave this function to chance. Caught up in the flurry of day-to-day activities, they often neglect this facet of their jobs. Consequently, employee relations either deteriorate or never fully develop.

Employee and pharmacy goals

One error commonly made by pharmacy owners when it comes to employee relations is that they forget that employees have goals too, or they assume that they know what their employees want in their professional and personal lives. This lack of understanding on the part of employers is highlighted in Table 14.2.

Employees work for a reason, be it to earn a living, pass idle time, or simply to meet the challenge of a difficult job. Whatever the case, employees expect to accomplish something through their employment. Whether their goals are similar to or even compatible with the pharmacy's goals varies according to the type of person and the characteristics of the pharmacy. Nevertheless, if an employee views the pharmacy's goals as counter to his or her personal goal achievement, it is most likely that the pharmacy will suffer. If they complement each other, the pharmacy will prosper with respect to its personnel relations.

Goal congruence

The shaded areas in Figure 14.1 show that the pharmacy and an employee will likely have at least some common goals. Although there may be many different areas of joint interest, the desire for the pharmacy to survive is one of the most important. If the pharmacy ceases to exist, the employee will be out of a job.

Areas of common interest could include profitability if the employee views personal income as being directly related to the pharmacy's financial success, and interest in the pharmacy's products and services. The employer must capitalize on these areas of common interest to develop good relations with personnel.

In some cases, however, there may be virtually no common interest (see Figure 14.1). Employees hired for the short term may not have sufficient time to develop much interest in the pharmacy or have much concern for its survival. Similar circumstances apply to an employee who takes a position on an interim basis. Finally, personal conflicts between the pharmacy owner and employees can result in the latter working in a manner counterproductive to the pharmacy's goals. Slowdowns and production errors frequently arise on these occasions.

Certainly an important area where employee–pharmacists and the employer may differ concerns the future. In most pharmacy settings there are limits to how high up in the organization the pharmacist can progress. There simply are not many positions. Unless the pharmacist wants to eventually move into a management position, there are relatively few opportunities for growth available.

The best interests of the employer are achieved when the goals of the pharmacy become those of the employee. To accomplish this, however, the pharmacy owner must set goals that also benefit the pharmacy's personnel (Table 14.3). This sounds easy, but what do employees want? How do their goals change over

Table 14.1 Tips on managing people

1.	Periodically review each position in the pharmacy. Take a quarterly look at the job. Is work being duplicated? Is it structured so that it encourages the employee to become involved? Can the tasks be given to another employee or employees and a position eliminated? Can a part-time person fill the job?
2.	Play a private mental game. Imagine that the pharmacy must get rid of one employee. If one person had to go, who would it be? How would jobs be realigned?
3.	Use compensation as a tool rather than viewing it as an evil. Reward quality work. Investigate the possibility of using raises and bonuses as incentives for higher productivity.
4.	Remember that there are new ways of controlling absenteeism through incentive compensation plans. For example, the owner–manager could eliminate vacations and sick leave and instead give each employee 30 days annual leave to use as he or she sees fit. At the end of the year, the employees could be paid at regular rates for the leave they didn't use.

Modified from Feller JH Jr. *Keep Pointed Toward Profit*. Management Aid No. 1.003. Washington, DC: Small Business Administration, 1985.

Table 14.2 What employees want from a job

Ranking by employees	What employees want	Ranking by management
1	Credit for all work done	7
2	Interesting work	3
3	Fair pay	1
4	Understanding and appreciation	5
5	Counsel on personal problems	8
6	Promotion on merit	4
7	Good physical working conditions	6
8	Job security	2

Modified from Bruce MM. *Human Relations in Small Business*. Management Series No. 3. Washington, DC: Small Business Administration, 1969.

time? The complex nature of goals makes answers to these questions not always easy to obtain.

Personal goal structures

Employees bring aspirations to the pharmacy in the hope that they will be satisfied. Although these goals can be classified in many ways, the grouping advanced by Abraham Maslow in 1943 still is one of the most frequently cited. Suggesting that there are five different sets of needs, Maslow sees them as arrayed in a hierarchy, beginning with the physiologic and moving through safety, social, esteem, and self-actualization needs (Figure 14.2). Thus, one set of goals does not become of much importance until more basic, lower level goals are satisfied.

The most elementary of all needs are those essential for survival. For the employer, it is important that the employee earn enough to survive economically. Wages well below the levels needed to purchase food and shelter make it necessary for the employee to work elsewhere.

Once the employee's physiologic needs are satisfied, the desire for safety and security takes on added importance. In addition to being physically safe, most people work more productively when they feel secure in their positions. The fear of being fired or laid off is not conducive to high levels of productivity. By maintaining rigorous standards in hiring and continually training employees, it becomes less likely that they will need to be fired. Building a stable work environment is a common goal.

After the employee achieves reasonable fulfillment of his or her physiologic, safety, and security needs, social needs become more prominent. The desire to belong and to be accepted by others, especially by the peer group, is important. Accordingly, the pharmacy owner should make developing a cohesive workforce a priority. Here, effective orientation and training can be of great value. The employer must make sure that both the trainee and the work group understand the role and position of the new employee. Neither party should feel uncertain or threatened. Rather, their mutual acceptance should be cultivated to establish the

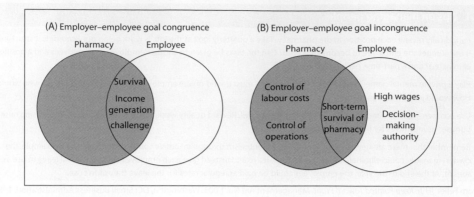

Figure 14.1 Employer–employee goal congruence. From Gaedeke RM and Tootelian DH. *Small Business Management*, 3rd edn. Boston: Allyn and Bacon, 1991: 462.

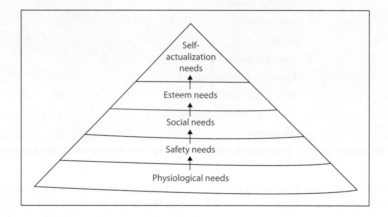

Figure 14.2 Maslow's hierarchy of needs. From Gaedeke RM and Tootelian DH. *Small Business Management*, 3rd edn. Boston: Allyn and Bacon, 1991: 464.

type of working environment that will satisfy the social needs of all.

The fourth need in Maslow's scheme is esteem, or ego fulfillment. Everyone likes to feel independent and self-confident, and wants to be recognized and appreciated from time to time. The extent to which the employer allows employees freedom to undertake important jobs and also recognizes their accomplishments is of critical importance to determining the extent to which employees will become emotionally involved in their work. If the opportunity for ego satisfaction is not present, employees will certainly look elsewhere. The job may simply become a vehicle to generate money so that other personal activities can be undertaken. That is, an employee may simply use the job to get money for skiing, boat-

ing, etc. When the employer provides the opportunity for employees to achieve their ego needs through the work experience, jobs take on added personal value.

The final and ultimate goal of most people is self-actualization—doing all that one is capable of. While few ever really achieve this, it is important that people have the opportunity to try. Chances for advancement, more challenging assignments, or perhaps part ownership in the pharmacy through stock ownership programs (ESOPs) deserve consideration. When employees feel they have gone as far as they can with the pharmacy, but still are not fully satisfied, they either look to other opportunities for employment or lose interest in their jobs.

Table 14.3 Employer–employee expectations and trouble spots

1. What the employee expects from the employer	Proper job instruction
	Impartial treatment and loyalty
	Fair production standards
	Good working conditions
2. What the employer expects from the employee	Cooperation
	Standard production
	Attendance
3. What the department manager expects from the top management	Clear line of authority
	Non-conflicting rules and regulations
	Reasonable production schedules
	Decisions backed by management
4. What top management expects from the department manager	Trouble-free leadership
	Carrying out pharmacy rules
	Meeting sales and expense budgets
	Keeping adequate records
5. Is the department manager "turnover conscious?"	The effect of turnover on costs
	The effect of turnover on morale
	Are the reasons given for discharges or quits sufficiently detailed to allow for complete analysis of trouble spots?
	Are grievances heard privately and are they resolved promptly?
6. The employee as an individual	What makes the employee different from others? (temperament, education, outside interests, etc.)
	What outside conditions affect the employee? (finances, marital troubles, transportation, children, etc.)
	Age and how it affects the employee
	Reasons for working? (support self, supplement spouse's earnings, buy clothes, etc.)
7. How to get the most out of an employee	Gain respect
	Let the employee know what is expected
	Be fair and impartial
	Be patient and understanding at all times
	Make each employee feel a part of your team

(continued)

Employee morale and motivation

The extent to which an employee can achieve personal needs affects motivation on the job. When personal goal achievement is closely intertwined with that of the pharmacy, the stage is set for high levels of employee motivation and productivity. But how does the employer tell when the employee perceives that personal goals coincide with those of the pharmacy? How can the pharmacy owner strengthen the employee's desire to perform well?

One well-known study on employee motivation was conducted by Frederick Herzberg in the 1950s on groups of accountants and engineers. Although

Table 14.3 *(continued)*

8. The problem employee	Lack of respect for supervisor
	Inefficiency
	Carelessness
	Rumormonger
	Time and material waster
	Privilege abuser
9. Causes of problem employees	The common denominator of all problem cases is the failure of employees to adjust themselves to the work situation. Principal causes for problem employees are:
	Poor selection and placement
	Inadequate training
	Incompetent supervision
	Failure to enlighten employees on management's attitude on matters of promotion, grievances, etc.
	Unsound personnel practices
	Off-the-job problems

Adapted from Loen EL. *Personnel Management Guide for Small Business*, 2nd edn. Washington, DC: Superintendent of Documents, Government Printing Office, 1974: 36–37.

these were atypical employees, two sets of factors that may play a critical role in many issues of employee motivation were identified: maintenance factors and motivation factors. Herzberg found that the lack of some variables would cause employee dissatisfaction, but that their presence would not move them to try to excel. These were the maintenance factors, and they included money, working conditions, and company policies and administration. Other variables, the motivation factors, could make employees strive for improved job performance, but their absence would not cause dissatisfaction. Motivation factors included recognition, challenging work, and opportunities for advancement and personal growth.

Employee morale

Attitudes that individuals and groups have on the job usually directly affect their work performance. Known as employee morale, these attitudes can be either favorable or unfavorable to the job and the work environment. Since attitudes can be defined as predispositions to behave in certain ways, favorable morale tends to result in employees performing at their best, while unfavorable morale results in poor or perhaps counterproductive performances.

Because attitudes cannot be seen or heard directly, the pharmacy owner must be alert for signs

of poor morale. Many employers believe that if employees are unhappy with something they will say so, or that their dissatisfaction will be readily apparent. Usually this is not true. Employees, fearful of losing their jobs or who may be simply too shy to complain, often resort to subtle ways of expressing their displeasure.

An obvious sign of poor morale is increased numbers of complaints or grievances from an individual or a group of employees. Whether the complaints are valid is not as important as the fact that they are being made. The employer should not only try to correct any real problems but should also probe for deeper issues not being discussed. Unanswered complaints decrease productivity.

A high employee turnover indicates intolerable work conditions or mismatch between employees and jobs. When turnover is not concentrated among a few jobs or within a single department (e.g. prescription, durable medical equipment, home healthcare supplies), it is most likely that a more general morale problem exists. A full evaluation of personnel policies and the work environment typically is necessary to determine the problems.

A third sign is an increase in absenteeism and tardiness. Some employees will not go to the extreme of quitting, but will become lax in coming to work. An increasingly frequent incidence of employees calling in sick, simply not showing up, or arriving late is an indication that they are not eager to work for the pharmacy. Since these symptoms can be costly in terms of lost productivity, the employer should determine their causes.

Another sign of low morale is when an increasing number of errors are made in prescription dispensing or cash register sales. Whether this indicates a deliberate attempt to hurt the pharmacy, or simply a lack of care and concern, the results are the same—decreasing profitability. In situations where there is considerable antagonism between the owner and employees, it is not unusual to find employees venting their frustrations on their jobs.

Finally, there may be an increase in the number of accidents. Perhaps this is the ultimate in carelessness. Often when people dislike some aspects of their jobs, they direct their attention elsewhere to mentally escape the unpleasantness. Unfortunately, their physical beings remain, and they make errors.

To be effective, the pharmacist must be able to recognize possible signs of poor morale and take corrective action before valuable employees are lost or costly errors are made. Some suggestions for employers on keeping morale high include:[2]

- Accept the fact that management and employees do not always see things similarly.
- In any differences of opinion, consider the possibility that the employee may have the right answer.
- Show employees that management is interested in them and that it wants their ideas on how conditions can be improved.
- Treat employees as individuals rather than dealing with them impersonally.
- Insofar as possible, give explanations for management actions.
- Provide information and guidance on matters affecting employees' job security.
- Make reasonable efforts to keep jobs interesting. This is especially important for pharmacists who have limited opportunities to move up in the organization. Try from time to time to offer some new challenges to professionals.
- Encourage promotion from within.
- Express appreciation publicly for jobs well done, and offer criticism privately in the form of constructive suggestions for improvement.

- Train managers to be concerned about the people they manage.

While many pharmacy owners watch for problems in employee morale, others rely on extensive personal interviews, open sessions with employees, and anonymous surveys in which employees provide written responses to general questions about their jobs and work conditions. Another useful approach is to use an employee suggestion system along the lines described in Figure 14.3. Such a method provides a confidential means for employees to air their complaints and make positive recommendations for pharmacy improvement.

Interviews and surveys tend to be a little more expensive to develop and may be inaccurate if employees perceive any danger in being honest. Nevertheless, they are useful in spotting troubles in their early stages. In addition, the simple fact that the employer cares enough to ask employees often bolsters morale by itself.

Leadership style

Leadership style refers to the approach the manager uses to direct the actions of employees.

How the pharmacy owner views and treats employees will have significant effects on worker morale and motivation. Perhaps the two most important aspects of developing a leadership style concern the degree to which the pharmacy owner allows employees to share in the management of the pharmacy, and the extent to which the employer is concerned about the human vs. the "production" management of the pharmacy.

The type of approach used by the manager can be either autocratic, democratic, or something in between. An autocratic style of leadership means that the manager retains absolute control by not allowing employees to make decisions or provide any input into the decision-making process. Some managers have little confidence in their employees' ability to make decisions. In addition, since all the risks are taken by the owner, why should anyone else determine the pharmacy's fate? In many pharmacies, too, there is little need for numerous decision-makers. Coordination and communication problems often are not worth the trouble involved.

In contrast to the autocratic style, some pharmacy owners consider themselves democratic managers.

The idea behind the suggestion plan is simple. The employees spend most of their workday performing one or more specific tasks. They know the details of their jobs better than anybody else, including the manager. Certainly, they look at the job fromadifferent point of view. They may, and in practice often do, have ideas that nobody else would think of about better ways to do the job.

Employees may have many good ideas for improving the preparation or sale of the pharmacy's products and services, but they may be reluctant to suggest them because:

- they fear that management will think itareflection on them for not having thought of the idea

- they believe that the pharmacy will get all the benefit from the suggestion and they will get none

- since there are no recognized channels for making suggestions, they are afraid that suggesting a new and untried idea will make them appear peculiar in the eyes of fellow employees and management.

If,however, all employees are encouraged to submit suggestion by provision of a formal suggestion plan, this reluctance can in most cases be overcome and valuable ideas obtained.

Inviting employees to make suggestions about that phase of the pharmacy with which they are most familiar — primarily their own jobs and surroundings on the job—is in effect asking them to lend a hand in planning plant processes and procedures. And *you* are providing them with a channel by which they can go right to "topside" with ideas.

There are five elements of an employee suggestion system:

1. a suggestion box to keep employees reminded of the plan and to receive their ideas
2. an administrator to gather suggestions, obtain evaluations from operating officials concerned, and otherwise see to the smooth functioning of the suggestion system
3. a committee to consider suggestions and approve rewards
4. recognition and rewards for ideas that are accepted and suitable explanations for those that are not
5. a follow-up system to see that good ideas are put to use, either immediately or whenever changing conditions make them applicable.

Figure 14.3 Employee suggestion system. Modified from Wilhelm D. *An Employee Suggestion System for Small Companies*, 3rd edn. Washington, DC: Small Business Administration, 1964: 2.

Here, decision-making within the pharmacy is shared fully between the owner and employees. The manager must have great confidence in the employees and their ability and desire to make decisions in the best interests of the pharmacy. The democratic style tends to get employees ego-involved in the pharmacy and serves to improve their morale and motivation. Sharing decision-making can complicate coordination problems, but at the same time improve the quality of decisions since they are being made more quickly and closer to the scene.

Although some managers are either autocratic or democratic, most are somewhere in between. They may seek the inputs of employees before making a decision, or they may allow them to make the actual decision within certain specified limits. In some instances, the manager will announce a tentative decision and ask employees for their opinions so as to provide them with opportunities to voice concerns or support. In other cases, the manager will provide employees with the authority and responsibility to make management decisions outright.

The style of leadership selected by a pharmacy owner depends on several factors, including the:

- degree of self-confidence the pharmacy owner has
- degree of confidence the manager has in subordinates
- importance of decisions to the survival or success of the pharmacy
- extent to which employees want decision-making responsibilities.

The pharmacy owner who has ample self-confidence will feel more secure in delegating decision-making authority. In addition, confidence in the work group, coupled with their desire to make decisions and a reasonably secure business climate, will be more conducive to democratic management. However, if the decision has a major impact on the pharmacy's survival, most employers will make the ultimate decisions themselves.

Such retention of decision-making authority can also be found among employers who have retired and turned operations over to their offspring. During difficult times or when critical decisions have to be made, founders often return to "their" companies. This occurs frequently in smaller pharmacies, in part because the founder may continue to have a great financial interest in the business.

Although there is no "right" method of leadership, it is highly important that the employer take into consideration the desires of employees. An autocratic approach may frustrate more creative employees who want some decision-making responsibility. Similarly, a democratic style may be unacceptable to employees who like structure and do not want extra responsibility.

One interesting theory on leadership style was advanced by Fredrick Fiedler in 1965.[3] Arguing that it was difficult and costly to try to change a manager's leadership inclinations, Fiedler suggested that the job be changed to fit the individual. For example, a manager who wants to control all aspects of the business and not delegate any decision-making authority should look for employees who prefer not to make decisions.

Production vs. personnel orientation

Related to the issue of autocratic vs. democratic management is whether the employer is more concerned about employees or the pharmacy's products and services. Explored by Blake and Mouton, this issue highlights some common pitfalls in managing a business.[4]

The "management grid" identifies two extremes in the employer's concern for production or the employees. The pharmacy owner may be a production manager who is totally concerned about the product and service aspects of the pharmacy and has no regard for the employees or their working conditions. Even though the employer should never lose sight of sales and customer satisfaction goals, such disregard for the employees will usually hinder achievement of pharmacy goals.

The opposite of the production manager is the personnel manager. This employer is concerned with employees and their work conditions. It is a true paternalistic approach to management. It is assumed that if the employees are well cared for, the productive effort will follow naturally. Unfortunately, pampering the workforce will not always lead to greater production. Indeed, some employees resent the paternal approach, while for others it might impede their own self-development.[5]

Organizational communication

One of the most critical factors in the area of personnel relations is that of organizational communications. Perhaps nothing creates more problems and destroys employee morale and motivation faster than a breakdown in the communication process within the pharmacy. Not knowing what is going on results in disruptions in operations and employee uneasiness. Employees need accurate and timely information if they are to avoid missing duties and making preventable errors.

Lapses in communication lead to rumor, innuendo, and general distrust. Since people typically fear the unknown, such gaps within the organization have a definite unsettling effect. In addition, without a formal communication process it is probable that an informal one, the grapevine, will develop. Although the grapevine can be an effective vehicle for communication, it generally is outside the employer's control.

To avoid or at least minimize potential problems with the grapevine, the pharmacy owner should be sure to set up at least a simple communications network so that rumors will not go unchallenged. The key to this process is identifying what information employees need to do their jobs, and what they want to provide an appropriate level of comfort about job security and related concerns.

Communication processes can flow in either one or two ways. One-way communications move from the top down and do not allow for much dialogue between the employer and the employee. In a pure sense, the employer gives orders and the employee accepts them or quits. There is no interchange. While one-way flow can be expedient, it often leads to employee dissatisfaction because employees are not involved in the management process. This approach also does not gain the input of employees who are closer to the pharmacy's basic operations.

Two-way communications allow for information to move from the employer to the employee and from the employee to the employer. This is generally preferred since it involves and utilizes employees to a greater extent.

The formal line of communication can be used to pass along information in non-productive areas when desirable. Information on the general success of the pharmacy, possible changes in the future, and social factors can be effectively communicated.

With the formal and informal lines for passing oral and written information, the pharmacy owner also must recognize such factors as mannerisms and body language. Employers, for example, often tell employees that they have an "open door" policy in being accessible. Then, they proceed to walk into their offices and close their doors—making it very difficult for employees to believe the policy.

Employee performance appraisal

A critical element in any personnel relations program is the appraisal of employee performance. This evaluation improves not only the quality of work but holds important implications for employee motivation and discontent. When used effectively, the appraisal identifies the individual's strengths and weaknesses and provides the employer with information relative to the employee's capacity for retention and promotion.

Methods of appraising performance

There are many methods available for evaluating effort and ability. For management positions in particular (e.g. prescription department manager, home healthcare manager), the "management by objectives" (MBO) approach is quite valuable. This is one of the most commonly used and desirable techniques available since it involves a joint effort and evaluation by both the owner and employee. The key to its use lies in establishing employee objectives by employees, developing action-oriented plans for their achievement, and periodically reviewing performance. Because it is an interactive approach, communication concerning performance is virtually assured.

For non-managers, including staff pharmacists, a host of evaluation techniques have been prepared. Two samples are presented in Appendix 14-A. The advantage of each of these is that they are reasonably comprehensive, yet easy to administer and understand. To the extent possible, the form used should be made available to employees at the time they are employed. By doing this, they will know the criteria to

be used to evaluate their performance and the method by which the evaluation will take place.

The desirability of any method of performance appraisal can be assessed on the basis of its ability to make a complete yet simple evaluation. Although the content will vary by type of job and pharmacy needs, some of the more common factors to be measured include:

- *Units of output*: This can be measured on an hourly, daily, weekly, or monthly basis. For pharmacists, this may be the number of prescriptions dispensed per day; for salespersons, it may be sales per day.

- *Quality of work*: Based on the number of prescription errors, incorrect transactions recorded, or number of complaints, some assessment of the employee's quality of efforts should be made.

- *Dependability*: Measured in terms of coming to work on time, one assessment will be the dependability to perform. Another dimension is the extent to which the individual can be counted on to do a good job. This is an intangible factor that is hard to measure. Perhaps the closest approximation is the quality of work.

- *Job knowledge*: A person's knowledge of the job, pharmacy, and parent company policies, and so on can be measured through objective testing techniques if desired. Informal questioning of the employee also can be used to assess this.

- *Ability and willingness to work with others*: Since the pharmacy relies on relatively few people, it is essential that they be willing and able to work in a cooperative spirit. This, however, is difficult to measure quantitatively. Observation of the employees' interaction as well as monitoring any conflict through grievances or other hostilities provides several bases for rather subjective appraisals.

- *Initiative and ability to handle ambiguity*: The extent to which individuals can work on their own and perform relatively unstructured tasks is a definite asset to the pharmacy. Measurement of these factors is difficult, short of psychological testing. Most pharmacy owners do not want to take the time or spend the money to conduct such tests. Thus, observation of the employees' work and the extent to which they take command is all that can be viewed. This is a crude measure and must be recognized as such.

The first three of these factors can be measured quantitatively with reasonable accuracy. The last three are qualitative and subject to considerable judgmental error.

Use of employee appraisals

However evaluated, the employee appraisal process is not complete until it has been personally discussed with the employee. Secret evaluations whose results are not conveyed to the worker will be of no value for improved performance, and in fact will be viewed negatively by employees. Not knowing where they stand or how they are rated has a destabilizing impact on the workforce.

Used properly, the evaluation form will be reviewed at a meeting between the employer and the employee. Each aspect of the individual's performance should be discussed in terms of strengths and weaknesses, and how the latter can be improved. Many managers require employees to sign the evaluations, stating that they have seen and discussed them with their immediate supervisor. This assures that such a meeting actually took place. As a positive assessment, this approach can do much to improve overall employee performance.

In addition to its use for strengthening employee performance, the assessment process also can be a vehicle for motivating people and an input to the promotion process. By showing employees how they can improve, and identifying possibilities for advancement through bettering themselves, the benefits of evaluation can be expanded. Most important, these evaluations over a period of time will show how well an employee is doing and where he or she is headed with respect to a career within the pharmacy. Such an assessment of the pharmacy's most valuable asset—its employees—is essential to the development and maintenance of sound personnel relations.

Improving employee relations

No matter how careful the pharmacy owner is in developing employment plans and practices, it is likely that employees at times will become dissatisfied. In some cases, this might be the result of poor working conditions or the job itself. In others, employees may be having personal problems that they unavoidably bring to work. Finally, there will be some bad days for both the employer and the employees—days when they wake up in a bad mood that gets progressively worse.

While these problems are to be expected when humans are involved, they should be dealt with quickly yet cautiously to avoid long-term problems. When handled properly, these difficulties can be resolved and in many cases used to solidify a strong bond between the owner and employees. When mishandled, the result typically is intense labor problems.

Handling employee grievances

To get the best from employees, it is important that they have opportunities to voice their opinions. Successful handling of employee dissatisfaction revolves around the following:

- recognizing problems quickly
- allowing grievances to vent themselves
- equitably resolving the problem(s).

Quick recognition

Whether a complaint is serious, valid, or resolved to the employee's satisfaction, the longer it lingers before being treated, the more it strains the long-term employer–employee relationship. If nothing else, a long recognition time is viewed as evidence of insensitivity to the cares and needs of the workforce. In addition, one irritant often sets the stage for other complaints that might never have arisen.

Consequently, the pharmacy owner needs to be alert for signs of employee discontent—slowdowns, tardiness, accidents, excessive waste. By identifying and focusing on those areas where problems are most likely to occur, the employer will increase the chances of early detection. Although these areas vary by pharmacy and mix of employees (e.g. pharmacists, technicians), in many instances they include jobs that are highly routine and those in adverse work environments (e.g. hot or cold, noisy, highly stressful).

Airing of complaints

Closely related to this early recognition is the need for an outlet for discontent. When employees have no established means of airing complaints, they often resort to counterproductive measures that are more difficult to recognize.

Since everybody needs to "blow off steam" at some time, the pharmacy owner should establish a mechanism through which employees can voice their complaints. This may to some extent be therapeutic, and some pharmacy owners regularly schedule open sessions with employees during which time they are encouraged to say what they like and dislike about the pharmacy and its management.

Other employers use "grievance boxes," which are similar to suggestion boxes. Employees can submit complaints, while maintaining their anonymity, which is impossible with the open-session approach.

While there are many approaches to bringing grievances to light, the success of any such process depends on the atmosphere created by the owner and manager. There must be a genuine concern conveyed to employees, and an assurance that grievances are free from management reprisal. If employees are not encouraged to be free and open with the owner, they will likely conceal their complaints and "get even" through various means.

Equitable resolution

Even if the pharmacy owner makes every effort to identify problems quickly and create an open employer–employee atmosphere, it will be of little value if grievances are not resolved equitably. Not eliminating the conflict will certainly damage this relationship.

This does not mean, of course, that the employer must give in on all areas of conflict. Rather, the owner should try to maintain an open mind and try to understand the problem from the perspective of the employee. By openly discussing the problem and methods of resolving it, the employer hopefully will find a solution that is fair and acceptable to all. In many cases, the true problem will be a personal one that is due to mental, financial, or health difficulties. Simply being willing to listen to the troubled employee and showing concern and sympathy may be all that is necessary. When employment-related issues are involved, the employer needs to assess the costs and benefits to be derived from all possible options.

The critical point is whether the employee views the solution as being equitable. When no changes or only partial changes are made, the employee should be told why complete action was not taken. In this way, the employee will at least understand the reasons and go away with the belief that the owner was being honest and trying to be fair.

Employee discipline and dismissal

Over the life of any business it is likely that there will be a need for employee discipline and dismissal. In some cases, it will simply be a result of an error in hiring—the employee did not fit the needs of the job or the "personality" of the organization. In others, it will be due to an evolutionary change in the business, including its objectives and the types of tasks to be accomplished, which made it different from what it was and what it needed in terms of personnel. Similarly, the needs of employees change over time, and the pharmacy may not be in a position to satisfy those needs and still accomplish its own objectives. Finally, there are instances where access to controlled substances makes drug abuse or theft particularly enticing.

Dismissing personnel can place great strains on a pharmacy and is never a pleasant experience. Whatever the cause, the pharmacy owner must be ready to deal with the fact that discipline or dismissal may be called for. Such actions have to be based on a clear understanding of the ground rules for employment. This necessitates identifying and publicizing actions like theft, fighting, continued tardiness, or other infractions which will result in discipline or dismissal.

Disciplinary actions should be prompt, commensurate with the violation, and clearly explained to all affected. Long delays between the time of the employee action and the resulting disciplinary steps usually are viewed as indecisive. Similarly, management over- or under-reaction generates little employee confidence and respect.

To be effective, therefore, employee practices calling for discipline or dismissal should be well communicated, and management actions promptly taken. Some of the more common grounds for discipline or dismissal are:

- refusal to work or take direction
- disorderly conduct
- tardiness and absenteeism
- poor treatment of customers
- stealing from the pharmacy or other employees
- destruction of pharmacy property
- violation of safety practices
- alcohol or drug abuse
- gambling while on the job.

What is most important is that the discipline be positive in nature and not a personal attack that embarrasses or destroys the employee's sense of self-worth. Thus, corrective action should be oriented toward improving future performance rather than punishing for past mistakes. Similarly, any discipline should be directed toward the mistake and not used to make an example of the person being disciplined. If the ground rules are well known, there should be no need to make anybody the "classic case." The process may begin with a verbal warning, followed by a written warning the next time, and dismissal thereafter. From a legal standpoint, however, all such actions should be documented for future reference.

While dismissing employees seldom is a pleasant experience, it may be necessary. Incompetent employees are a drain on the limited resources of a pharmacy. Insubordinate employees who have been disciplined two or three times are an added headache to the already overworked manager's life. Neither can be tolerated for long if the pharmacy is to survive and have a chance to prosper.

Perhaps the most difficult termination is the one where there is insufficient work or a change in the direction of the pharmacy's efforts. At this point, a good employee's job must be terminated. Some actions can be taken to ease the damage this causes. First, the employee can be given sufficient notice so that he or she might find employment elsewhere before leaving. Second, the employer can assist the employee to find other employment through business contacts and letters of recommendation, making the employee's search for a new job more tolerable.

Disciplining or dismissing employees is a particularly sensitive activity in a pharmacy since there are fewer people and they tend to know one another well. However, the employer must take action when necessary or the pharmacy will not survive.

Union–management relations

The inability of management to resolve employee grievances is one of the more common reasons cited for unionization within business in general. Other reasons include employee desires for higher wages, greater job security, and a voice in the overall management of the pharmacy. To be sure, many pharmacy owners protest, "It won't happen to me—my employees are my friends!" More often than not, this is naive. "It" frequently transcends the question of employer–employee friendship. In many cases, it is a simple question of economics. Union representation provides employees with some degree of security, protection from arbitrary management actions, and the hope of higher wages.

Since employees do have the ability to unionize, the employer must decide whether or not to fight it or encourage it. Some consider unionization a fate worse than death. These employers adopt exotic policies and practices designed to keep employees happy and avoid hiring union instigators. Other employers actually prefer to deal with one entity rather than try to negotiate with employees one by one.

Although pharmacy owners at times can deter or delay unionization, in some cases it is best to recognize the union's right to exist and strive for a rational and harmonious relationship. Interfering with employee rights to organize can violate federal law, the National Labor Relations Act. In addition, such a fight creates a poor basis for building future relationships.

Summary

- Good employee relations are as necessary as the care and upkeep of a pharmacy's physical equipment.
- Employers should set pharmacy goals that also provide for the benefit of the employees.
- Personal goals of employees are related to Maslow's hierarchy of needs, which move from survival to self-actualization.
- The extent to which personal goals are intertwined with pharmacy goals affects the levels of employee motivation and productivity.
- The employer must be aware of morale problems. Some of the signs may be increased

private insurance programs. We still sell a fair amount of prescriptions on a private pay (cash) basis, but usually this is to people who do not have insurance and are at the very low end of household incomes. So even there, we are limited to what we can charge them. And, we were taught as kids not to try to take advantage of people who were down on their luck. Our parents said that we could end up in a similar spot someday, just like our grandparents were when they started out.

As a result of all this, we tried to make sure that we keep some balance between prescription and non-prescription sales. This means that we have to be very careful to carry non-prescription merchandise that will sell to our customers. We think that store managers are much closer to our customers than we are at the corporate level. For this reason, we pretty much allow them to decide what to buy, within some limits of course.

The organizational structure of Garcia's Rx Drugs is presented in Figure V.4.1. In addition to discretion regarding purchasing, store managers also were given authority to hire and fire personnel. The general company policy was to try to hire people who resided in the immediate neighborhoods whenever possible. This was thought to help build customer relations and loyalty to Garcia's Rx Drugs.

However, because the Garcia brothers had a large extended family, they tried to mainly hire family members to be store managers and department managers. Overall, more than half of the managers in the stores, whether at the store or department level, were related in some way to Robert or Carlos. Robert commented on their hiring practices:

We have a very large family, and we feel some responsibility to hire our own when we can and it makes sense to do so. We would like to hire the best people possible, but sometimes we will hire within the family—cousins, nieces, nephews, or some other relatives—even though they may not be the most qualified.

This has caused us some problems over time. For one thing, in locations that are not mainly Hispanic, we have tried to be sensitive to the local area and employ people of ethnicities that are highly represented rather than family. On the other hand, some of our store and

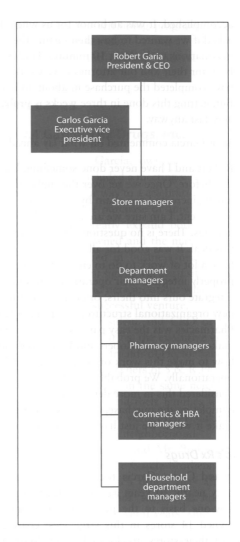

Figure V.4.1 Organization of Garcia's Rx drugs.

department managers probably feel that we will give preferential treatment o family members over non-family. I'm sure it looks that way at times, but we don't always do that intentionally. But, this is a sensitive area, and while we would like to keep everybody happy, there is no question that we will try to help our family but that doesn't mean we will hurt non-family employees. We try to be fair to everybody.

S & R Pharmacies, Inc.

Hector Sanchez and Manuel Rodriquez started S & R Pharmacies about 12 years ago. After working for a discount drug chain, they decided to join forces with several other pharmacists who already had a small chain of medical pharmacies. Eventually, Mr. Sanchez and Mr. Rodriquez bought out their partners and renamed the group of pharmacies S & R Pharmacies, Inc. From relatively modest beginnings, they grew the volume of business from an average of about $1.7 million per pharmacy to more than $3.5 million per store. During the growth period, they also acquired four pharmacies to give the chain eight pharmacies located within the city. Although they all had a medical focus, they were in neighborhood centers rather than in medical office buildings. Carlos Garcia commented on the S & R Pharmacies:

My brother and I call Hector's and Manuel's pharmacies "tweeners." They are bigger than traditional medical pharmacies but not as big as most community chain pharmacies. It's interesting because they have been very successful with this little niche of doing mostly prescriptions, but having just enough front-end merchandise to make that profitable. This is one of the good and bad things about our buying their company. On the good side, we don't feel that we ever really competed with them because our stores are so different. The bad thing is that our stores are so different. I doubt that we can

run them all the same, but that is what we are wrestling with now.

S & R Pharmacies' stores are considerably smaller and newer than those of Garcia's. They average about 5,500 square feet and average 6 years old versus Garcia's average age of 11 years.

The merchandise mix of S & R Pharmacies is oriented mainly around healthcare. The company's sales are mainly prescriptions, averaging 62.8 percent of total sales. They also have substantial sales in over-the-counter medications and about 9.0 percent of their sales are in home health supplies and durable medical equipment. While they carry adequate lines of over-the-counter medications, home health supplies, and durable medical equipment, their other product lines are very limited due to space constraints.

Both Hector and Manuel believed that the key to success with a chain of pharmacies was central control and decision-making. Accordingly, unlike Garcia's, they hired several vice presidents to manage various aspects of their operations. Decisions were made at the vice presidential level and carried out by the store managers. The organizational structure of S & R Pharmacies is presented in Figure V.4.2. Robert Garcia commented on the organization of

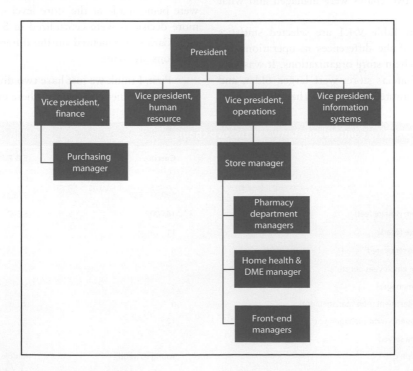

Figure V.4.2 Organization of S & R Pharmacies.

S & R Pharmacies:

> The structure set up by Hector and Manuel is very different from ours. I guess this is proof that there is no single correct way to organize a pharmacy because both of our companies have been quite successful.
>
> They wanted to keep control over every aspect of their operations and make them as similar as possible. So, they make the decisions at the top and leave very little room for discretion as to what to purchase, whom to hire, and so on. What this means is that they have more staff and costs at the top, but then they can hire managers who do not have to make all of the decisions, so they can pay them less at the lower levels. I think they still spend more overall on managerial compensation than we do, but all of this is very different.

Comparisons between Garcia's Rx Drugs and S & R Pharmacies

To begin their assessment, Carlos put together some comparisons in operations between the two chains. He thought that this would be helpful in getting a clearer picture of how much difference there was between how the two chains were managed and what they did.

Presented in Table V.4.1 are selected statistics showing some of the differences in operations between the two chain store organizations. It was very apparent that Garcia's stores were larger, older, and had not been renovated as recently as had the stores of

S & R Pharmacies. The age and years since renovation were not surprising to Carlos since the entire chain was newer and more of the stores had been started new.

What did catch Carlos's attention was the average number of non-management employees in the stores of the two chains. S & R Pharmacies had less than half the number of non-management personnel of Garcia's. Carlos attributed this to the fact that most decisions are made at the upper level and the stores were smaller and had more limited lines. However, because S & R Pharmacies sold home health supplies and durable medical equipment, he thought they would need more personnel to serve those patients.

Also of interest to Carlos was the fact that their two chains appealed to somewhat different clientele. He considered this good because it allowed Garcia's Rx Drugs to have a better chance to enter into different market segments. But, it also meant that some of Garcia's operating practices may not be as appropriate when dealing with an older and somewhat more affluent customer. These are issues that he figured would have to be addressed at some point.

Presented in Table V.4.2 are comparisons of how decisions were made in selected areas of operations by both chains. It was clear that many more decisions were being made at the store level in Garcia's, and more decisions were centralized in S & R Pharmacies. Carlos commented on the differences in where decisions are made:

> First, I think we just have two different philosophies concerning where major decisions

Table V.4.1 Operating comparisons between the two chains		
	Garcia's	**S & R Pharmacies**
Number of stores	14	8
Total sales last year	$90,978,454	$28,231,528
Average size of store (square feet)	14,000	5,500
Average age of store (years)	11	6
Average years since renovated	6	2
Average number of employees per store		
Department managers	3	3
Pharmacy department (non-management)	6	4
Other departments (non-management)	12	3
General market area served		
Age demographic	Young to middle	Middle to older
Income demographic	Lower to middle	Middle

Table V.4.2 Comparison of operating decision-making

	Garcia's	S & R Pharmacies
Support services		
Purchasing	Store level	Central
Hiring	Store level	Central
Accounting	Central	Central
Information systems	Central	Central
Payroll	Central	Central
Merchandise decisions for stores	Store level	Central
Advertising and other promotion	Store level	Store level
Goals, policies, procedures		
Sales goals	Central	Store level
Profit goals	Central	Store level
Policies and procedures	Central	None
Training manual	Central	None
Job descriptions	Store level	Central
Performance appraisals	Store level	None
Decisions		
Merchandise to purchase	Store level	Central
Wages	Store level	Central
Benefits	Central	Central
Bonuses	Store level	Central
Store layout	Store level	Central
Physician relations efforts	Store level	Store level

should be made. Our approach has been to make them at the point closest to the customer. Since we have different customer groups, we felt that this was the best way to ensure that we stayed connected to the marketplace.

S & R Pharmacies make the decisions at the upper management level. This may be best since they do not have quite the variation in customers and geographic areas as we do. Also, they may be able to get more economies of scale in purchasing and more efficiency in store management because so much is standardized.

It does seem a bit ironic, however, that despite all of the centralization they use, the sales and profit goals are set at the store level. We give store managers a lot of discretion in decision making, but we set their sales and profit goals to give them the direction to make the decisions that give us the results we want. This definitely will have to be addressed when we merge organizations.

The differences in product lines carried and the percentages of sales of each line in relation to average store total sales are presented in Table V.4.3. As both Robert and Carlos knew, there were differences in what each chain carried. What was most striking to them was how much more prescription sales were of the total for S & R Pharmacies in comparison to Garcia's. While S & R Pharmacies was more of a chain of medical pharmacies, Garcia's had considerably more store traffic. Robert commented on this:

I expected prescription sales in S & R Pharmacies to be a higher percentage of total sales than we have. But, what concerns me is that Garcia's has considerably more store traffic. This suggests to me that our current stores are not maximizing their potential for generating prescription revenues. It may be that customers are coming into Garcia's and buying front-end merchandise but having their prescriptions filled elsewhere. We need to capture more of this business.

Table V.4.3 Comparative product lines and sales by product lines

Departments/product lines	Garcia's	S & R Pharmacies
Product lines carried		
Prescription	Yes	Yes
Over-the-counter medications	Yes	Yes
Cosmetics	Yes	No
Health and beauty aids	Yes	Yes
Home health supplies	No	Yes
Durable medical equipment	No	Yes
Gifts	No	No
Cards	Yes	No
Candy	Yes	No
Books/magazines	Yes	Yes
Electronic products	Yes	No
Household supplies	Yes	Yes
Packaged foods—general	Yes	No
Packaged foods—ethnic	No	Yes
Sales by product lines		
Prescription	49.2%	62.8%
Packaged foods—general	9.3%	n.a.
Household supplies	9.2%	3.6%
Over-the-counter medications	8.2%	14.9%
Health and beauty aids	7.2%	6.8%
Cosmetics	6.5%	n.a.
Electronic products	3.5%	n.a.
Candy	2.9%	n.a.
Cards	2.8%	n.a.
Books/magazines	1.2%	0.7%
Home health supplies	n.a.	5.2%
Durable medical equipment	n.a.	3.8%
Gifts	n.a.	
Packaged foods—ethnic	n.a.	2.2%
Total	100.0%	100.0%

n.a., not applicable.

The future

In reviewing the data from Figures V.4.1 and V.4.2, and Tables V.4.1 through V.4.3, Robert and Carlos Garcia knew they had some major decisions to make. Although they strongly felt they made the right decision to purchase S & R Pharmacies, they were uncertain as to how to merge the organizations, or whether it might be best to leave them as they are and basically have two different companies.

Robert summarized what he saw as differences:

When Carlos and I look at this, we see that there are two different cultures with respect to whom we hire, and how and where decisions should be made. We also see that there are differences in the merchandise carried and the target markets served. Some of this is good because it allows our company to expand its horizons. Our greatest fear, however, is that if we merge the two organizations and change much of the way things are managed and operated, it will cause chaos in the stores. We could lose very good people, and it could hurt customer service in both chains. One part of us says that we should just leave the two chains alone and not try to merge them. But, that would mean a lot of duplication and much higher costs. We don't need two sets of accounting systems and departments, and it would be good to do joint purchasing so that we can get better economies of scale in our buying. Probably, each organization does some things right and some things wrong. We just need to figure out what is right and what is wrong and how to blend all of this. I think the fun part of this is over.

Possible discussion questions

1 How significant are the differences in the cultures of the two organizations and how can they be merged? Or can they be merged?
2 What are the advantages and disadvantages of keeping the two companies separate versus merging them into one?
3 What does each organization do well and do poorly, and how can a single organization be created that takes the best of each?

Case V.5 Hat's Stores, Inc.

Edward Mann, president and chief executive officer of Hat's Stores, Inc. (Hat's), was in deep discussion with Richard Shimura (vice president of operations) and Helen Ng (vice president of finance) concerning the future expansion of Hat's. Based on their recommendations, the board of directors approved opening pharmacies in six of their 11 stores. While the legal department was working on obtaining the necessary permits to operate pharmacies, they had to decide whether they needed to reorganize the company and how to proceed to hire the necessary staff for the pharmacy.

Hat's is a relatively small mass merchandise chain located in the Midwest. The chain has been in existence for more than 20 years, but has changed ownership on two occasions. Nearly a year ago, Mr. Mann thought it was important for the company's growth either to expand the number of stores in the chain or to try to increase the offerings of the present stores. He did not think there were opportunities for growth otherwise:

> I have been in the department store and mass merchandise store industry for nearly 15 years. In this business, you either grow or die. That was what happened to this chain in its earlier years. The previous owners did not want to take the steps to increase revenues. As a result, the stores stagnated. The current owners have many years of retail experience and realize that we needed to avoid making the same mistake.
>
> So, when I proposed the options of adding stores or altering what we sell, the owners were receptive to altering our lines to include pharmacies. One of them is a pharmacist by training, and I think that probably swayed the three other major shareholders.
>
> Now, we have to figure out how to best organize our company and staff the new departments that will be created. It is a bit problematic because we are not adding pharmacies to all of our stores. This is partly because we are not sure all of the stores could handle pharmacy operations, and partly because the owners want to try this out first on a smaller scale and then add more pharmacies if they work out. But, this approach makes it more difficult to really gear up organizationally.

The two big issues being discussed centered on whether it was necessary to bring on another vice president of pharmacy operations, and how to set up the organization of the prescription departments within the stores.

Hat's Stores

Hat's was started more than 20 years ago with two stores. This occurred when the owners of the two department stores decided to merge operations in order to obtain better negotiating power with suppliers and to better utilize their individual advertising dollars. Shortly thereafter, they purchased a small chain of department stores that was having difficulties. The owners primarily wanted the locations and leases on the stores in the chain, and quickly converted them and their two existing stores into what are now considered mass merchandise stores.

Within a year, a group of real estate investors made the owners a very attractive offer and purchased the chain. Unfortunately, none of the investors had retail experience, and the chain suffered from the beginning. Deciding to cut their losses, they sold the chain to the current owners.

The new ownership group had considerable retail experience with both department store and deep discount store operations. They immediately closed two of the stores that were not profitable and then opened four others in what they considered to be more viable markets. At this time, the chain consists of 11 stores. Four of these stores are located in metropolitan areas and seven are in smaller towns that are more rural based.

Compared to the national mass merchandise stores, Hat's stores are relatively small in size. While many of the national chain stores have about 125,000 square feet, the average Hat's store is about 85,000 square feet in size. Mr. Shimura commented on the store sizes:

> There is no question that our stores are smaller than many of the national chains. We didn't have large footprints (store sizes) with the original stores and the owners made the decision that it was better to have all stores about the same size rather than some very large and others quite small.
>
> Being somewhat smaller presents problems for us in the metropolitan areas where we really go head-to-head with the national chains. We just don't have the selection of merchandise that they do. But, in the more rural area, where most of our stores are located, our size can work to our advantage. People in the smaller towns like stores which are not intimidating and don't take forever to navigate until they reach the checkout stands.

Overall, Hat's stores tend to carry a reasonably wide range of merchandise. However, the selection available is more limited due to space constraints, so it is common for customers to experience stock-outs of merchandise and not find the particular styles or sizes they want. The product lines carried and the percent of floor space allocated to each line are shown in Table V.5.1.

To compensate for this, Hat's emphasizes its willingness to special order almost anything not found in the store. In fact, it has used a slogan "If we don't have it, we'll get it for you within 36 hours—that's our guarantee." While this has been somewhat costly, the management team (i.e. Mr. Mann, Mr. Shimura, and Ms. Ng) feel that this has been a strong competitive advantage.

The focus of their marketing efforts, therefore, has been on convenient location, easy shopping, and special ordering. Even though they advertise weekly in the Sunday newspaper, the management team has not wanted to compete on a price basis. As Ms. Ng noted:

> Although our prices are lower than some specialty stores, we do not try to compete with national chains. That would be foolish because we do not have their buying power and volume to get the best prices. Edward and Richard are always saying that they do not want to get into any war they cannot win, and pricing is one that we cannot win. So, the advertisements

Table V.5.1 Product lines carried in Hat's stores

Product lines	Proposed percent of floor space in store
Food	18.0%
Apparel	13.5%
Pharmacy (proposed)	7.5%
Household supplies	7.0%
Toys	6.5%
Baby products	6.0%
Garden supplies	6.0%
Jewelry	6.0%
Over-the-counter medications	5.5%
Cosmetics	5.0%
Games	5.0%
Shoes	5.0%
Sporting goods	4.0%
Automotive supplies	2.5%
Hardware	2.5%
Total	100.0%

Richard runs on Sundays tend to be only for items in which we get promotional allowances or discounts from the manufacturers.

Organization of Hat's

With only 11 stores, the owners of Hat's wanted to keep the management team small. The overall organizational chart for Hat's is presented in Figure V.5.1.

Mr. Mann, the president and chief executive officer, has been in his position for nearly 5 years. He was hired by the owners from a large department store chain where he served in various capacities, ranging from purchasing manager to vice president of regional sales.

His vice president of operations, Mr. Shimura, rose through the ranks from being a department manager and eventually a store manager. He was promoted to his current position 3 years ago. Prior to working for Hat's, he had worked for a large pharmacy chain as a store manager. His experience with pharmacy operations was limited because he only worked for the chain for 4 years, and did not oversee any of the pharmacy activities. Mr. Shimura was responsible for all of the operations within the stores except purchasing. He is in charge of human relations and staffing, deciding what merchandise to carry, overall pricing, and overall allocation of space to product lines.

Ms. Ng is the vice president of finance, and has been with the chain for less than 2 years. Although she worked for the company briefly while going to graduate school, her experience was mostly with an accounting firm working as a certified public accountant. Ms. Ng was responsible for the financial aspects of the company, and she managed the purchasing department. Mr. Mann moved control over purchasing from Mr. Shimura to Ms. Ng to have some separation between ordering and paying the bills. Mr. Mann commented on this:

> The reason I moved purchasing to be under Helen's control was to ensure that there was a separation between ordering and paying the bills. It has nothing to do with Richard's abilities, he is a good VP. But, this helps keep anybody in that position from going crazy with the ordering. When Richard and the store managers want to buy something, we have Helen taking a look at the dollars involved to be sure that it is not out of line. Helen rarely

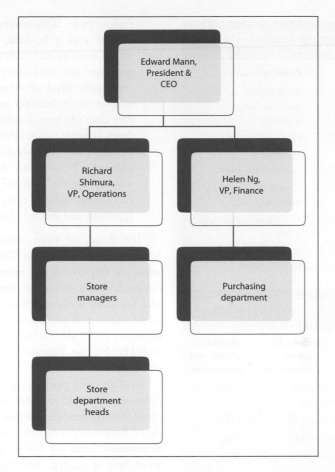

Figure V.5.1 Organizational chart for Hat's.

looks at the merchandise mix Richard and the store managers want to order. She is just concerned about the costs, total dollars spent, and dollars in inventory.

Within each store, there was a store manager and currently three department heads. A fourth department head was being planned for the prescription department. The product lines were divided into seven "product categories" for organizational purposes, which then were grouped and assigned to the department heads. Currently, over-the-counter medications is part of food and household supplies, but Mr. Mann had already decided to move that to the new prescription department.

The proposed grouping of product categories and assignments to department heads is presented in Table V.5.2. Past sales and expected sales with the addition of the pharmacies are shown in Table V.5.3. Although Mr. Mann and Mr. Shimura had proposed

these groupings to the board of directors, they were given the freedom to make any changes they wanted with respect to the groups. As Mr. Mann noted:

We have a good board of directors. They basically approved of moving forward with the pharmacies in some stores and gave us the discretion to organize any way we want. Richard and Helen agreed with me that it would be best to move the over-the-counter medications (OTCs) to be with the prescription department rather than with foods. We also thought it would be best to have an additional department head to be in charge of the pharmacy and OTCs. We hate to add the cost of another department head, and Helen is somewhat against increasing our costs this way, but Richard and I think it is necessary. We have not finalized that yet.

Table V.5.2 Proposed organization of product categories into departments

	Product categories
Head, prescriptions and OTCs	Pharmacy
	Over-the-counter medications
Head, food, cosmetics, and jewelry	Food and household supplies
	Cosmetics and jewelry
Head, apparel and shoes	Apparel, shoes, and baby products
Head, entertainment and home and auto	Toys, games, and sporting goods
	Automotive, hardware, and garden supplies

Table V.5.3 Past and expected sales by product categories

Product categories	% of sales before pharmacies	Expected % of sales after pharmacies
Pharmacy and over-the-counter medications	2.5%	10.5%
Food and household supplies	19.5%	17.5%
Cosmetics and jewelry	19.5%	16.5%
Apparel, shoes, and baby products	31.5%	30.0%
Toys, games, and sporting goods	16.5%	15.0%
Automotive, hardware, and garden supplies	10.5%	10.5%
Total	100.0%	100.0%
Total sales of average store	$32,450,000	$36,000,000

Duties and operations

By consolidating the product lines into product categories and then assigning categories to department heads, Hat's was able to keep the number of managers to a minimum. As Mr. Shimura commented, this was done for several purposes:

> We set up this organizational structure for several reasons. First, we wanted to minimize the number of managers in order to control our costs. Being a smaller chain and up against big companies, we felt that it was critical to keep our costs as low as possible. In addition, we wanted to encourage a team approach to

management. With fewer department heads and a lot of work to be done, we thought they would learn to help each other as time permitted because sooner or later every department head would get buried and need the others to help them get out of a mess. So, if they didn't help each other, they all would go down at some point. I think they recognized this and generally they do what they can to help each other because the "helper" at some point will become the "helpee." It doesn't work in every department in every store, but it's a novel approach and seems to be working ok.

The duties of store managers and department heads are summarized in Table V.5.4. Store managers are responsible for managing operations on a day-to-day basis. While they have the authority to hire and fire staff, make purchase decisions, and recommend wages and benefits, in reality they have to get clearance from Mr. Shimura for personnel decisions and Ms. Ng for purchase decisions above normal stock replenishment.

In addition to performing their duties, department heads are expected to assist each other in both managing the departments and providing staff during busy times. Frequently, a department head will ask another department head for use of some the latter's staff when help is needed. This can be for assisting customers, stocking the shelves, changing merchandise layout, etc.

Purchasing has been somewhat complicated at the store level. Department heads will make recommendations to the store manager. Although the store managers report directly to Mr. Shimura, they have to get the approval of Ms. Ng to actually purchase the merchandise they need for the stores for anything other than stock replenishment. At times, this has caused problems because Mr. Shimura and Ms. Ng may not agree as to what to purchase or in what quantities, and the store managers are caught up in the disagreement.

Staffing and compensation

Staff turnover tends to be relatively low, especially in the rural areas. There appears to be some variation in the number of years employees stay at Hat's based on whether they work in the urban or more rural stores. As shown in Table V.5.5, turnover levels are higher in urban areas than in rural areas. Mr. Mann

Table V.5.4 Duties of store managers and department heads	
Store manager	Approve department head recommendations for products to carry
	Conduct performance appraisals of department heads
	Coordinate activities between department heads
	Decide on space allocation for departments in store
	Ensure store cleanliness
	Hire and terminate employees in all departments
	Interact with community
	Recommend advertising promotions for all departments
	Recommend bonuses for department employees
	Recommend bonuses for department heads
	Recommend wages and salaries for all employees
	Resolve customer complaints
	Resolve issues between department heads
	Review employee performance appraisals by department heads
	Submit all expenses to VP of finance
	Submit purchase orders for all merchandise to VP of finance
	Perform other duties as assigned by VP of operations
Department heads	Assess own performance and report to store manager
	Assign department employees to other departments when needed
	Assist other department heads when needed
	Decide how to utilize space with department
	Ensure department is clean and well maintained
	Evaluate department employees and report to store manager
	Interview job applicants and make recommendations to store manager
	Manage department employees
	Manage inventory
	Recommend bonuses for department employees
	Recommend merchandise to carry
	Recommend quantities to purchase
	Set employee hours
	Perform other duties as assigned by store manager

attributes this to both the competition for good people being more intense in urban areas and Hat's

salaries generally being lower than what is offered by other retailers:

We have done quite well with retaining good employees in the more rural areas. Of course, the costs of living are somewhat less so the fact that we offer lower salaries and bonuses than many other retailers makes this a little more tolerable. I also suspect that employees in the more rural areas do not have as many employment opportunities as their counterparts in the cities. But, we also treat our employees very well. For example, while they have set numbers of days for vacations and sick leave, we frequently give them a few extra days to help them out when they need it. And if someone has to take some time off during the day to go for a doctor's appointment or take their child to something, we try to flex and allow them to do so without docking their pay. Since they don't abuse this, we feel that this is a great way to keep employees. Overall, other employees step in to help each other so it does not disrupt operations. We try to operate as a family.

As Mr. Mann indicated, salaries tend to be below the average for retailers. Generally, salaries for store managers are thought to be between 5 and 10 percent below the national chains, and department heads make between 5 and 7.5 percent less than their counterparts in other retail stores. Non-management hourly wages are about 5 percent below the average. Benefits are thought to be only slightly below average because of the liberal allowances for vacations and sick leave time actually given.

One of the main problems Hat's experienced with salaries and wages was the management team's insistence that all base salaries and hourly wages be the same across the stores. This tended to be a problem for store managers who worked in the more urban areas making the same base salaries as those in rural areas where the costs were lower and competition not as intense. It also had caused some complaints among some department heads who felt they had more responsibilities than others. Mr. Shimura commented on the issue of comparable salaries and wages:

There may be some valid reasons for paying store managers more if they are in urban areas, and it might be reasonable to pay some department heads more than others. However, be willing to hire another pharmacist, nothing has happened yet.

In recent months, the pharmacy services department has been under some pressure to improve its performance. The main issues that Dr. Geede and Ms. Greg have with the department are the high costs of medications and the department's lack of interaction with other departments in the hospital. Both feel that the department could do more to reduce the costs of medications and become more of a "profit center" within the hospital. They also think that the outcomes of the hospital could be improved if pharmacists worked more closely with physicians, nurses, the various therapists, and others. Ms. Greg commented about these issues:

> Pharmacy services is an area where we can make some significant improvements in services and the hospital's bottom line. Both Ralph and I have a great deal of respect for the department's staff and for Kathryn. We just think they could do more to help us. At times, it feels like all they do is fill the orders for medications and do not apply their skills to finding better solutions.
>
> To be perfectly honest, I also do not know how well their recommendations would be accepted by the other healthcare professionals in the building. Everybody has a bit of a turf they protect. But, I do know from my past experience that pharmacists can make a difference in hospital outcomes. We just are not reaching our potential. That's why Ralph and I are pushing the pharmacy services department to become more assertive and take the initiative to be more involved. We'll all have to deal with turf matters if they become issues.

The future

After reviewing Dr. Geede's memorandum, Dr. Chin decided to hold a department meeting to find out what concerns the staff had about the expansion and comments of Dr. Geede and Ms. Greg relative to the department. Upon completion of the meeting, she made a list of the ten most common concerns expressed by staff in the order of the number of times they were mentioned:

1 The expansion will create more work, but will the department be given additional positions for pharmacists or technicians?

2 Even if new pharmacists and technicians are hired, how well will they fit in with a group that has worked together for a long time?

3 If the expansion creates more work, the space within which pharmacy services operates will not be adequate. Will the department be moved or the space allocated to it be expanded?

4 What will happen to the work schedules of the pharmacists and technicians when the expansion takes place? Will this change the current work schedules of individuals?

5 With the addition of Alzheimer's and RA, will there be any changes in the computers and information systems currently being used? Will it affect how the pharmacy operates?

6 What role will pharmacists have in the Alzheimer's and RA care?

7 Will there be a need for special training if pharmacists are involved in Alzheimer's and RA care? If so, when will it be provided, who will pay for it, and how much time will it take?

8 To what extent does NRCCH want pharmacist involvement in patient treatment and care? While Dr. Geede and Ms. Greg want pharmacists involved, is this feeling held by the other medical staff?

9 What does the hospital want from pharmacists and who will ensure that pharmacists integrate into medical teams?

10 To what extent will individual pharmacists and the pharmacy services department be held to outcomes measures? If they are held accountable, what are the measures that they will use?

Based on the memorandum, the comments of Dr. Geede and Ms. Greg, and the concerns expressed by her staff, Dr. Chin wanted to put a plan together to address several matters:

- What information NRCCH should provide the pharmacy services department and other hospital departments concerning the future expansion.
- What information NRCCH should provide the pharmacy services department and other hospital departments concerning how staff pharmacists should be more involved in patient care.
- How pharmacists could become more integrated into current patient care.
- How pharmacists could become integrated into patient care for Alzheimer's and RA.

- What the pharmacy services department needed to do to make pharmacists available for involvement in current and future patient care.
- What information about pharmacists' services could be conveyed to other healthcare professionals within the hospital.
- How information about pharmacists' services should be conveyed, and how often communications should take place.

Currently, the hospital held all-staff meetings on a quarterly basis, issued an internal staff newsletter on a monthly basis, and put information on bulletin boards in staff areas (e.g. lunch rooms, conference rooms). It also distributed more immediate memorandums through supervisors when the need arose.

Dr. Chin felt that the only way to build a role for the pharmacy services department and its pharmacists was to take a proactive approach. She wanted to tell Dr. Geede and Ms. Greg how things should be done. She commented on this:

> I have been here a long time, and I know that either we tell them how it should be done, or they will tell us how to do it. I'd prefer we take the initiative. That will show that we are responsive, and it is more likely that we can get things done our way. If we wait for them, the odds are that we won't like what they want done and how they want us to do it. So, we need to make the plan first and then let them react to it.

Possible discussion questions

1 How big an impact will the expansion of medical care and staffing have on the NRCCH and the pharmacy services department?

2 What plans should be developed by the pharmacy services department to increase both involvement in current healthcare and the expansion?

3 What information should the pharmacy services department develop to convey to other healthcare professionals regarding what pharmacists could do to improve patient outcomes? How and how often should this be conveyed?

4 How reasonable are the concerns expressed by Dr. Geede and Ms. Greg?

5 How valid are the concerns expressed by the pharmacy services department?

PART **VI**

Pharmacy operations management

15

Purchasing and inventory control

Learning objectives

The objectives of this chapter are to assist you to be able to explain:

- the common objectives of purchasing management
- the common objectives of inventory control
- the major decisions that need to be made in purchasing management
- the major decisions that need to be made in inventory management
- the policies and procedures that can be developed for effective management of pharmacy purchasing and inventory control.

Key terms

Carrying costs
Cash discounts
Cooperative buying groups
Economic order quantity (EOQ)
Inventory turnover rate
Open-to-buy (OTB)
Order lead time

Procurement costs
Promotional discounts
Quantity discounts
Reorder point
Safety stock
Trade (functional) discounts
Usage rate

Table 15.1 Assessing purchasing policies and procedures

Question	Comments
1. Do you have specific policies and procedures regarding who is authorized to purchase goods or services? Receive salespersons' calls? Place requisitions? Process records?	In a small firm the manager will usually do all the purchasing, but this may not always be possible. Therefore the manager must control the purchasing function to prevent possible deception or fraud. The first step toward control is to carefully select the person authorized to do the buying. Then records to indicate need, receipt of purchase, and subsequent payment should be maintained
2. Have you ever reviewed existing purchasing procedures to see if they meet your needs?	The size and nature of purchases change as a pharmacy grows in size. What worked when a pharmacy or chain of pharmacies was small will not necessarily be appropriate as it starts to be able to take advantage of greater quantity discounts and more electronic methods of purchasing. A review of how decisions are made as to what to purchase, when, and in what amounts should be conducted at least annually
3. Have you ever discussed your purchasing function with other firms or with local trade associations to obtain suggestions or techniques?	An easy way to develop a working purchasing method is to review your needs. An extremely sophisticated procedure is not necessary if you purchase only a few or relatively inexpensive outside products or services. Good sources of data or ideas are the local purchasing association, a business similar to your own, and trade or craft associations
4. Do you request prices from several vendors for each product or service you purchase?	Prices do differ from vendor to vendor because of their cost structure, quality of materials and services, location, and so forth. To obtain the best price consistent with quality and service, shop around
5. Have you ever visited or investigated your existing or potential vendors to verify that they can meet your requirements in terms of price, quality, quantity, and service?	Your commitments to your customers are quite often, if not entirely, based on the promises your vendors make to you. Therefore, it is essential for you to know your vendors' limitations and strengths. If they continually delay or provide inferior-quality products, this will reflect on your services and must be corrected
6. Does your volume of purchasing for any particular item warrant your dealing directly with its manufacturer?	If the key ingredient to the service you offer is some manufactured product, you might consider direct buying to reduce the costs associated with middlemen. Communications with regard to technical problems may also be made easier
7. Do your vendors have regular and competent sales personnel?	Salespeople are more than just nice guys. If they know their products, they can be an aid to you and make recommendations when you encounter special problems. They will not waste your time either, but will make themselves available when you need them by helping you with expediting and order follow-up
8. Have you had problems with suppliers in regard to shortages? Backdoor selling? Delivery delays? Unsolicited favors and gifts?	Ethical suppliers will rarely ship shoddy merchandise intentionally. But on occasion they may ship substandard material owing to error or failure of internal production processes. On the other hand, if your supplier makes a habit of questionable or unethical selling practices, you can also be certain that you are paying for it in the form of inferior goods or services, inflated prices, or some other way

Adapted from Small Business Administration. *Management Audit for Small Service Firms.* Management Series No. 38. Washington, DC: Small Business Administration, 1982: 1–2.

Purchasing policies should be flexible and reflect the pharmacy's objectives and plans. They must leave room for discretion to allow the pharmacy to respond to unanticipated events such as unusual demand fluctuations and special price incentives offered by suppliers.

As should be evident from the objectives associated with purchasing, effective buying is the culmination of numerous decisions, including:

- buying merchandise in the right quality and quantity
- buying merchandise from the right suppliers
- buying merchandise at the right time
- buying merchandise at the right terms.

Merchandise mix decisions

Merchandise mix decisions (i.e. determining what prescription and front-end goods to carry) are the most critical for both medical and community-oriented pharmacies. After all, it makes little difference how well the purchasing tasks are carried out if the merchandise bought is the wrong variety or the wrong quality.

In some respects, decisions relative to prescription inventory are somewhat easier to make. In an average pharmacy, roughly 50 percent of all prescriptions dispensed are refills, so the pharmacy manager has the data available to determine in half of the cases what drugs will be needed, in what quantities, and when they should be delivered.

To the extent that this information is compiled from patient profiles, there may be relatively few problems in determining what to purchase. For the other 50 percent of prescriptions, industry data are available to help identify what drugs are likely to be prescribed, as are sources such as physicians in the immediate area, suppliers, published reports of the 50, 100, and 200 most commonly prescribed drugs, and professional, scientific, and trade journals.

Customer purchases of front-end items are less rational, more sporadic, and considerably trendier than prescription purchases. Consequently, the pharmacy manager may have to spend considerable time in determining what customers will want and for how long. Even a medical pharmacy, with a small front-end, has to be stocked properly. Rent is being paid on this space, and the front-end is all the customer ever sees. It is this space that often creates the customer's image of the pharmacy.

Of particular concern related to merchandise variety decisions are the different lines of merchandise, the assortment within the lines, and the extent to which new and seasonal items are stocked. The lines of merchandise carried will depend first and foremost on the needs and desires of the target market. Other factors influencing the variety of merchandise carried include the image to be conveyed to customers, the lines carried by competitors, the size of the pharmacy, and financial limitations on investing in inventory.

The assortment within each line of merchandise refers to how many versions are offered of each product in each line. Several factors should be considered in this decision, including sales response and space requirements. Sales should be evaluated to determine whether, if product variety is increased, the overall sales will go up and overall profits rise.

Carrying ten varieties of shampoo will not necessarily produce greater sales or profits than stocking five varieties. Space requirements should be examined for each product category. How much space is available? Because available selling space is limited, it should be allocated to those items generating the greatest customer traffic and sales. Stock turnover (discussed later in this chapter) should also be considered in the assigning of shelf space.

Special consideration also should be given to stocking new merchandise and eliminating existing lines from time to time. New items generate interest

in the pharmacy's front-end and may sell well and enhance overall front-end sales and profits. Similarly, eliminating slow-moving merchandise improves the profit potential of the space available by making room for more salable merchandise.

A final consideration in a pharmacy's merchandise mix is the quality of merchandise. The quality, including commensurate prices, must be appropriate for the clientele and the image desired for the pharmacy. It is also dependent on the pharmacy's financial ability to invest in inventory—an especially important issue when high-quality merchandise is needed.

Purchase quantity decisions

A common fear among people in all types of business is that they will run out of whatever it is they are making or selling. The concern about lost sales due to stock-outs, then, becomes a primary reason for carrying excessive inventory. Unfortunately, such concerns carry very high price tags. Yet, frequent stock-outs certainly risk alienating and losing customers.

To the extent that demand for specific items is known, one can calculate the appropriate order quantities that will minimize overall purchasing costs. This is known as the economic order quantity (EOQ) formula and is discussed later in this chapter. For items which have relatively uncertain demand, one can make estimates based on past sales and purchasing records and then use the average as the basis for projecting future sales.

Sources of supply decisions

In selecting sources of supply, the pharmacy manager has several options, including buying from manufacturers, wholesalers, or buying groups. Purchases of selected items may be made directly from manufacturers. Pharmacy managers often prefer to buy merchandise directly, especially if such purchases result in lower prices and more specialized assistance in the form of promotion, display materials, and merchandising advice that can be obtained from wholesalers. Most of the merchandise sold in retail pharmacies, however, is supplied by wholesalers.

Wholesalers may perform numerous marketing functions for the pharmacy manager, including:

- providing a wide assortment of products
- extending credit

- supplying information about markets and products
- providing advertising, sales promotion, and merchandising assistance
- supplying customized price stickers and permanent shelf labels
- providing electronic order-entry hardware
- providing purchase analysis reports.

Purchase analysis reports can help the pharmacy manager control inventories better, thus improving in-stock position, increasing sales, and enhancing customer satisfaction with service.

Monthly purchase reports can be used to compare purchases in the current month against previous months by department to determine if purchases meet sales needs. They can also be used to allocate shelf space; review item selection, gross profit, retail pricing, price changes, and items purchased to identify areas for adjustment; and determine gross margin and evaluate the impact of pricing decisions for individual items or departments on total profitability.

Cooperative buying groups

Independent pharmacies have made arrangements in recent years for central purchasing through the formation of cooperatives or buying group services. The purpose of such buying groups is to promote the economic welfare of independent community pharmacies by utilizing their combined efforts for efficient and economical distribution through buying merchandise at the lowest possible price. Indications are that for the most part these arrangements have been successful because they have reduced the cost of doing business.

In the pharmaceutical industry, cooperative purchasing is best known as "group purchasing" and is organized through group purchasing organizations or GPOs. Buying group benefits include:

- *Purchasing power*: Pharmacies have translated their combined purchasing power into lower acquisition costs and increased margins resulting in maximum profitability.
- *One-stop shopping and no minimum orders*: Participants save time by not ordering from numerous sources. With one-stop shopping, next-day delivery is received, inventory is reduced, and the number of checks generated from accounts payable is eliminated.

- *Choice of wholesalers*: Participating pharmacies are not restricted to one wholesaler. Therefore, pharmacists do not need to change wholesalers to participate.
- *Increased profit margin*: Since most third-party prescription programs are encouraging the use of lower cost generic drugs, it is important that pharmacy generic purchases allow for maximum profitability. Pharmacies participating in buying groups have this advantage.

Selecting vendors

The objective of careful vendor selection is to find the one most satisfactory source, or a number of alternative sources with adequate comparable qualifications. Thus succeeding orders for the same item can be placed with these same suppliers with confidence in the original selection. In other words, the decision as to a source of supply contemplates a continuing relationship.

Several criteria should be considered in selecting vendor sources, including:[1]

- *Reliability*: Will the vendor fulfill all promises?
- *Price and quality*: Who provides the best merchandise at the lowest price?
- *Order-processing time*: How fast will a delivery be made?
- *Functions provided*: Will the vendor provide storage, market information, and other functions, if needed?
- *Guarantee*: Does the vendor stand behind the products?
- *Financing*: Does the vendor provide credit?
- *Long-run relations*: Will the vendor be available over an extended period of time?
- *Innovativeness*: Are the vendor's product lines innovative?
- *Risk*: How much risk is involved in dealing with the vendor?
- *Investment*: How large are total investment costs?

The real test of vendor selection is, of course, the test of experience, or satisfactory performance by the vendor once the order has been placed.

Working with wholesalers

Selecting and working with capable wholesalers is a significant function of purchasing. Probably no one is more important to the operation of a pharmacy than the wholesaler. Yet many pharmacy managers have not recognized that good supplier relationships result in wholesaler goodwill.

Instead, wholesalers are often treated in a suspicious and even ill-mannered fashion. It is mutually advantageous to have a positive buyer–seller relationship. There have been numerous instances when an unexpected customer problem or emergency was solved with the help of a friendly wholesaler. The pharmacy manager must have wholesalers motivated by goodwill to cooperate with them in such situations.

Number of wholesalers

The question of how many wholesalers to use has no definitive answer. As is true for so many business decisions, it depends on many factors. Many buyers have found it advantageous to spread purchases among many wholesalers to gain the advantage of the most favorable prices, best delivery schedules, and promotional material offered. Another reason for relying on several wholesalers is that it gives buyers an opportunity to continually evaluate alternative sources of supply, to have greater assurance of supply reliability, and to keep wholesalers competitive with one another.

On the other hand, several distinct advantages of concentrating purchases from one wholesaler (i.e. the primary vendor) can also be cited. For example, the argument for doing the bulk of buying from a single wholesaler is that in times of shortages, the primary vendor will take better care of its customers. Other possible advantages include receiving more attention and help from a wholesaler who knows it is receiving most of the pharmacy's business; having a smaller inventory investment; having larger purchase orders, which may permit larger discounts; and simplifying credit problems. These advantages are convincing arguments as to why it is often better for a pharmacy to concentrate its purchases and work closely with a few wholesalers.

Purchasing policy in most companies traditionally requires at least two supply sources for each item as being in the best interest of the company. Whether there should be more than two, and how many, is a matter of purchasing judgment. It depends partly on the importance of the item, on competitive conditions in the industry, and on the quantities involved, which might make it practicable to divide the business among several vendors.

Purchase timing decisions

Decisions concerning the timing of purchases must closely coincide with consumer demand and minimize the amount of inventory investment. One means of doing this is to establish stock levels at which new orders must be placed. The stock levels are called *reorder points*.

Determining reorder points depends on the length of order lead time, usage rate, and the amount of safety stock to be kept on hand. *Order lead time* is the time span from the date an order is placed to the date the merchandise is received, priced, and put on the selling floor. Usage rate refers to average sales per day, in units, of merchandise. *Safety stock* is the amount of extra inventory kept on hand to protect against running out of stock owing to unexpected demand and delays in delivery. Safety stock should be planned in accordance with the pharmacy's policy toward running out of merchandise. The formula for when to reorder, assuming the pharmacy incorporates safety stock into its planning, is:

$$\text{Reorder point} = (\text{usage rate} \times \text{lead time})$$
$$+ \text{safety stock}$$

Ideally, orders should be placed at the precise point in time at which sales during the order lead time will just have depleted all of the inventory on hand, so that no safety stock is needed. Unfortunately, "ideal" conditions seldom, if ever, occur.

To establish effective safety stock policies, it is necessary to make a tradeoff between two opposing factors: the cost of carrying the safety stock and the cost of being out of stock. Normally, inventory carrying cost is easier to measure than the cost of running out of inventory. It includes (1) capital costs (inventory investment and investment in assets required by inventory), (2) inventory service costs (insurance and taxes), (3) storage space costs (warehousing costs), and (4) inventory risk costs (obsolescence, damage, pilferage).

Out-of-stock costs are the costs incurred by the pharmacy when an item is demanded but is not immediately available for sale. The cost of a stock-out is determined by the reaction of the customer. For example, the customer may simply wait to buy the item the next time it is available; thus the pharmacy would experience no apparent loss. However, the customer may purchase the item from a competitor, thus causing the out-of-stock pharmacy the lost profit on the sale. If stock-outs occur too often, the pharmacy may lose a customer forever.

Another dimension of the timing issue in purchasing is whether buying will be conducted at random points in time or restricted to defined periods. Left unrestricted, purchasing can become a daily activity conducted in bits and pieces, and hurriedly on a time-available basis. As such, purchasing control tends not to be very stringent, as no consideration is given to monetary investments in inventory or the tradeoffs in the use of limited purchasing dollars.

For this and other reasons, the pharmacy manager may want to use an open-to-buy/closed-to-buy system. Although there are several different forms of open-to-buy/closed-to-buy, the more common ones limit purchasing to defined periods, such as the first two days of each week or month. By doing this, the purchasing process becomes more deliberate as additional consideration can be given to what is being bought, when it will be sold, and what prices are being paid for the merchandise.

Another form of open-to-buy/closed-to-buy is one in which specific dollar limits are set on purchasing for a predetermined period of time. *Open-to-buy (OTB)* is a budgeting tool by which retailers regulate and coordinate the timing of purchases. OTB helps the pharmacy manager monitor actual purchase commitments in relation to planned amounts. It specifies how much of an item to buy for delivery during a specified time period to avoid exceeding planned purchase amounts for that time period.

The amount of OTB equals the difference between the planned purchase amount during a time period and the amount of merchandise already received together with the amount on order for delivery during the period. When the residual balance reaches zero, the pharmacy moves into a closed-to-buy condition until the next open period.

Purchase terms decisions

Pharmacy managers must negotiate the best deal they can with each supplier to improve profit. Five factors are especially important in supplier negotiations: (1) quantity discounts, (2) cash discounts, (3) trade discounts, (4) promotional discounts, and (5) return goods policies.

Unfortunately, not all deals may be worth while. The quality of a cash or quantity discount, for example, depends on the amount of discount being offered,

the carrying cost of holding inventory, the retail price charged for the item, and the time it takes to turn the merchandise into sales. Most important, a deal can only become profitable when the sale, not the purchase, is completed. Thus, a 25 percent discount on an item that will not sell is not much of a deal. On the other hand, a 1 percent discount on merchandise that is sold and replaced weekly may represent a very good deal for the pharmacy.

Quantity discounts are reductions in price allowed for buying certain quantities. They are generally expressed in terms of total dollars purchased (value) or number of units (quantity) ordered. For example, a supplier might offer a 5 percent quantity discount for orders over $500, or 100 units. Sometimes these discounts are graduated (e.g. over $500, or 100 units, a 5 percent discount is offered; over $1,000, or 200 units, a 7 percent discount; and over $5,000, or 1,000 units, a 10 percent discount).

Another variation of quantity discounts is *cumulative discounts*. They represent discounts calculated at the end of specified time periods. For example, a 10 percent discount may be offered if a pharmacy's purchases total over a certain dollar amount or units of merchandise purchased during a year. These discounts tend to build loyalties to a single supplier.

The disadvantages of taking quantity discounts, however, must be considered. Larger purchases increase the risks of loss resulting from stocking unsalable merchandise—unwanted by customers or dated because it could not be sold with reasonable speed. In addition, large purchases serve to increase the dollar investment in inventory and worsen the pharmacy's cash position. If the pharmacy faces cash flow problems, these can be critical problems.

Cash discounts are reductions in price offered to those who pay their bills promptly. They are offered by suppliers because it saves them money by reducing credit risks and losses from bad debts. They also permit suppliers to reinvest the money from early payment of bills or use it to pay their own bills.

It is prudent to deal with suppliers who offer the best cash discounts. Supplier credit terms normally vary from 30 to 90 days and up to six months in special cases. Cash discounts are often available if a bill is paid within 10 days.

A sales term quoted as "2/10, net 30" or "2/10 n/30," means the supplier gives a cash discount of 2 percent if the bill is paid within 10 days of the invoice date. The 30 represents the number of days within which payment must be made. A sales term quoted "2/10 EOM n/30" means that the dating period does not begin until the end of the month (EOM) of the date shown on the invoice. If the buyer has cash available, payment should be made within 10 days of the invoice date or the end of the month because the approximate cash discount value is 36 percent a year. Other examples of the approximate cash discounts available on an annual basis are:

- 1 percent in 10 days, net 30 days = 18 percent a year
- 2 percent in 10 days, net 60 days = 14 percent a year
- 2 percent in 30 days, net 60 days = 24 percent a year
- 3 percent in 10 days, net 30 days = 24 percent a year
- 3 percent in 10 days, net 60 days = 21 percent a year.

These examples show why it may be prudent to take advantage of cash discounts. If a buyer is considered a credit risk, suppliers will normally require COD (cash on delivery).

Although the benefits of taking cash discounts can be substantial, there are some important disadvantages as well. Not all cash discounts represent good deals—it depends on the time difference and the percentage offered. More important, however, is the cash drain these deals tend to cause. Designed to speed cash inflows to the supplier, they serve to deplete cash resources. If a pharmacy is experiencing cash flow shortages, these discounts will magnify the frequency and severity of the problem.

Trade (or functional) discounts are given to middle-men or others who act in the capacity of performing distributive services which would otherwise have to be performed by the manufacturer. For example, a manufacturer may offer a discount of 40 and 10 percent off the list price of $5 to a wholesaler. The 40 and 10 percent reduction would go to the wholesaler, who would then pass on the 40 percent to the retailer. Thus, on a $5 item, the wholesaler would pay $2.70 [$5 − (0.40 ×$5) = $3, and $3 − (0.10 ×$3) =$2.70], and the retailer would pay $3 [$5 − (0.40 × $5) = $3]. This general method of discounting the list price is relatively popular, although the exact form varies from manufacturer to manufacturer.

Promotional discounts (or allowances) may be provided for undertaking certain advertising, selling,

or merchandising activities (e.g. providing preferred window and interior display space) to promote a product. Various types of allowances include an actual cash payment or an extra amount of "free goods." A portion of these savings frequently are passed on to the consumer.

Returned goods policies are typically established by manufacturers and wholesalers. These policies indicate under what conditions merchandise will be accepted back from a pharmacy. The pharmacy manager should be fully aware of what items qualify under returned goods policies and what time limitations are in effect. To maintain an orderly return system, returns should be made on a regular, periodic basis.

Legal aspects of purchasing

Purchasing decisions must be legally as well as economically sound. Sales agreements of doubtful legality can lead to ill-will among buyers and sellers, to confusions about the rights and obligations of the parties involved, and to expensive and time-consuming litigation. Obviously, unfavorable decisions in such litigation can mean substantial economic loss to the losing parties.

Pharmacy managers must keep current of the legislation pertaining to purchasing and inventory decisions. This is particularly true today in the highly complicated and ever-changing environment of pharmacy, particularly in view of the increasing intervention of government in pharmacy. In any situation where the legality of a sales agreement, contract, or business practice seems doubtful or controversial, legal counsel should be consulted.

Major inventory control decisions

Inventory control is the process of managing inventory in order to meet customer demand at the lowest possible cost and with a minimum of investment. Unlike many factors in pharmacy management, inventory is controllable by management. The pharmacy manager decides how much inventory investment to make, when to reorder, and in what quantities.

Typically, the largest investment in the average independent retail pharmacy is merchandise inventory, and, as such, its control significantly influences profit. A successfully implemented inventory control program takes into account such things as purchasing goods commensurate with sales, seasonal variation, changing usage patterns, and monitoring for pilferage. The challenge of productive inventory management is how to support an upward trend in sales while keeping the investment at the lowest level consistent with adequate customer service.

In attempting to control inventories, managers often lean toward keeping inventory levels on the high side, yet this greater investment (given a constant amount of profit) increases risk and yields a lower return on the dollar invested. This is one of the contradictory demands made upon the manager with respect to keeping inventory. Others include:

- maintaining a wide assortment of stock—but one should not be spread too thin on the rapidly moving ones
- increasing the inventory turnover—but one should not sacrifice service level
- keeping stock low—but one should not sacrifice service or performance
- obtaining lower prices by making volume purchases—but one should not end up with slow-moving inventory
- having an adequate inventory on hand—but one should not get caught with obsolete items.

Successful inventory management involves simultaneously attempting to balance the costs of inventory with the benefits of inventory. Many small business owners often fail to appreciate fully the true costs of carrying inventory, which include not only the direct costs of storage, insurance, taxes, etc., but also the cost of money tied up in inventory. Inventory also ties up capital, which may strain a pharmacy and lead to a severe cash crisis. Good inventory management improves customer service, increases sales, increases profit, and increases working capital without having to borrow money.

Deciding on what to control

Despite the importance of inventory control in the overall management of a pharmacy's assets, there is no denying that this activity can be time-consuming and expensive. And it is not uncommon to find even the most adamant supporters of inventory control spending more for control than they would lose by having a less efficient system. Normally, however, it is more likely that inventory is not being controlled to

the extent that it should, and store profits are being lost.

A preliminary step in the process of inventory control is to determine the approximate costs of carrying inventory. These costs include such expenses as storage costs (taxes, insurance, rent), inventory risks (inventory deterioration, pilferage and theft, price reductions) and the loss-of-opportunity costs associated with tying up capital. Obviously, many of these costs are difficult to determine precisely. Nevertheless, it is possible to approximate most of these for management decision-making.

The costs of capital and opportunity are the most important of those associated with holding inventory. By investing in inventory, other uses for money are lost—uses which could provide greater returns. The most commonly used benchmark for measuring the costs of capital is the prevailing interest rates. Ideally, this measure should be for an investment of comparable risk, but that is seldom possible. Consequently, some nearly risk-free investments, such as treasury bills, are often used instead.

Closely related to the costs of capital are the opportunity costs of using space for one type of merchandise rather than another. At times the difference between these costs may appear insignificant. Yet, the costs of capital represent the fundamental decision as to whether to invest in inventory, while the opportunity costs concern what types of inventory are held.

Irrespective of what the actual costs are of holding specific items in inventory, there is little doubt that some items need to be controlled more than others. Some cost more, and therefore represent a greater financial investment. Some are dated and have only a relatively short shelf life, and others may be important for other reasons.

Because of this, inventory can be labeled as being A, B, or C merchandise. This gives recognition to the varying importance of different types of pharmacy inventory. Consequently, classifying merchandise into A, B, and C items allows the pharmacy manager to better identify and control items of greater importance.

What constitutes A, B, or C merchandise varies by pharmacy and its clientele. The classification for particular items also will change over time based on product demand and cost. So, this system needs to be adapted to the needs of the individual pharmacy and reviewed and adjusted periodically.

As shown in Figure 15.1, a relatively small percentage of total merchandise will represent a very large percentage of dollar investment in inventory. For example, approximately 20 percent of the inventory items should receive much greater attention than the remaining 80 percent since they may account for 90 percent or more of inventory investment. Loss of control over a few of these items is considerably more serious than loss of control over a large number of other items.

"A" merchandise would be considered the most important to control. Typically, this includes prescription department inventory, high-cost front-end merchandise, and those traditionally considered essential in a full-line pharmacy (e.g. over-the-counter drugs such as aspirin, cough syrup, and antacids). Of course, prescription department inventory generally is most important since it is expensive, essential to store operations, and has a limited shelf life. However, high-cost front-end items and those necessary to the image of the store must be carefully controlled as well. Accordingly, these "A" items should be the primary focus of the pharmacy manager's efforts to control inventory.

"C" items, on the other hand, would be considered the least important to control, and not worthy of the more elaborate system used to control "A" items. Typically these would be the less expensive items which account for a small dollar investment in inventory, and are not especially bulky so as to consume disproportional amounts of shelf space. "B" items would be somewhere in the middle, and their control would depend on the actual cost of inventory control.

Measuring the inventory turnover rate

One method of assessing the effectiveness of an inventory control system is the turnover rate. The inventory turnover rate represents the average number of times inventory is sold and replaced during a given period (usually a year). In general, a high turnover rate indicates that merchandise is selling well relative to the average amount of inventory kept in stock. A low turnover rate indicates that merchandise is not moving very quickly relative to average inventory.

Inventory turnover rate (ITR) is calculated by dividing average inventory into sales. It can be calculated on the basis of retail sales dollars, costs, or units.

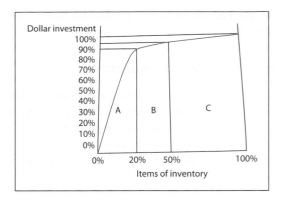

Figure 15.1 Dollar investment in items of inventory grouped as "A," "B," and "C" merchandise. For explanation, see text.

Each of the following formulas will provide identical inventory turnover rates for a given situation:

$$ITR = S/AIRD = SC/AIC = U/AIU$$

where ITR is inventory turnover rate; S is net sales dollars; SC is sales at cost (or cost of goods sold); U is number of units sold; AIRD is average inventory in retail dollars; AIC is average inventory at cost; and AIU is average inventory in units.

To illustrate how these formulas work, assume a pharmacy sells 300 bottles of an over-the-counter (OTC) medication in a year. The OTCs cost a total of $3,000 and the pharmacy has net sales of $6,000. If the average inventory was 50 bottles that cost $500 and were valued on a retail basis at $1,000, then:

$$ITR = \$6,000/\$1,000 = \$3,000/\$500$$
$$= 300/50 = 6$$

Turnover rate can be used as a standard for inventory control purposes. After establishing turnover standards, the pharmacy manager should compare actual inventory turnover rates to the industry standard for pharmacies.

By controlling inventory investment and maintaining a high turnover rate, pharmacies can improve their income as a percentage of total sales. Pharmacies with high turnover tend to have lower inventories as a percentage of sales; however, the cost of goods sold might be higher, resulting in a gross margin lower than that in the low-turnover group of pharmacies. The lower gross margin may be compensated for by the lower costs associated with carrying a smaller inventory. Because of this expense control, pharmacies

discounts, number of suppliers, special orders, and new merchandise to seek.

- Major inventory control issues to consider in establishing inventory control policies include merchandise variety and quality, unit inventory levels, dollar levels of investment, and what to do about slow-moving merchandise.

Questions for discussion

1 What are potential drawbacks of relying solely on the sophisticated and efficient purchasing programs offered by many wholesalers?

2 What are some major objectives in purchasing?

3 What are important objectives in inventory control?

4 Why should purchasing policies be flexible and reflect the pharmacy's objectives and plans?

5 What are major considerations in merchandise mix decisions?

6 What are the typical marketing functions performed by wholesale suppliers?

7 What are the advantages of joining cooperative buying groups?

8 How many suppliers should a pharmacy use?

9 What decisions need to be made regarding the timing of purchases?

10 What is the objective of open-to-buy/closed-to-buy systems?

11 What aspects should be addressed in negotiating purchase terms?

12 What is the largest investment in the average independent retail pharmacy?

13 What specific costs are included in inventory costs?

14 How is inventory turnover rate calculated?

15 What are the advantages and disadvantages of using the EOQ?

16 What are characteristics of visual, periodic, and perpetual inventory control methods?

17 What procedures can be used to identify and weed out slow-moving inventory?

18 Why should a pharmacy establish policies and procedures for purchasing and inventory control?

Self-test review

True/false statements

1 Consumer purchasing tends to be more sporadic for prescriptions than for front-end merchandise.

2 The greater the amount of time that elapses between ordering and sale of goods, the easier it is to balance supply and demand.

3 The lines of merchandise carried will depend first and foremost on the needs and desires of the target market.

4 To the extent that demand for specific items is known, one can calculate the appropriate order quantities that will minimize overall purchasing costs.

5 Indications are that, for the most part, cooperative buying group arrangements have been successful in reducing the cost of doing business.

6 By and large, pharmacy managers have recognized that a good supplier relationship results in supplier goodwill.

7 The question of how many suppliers to use has no definitive answer.

8 Open-to-buy policies specify how much of an item to buy for delivery during a specified time period.

9 Unlike many factors in pharmacy management, inventory is not controllable by management.

10 The costs of capital and opportunity costs are the most important of those associated with holding inventory.

Multiple choice questions

1 Which of the following is the single most important factor to consider in a pharmacy's purchasing decisions?

(A) Buying the right quantity.
(B) Buying at the right price.
(C) Buying from the right supplier.
(D) None of the above.

2 An advantage of buying from one supplier is:

(A) Having greater assurance of supply reliability.
(B) Receiving more attention and help.

(C)   Both A and B.

(D)   Neither A nor B.

3 Which of the following is not an objective of inventory control?

(A)   Minimizing carrying costs.

(B)   Balancing supply and demand.

(C)   Maximizing inventory investment.

(D)   Maintaining an up-to-date inventory control system.

4 An inventory control system that allows a pharmacy to know how much of any item is in inventory at any given time is a:

(A)   Physical system.

(B)   Perpetual system.

(C)   Periodic system.

(D)   Both A and B.

5 Which of the following criteria should be included when evaluating whether a product should be removed from inventory?

(A)   The product's expiration date.

(B)   The product's gross margin return on investment.

(C)   The product's turnover rate.

(D)   All of the above.

References

1. Berman B and Evans JR. *Retail Management*, 3rd edn. New York: Macmillan, 1986: 303.

16

Operations management

Learning objectives

The objectives of this chapter are to assist you to be able to explain:

- how managers convert sales plans to operations plans
- how work is scheduled to achieve an efficient operating process
- how operating processes and quality are controlled
- what role computers can play in the pharmacy
- what process the pharmacy owner would use to acquire a computer system.

Key terms

Hardware
Methods of operation
Operations control
Operations process chart
Operations scheduling

Payback period
Pharmacy layout
Product inspection
Quality control
Software

Most of the processes used to manage a pharmacy have been described in the previous chapters. However, all of these facets do not operate independently of one other. It takes considerable time, effort, and skill to bring all of the accounting, marketing, human resources, and workflow processes together to operate as a cohesive and seamless unit. If the management activities do not work together, it is highly likely that the pharmacy will operate inefficiently and costs will be higher than they need to be. Perhaps most importantly, clinical outcomes and overall customer service will suffer. In a highly competitive market environment in community settings, pharmacies only survive if they operate at peak effectiveness.

Similarly, in institutional settings, pharmacies provide critical clinical and support services. Inefficient and ineffective operating processes will not be tolerated for long by administrators and the other medical staff.

From a business perspective, pharmacists face the dual problem of "producing" and selling their products. While any business is essentially involved in producing or buying goods or services and selling them, pharmacies face a more complex task. They must serve several constituencies at once, including patients, physicians, insurance companies, federal and state agencies, etc.

Patients and physicians look predominantly at quality of care, therapeutic outcomes, and convenience. Issues of cost management are of considerably less importance to them than they are to insurance companies and governmental agencies. While therapeutic outcomes are important to the latter groups as well, budgetary constraints play a critical role in their perceptions of healthcare delivery. Operationally, the pharmacist must blend all these considerations into a single set of products and services—the provision of consistently high-quality drugs at the lowest cost possible. To do this, the pharmacy's operating processes must be efficient. There is little room for error.

Operations management

To make the pharmacy's operations as efficient as possible, plans must be formulated as to how prescriptions are to be filled and dispensed, what varieties of non-prescription merchandise are to be sold, etc. Since inefficient operations and unnecessarily high costs will all but destroy a pharmacy's chances of survival, the process of planning and implementing an operating plan is of great importance.

Fortunately, many of the pharmacy's operations are now based on advanced technology. Electronic medical records, programs that identify potential drug interactions, purchasing and inventory control, and a variety of other critical pharmacy activities can be managed much more effectively with even basic computer systems. The results are improved patient monitoring and care and more effective management of the business aspects of pharmacy operations.

Dispensing prescriptions efficiently and allowing sufficient time for appropriate counseling, and making available the right non-prescription merchandise can be a challenging process. Blending all of the components of what a pharmacy is and does, including its personnel, inventory, equipment, etc., into a unified whole that operates efficiently, involves many interrelationships. Dispensing a prescription, for example, requires bringing a pharmacist, a drug product, supplies, patient profile, and the patient together—sometimes at an instant in time. If any one of these components is not there, the operations break down. If some components (e.g. a drug product) arrive early and have to wait, there is inefficiency (e.g. inventory carrying costs). Thus, the possible interrelationships are nearly endless, but they must be coordinated into a viable operating process.

The planning process

A smoothly and efficiently operating pharmacy is the result of deliberate and detailed planning of the entire process from buying inventory, equipment, and supplies, to hiring and scheduling personnel, and dispensing prescriptions and selling non-prescription merchandise to customers. Specific areas of focus are shown in Figure 16.1.

Prescription product and service development

Determining what prescription and non-prescription products are to be bought and sold is a prerequisite to further planning. This is especially important as it relates to compounding prescriptions, preparing home intravenous (IV) solutions, preparing unit doses for skilled nursing facility patients, and other pharmacy services. Special services need to be defined so that they can be incorporated into normal work flows.

Developing the product and services

Designing and laying out the operating facilities

Determining inventory and materials needs and sources of supply

Acquiring capable labor

Scheduling tasks

Figure 16.1 The operations planning process.

Furthermore, management needs to decide the extent to which consulting and other services are to be offered. These services will take time and need to be planned in the operating process.

Facilities and layout

Once the particular products and services to be offered by the pharmacy are defined, management can begin to assess the need for various types of fixtures and equipment. In addition, the physical spacing and general layout of workstations and equipment will directly affect the pharmacy's ability to maximize output and provide high-quality prescriptions and services. If not arranged in an orderly manner, employees will either be bumping into one another or making unnecessary movements that create delays and reduce output.

Inventory and supply needs and acquisition

Proper equipment and excellent layout will be of little value if inventory and supplies are not available. Consequently, obtaining the right components of a prescription at a reasonable price and at the right time is critically important. Thus, management should give high priority to maintaining dependable sources of supply.

Acquiring capable labor

Even in the most highly mechanized pharmacies, there is still a need for pharmacists and other employees who can skillfully convert "raw materials" to sold products and services. Capable employees are assur-

ance that the pharmacy's resources will be put to their best use.

Scheduling operations

Once all of the productive resources are accumulated —equipment, inventory and supplies, and labor— they should be scheduled to provide an orderly process of converting inputs (i.e. inventory and supplies) into outputs (i.e. prescriptions). Since a great many different types of prescriptions are to be filled, decisions have to be made as to which are to be done first, who will fill what types of prescriptions, etc.

For example, will prescriptions be filled on a "first-come, first-served" basis? Or by those that are easier to fill before those harder to fill? Or by urgency (e.g. acute care before maintenance prescriptions)? By therapeutic category, etc.? Will an individual pharmacist fill all types of prescriptions? Or just those in specific therapeutic categories? Or those for which prescription inventory is physically nearby?

Some system needs to be designed so that the "production" of prescriptions is in place. Otherwise, decisions to the questions posed above will have to be made for each prescription. This is an expensive waste of time for the pharmacist, and an inconvenience to the patient. While there are occasional exceptions, a work schedule should be prepared to standardize the work flow to the extent possible.

Converting the sales plan to an operations plan

The interaction between sales and operations should be a source of serious concern to management. While the manager will want to increase the number of prescriptions dispensed and the amount of non-prescription products and services sold, care must be taken to ensure that the pharmacy has sufficient capacity to do so.

Essentially, there are two main operating issues to be resolved. First, the manager must ensure that the products and services the pharmacy is capable of providing are the same as those being demanded by customers. Second, scheduling work flows must be done in a way that both minimizes delays in filling prescriptions and making sales, and controlling the amount of inventory carried and the number of personnel employed.

Products available are the same as those demanded

To the frustration of many customers and pharmacy personnel alike, there often are differences between what customers want and expect, and what pharmacies can or do offer. If viewed from a purely economic standpoint, there would have to be a divergence. Consumers want the most for their purchasing dollars, while businesses want to give the least. In addition, consumers may well expect certain services that the pharmacy may find too difficult or costly to provide.

One of the most significant issues for prescription products concerns quality. Pharmacists and healthcare professionals agree that prescription drugs should be of high quality to provide positive therapeutic outcomes. In some cases, this can be accomplished through the dispensing of generic products. However, to consumers, generics in some therapeutic categories tend to be viewed as being of lesser quality. The scandals of the late 1980s and early 1990s concerning alleged falsifying of laboratory tests served to solidify this perspective. While consumers generally have more confidence in brand-name products, they and their insurance companies are unwilling to pay the higher costs of these medications. Consequently, the pharmacist is placed in the position of having to balance customers' fears against the economic realities of drug therapy.

A second issue relates to the variety of non-prescription products offered. While wide variations in color, style, and size will appeal to a larger number of consumers, it creates immense challenges for pharmacists. Not only will there be added purchasing, there will almost always be buildups in inventory. And, invariably, some items will prove to be unsalable. All of these factors can translate into higher operating costs. Here again, the manager must try to reconcile demands for variety with the realities of space and financial limitations.

Producing to order vs. in anticipation of orders

Although specific scheduling techniques are described later in this chapter, one interesting issue concerns how filling prescriptions is to be related to expected demand. With respect to refills, should the pharmacist fill prescriptions to order or in anticipation of orders?

Since there are uncertainties as to when consumers will bring in new or refill prescriptions, and in what quantities, the manager must try to arrive at a method of scheduling that is both conducive to sales and reasonably inexpensive. This is no simple task. When consumers want something, they typically want it instantly, especially if they are ill. If the pharmacy cannot provide the item promptly, some consumers will go elsewhere if there are alternatives available. But it would be too costly to have extra pharmacists and large quantities of inventory on hand just in case some customers come into the pharmacy.

Because of the risk involved in exclusively filling to order, many pharmacists have moved to producing in anticipation of sales. They are willing to track customers on maintenance drugs and automatically fill their prescriptions during slack times. They are willing to accept the risk that the prescriptions will have to be returned to stock. But they are able to better schedule their personnel. In addition, by sending refill reminders, or calling patients, they can reduce the number of prescriptions unclaimed and provide better patient services.

Methods of operation

Most businesses in their very basic form are processes of converting inputs to outputs, and selling those outputs. Inventory and supplies, labor, management time, facilities, utilities, and other factors are turned into finished products ready for sale.

Methods development

For a manager to get the best results from an operating process, it must consider the type and quality of equipment and fixtures needed, how they are spatially arranged within the prescription and non-prescription areas, and how employees should be scheduled and the physical design of their workstations.

Equipment and fixture considerations

In many instances, pharmacy owners cannot afford to have the newest and best equipment and fixtures available. Their limited resources force them to use more dated equipment whose quality is not of the highest caliber. Modern equipment and good fixtures can improve operations. However, they may not make radical differences in efficiency that warrant the costs involved. Assessing the cost vs. efficiency tradeoff is an important operating decision for the manager.

Even if the pharmacy had the financial resources to buy ideal equipment and the newest fixtures, this might not be advisable. Just because new equipment is brighter and shinier does not mean it will work better. A new pair of shoes, for example, does not necessarily protect the feet any better than an old pair, nor do they necessarily make the wearer walk faster or straighter. All they really do is look better. Many pharmacies have installed highly sophisticated computer systems only to find that they did not need all the functions available, and did not have the trained staff to gain the real benefits from the systems.

One major question in deciding whether to purchase a new computer or other piece of equipment is how long it will take to pay for itself.

Calculating the payback period—the time it will take for increased revenues or reduced costs to pay for the equipment—provides a means of evaluating the wisdom of making a major purchase. The formula for this is:

Payback period (years)

$$= \frac{\text{Total costs of purchase}}{\text{Yearly cost savings or profit increases}}$$

Although there is no set rule as to how quickly the equipment should pay for itself, it certainly should do so before its useful life is over. Thus, if a computer has a 5-year life and the payback period is 7 years, it is likely that it will never pay for itself. Consequently, the philosophy regarding payback periods is: the sooner, the better. Typically, pharmacies look for a payback within 2–3 years.

Pharmacy layout

The manager also must be sure that the appropriate equipment and fixtures are arranged for an orderly flow within the overall operating process. Spatial considerations are important in improving operating efficiency.

Of particular concern is ensuring that the flow is efficient in that it eliminates unnecessary movements and backtracking. There are innumerable layout possibilities, depending on both the overall size and the shape of the pharmacy and the prescription department work area.

Basically, the prescription dispensing area should be arranged to provide the pharmacist with good visibility of the pharmacy. Similarly, it should allow patients clear visibility of the pharmacist, and be designed to minimize the physical barriers between the pharmacist and the patient.

Within the dispensing area, the placement of the pharmacy computer, inventory, refrigerated cabinets, etc., should be undertaken with considerable care. Every effort should be made to make equipment and inventory readily available so as to reduce wasted motion and the time it takes to dispense the prescription.

One key to efficient pharmacy layout is to maintain some degree of flexibility in the overall design. As the pharmacy's operations change, so will the need for particular space and physical layout. More space may be needed for private consultations, changing rooms may be needed to fit prostheses and other items, and more room will be needed for additional pharmacists as prescription volume grows.

Just as there should be careful planning of the filling of prescriptions, consideration should be given to the delivery of pharmacy services. How will patients be consulted? Where will this happen? Since the role of pharmacists will expand with the provision of cognitive services, and technicians may handle more of the physical filling of prescriptions, plans for service delivery are critical. Work flows, pharmacy layout, etc., need to be carefully planned to gain the best use of the physical space available within the pharmacy.

Work scheduling

Once the most effective methods of dispensing prescriptions are decided upon, and the physical layout is made conducive to efficient operations, the work must be scheduled appropriately. Confusion in scheduling the various elements of the operating process typically results in delays in dispensing and lost sales.

Timing issues related to purchasing inventory, scheduling pharmacists and other personnel, etc., must be undertaken based on the expected demand for pharmacy services. To the extent that estimates of demand can be predicted with some degree of accuracy, the pharmacy's operations can be made more efficient.

Some factors, such as busy Mondays and Fridays and slow Wednesday afternoons, are well known. However, revenue patterns for days, weeks, and months need to be considered to control labor costs and the purchase of inventory. In existing pharmacies, track records of the volume of activity can provide good clues as to what should be expected. For new pharmacies, past experiences of pharmacists and management may serve as the basis for initial estimates until track records are established.

One of the most useful tools in planning operations process is the *operations process chart*, which is a graphic representation of the various operations, time allowances, and materials used to dispense a prescription. This chart clearly delineates each step so that none will be forgotten or ignored. In graphic form, this approach allows the manager to visualize each aspect of operations and each decision point in the overall process. A sample operations process chart for dispensing a prescription is shown in Figure 16.2.

Another important consideration is the productive capacity of the pharmacy. The manager should test the operating process and time it at slow, normal, and high speeds. By timing the speed at which prescriptions can be dispensed, the overall capacity per hour can be assessed. This, of course, does not mean that pharmacists will be given time standards. However, it will provide an estimate of the volume that can be achieved with an existing staff under ideal, and not so ideal, conditions.

Controlling the operating process

Controlling the operations process is necessary to the success of any business. When operations go out of control, costs become excessive, delays occur in customer service, and the overall quality of care tends to suffer.

Product control

The issue of what prescriptions to dispense, and what non-prescription merchandise to sell involves marketing decisions. Determining what quantity of prescriptions the pharmacy will be able to dispense is of great concern because of the high cost of excess capacity. For very small pharmacies, where the owner serves as

the only staff pharmacist, the capacity decision is relatively simple. But what if the number of prescriptions should range from 300 to 600 per day? How many pharmacists and technicians should be employed, and at what times? How much prescription inventory, and what types, should be on hand at all times?

Product control for non-prescription sales focuses mainly on what types of merchandise to purchase and in what quantities. How wide a range should there be of health-related merchandise? Should products that have no relationship to traditional pharmacy practice be carried? Should the merchandise be of very high or lesser quality? Owing to space and financial limitations, managers in community settings have to make decisions such as these. In hospital inpatient pharmacies, the merchandise usually is limited to over-the-counter products that are "companions" to prescription drugs.

Inventory levels

Keeping some inventory on hand usually is advisable since it guards against stock-outs and lost sales as well as reducing the need for special ordering, and dealing with disgruntled customers. On the other hand, there is a fine line between holding too much inventory and too little.

The costs of maintaining certain levels of inventory must be correlated to the cost savings of larger purchases and their associated discounts and the increased likelihood of being able to fill incoming prescriptions or requests for non-prescription merchandise. Regulating the inventory levels for each product is a focal point for operations control. Economic order quantities can be calculated using the formula shown in Figure 16.3.

Quality control

Control of the operating process includes not only the number and type of prescriptions dispensed and the non-prescription merchandise carried but also the quality of the products and services. It makes no sense to dispense a large quantity of incorrect prescriptions efficiently. However, making sure that each prescription and associated service meets the absolutely highest-quality standard possible will be very expensive.

Thus management must develop a control process that effectively maintains a high quality of

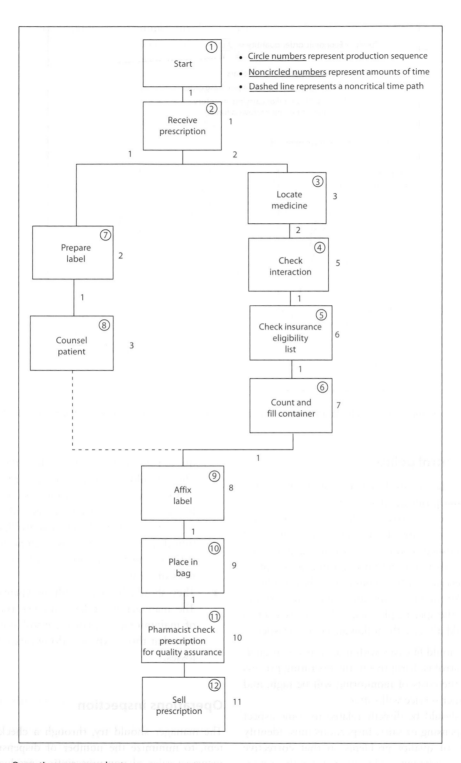

- Circle numbers represent production sequence
- Noncircled numbers represent amounts of time
- Dashed line represents a noncritical time path

Figure 16.2 Operations process chart.

service at a reasonable cost. To do this, a manager may establish some minimum level of qual-

ity as the standard against which services can be compared.

manager can automatically produce a sales journal and an income statement and balance sheet, accounts receivable and payable lists, cash flow statement, and an updated inventory status report. With such computer-generated reports, management would have accurate information to help operate the business without the burden of a large clerical staff.

Computers, of course, cannot operate without people. Computers can do only what humans have told them to do. They must be directed in each step by people-produced programs. Pharmacists still need to dispense the prescriptions and counsel patients, they must also undertake some clerical efforts. Nevertheless, the amount of labor can be reduced as more management functions are computerized. While this will result in savings in labor costs, it is not always as great as expected. Pharmacists and other personnel involved with the computer process tend to be higher paid individuals within the pharmacy. It is the faster, more accurate, and more complete reporting and greater efficiency that justifies the use of computers in many pharmacies.

To get the maximum benefit, management needs to evaluate what benefits can be obtained from using the computer for more than the dispensing process. The steps involved in acquiring computer hardware and software for management purposes can be grouped into a series of six steps described below.[2] Ordinarily, these steps should be undertaken in sequence.

Step 1: Prepare a "job description" for the computer

The most important step in the process of acquiring a computer is to determine just what it is to do, what benefits it will provide, and who is to operate the system. Deciding on these factors is very similar to preparing a job description for a new position within the pharmacy. This job description should be developed with the focus on not only the immediate needs of the pharmacy, but also for 1–2 years in the future. To the extent possible, a system should be acquired that will—with possible modifications—serve the pharmacy for a period of 2–3 years.

Pharmacy computers are costly, and they become technologically obsolete relatively quickly. Accordingly, management must consider whether it is best to purchase or lease a system. Purchasing can be less expensive over the long run, but leasing reduces the initial expenditure and provides more flexibility in replacing a system when the current one is no longer adequate. Advances in computer technology are always a concern when deciding whether to acquire a new system.

Step 2: Select the software

Some pharmacy owners mistakenly select hardware (Step 3) before software. Because hardware tends to be a more expensive element in computerizing, management tends to focus its attention on this component. Unfortunately, the hardware is of little value without the proper software—and some programs will only work with certain types of hardware.

Since the software tells the computer what to do, management should find the programs that will perform the desired tasks as specified in Step 1.[3] In some instances, it may be necessary to combine Steps 2 and 3 when the choice of software will have a major impact on the type and cost of hardware to acquire. For example, if management has the choice of two software programs that will perform the needed tasks adequately, consideration should be given to the type and costs of hardware each would need. One software alternative may require hardware that is more costly or configurations that limit the use of the hardware for other purposes.

The ultimate evaluation of software includes answers to the following questions:[4]

- How efficient is it in serving the pharmacist's needs for dispensing prescriptions? Will it continue to be efficient if the number of prescriptions increases significantly?
- To what extent will it require changes in current operating practices?
- Will it provide accounting and management information?
- How easy is it to use?
- How easy will it be to change? To expand?
- What control and security features does it incorporate?
- If the software is being written for the pharmacy, who will own the program(s)?
- How well is it documented (i.e. have written descriptions of what it does)?

Step 3: Select the hardware

Selection of hardware should be based on the needs of the software. In many instances, this will be decided by the type of software to be used. However, there are times where software will be available only for certain types of systems, and management will have to choose one or the other. Advantages and disadvantages of each should be carefully evaluated based on cost, speed, expandability, etc.

Another decision concerns whether to acquire a brand name or "clone." Brand-name hardware tends to be more expensive, but may offer some advantages in quality, servicing and repair, life expectancy, and trade-in value. Clones are computers that do not carry a national brand name, and often are assembled by individual retail stores or purchased from another business. They vary considerably in terms of their component parts and configurations, and therefore may need to be serviced by the sellers. Servicing of national brands tends not to be so limited. There has been considerable debate about the relative advantages and disadvantages of brand names versus clones. The ultimate decision often depends on budget and availability and convenience of service.

A third set of decisions will center on the components of the system in terms of computer speed, the number of disk drives, the number and size of hard drives, etc. The components of the hardware will be influenced by a variety of factors, including the software to be used, how fast the system must operate, the number of workstations to be used, and cost.

Step 4: Select the vendor

In addition to assessing software and hardware alternatives, management must evaluate the vendors. Of critical concern here will be expertise in the field, price, support services capabilities, amount and speed of service available, and stability and reliability.

In general, it is best to acquire both the software and hardware from the same vendor to ensure their compatibility. When this is not possible, or where there are substantial cost differences between using one versus multiple vendors, management must be sure that the software and hardware are integrated into a single overall system. If management does not have the technical expertise to do this, consideration should be given to hiring a consultant that will assemble the total system and install the unit and train the individual who will be using the computer.

Step 5: Install and implement the computer system

Converting from one type of system to anther can be an arduous task. Old methods of conducting day-to-day operations will change, and this conversion process will take time and generate at least short-term inefficiency.

Of particular concern in this process is whether the conversion will be phased in over time, installed at an instant in time (e.g. over a weekend), or undertaken in parallel. Phasing in the computerization over a period of 3–6 months allows management and staff pharmacists time to become accustomed to the system and may be least disruptive to daily operations. However, this means that the benefits of changing a system will not be achieved for a longer period. If the system is to be installed within a very short period, some degree of pre-training may be needed so pharmacists will know how the new system works before it is "on line."

A parallel conversion involves continuing the old methods of operation while also initiating the new computer system. This means that the work is being duplicated, but it reduces the risks of errors and provides a method for checking the accuracy of the computer system. While this approach is more costly because of the extra work involved, it helps illustrate the benefits of the new system since direct comparisons can be made.

Step 6: Establish systems for backup and security

No computer system is foolproof and completely secure. Because erasures of files, power failures, and other computer "disasters" do occur, some backup system must be built into the system.

Pharmacies that rely heavily on computers to continue daily activities must have some alternative means of remaining operational when the computer is out of service. This may involve having a manual backup system ready, contracting with a company who supplies backup services, or some other alternative. At minimum, data on a computer system should be backed up very quickly to ensure that if the system fails that information will not be lost.

In addition to backup procedures, management should have some process for ensuring the security of the system. Access to the system should be limited to

(C) What control and security features it incorporates.

(D) All of the above are criteria.

References

1. McKesson Corp. website (2011). www.mckesson.com/en_us/McKesson.com/.

2. Business computers from A to Z. *Small Business Reporter*, San Francisco, CA: Bank of America NT& SA, 1986: 5–52.

3. Karasik M. Selecting a business computer. *Harvard Business Review*, January–February, 1984: 26–30.

4. Kramer EC. *Can You Use a Minicomputer?*, *Management Aids No. 2.015*, Washington, DC: Small Business Administration, 1982: 1–8.

17

Measuring the success of the pharmacy

Learning objectives

The objectives of this chapter are to assist you to be able to explain:

- the most important dimensions of performance
- for what purposes performance measures are used
- the differences between conducting annual and periodic performance measurements
- the attributes of good performance measures
- the different types of clinical, financial, operating, and competitive measures that can be used
- what sources of internal and external information are available for measuring performance.

Key terms

Activity
Appropriateness of variables being measured
Clinical performance
Competitive advantage

Competitive measures
Competitive performance
Financial measures
Financial performance
Leverage

Liquidity
Market share
Method of measurement
Nature of the measurements
Operating measures
Operating performance
Patient behavior
Patient outcomes
Performance measurement
Profitability
Quantitatively measureable

Irrespective of the practice setting, every pharmacy will experience good and bad times. Some of the reasons for successful and not so successful times will be due to the actions of the pharmacy manager and employees, and some will be totally beyond their control. A good owner or manager will understand that not everything will run perfectly or according to plan all the time.

In fact, what separates the successful and not-so-successful managers is their ability to monitor the activities of the pharmacy and take steps to build on current and anticipated successes and minimize or mitigate current and anticipated difficulties. Good managers are proactive in keeping track of the activities of the pharmacy and seemingly constantly making adjustments based on a wide variety of external and internal conditions. The performance of the pharmacy should be the result of what the owner or manager does, not just what "happens."

Measuring the performance of the pharmacy is not a new concept. Performance measures have been used from a business perspective for many decades. Historically, they have been used at the end of the year to see how well the pharmacy did financially. This was not an especially useful practice except that it forced owners and managers to view operations more critically—sometimes it is hard to see what is going on when viewed on a daily basis "in the trenches."

Over the last 20 years, however, performance measures have evolved to not only serve as end-of-year processes, but to help manage operations so that goals can be achieved. Making mid-year assessments, for example, allows pharmacy owners and managers to take proactive corrective actions. As drug reimbursements and dispensing fees have shrunk, there is little room for inefficiency. From a business perspective, pharmacies in outpatient and inpatient settings have to operate at peak efficiency in order to achieve any reasonable degree of success.

More recently, numerous efforts have been made to measure the clinical success of pharmacy practices to improve patient outcomes and reduce healthcare costs. Many studies have been undertaken to demonstrate that good pharmacy service can enhance patient compliance with their drug therapies, improve the success rates of medication therapy, and keep patients out of hospital emergency rooms and physician offices. Much of this has been conducted to justify expanded roles for pharmacists in medication therapy management (MTM) and increased compensation for consultations. These studies of performance were designed to show that there is considerable value in expanding the role of pharmacists in overall healthcare delivery.

So, performance measures have both their traditional and newer roles in pharmacy operations. Today, pharmacies and the profession in general need effective performance measures to succeed.

What performance measurement means and why it is important

Performance measurement is the process of monitoring the activities of the pharmacy in a way that allows the owner or manager to take corrective action during and at the end of the fiscal year. In some respects, waiting until the end of the year to see how well the pharmacy did in terms of patient care, financially, and competitively is too late—whatever has happened cannot be changed. However, measuring the pharmacy's performance at strategic intervals within the fiscal year gives the owner or manager time to make adjustments. Year-end reviews are mainly valuable in helping plan strategies for the next fiscal year and determining if initiatives undertaken during the last year should be continued, modified, or discontinued.

"Performance," of course, has many dimensions. Perhaps, the four most important of these from the perspective of measuring the overall success of a pharmacy in any practice setting are:

- clinical performance
- financial performance
- operating performance
- competitive performance.

Clinical performance

In many respects, the clinical performance of the pharmacy is the most important measure of all. If the pharmacy does not serve its patients well, it is almost impossible to be successful financially and competitively over the long term.

In outpatient settings, poor customer service can drive patients to other pharmacies and possibly cause payors not to include the pharmacy in their networks of service providers. Similarly, physicians are not inclined to suggest pharmacies to their patients if they have any concerns about the quality of service their patients will receive. Patients, physicians, and payors have numerous options when it comes to patronizing a pharmacy, and their tolerance for inadequate clinical care will be low. Furthermore, the liability created by inadequate care will put the pharmacy and its professional staff at risk—something that cannot be sustained for any period of time.

In inpatient settings, poor patient services undoubtedly will generate complaints to hospital administrators from physicians and nurses. Obviously, hospitals cannot afford to operate a pharmacy that does not produce the patient care desired by the hospital and needed by its medical personnel. After all, the reputation of the hospital and staff is at risk, and the potential liability for improper or inadequate care is high.

Accordingly, the quality of patient care from a clinical perspective must be maintained to meet the needs and expectations of patients, physicians, and payors. Conducting periodic performance assessments helps ensure that the pharmacy is providing the appropriate services and level of care.

Financial performance

The financial performance of the pharmacy is nearly as important as the clinical performance, especially in outpatient settings and only to a slightly lesser extent in inpatient settings. After all, if the pharmacy loses money, it cannot continue to provide clinical services.

Whether it is an independent or chain pharmacy, no store can survive over the long term if it is operating at a loss. It is possible for some individual pharmacies within a chain to lose money but continue to operate in instances where the chain wants to provide full market coverage. However, it is unlikely that the chain's management will accept losses over

an extended period of time. Most likely, it will either close the pharmacy or restructure its personnel and/or operations to ensure that it at least operates at a "break-even" level (i.e. revenues just cover expenses).

In inpatient settings, "profits" may not be as critical, but expense control certainly will be. Some hospitals tolerate losses in the pharmacy and make them up in other operating divisions. However, this is still not considered desirable, and it is most likely that hospital administrators will expect the pharmacy to operate on a break-even basis or generate a profit. As in the case of clinical performance, hospital administrators are not going to accept financial losses in the pharmacy over the long term. They will make adjustments in personnel and/or operations to ensure that it operates as cost-effectively as possible.

Operating performance

Sometimes, the pharmacy's operating performance is not included as a separate category for measurement. The rationale is that how well operations are performed will directly impact the pharmacy's clinical, financial, and competitive performance. A smoothly and effectively running pharmacy has a much better chance of providing good clinical services, achieving financial success, and being a strong competitor in the marketplace. Conversely, if operations are not efficient and managed properly, the results will be less-than-desirable clinical services, lower financial profits or even losses, and will cause patients to switch patronage to competing pharmacies.

In outpatient settings, operating performance encompasses all of the activities conducted within the prescription department and in the front-end. It includes what products and services to offer, how well they are merchandised and displayed, service levels in assisting customers from the time they enter the pharmacy until they leave, purchasing merchandise, store appearance and cleanliness, and many other dimensions. Essentially, it includes everything that is done from making the pharmacy ready to receive customers to actually serving customers and following up with their care as necessary.

In inpatient settings, operating performance includes much the same. However, it also includes to a greater extent the interrelationships between pharmacy personnel and hospital staff. In these settings, the "output" of the pharmacy tends to involve more members of the healthcare team and less emphasis on non-prescription sales. Since most of the pharmacy's operations center on the provision of clinical services, the activities of the pharmacy are much more directed to providing these services effectively and in a cost-efficient manner.

Competitive performance

Pharmacies in every practice setting compete in some manner. Therefore, the fourth major area of performance is how well the pharmacy competes for customers in outpatient settings and budgetary dollars in inpatient settings. In general, if a pharmacy cannot compete successfully with other pharmacies in outpatient settings, or other departments within inpatient settings, its clinical and financial performance will be adversely impacted.

In outpatient settings, a pharmacy has to be able to compete with other pharmacies if it is to survive. If a pharmacy loses market share to other pharmacies (i.e. has less of a percentage of the total market in terms of numbers of customers, dollar sales, and/or number of prescriptions dispensed), its image is likely to suffer and that ultimately results in reduced patronage. Accordingly, the pharmacy needs to be able to at least retain its market share and not lose customers to competing pharmacies. Losses in market share can be the result of a relatively poor location, poor service, higher prices, or some other reason that is sufficiently important to cause patients to go elsewhere. And, sooner or later, not being competitive will result in diminished profits or financial losses.

In inpatient settings, every organizational unit within the hospital competes with one another for budgetary dollars, management attention, recognition, etc. While nobody will dispute the importance of the pharmacy in the overall provision of hospital care, the hospital's resources for staffing, facilities, equipment, and virtually everything else have to be allocated among the demands of every organizational unit. And, this is somewhat of a "zero sum game" in that when more financial and staffing resources go to one department, it means equivalently less must be allocated to other departments.

How performance measurements are used

Pharmacy owners and managers use performance measures in a variety of ways. As previously indicated,

they are most commonly used to assess how well the pharmacy has conducted its clinical, financial, operating, and competitive operations within some defined period of time (e.g. monthly, quarterly, semi-annually, annually). However, they also can be used to help market the pharmacy to targeted constituent groups.

In outpatient settings, for example, clinical performance results can be used to help become part of payor networks, justify better compensation terms from payors, encourage physicians to refer patients to the pharmacy, etc. Within hospital settings, demonstrating clinical successes can help show that the activities of pharmacists improve patient outcomes and potentially reduce expenses. These types of results help justify enhanced pharmacy department budgets and expanded roles for pharmacists in inpatient healthcare teams.

In general, performance measures are used for four purposes:

- to assess annual performance
- to monitor performance during the fiscal year
- to conduct performance reviews of key personnel
- to demonstrate the value of the pharmacy's services to targeted audiences.

Assessing annual performance

Historically, most performance measurements were used by management to try to figure out how well the pharmacy did over the last fiscal year. Typically, owners and managers would await the year-end profit and loss statement and balance sheet, and count the number of prescriptions dispensed. These would be compared to what was forecasted and budgeted at the beginning of the year to see if the pharmacy sold more, dispensed more, and spent less than what was budgeted. These figures would also be compared to prior years to see if pharmacy sales and profits rose, remained the same, or declined.

This exercise was and is useful. If nothing else, it tells the owner and manager where the pharmacy stands at the end of the year. This is important to determining whether the pharmacy is achieving goals and sets a baseline for what is to be achieved in the next 1–5 years. Unless the owner or manager knows where she or he is, it is hard to try to figure out where the pharmacy should go in the future. It is just like using a map. Unless you know where you are, the map is worthless in trying to determine how to get to your destination. Similarly, the annual performance measurement tells the owner and manager where the pharmacy is.

In addition, the year-end performance measurement does provide insights to what went on in the previous year. Hopefully, the owner and manager can learn what was done right and what needs to be improved going forward. Whether in an outpatient or inpatient setting, it often is not possible to see the good and bad when dealing with all of the day-to-day activities associated with managing the pharmacy.

In practice, these annual performance assessments primarily focused on three factors: revenues, expenses, and number of prescriptions dispensed. While all three are critical to the success of the pharmacy from a business perspective, there are many more factors that need to be considered. These are discussed later in this chapter.

Annual performance measurements generally suffer from two major problems. First, they are made after the year has ended. There is nothing the owner or manager can do at that point to rectify less-than-desirable results. It is done, and the goals were either reached or not. Either the pharmacy's clinical services were well done or they were not. Either the pharmacy generated a satisfactory profit or it did not. Pharmacy personnel either did their jobs well or they did not. While determining all of this and more could be useful going into the next fiscal year, it does not make the previous year any better.

Second, most annual performance assessments were very limited in scope. Knowing that "what's done is done," the owner and manager tend not to make an exhaustive analysis of how the results were achieved. They do not take the time to fully identify the causes of last year's outcomes and assess whether they can make changes in the future which will ensure better outcomes are achieved next year. Sometimes the review is just a quick glance at the "bottom lines" for revenues, expenses, and profits—certainly not a sufficient review to understand the interrelationships in operations and internal and external market forces that caused the results. There is a big difference between knowing what the results were and knowing why the results occurred. All too often annual performance measurements focus on the "what" rather than the "why."

Monitoring performance during the fiscal year

Modern businesses monitor performance during the fiscal year in addition to making year-end performance assessments. This way, owners and managers can evaluate how well the pharmacy is doing at set intervals and take actions to adjust operations to help ensure that goals are achieved.

Monitoring performance is considerably different from conducting annual performance measurements. While some of the measures to be described later in the chapter are the same, they differ in two ways. First, they focus on both the "what" and "why" because the latter is critical to making any changes. For example, even though it is important to know that pharmacy sales are not reaching desired levels, it is more important to know why that is occurring. Is it prescription sales that are lagging? Are dollar sales declining because the number of prescriptions has dropped or because the mix of prescriptions being dispensed is such that average prices are lower? Are patients bringing in multiple prescriptions and not having all dispensed because of costs and medical coverage, or are they not refilling prescriptions as often as they should—suggesting they are not adhering to the proper drug therapy regimen?

Second, the measures tend to focus more on those variables within the pharmacy that are controllable. Since the purpose of monitoring performance is to make adjustments as appropriate, priority should be given to studying things that can be changed during the year. For example, it may not be possible to make radical changes in the physical layout of the front-end in the middle of the year. Major capital expenditures are typically planned for at the beginning of the year and authorizing funds in the middle of a year is less likely unless absolutely necessary for the survival of the pharmacy. In general, monitoring during the year focuses more on sales by product/service lines, purchasing as it impacts costs of goods, staffing levels, and wages and salaries since they are major components of total expenses, etc.

This is not to say that everything could be monitored. But the emphasis is on what is most controllable and what has the greatest impact on the achievement of goals by the end of the year. As such, the measures that are most important could change over the course of the year. For instance, once staffing levels are under control and wages and salaries are at desired levels, less attention could be given to these variables and additional attention given to more effective and efficient purchasing in the next cycle of reviews.

Conducting performance reviews of key personnel

Because employees are so critical to the success of any pharmacy, there are some performance measures that can be used to assess the activities of key personnel (e.g. pharmacists, technicians, department managers). Most commonly, these are included in annual performance reviews that should be conducted for every pharmacy employee. However, as previously indicated, the purpose of performance measures is not only to determine how well the pharmacy and its personnel performed over the fiscal year, but also to monitor along the way and take corrective action so that the end-of-year results are desirable.

Performance measures used to evaluate pharmacy personnel need to satisfy two conditions. First, to the extent possible, whatever variables are used should be directly linked to individual employees. For example, if a measure of performance is the percentage of patients who are counseled about their medications, the percentage should be for each pharmacist and not just an average for the entire pharmacy.

Second, the variables need to be within the control of employees. It is unreasonable to measure factors over which employees have little control. For example, pharmacists have no control over the number of new prescriptions that come into the pharmacy, so they should not be held accountable for dispensing a targeted number of new prescriptions within some time period. If the pharmacy is focusing on ensuring compliance with drug therapy, measures can be created for the percentage of refills actually achieved, recognizing, of course, that not all drug therapies will continue and some refills will not be made because of changes in drug therapy.

A common method that has been used in all types of retail outlets, including pharmacies, to evaluate store personnel is the "mystery" shopper. Here, the pharmacy owner or manager hires an outside firm to send someone into the pharmacy disguised as a customer. Mystery shoppers engage pharmacy personnel as if they are actual customers and then rate the personnel on the basis of a variety of knowledge and service dimensions. Ratings could focus on politeness,

efficiency in conducting a transaction, knowledge of the pharmacy and the locations of front-end merchandise, knowledge of merchandise, etc. These ratings are then reported back to the pharmacy owner or manager.

For managers and executive staff in all types of practice settings, some ratings are conducted using "management by objectives" (MBO) or "360 reviews." The MBO approach has been used for many years, and consists of an executive developing a set of objectives and then presenting them to her or his superior. The executive and superior then agree on a set of objectives and the executive is then evaluated against those objectives at set intervals (e.g. end-of-year performance appraisal). The "360 review" consists of having an executive evaluated by both her or his superior and her or his subordinates. The reviews conducted by subordinates are, of course, conducted anonymously. The combined reviews are then discussed by the executive and her or his superior at set intervals.

Demonstrating the value of the pharmacy's services to targeted audiences

One of the more recent uses for performance measures is to demonstrate to targeted audiences how well the pharmacy performs its activities. Historically, this has only been used to show creditors (e.g. banks, suppliers), owners (e.g. shareholders in independent and chain pharmacies), and administrators and boards of directors (e.g. hospital administrators, board of trustees/directors) the financial performance of the pharmacy. Typically, those measures focus on the pharmacy's ability to pay its bills and generate acceptable levels of profits.

Clinical measures are increasingly being used to demonstrate to physicians and payors how well the pharmacy delivers clinical services and impacts patient outcomes. Physicians want to know that referrals they make to particular pharmacies will meet with their patients' satisfaction. If patients are satisfied with their pharmacy experience, there is greater likelihood that drug regimens will be adhered to and treatment outcomes will be enhanced.

Payors want to know that they are getting the services they are paying for, and that their customers (i.e. pharmacy patients) are being treated well and receiving proper care. When pharmacies take proper care of their patients, this creates fewer problems for payors.

In more recent times, pharmacists have sought to be reimbursed for services other than just those associated with dispensing functions. Numerous demonstration projects have been conducted to show that medication therapy management (MTM) can result in improved patient compliance with their drug therapies, improved outcomes, and reduced overall cost to payors. However, before payors are willing to fund these activities, they need to be assured that the services are being provided and patients are benefiting from the process. Clinical performance measures, such as increased refill rates, lower blood pressures, lower cholesterol levels, etc., can provide useful information for pharmacies to show their value to payors, physicians, and patients.

Attributes of good performance measures

There is little reason to conduct performance assessments if the measures being used cannot help the owner and manager achieve the goals of the pharmacy. Special care needs to be taken in developing measures of pharmacy performance that can help management determine the success of pharmacy operations, identify areas for improvement (if any), and better understand the interrelationships between finances, operations, marketing, and clinical services.

In general, the attributes of "good performance measures" can be viewed along three dimensions. These are the *appropriateness* of the variables that are being measured, the *nature* of the measurement, and the *method* by which measurements are made.

Appropriateness of variables being measured

The first attribute is the appropriateness of the variables being measured. All of the variables should have some direct or indirect link to the ultimate success of the pharmacy in terms of its clinical, financial, operating, and competitive positions. These are described later in this chapter, but typically relate to the provision of clinical services (e.g. accuracy of prescriptions

dispensed, speed of prescriptions dispensed), revenues (e.g. total pharmacy sales, non-prescription department sales), expenses (e.g. costs of goods sold, salaries and wages), profits, and staff performance.

In addition, it usually is best to focus more on variables that the pharmacy owner or manager can adjust often and in a relatively short period of time. For instance, wages, maintenance costs, and advertising can be modified much more readily than can such factors as rent, depreciation, business taxes, and insurance. While all of these are important to the overall success of the pharmacy, it is typically preferable to monitor controllable expenses during the year and more "fixed" expenses as part of the end-of-year performance measures.

Nature of the measurements

The second dimension of good performance measures is that the variables be quantitatively measurable to the extent possible. In order to assess the pharmacy's performance, it is important to be able to examine it objectively and accurately. Numbers tend to be more objective than opinion, and are more likely to be interpreted consistently by those making the assessments. For example, if the costs of goods for front-end merchandise are 90 percent of non-prescription revenues, that is what it is. There is no misunderstanding of the statistic. Most likely, too, it will be interpreted the same by whoever examines the statistic—it is too high and either costs need to be reduced or prices need to be raised, or both.

Even though some qualitative measures can be used, they are much more difficult to interpret and use for management decision-making. For instance, while the appearance of the front-end is important to the professional image of the pharmacy and its sales, the assessment will be more subjective in nature. Some people will look at the front-end and think it is perfectly merchandised while others will think it is disorganized and/or messy. In fact, there may be no right answer to qualitative measures.

Accordingly, it is best to try to use measures that are quantitative in nature. This makes it somewhat easier to identify and evaluate variations from goals and from past performance. The more definitive the measures are of the true performance of the pharmacy, the better it will be to use those to make decisions about the store's future operations. Although some qualitative measures can be included in an assessment, they should be used sparingly and with caution.

Method of measurement

The third dimension of good performance measures is that the manner in which the variable is measured adheres to proper and consistent practices. For performance data to be accurate, the manner in which the statistics are generated needs to be correct. To the extent that performance data for one time period are compared to those of another time period (e.g. first quarter of year 1 to first quarter of year 2), the manner in which the data are collected needs to be the same.

Different performance results can be obtained depending on how the data are collected and analyzed. Collecting information from the pharmacy computer in real time could show statistics that could be quite different than what comes from financial reports that tend to be about one or more months behind. For example, prescription inventory is commonly kept in real time in the pharmacy computer based on dispensing volume. However, the financial statements usually are based on physical inventory counts and estimates on a monthly basis. So the numbers in the pharmacy's computer and balance sheet may differ depending on when they are observed.

In general, it is important to measure the variables as accurately as possible, using as few estimates as possible. Yet, consideration should be given to the time and cost to get precise measures with how important precise information is. In some cases, estimates may be adequate and justified if the time and costs to obtain exact information are too high. For instance, physical inventory counts are necessary from time to time, but may not be needed for monitoring purposes if reasonably good estimates can be obtained from the pharmacy computer and possibly cash registers at significantly lower costs.

Importantly, too, the methods used to measure the pharmacy's activities should remain consistent over time to the extent possible. This will allow the owner or manager to compare measures from the past to the present. If the methodologies for collecting the data vary from the past, it will be difficult to know whether differences in results are due to actual activities of the pharmacy or the manner in which the information was accumulated.

Possible performance measures

Every pharmacy will utilize somewhat different performance measures depending on the needs and goals of the owner or manager and the financial and competitive condition of the pharmacy. An owner who is nearing retirement and wants to position the pharmacy for sale will have different needs and goals than will an owner who plans to keep the pharmacy for another 20 years. Managers of chain pharmacies will use different performance measures than will owners of independent community pharmacies. And hospital pharmacies which are very active participants in medical teams will have different performance measures than ones which are strictly conducting dispensing functions.

In reality, too, performance measures can change over time. For example, the performance measures for a new chain pharmacy located in a new housing development will be different from those used 5–10 years from now when both the pharmacy and development are well established. Pharmacies that are experiencing significant growth will probably use different measures than will those that are having financial difficulties.

In effect, there is no one absolute set of performance measures that all pharmacies should use. The main considerations are that whatever measures are used be meaningful and useful to the owner or manager and that the data are collected in a manner that is both time and cost efficient.

There are numerous ways to categorize measures. In general, however, they can be grouped based on:

- clinical performance
- financial performance
- operating performance
- competitive performance.

Most performance measures can be positioned within one of these categories. Some, however, may span multiple categories. For example, establishing an MTM program could include goals and measures within all four categories. Specifics related to the actual activities of the MTM program could be part of the clinical performance, the costs to establish and market the program could be included in the financial performance, which staff will provide the actual services could be included in the operating performance, and aspects of the program that make it unique in the marketplace could be included in the competitive performance.

Clinical measures

Clinical measures of performance can be grouped into several categories: satisfaction, dispensing, patient behavior, and patient outcomes. Examples of the specific variables that can be measured are listed in Table 17.1. Some of these are specific numbers while others can be expressed as percents of a total.

Financial measures

There are a variety of measures that can be used to assess the financial health and success of a pharmacy. Some of these were described in Chapter 7, but will briefly be reviewed in this chapter. Comparisons to budget typically can be used for pharmacies in any practice setting. Financial ratios can be used

as performance measures in independent community pharmacies and some community chain pharmacies. In hospital settings, some ratios are difficult to use because it all depends on how financial records are maintained by the hospital and the extent to which they are accessible to department managers.

Comparison to budgets

The most common measure of financial performance is how well the pharmacy is doing in comparison to its budget. As previously indicated, historically this was done at the end of the fiscal year to determine how well the pharmacy performed. However, to use budget comparisons effectively, an annual budget needs to be broken down into at least quarterly budgets and in some cases even monthly budgets. Quarterly comparisons to budget provide good snapshots of what has transpired and allow the pharmacy owner or manager time (i.e. the next three months) to make adjustments.

Table 17.1 Specific clinical variables that can be measured

Satisfaction (specific numbers)	Level of patient satisfaction with services received
	Level of physician satisfaction with services received
	Level of physician satisfaction with services provided to her or his patients
	Level of employee satisfaction within the prescription department
	Pharmacist satisfaction
	Technician satisfaction
	Pharmacy clerk satisfaction
Dispensing (specific numbers)	Number of prescriptions dispensed per day
	Number of consultations provided to patients per day, or number of consultations given as a percent of the number of new prescriptions dispensed
	Number of errors found in prescriptions written by prescribers
	Number of errors in filling prescriptions per month
Patient behavior (number or percent of patients)	Patient compliance in having prescriptions actually filled (if sent in directly by physicians)
	Patient willingness to accept generic substitutions if recommended by pharmacist
	Patient compliance with medication therapy as measured by prompt refills
	Number of consultations requested per day by patients for prescription medications
	Number of consultations requested per day for non-prescription medications
	Number of vaccinations provided at the pharmacy per month
	Number of blood pressure checks provided at the pharmacy per week
	Number of cholesterol tests conducted at the pharmacy per week
Patient outcomes (number or percent of patients for which there is interaction on their healthcare)	Blood pressure within normal level
	Cholesterol within normal level
	Blood sugar below acceptable level
	Weight within acceptable level

Monthly reviews can be used as necessary to help identify and track any potentially serious problems.

Quarterly comparisons of financial performance are made by comparing a three-month profit and loss statement to a budget that has been established for the same period. For example, the budget for the first quarter of the year (i.e. January through March) can be compared to a profit and loss statement for this period. This, of course, requires the pharmacy to develop budgets in quarterly increments and compile revenues and expenses for the same period of time.

The focus of these comparisons should be on the largest revenue and cost items and those which can be controlled in the short term. Depending on what the pharmacy sells and how it is organized into departments, revenues can be broken down by prescription sales, over-the-counter medications, cosmetics, health and beauty aids, greeting cards, gifts, food, etc. For prescription sales, it is sometimes best to break down new and refill prescriptions as this will provide an indication of what percent refills comprise total sales. If refills are a very high percent of the total, it may provide one indication that the pharmacy is not attracting new customers.

In terms of expenses, it is best to focus on those that have the greatest impact on profits and those that can be controlled in the short term. For example, costs of goods and wages have greater impacts on profits than do business taxes and maintenance costs. Similarly, the focus should be on those expenses that can be controlled and adjusted in a three-month period.

One of the difficulties in making expense comparisons to budget is that expenses are a function of revenues. If revenues are well above expectations as reflected in the budget, expenses are likely to be greater than budgeted as well. This problem can be resolved by using "flexible budgets" or monitoring expenses as a percent of revenues.

Flexible budgets are based on different assumptions as to revenues. For instance, expenses can be budgeted for situations where revenues are 5 percent greater than expected, 10 percent greater than expected, 5 percent lower than expected, 10 percent lower than expected, and so on. In this way, the owner or manager can determine what the revenues are for the quarter and then compare budgeted expenses based on that sales level. This provides a better perspective of whether expenses are being controlled adequately than just using percentages of revenues

as the measure. When sales are considerably higher or lower than expected, the percentages used for expenses may need to be adjusted for volume. For instance, if revenues are greater than anticipated, it is possible that the percentage cost of goods sold should be lower to reflect achieving economies of scale in purchasing. If revenues are lower than anticipated, the percent may be higher because volume discounts cannot be achieved.

Financial ratios

Depending on the practice setting, some or all of the following areas of financial measurement also can be used: liquidity, leverage, activity, and profitability.

Liquidity refers to the pharmacy's ability to meet its current obligations from current assets. In effect, can it pay its bills and pay them on time? These are critical measures to any organization, whether an independent community pharmacy or a not-for-profit hospital. Employees and suppliers need to be paid for their services and goods. If the pharmacy or hospital cannot make these payments, it will cease to exist.

The main measures of liquidity are the financial ratios described in Chapter 7:

- current assets divided by current liabilities (current ratio)
- (current assets minus inventory) divided by current liabilities (acid test ratio)
- difference between average collection period and average payables period.

Leverage ratios relate to how much debt the pharmacy has incurred. This impacts both its operating costs associated with interest expenses and its ability to borrow additional funds or obtain additional lines of credit should the need arise. Clearly, as the amount of debt increases relative to the total assets of the pharmacy, the risks to creditors rise and the cost of obtaining additional funds increases.

The main measures of leverage for performance measurement purposes are (see Chapter 7 for explanations of some of the specific ratios):

- (net profit minus interest expense) divided by interest expense (i.e. times interest earned)
- total liabilities divided by net worth
- current liabilities divided by net worth
- current liabilities divided by current assets
- current liabilities/(current assets minus inventory).

Activity ratios are designed to measure the ability of the pharmacy to use its assets to generate revenues. In its most basic sense, a pharmacy buys and sells goods and services. It generates revenues by using the assets at its disposal, including pharmacy staff, and turns them into sales. This is what activity ratios measure. If the pharmacy cannot generate adequate sales, it cannot pay its bills, pay salaries and wages to its employees, and generate a profit or at least cover all of its costs.

This set of ratios is often overlooked because the emphasis tends to be on liquidity and profitability. But, neither of those measures can come out positive if there are no revenues. The main measures of activity for performance measurement purposes are (see Chapter 7 for explanations of some of the specific ratios):

- cost of goods sold divided by average inventory (i.e. inventory turnover)
- net sales divided by total assets (i.e. asset turnover)
- net sales divided by (current assets minus current liabilities)
- average number of transactions per day in total and by department
- average dollar value of a transaction in total and by department.

Profitability ratios measure how much profit the pharmacy earns on the assets it employs. These are usually measured before taxes because the tax liability is generally not associated with operations or the performance of the pharmacy.

These measures tend to be of most concern to owners and managers because they focus on the profits of the pharmacy. While important, these ratios should not be used exclusively. In some respects, profitability is the result of managing the liquidity, leverage, and activity of the pharmacy. If the pharmacy is not well managed in terms of these three other sets of measures, profitability is likely to be less than desired or non-existent.

The main measures of profitability for performance measurement purposes are (see Chapter 7 for explanations of some of the specific ratios):

- cost of goods sold divided by net sales (i.e. percentage gross margin)
- net profit before taxes divided by net sales

- net profit before taxes divided by net worth (i.e. return on investment)
- net profit before taxes divided by total assets (i.e. return on assets).

It is important to note that the percentage gross margin is not a true measure of profitability. But because costs of goods are such a large part of total expenses, they have a direct impact on profitability performance. If the costs of goods are too high relative to sales, profits will undoubtedly suffer.

The best measures of profitability are return on investment and return on assets. They are the true measures of success—how much profit is earned on how much is invested by the owner (net worth) and how much is invested by both the owner and creditors (total assets).

Operating measures

Operating measures tend to be oriented on the pharmacy's human resources, non-prescription activities, and the physical facilities. Measures in this category focus on how well the pharmacy operates in terms of efficiency and ability to generate sales. As such, some of the specific variables are closely tied to both clinical and financial performance measures.

Human resources

The human resources of the pharmacy are among its most important "assets." Without a competent staff, customer service will suffer. However, human resources also are among the most expensive components of a pharmacy's operations, irrespective of practice setting. Therefore, the pharmacy owner or manager needs to monitor staffing levels, costs of staffing, productivity of the staff, and how well the staff functions with customers and each other.

Variables commonly used to measure human resource performance include:

- total cost of salaries and wages paid to staff
- total cost of benefits paid for staff
- total cost of benefits divided by total cost of salaries and wages
- total costs of salaries, wages, and benefits divided by total sales
- sales divided by the number of full-time employees
- employee turnover

- employee absenteeism
- total cost of salaries in comparison with the marketplace (i.e. total salaries that would have to be paid to new hires)
- total cost of wages in comparison with the marketplace (i.e. total wages that would have to be paid to new hires)
- total cost of benefits in comparison with the marketplace (i.e. total benefits that would have to be paid to new hires).

Non-prescription activities

Although the "front-ends," or non-prescription areas, of many independent community pharmacies are relatively small, they are important for at least four reasons. First, and perhaps most importantly, this is the area that most customers first see when they enter the pharmacy. This area will create the first impression of the store and its people and services. And since customers are not pharmacists, this area also is the one to which they can best relate because they are familiar with the products stocked on the shelves and can formulate opinions about their attractiveness, price, etc.

Second, the staff in the front-end are also the first line of contact with the customer. If the staff are competent and friendly, it will create an immediate positive image of the pharmacy. Undoubtedly, the pharmacist is the key person in terms of building relationships with the customer. But a poor front-end staff can do much to destroy that relationship because they often are the last line of contact with the customer as well.

Third, the front-end contains merchandise that adds to the cost of holding inventory. While the owner's investment in inventory typically is less in the front-end than the prescription area, it still can be sizable, especially if it offers much in the way of durable medical equipment or home healthcare supplies. In community chain pharmacies, the front-end inventory could even exceed the value of the prescription inventory if they carry a wide range of products not directly associated with healthcare (e.g. food, gifts, electronics).

Fourth, merchandise held in the front-end can generate significant profits for the pharmacy. Some merchandise will carry better profit margins than prescriptions, and some will be purchased more often.

Common measures of performance related to non-prescription activity include:

- customer satisfaction with the non-prescription merchandise available
- customer satisfaction with the non-prescription services available
- total sales divided by hours the pharmacy is open
- total sales by department (e.g. over-the-counter medications, cosmetics, health and beauty aids, gifts, greeting cards)
- total sales divided by square feet of store space (in total and by department)
- expenses by department
- total sales divided by number of employees (in total and by department)
- total sales divided by total salaries and wages (in total and by department)
- inventory turnover in total and by department
- average value of inventory in each department
- average value of inventory divided by square feet of store space (in total and by department)
- average age of inventory in total and by department.

Physical facilities

Customers typically judge a pharmacy on the basis of the service they receive and the merchandise available in the store. However, the physical facilities also create an image, and can be especially important in ensuring staff productivity, distinguishing one store from another, and enhancing the "shopping experience." In community settings, the exterior and interior of the pharmacy need to be visually appealing as well and laid out to maximize sales and staff efficiency. In hospital settings, operating efficiency is most important, but employees also want a work environment that is pleasant and contains the right equipment located in the correct places to allow for proper work flow.

Although there are some quantitative measures that can be used to assess performance of the physical facilities, most are more qualitative in nature. In essence, how the facilities, including shelving, decorations, etc., look and how well the equipment and merchandise are arranged commonly are based more on impression than on hard quantitative factors.

Variables commonly used to measure the physical facilities include:

- general image of the external signage

- average age of the shelving and other display cases
- average age of the equipment
- general image of the pharmacy with respect to cleanliness, organization, use of attractive colors, lighting, and signage
- amount of time the merchandise has stayed in its current location within the store (e.g. relocating merchandise within the store periodically generates renewed interest)
- facilities available to targeted audiences (e.g. seating and wide aisles for elderly customers).

Competitive measures

In many respects, pharmacies in all practice settings operate in a competitive environment. Independent and chain pharmacies function in a community environment in which they must compete with each other, mail order, mass merchandisers, grocery stores, discount warehouses, and others. Hospital pharmacies face a different type of competition, that being for funding given the limited resources institutions have to distribute among departments.

Competitive measures in community settings

To effectively function in community settings, independent and chain pharmacies need to have a "competitive advantage"—a reason why consumers should patronize their pharmacies rather than other options for prescriptions and non-prescription products and services. This was discussed briefly in the marketing chapters (Chapters 8 through 11). Their advantages can be real (e.g. more convenient location, lower prices) or imaginary (e.g. perceived to offer more knowledgeable services, perceived to have friendlier and more helpful staff). What matters is that consumers think the pharmacy is better than its competitors in some way that is important to them.

Competitive environments are always in a state of flux because competitors frequently change their prices, merchandise, and promotional programs. Therefore, it is important for the pharmacy to develop performance measures that consider how well they are doing vis-à-vis their competitors. For example, having "fair" prices may be a goal of the pharmacy, but if its prices are still considerably higher than the competition, being "fair" will not attract customers who are price sensitive. Similarly, offering "fast" service that is still slower than what is available from

competitors may not be adequate to attract and retain customers.

Variables commonly used to measure how competitive the community pharmacy is versus its competitors include:

- pharmacy awareness and recognition in the community
- range of clinical services offered in the prescription department
- speed of prescription services
- range of merchandise offered in the non-prescription departments
- depth of merchandise choices offered in the non-prescription departments
- appearance of the pharmacy's exterior
- appearance of the pharmacy's interior
- how visibly attractive its non-prescription merchandise is in terms of where it is located, colors, etc.

Competitive measures in hospital settings

Hospital pharmacies face a different type of competition. While there are some aspects of the clinical services that might be outsourced, the real competition is for support from the other medical staff (e.g. physicians, nurses) and for funds to operate the department. Sooner or later, all departments compete for scarce funding and space, and the pharmacy needs to compete for those resources.

Variables commonly used to measure how competitive the hospital pharmacy is versus competing staff and departments include:

- range of clinical services offered in the prescription department
- level of awareness and recognition of pharmacy services among the hospital administrators
- level of awareness and recognition of pharmacy services among the medical staff
- speed of prescription services
- speed of consulting services available to the medical staff and patients.

Collecting performance information

Collecting and interpreting performance data depends on what measures are employed and how they are to be used. For instance, if the owner or manager plans to use several of the performance measures identified earlier in this chapter to assess individual personnel performance, the collection and interpretation of the measures will have to be substantially more rigorous than if the same information is used to conduct an overall evaluation of how well the staff collectively are performing their duties.

There are several sources of information for measuring performance, depending on the specific variables being assessed. In general, these include both internal and external sources.

Internal sources

Most of the data that are used to measure pharmacy performance can be collected internally. The pharmacy computer has a wealth of information related to the clinical activities of the prescription department. Depending on the operating system being used and how the system is configured, nearly all of the information concerning dispensing can be obtained from the pharmacy's computer. To the extent that the computer is used to keep records on patients in addition to their prescription activity, the computer can also be configured to track some patient behavior and outcome variables (e.g. vaccinations received, blood pressure levels).

Special records, either maintained manually or on the pharmacy's computer or within an independent system, can be used to record nearly all patient behavior and outcomes measures. Although this information is good for tracking overall patient care, it can be time-consuming to maintain for every patient that has a prescription filled at the pharmacy. The owner or manager may designate criteria for deciding which patients should be included in the information system. This may be based on a variety of criteria, including those who have had refills, those who are at most risk, and those who have patronized the pharmacy for at least some specified time period. For strictly performance measurement purposes, the goal is to get a good sample of patients for tracking.

Depending on the type of cash register system being used in the front-end, the equipment can capture substantial information useful for monitoring performance. Total sales, the average size of each transaction, sales by product category, and other factors can be retained in some systems and extracted for performance assessment purposes.

Financial data, including budgets and ratios, can be computed from the pharmacy's profit and loss statement and balance sheet. This information should be available on a monthly basis, and is best reviewed at least quarterly. Most pharmacies also maintain some of the financial information on their cash registers and pharmacy computers. But, the financial statements are convenient sources of much of the data other than transactional information (e.g. transactions per day, average dollar value of a transaction).

External sources

Clinical, financial, and some operational measures can be compared to industry averages to evaluate how well the pharmacy is doing relative to others. There are several sources of industry averages. Some national pharmacy associations collect operating data on their pharmacies and publish the results for their members. This is done for both community and hospital pharmacies. The advantages of using this information is that it typically is segmented based on pharmacy characteristics so the pharmacy owner or manager can match the characteristics of her or his pharmacy to appropriate industry averages.

Other industry sources include private companies that collect and publish financial information for a wide range of industries. Dunn & Bradstreet, Risk Management Association, and the Almanac of Business are three well-known companies. These results usually are reported by Standard Industrial Classification Code (SIC) and contain some breakdown by asset size. However, most do not distinguish pharmacies by practice settings. These sources collect data annually and usually are available in public libraries.

Measuring patient and prescriber satisfaction is more labor intensive. It involves conducting periodic surveys to assess how satisfied customers are with the services they receive. This could be done on a quarterly, semi-annual, or annual basis. Typically, it is done semi-annually or annually to minimize the cost to the pharmacy and inconvenience to respondents.

A sample set of questions for patients is shown in Figure 17.1. This type of questionnaire can be mailed or handed to a sample of patients. On-line customer surveys are reasonably easy to conduct, and the results generally are provided in a convenient form. The difficulty with this method is that the pharmacy needs to develop and maintain email addresses of patients. Since people tend to change Internet providers with some degree of frequency, maintaining an accurate set of email addresses can be time-consuming.

For prescribers, it is best for the pharmacist to contact the prescriber and ask similar types of questions directly. Prescribers are less likely to respond to a survey and the direct contact helps build pharmacist–prescriber relationships.

While satisfaction surveys are somewhat tedious to conduct, they offer two benefits. First, they provide valuable information on how well the pharmacy is meeting the needs of those being surveyed. If there are problems, they can be addressed before patients and prescribers are lost. Second, there is considerable public relations value in asking these groups for their inputs. It demonstrates that the pharmacy cares about the services it provides. This tends to strengthen the relationships the pharmacy has with patients and prescribers. The risk, however, is that if areas of dissatisfaction are uncovered, they need to be addressed by the pharmacy.

Using performance measures for management decision-making

There is no value in conducting performance measurements if the information is not used to improve pharmacy operations. All of the information that is collected should have some identified purpose and be useful for management decision-making.

To the extent that the performance measures are relevant and collected in an appropriate manner, they can be powerful tools for tracking the success of pharmacy operations. This information can also be shared with employees as an indication of what is expected of them and how their overall performance contributes to the well-being of customers and the pharmacy.

An increasingly common use for performance measures is to build a data base to show prescribers and payors how well the pharmacy is providing its clinical services. Being able to show that the pharmacy is providing value-added services in terms of patient care can help pharmacies to participate in more attractive contracting opportunities. In hospital settings, clinical measures can assist the pharmacy manager to build the role of pharmacy staff on medical teams and broaden the value of the pharmacy in healthcare delivery.

It is important to recognize, however, that there are dangers in using performance measures. One set of measures at a point in time may not provide a clear picture of pharmacy operations. Accordingly, when possible, the owner or manager should look for trends or continued undesirable results over time before taking any drastic actions. It is common for performance to vary from time-to-time despite the best efforts of the pharmacy staff, and sometimes it will vary for reasons beyond control.

The best use for performance measures is to identify areas of pharmacy operations that need special attention. Performance measures do not always provide answers and cannot be used entirely as a substitute for management judgment. But, they can assist owners and managers to set directions and monitor activities to ensure the pharmacy's success.

Summary

- What separates the successful and not-so-successful managers is their ability to monitor the activities of the pharmacy and take steps to build on current and anticipated successes.

- Performance measurement is the process of monitoring the activities of the pharmacy in a way that allows the owner or manager to take corrective action during and at the end of the fiscal year.

- The financial performance of the pharmacy is nearly as important as the clinical performance, especially in outpatient settings and only to a slightly lesser extent in inpatient settings.

- In outpatient settings, operating performance encompasses all of the activities conducted within the prescription department and in the front-end.

- In inpatient settings, operating performance includes much the same but also includes to a greater extent the interrelationships between pharmacy personnel and hospital staff.

- Pharmacies in every practice setting compete in some manner. Generally, if a pharmacy cannot compete successfully with other pharmacies in outpatient settings, or other departments within inpatient settings, its clinical and financial performance will be adversely impacted.

- The year-end performance measurement does provide insights in what went on in the previous year.

The following questions can be used in a survey. This list is neither complete nor presented in a format that could be used directly.

1. Overall, how satisfied are you with how quickly your prescriptions are ready for you?
   1) Very satisfied
   2) Somewhat satisfied
   3) Uncertain
   4) Somewhat dissatisfied
   5) Very dissatisfied
2. How frequently do you receive consultations when you obtain a prescription?
   1) 75% to 100% of the time (Please go to Question 3)
   2) 50% to 74% of the time (Please go to Question 3)
   3) 25% to 49% of the time (Please go to Question 3)
   4) 1% to 24% of the time (Please go to Question 3)
   5) Never (Please go to Question 4)
3. Overall, how valuable have the consultations been?
   1) Very valuable
   2) Somewhat valuable
   3) Uncertain
   4) Not very valuable
   5) Not at all valuable
4. How knowledgeable do you consider your pharmacists to be concerning your medical condition?
   1) Very knowledgeable
   2) Somewhat knowledgeable
   3) Uncertain
   4) Not very knowledgeable
   5) Not at all knowledgeable
5. How would you rate the courtesy of the employees when you come into our pharmacy?
   1) Very courteous
   2) Somewhat courteous
   3) Uncertain
   4) Not very courteous
   5) Not at all courteous
6. How would you rate the attentiveness of the employees when you come into our pharmacy?
   1) Very attentive
   2) Somewhat attentive
   3) Uncertain
   4) Not very attentive
   5) Not at all attentive

Figure 17.1 Sample patient satisfaction survey questions *(continued)*.

- Whether in an outpatient or inpatient setting, it often is not possible to see the good and bad when dealing with all of the day-to-day activities associated with managing the pharmacy.
- Annual performance measurements generally suffer from two major problems. First, they are made after the year has ended. Second, most annual performance assessments were very limited in scope.
- Monitoring performance is considerably different from conducting annual performance measurements.
- Clinical measures are increasingly being used to demonstrate to physicians and payors how well the pharmacy delivers clinical services and impacts patient outcomes. Clinical measures of performance can be grouped into several categories:

satisfaction, dispensing, patient behavior, and patient outcomes.
- All of the variables should have some direct or indirect link to the ultimate success of the pharmacy in terms of its clinical, financial, operating, and competitive positions.
- In order to assess the pharmacy's performance, it is important to be able to examine it objectively and accurately. It is best to try to use measures that are quantitative in nature. This makes it someone easier to identify and evaluate variations from goals and from past performance.
- For performance data to be accurate, the manner in which the statistics are generated needs to be correct and performance data for one time period is compared to that of another time period.

7. How satisfied are you with the variety of non-prescription merchandise we have in our pharmacy?
   1) Very satisfied
   2) Somewhat satisfied
   3) Uncertain
   4) Somewhat dissatisfied
   5) Very dissatisfied

8. When you come into our pharmacy to obtain a prescription, what percent of the time do you also purchase non-prescription merchandise?
   1) 75% to 100% of the time
   2) 50% to 74% of the time
   3) 25% to 49% of the time
   4) 1% to 24% of the time
   5) Never

9. Overall, how satisfied are you with our pharmacy?
   1) Very satisfied
   2) Somewhat satisfied
   3) Uncertain
   4) Somewhat dissatisfied
   5) Very dissatisfied

10. On the average, how many times per month do you come into our pharmacy?
    1) More than 4 times per month
    2) 2 to 3 times per month
    3) 1 time per month
    4) Less than 1 time per month

11. Do you have prescriptions filled at pharmacies other than ours?
    1) Yes (Please go to Question 12)
    2) No

12. What is your **one main reason** for having prescriptions filled at other pharmacies?
    1) Convenient location
    2) Physician recommended other pharmacy
    3) Mail order
    4) Price
    5) Other (please specify) _____

Figure 17.1 *(continued).*

- The most common measure of financial performance is how well the pharmacy is doing in comparison to its budget. However, to use budget comparisons effectively, an annual budget needs to be broken down into at least quarterly budgets and in some cases even monthly budgets.

- Depending on the practice setting, some or all of the following areas of financial ratio measurement also can be used: liquidity, leverage, activity, and profitability.

- Operating measures tend to be oriented on the pharmacy's human resources, non-prescription activities, and the physical facilities. Measures in this category focus on how well the pharmacy operates in terms of efficiency and ability to generate sales.

- The human resources of the pharmacy are among its most important "assets." Without a competent staff, customer service will suffer. However, human resources also are among the most expensive components of a pharmacy's operations, irrespective of practice setting.

- Customers typically judge a pharmacy on the basis of the service they receive and the merchandise available in the store. However, the physical facilities also create an image, and can distinguish one store from another, and enhance the "shopping experience."

- To effectively function in community settings, independent and chain pharmacies need to have a "competitive advantage"—a reason why consumers should patronize their pharmacies rather than other options for prescriptions and non-prescription products and services.

- Hospital pharmacies face a different type of competition. While there are some aspects of the clinical services that might be out-sourced, the real competition is for support from the other medical staff (e.g. physicians, nurses) and for funds to operate the department.

- Most of the data that are used to measure pharmacy performance can be collected internally. Clinical, financial, and some operational measures also can be compared to industry averages to evaluate how well the pharmacy is doing relative to others.

- The best use for performance measures is to identify areas of pharmacy operations that need special attention. Performance measures can assist owners and managers to set directions and monitor activities to ensure the pharmacy's success.

Questions for discussion

1 Why is it important to monitor a pharmacy's performance on an annual basis? On a quarterly or monthly basis?

2 How do clinical, financial, operating, and competitive performance interrelate?

3 When is each type of performance measure the most important in an outpatient pharmacy? In an inpatient pharmacy?

4 Why does conducting performance reviews of key personnel require more careful analysis than other types of reviews?

5 Why is it more desirable to conduct quarterly than monthly reviews? When are monthly reviews most appropriate?

6 How can performance measures be used to show the value of an outpatient pharmacy to targeted audiences? The value of an inpatient pharmacy?

7 How can the pharmacist be sure that the variables being used to measure performance are appropriate?

8 Why is it important to use the same methodology over time to measure a pharmacy's performance? When is it appropriate to change the methodologies?

9 Why should most of the performance measures be quantitatively-based instead of qualitative?

10 How should performance measures be used in the overall management of an outpatient pharmacy? Of an inpatient pharmacy?

Self-test review

True/false statements

1 In outpatient settings, operating performance encompasses only those activities conducted within the prescription department.

2 Pharmacies in every practice setting compete in some manner.

3 Historically, annual performance assessments primarily focused on revenues, expenses, and the number of prescriptions dispensed.

4 Generally, annual performance assessments are more useful to managers than are quarterly performance assessments.

5 Most performance measures should be qualitative rather than quantitative.

6 There is no one absolute set of performance measures that all pharmacies should use.

7 The most common measure of financial performance is whether the leverage ratios remain stable over time.

8 Patient outcomes measures are part of the pharmacy's operating performance.

9 The best measures of profitability are return on investment and return on assets.

10 In most outpatient pharmacies, how well the front-end is merchandised is not especially important.

Multiple choice questions

1 Which of the following is normally the most important performance measure?

   (A) Clinical performance.
   (B) Financial performance.
   (C) Operating performance.
   (D) Competitive performance.

2 Which of the following is not a common purpose for performance measures?

   (A) Assess annual performance.
   (B) Monitor performance during the fiscal year.
   (C) Conduct reviews of every employee within the pharmacy.
   (D) Demonstrate the value of the pharmacy to targeted audiences.

3 Which of the following is not true?

   (A) All variables being measured should be linked to the success of the pharmacy.
   (B) Even if the pharmacy manager cannot control a variable, it should be included in the performance measures.
   (C) Most variables should be measured quantitatively.
   (D) All of the above are true.

4 The pharmacy's ability to meet its current obligations from its current assets is known as:

(A) Liquidity.
(B) Leverage.
(C) Activity.
(D) Profitability.

5 Variables used to measure human resource performance are part of:

(A) Clinical measures.
(B) Financial measures.
(C) Operating measures.
(D) Competitive measures.

Cases for Part VI*

Short cases

Case VI.1 Central Drugs

Central Drugs was a relatively new pharmacy in a medical complex within a large subdivision of this city in the upper Midwest. This subdivision was the third stage of the much larger planned development. The first two stages contained 500 homes, and 300 were planned for the third stage. Ultimately, over 1,000 homes and condominiums were expected to be built.

Despite intense competition from a chain drugstore, Danielle Granger, the owner of Central Drugs, has prospered in her first 2 years of business. Sales have grown at an annual rate of nearly 30 percent, and profits have increased approximately 5 percent each year. The number of prescriptions has increased 20 percent from the time she opened the pharmacy.

This rapid growth, however, began to cause some potentially serious problems. During the first 2 years, Ms. Granger was able to fill a walk-in prescription within 10 minutes, giving her a significant advantage over competitors who took from 15 to 60 minutes to fill a prescription. In fact, she guaranteed that a prescription would be filled within 15 minutes, and if it was not, she would give the patient a $5 gift card for use at a local theatre. Now the same process was taking 10–18 minutes, even though she had added a technician. With a 10- to 18-minute dispensing period, Central Drug's time advantage was

*Names of the organizations, individuals, and locations of all cases are fictional. Any likeness to actual organizations and/or individuals is purely coincidental.

only marginal at best. The chain drugstore was filling prescriptions within 15–20 minutes.

An additional concern was that the chain drugstore was offering ever-wider ranges of non-prescription merchandise. Ms. Granger did not have the space or the time to add and drop non-prescription merchandise lines to anywhere near the degree that the chain could. She knew it was important to have an attractive range of non-prescription merchandise both to attract customers and to generate profits. In many cases, this merchandise was more profitable on a percentage basis than some of the prescriptions she dispensed.

Because speed was such an important selling point, Ms. Granger thought she had taken the necessary steps to ensure fast and high-quality service. Initially, she did all of the prescription dispensing and ordering of non-prescription merchandise herself. Later, she assigned a clerk to buy part of the non-prescription merchandise and hired a part-time technician to assist in the prescription department.

From the beginning, she wanted to have prescriptions filled on a "first-come, first-served" basis—whether the prescription was a walk-in or telephoned in by the physician. This simplified the dispensing process, and assured physicians that their patients' prescriptions would be ready when they arrived. While Ms. Granger was not getting any complaints from patients who had their prescriptions submitted electronically by their physicians, there were problems when a prescription was not filled within the guaranteed time of 15 minutes. In two recent instances, patients walked out and said they would not return. In another case, the patient demanded $10 because he had waited 25 minutes.

In trying to resolve the scheduling problems, Ms. Granger knew that the employees were working with reasonable speed and care. But somehow there always seemed to be delays, especially with new prescriptions, which required more counseling.

Even with more personnel to handle the greater volume, the problem of delays was not resolved. Ms. Granger is now wondering whether she needs to add another technician or pharmacist, or whether the problem is in the workflow she had first established for the pharmacy. She thinks that if the problem is not solved soon, she will face the prospect of changing her guarantee and losing the time advantage or having to turn away business in order to keep the time factor as a competitive advantage. Neither of these alternatives seems satisfactory, but it was necessary to control costs.

Questions

1 How can the problems of customer waiting time be mitigated? What could Central Drugs do to ensure that customers do not complain about the wait time?

2 Evaluate the first-come, first-served policy originally developed for Central Drugs. Is it still appropriate?

3 Other than taking more time and turning away business, what options does Ms. Granger have?

Case VI.2 Tri-City Pharmacy

Tom Gomez owns and operates a neighborhood pharmacy in a rapidly growing West Coast city. The store, which opened 5 years ago, has experienced an annual sales growth of 25 percent. This growth can be attributed to the following factors: knowledgeable, helpful, friendly pharmacists and salespeople; the most extensive selection of home health supplies in the city; its location at the major intersection of the city, and Tri-City's advertising promise, "We Will Match Anybody's Price."

Dr. Gomez uses both a computerized and visual inventory method to keep track of prescription drugs and front-end merchandise on hand. Although it is time-consuming, he has one or more of his non-prescription department employees conduct a visual count of front-end merchandise on a weekly basis during slack business hours. The employees devote a total of between 10 and 20 hours per month to taking physical inventory and comparing it to what

his computer system shows. Their other duties are operating the cash register and stocking shelves. The two full-time pharmacists are responsible for inventory control of prescription drugs.

Tri-City Pharmacy's inventory consists of the typical front-end merchandise, including health and beauty items, gift cards, and seasonal gift items. The bulk of the time taking inventory of non-prescription merchandise is with the physical count and verification of home health supplies. Dr. Gomez believes this has the highest value and should be watched very closely.

Based on weekly inventory summaries, Dr. Gomez decides which items should be reordered or dropped. He estimates that $750–$1,000 in monthly sales is lost or costs incurred because a requested item is out of stock and either results in lost sales or has to be ordered specially. Dr. Gomez does not know the turnover rates for individual items, but he has a "feel" for what they are. "This is basic business, no matter how sophisticated my computer system might be at inventory control," he says. "If you keep a pharmacy with fully stocked front-end merchandise most of the time and can get employees to help customers and smile at all times, you do all the business you can handle."

Frequent customer requests for special home health items and seasonal gift items prompted Dr. Gomez to stock increasing amounts of inventory, increasing the total by 18 percent. He estimates that about 2–5 percent of this inventory becomes dated, obsolete, or somehow damaged or lost.

Dr. Gomez decided to use visual inventory control on a daily basis for the new items in order to monitor sales of these items. Typically, there are 5–10 new gift items purchased each month, and the number of other new items varies between 2 and 20 depending on the season. This usually takes an employee about 30–60 minutes per day to make the counts and reconcile them with the computer count.

Overall, he feels that the visual approach to controlling inventory is better than the computer-generated reports since there often is anywhere from a 5 percent to 15 percent discrepancy between the two. Typically, the visual inventory count proves to be the correct number.

While he collects a lot of data on inventory levels, he is not sure how to get the most use of the information. Some of his employees complain that they do not have the time to do the counts each day or week, but Dr. Gomez made that part of the job description and continually points out that it is all part of what he needs his employees to do.

Questions

1 What are the strengths and weaknesses of Dr. Gomez's inventory control methods? Is it worth the effort?

2 How could the data on inventory be used to improve the operations of the pharmacy?

3 What would cause the computerized inventory control system to be less accurate than the physical count?

Case VI.3 Valley Pharmacy

After considerable searching and deliberating about the site with colleagues, Dr. Larry Lee recently opened a 3,000 square foot pharmacy located in a neighborhood shopping center. It was not an ideal site for the pharmacy but was the only space available with any amount of foot traffic in the area.

The shopping center consisted of 20 stores that sold everything from pet supplies to dental services. The tenant mix had changed considerably over time as businesses closed due to insufficient business or the owner's retirement, or relocated to another area of the city. The shopping center is 25 years old and caters principally to middle-income, price-conscious working women between 25 and 50 years old.

The main anchor store in the shopping center is a supermarket. It is located next door to the pharmacy and has always done a reasonably large business. Dr. Lee feels this creates the foot traffic that should help his pharmacy. Unfortunately, however, the supermarket also added a prescription department to the store about 3 years ago. While it seems to be doing a decent prescription volume, Dr. Lee is most concerned about having to compete with it for non-prescription merchandise sales. Since the supermarket is an independent store, it does not having the buying power of major chains, but it still is bigger than Valley Pharmacy and should be able to obtain better discounts due to volume purchases.

Dr. Lee plans to reorganize the pharmacy because 20 percent of its space is not being used. At present, he is outlining plans for a distinctive interior store design featuring a large checkout counter on which to display new products and impulse items, permanent end-cap displays for seasonal and promotional tie-in merchandise, and permanent floor stand displays.

The current layout of the store features five gondolas plus the prescription department which is situated at the back-end of the store. As shown in Figure VI.3.1, two of the gondolas are unused. Dr. Lee preferred not to stock any inventory on them rather than put merchandise on the shelves that would not sell. He recognized that this did not create the most desirable image for the pharmacy, and that was one of the main motivating factors for the reorganization.

The present location of the over-the-counter medicines is near the front of the store and this is a major concern to him. He believes that this should be positioned near the prescription department which is currently located three aisles away. His reason for putting the cosmetics and health and beauty aids close to the prescription area was due to this merchandise being the most valuable and it would be easier to protect against shoplifting.

After going into the supermarket, Dr. Lee also noticed that the pharmacy's prices of popular

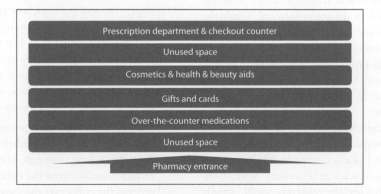

Figure VI.3.1   Current pharmacy layout.

brand-name over-the-counter medications especially are not competitive with those of the supermarket. He wonders whether or not his pricing strategy is the right one. He also wonders whether he should try to carry more merchandise that is not found in the supermarket, or at least not carry the same brand-named products.

Questions

1 What factors must Dr. Lee consider in changing the overall store layout?

2 What are the pros and cons of locating merchandise close to the prescription department?

3 Should Valley Pharmacy carry products that directly compete with the supermarket? If it does not do so, it will have to carry products with less well-known brand names—would this be advisable? Why or why not?

4 Should Valley Pharmacy's prices for popular products be competitive with those of the supermarket? If not, how much different could the prices be?

Major cases

Case VI.4 Professional Medical Pharmacies, Inc.

Clark Gust, president of Professional Medical Pharmacies, Inc. (PMPI), just returned from the annual shareholders' meeting and started outlining what had transpired over the course of the three-day meeting. He felt the meeting had been very productive, and there were a lot of positives in terms of the company's financial performance over the last 5 years. However, he was both enthused and troubled about what the shareholders wanted to do going forward. While the company was in very good shape in terms of its operations and financial situation, he was concerned that what was being proposed was too ambitious and might turn a nice solid company into one that loses control over what it is supposed to do and how it is supposed to operate.

Based on the shareholders' desires, the board of directors of the company decided to expand significantly over the next 3 years. Currently, PMPI operates 11 community pharmacies in a western state. Generally, these pharmacies are relatively small, mostly located in medical office buildings, and focused on

prescription sales rather than front-end sales. At the end of the shareholder meeting, the board set a goal of expanding the number of pharmacies to 20 in the next 3 years. Dr. Gust commented on this goal:

We have done very well, especially over the last 5 years. We are a relatively small chain of pharmacies, but quite disciplined. While each one operates somewhat differently, it works. When we try to expand from 11 to 20, the company will change. It will be much harder to keep track of what every one of the 20 pharmacies is doing, how well they are doing financially, and especially the quality of patient services each provides. If we are going to do this expansion, we need to develop some performance standards and means for monitoring our operations so that we stay on track and remain successful in every way. Fortunately, the board understands this, but the great results we have had may have made the shareholders overly ambitious.

Acknowledging Dr. Gust's concerns, the board asked Clark to develop a set of performance measures that could be used within individual pharmacies and for the company as a whole. These measures would then be used to monitor the performance of the company and possibly as a selling point when negotiating with contractors for services. As Dr. Gust noted:

The board wants to develop a process for measuring the success of the current pharmacies and those that will be added over the next 3 years. They feel, and I agree, that this will give us better information on how well individual pharmacies are doing, what needs to be improved, and perhaps how to divide the profits of the company among shareholders based on performance rather than just the number of pharmacies they have. We also think that if we can show good performance and have solid outcomes measures in place, it may be useful when we contract as a group with insurers.

So, this is the main charge they gave me and they want it soon. We probably should have done this a long time ago, but that doesn't matter now. We need the measures to use, the process for collecting the measures, and some idea as to how to use them.

Professional Medical Pharmacies, Inc.

Formed nearly 9 years ago, PMPI is a holding company consisting of a group of 11 medical pharmacies located in a large city in the western part of the USA. Originally, the company was formed by four pharmacy owners as a buying cooperative so they could try to negotiate better terms from wholesalers and possibly buy some products directly from manufacturers. They felt that if they could pool their purchases in some way, they might be able to obtain more attractive quantity discounts and/or better payment terms. Because the pharmacies were located in different parts of the city, the owners did not feel that they were competing with each other. They continued to operate their pharmacies individually.

After 2 years, they decided to merge their pharmacies into PMPI and try to both purchase and contract with insurance companies on better terms. They issued 100 shares of stock for each of the owners of those pharmacies. Although there were some differences in the revenues and profits of each pharmacy, the assets each was bringing into the company were nearly identical. Based on this, they all agreed that it would be best to pool their pharmacies into one entity and share equally in the profits. Dr. Gust commented on the creation of PMPI:

> I was hired to run PMPI when it was formed. It was an amazing process. We had four owners who ran their pharmacies differently and there were some real differences in profit levels. Instead of quarreling about who got what number of shares based on revenues and profits, they set aside possible differences and just said "let's do this, and the simplest way is to make everybody equal owners." They realized that they would all benefit in the long run if this worked out. I also think that the ones who were making more felt that the others had some real growth potential, so they were looking at the long run rather than just what it immediately meant to them. You don't see this happening very often.

Very quickly, however, it became apparent that even though they received slightly better deals with wholesalers, they needed to be a larger group to have any real chance to negotiate successfully. As a result, they added five owners who had a total of seven more pharmacies to the group. Two of the owners had two pharmacies each.

PMPI has a total of 11 medical pharmacies and nine shareholders. Keeping with the agreement they started with when forming PMPI, each pharmacy is worth 100 shares. So, there are seven shareholders who have 100 shares and two shareholders who have 200 shares each.

The board of directors comprises five of the nine shareholders. They each serve a 2-year term on a rotating basis. Because the terms are staggered, two board members are replaced each year. Each shareholder gets one vote, irrespective of the number of shares held. However, profits of the company are shared based on the number of shares held.

All the shareholders are paid a standard salary. The two shareholders who have two pharmacies each receive double salaries.

Each shareholder manages the pharmacy(s) she or he brought into PMPI. The two shareholders that have two pharmacies continue to manage those pharmacies. Dr. Gust developed programs to standardize operations to the extent possible. PMPI negotiates contracts with a primary wholesaler, tries to make some purchases directly from manufacturers, and negotiates all insurance contracts. Although the amount of advertising is very limited, any advertisements, circulars, or other promotional materials are managed centrally.

While Dr. Gust manages day-to-day operations of the company, Dr. Eric Skall is the vice president and is primarily responsible for financial matters, contracting, purchasing, and promotion. Dr. Skall was hired about six months after the company was formed. An organization chart for PMPI is presented in Figure VI.4.1.

Characteristics of the pharmacies

The characteristics of the pharmacies are summarized in Table VI.4.1. The pharmacies range in size from just over 1,500 square feet to more than 2,800 square feet, with the average being 1,987 square feet. Most of the pharmacies (54.5 percent) are located in medical office buildings. The others are in small strip shopping centers (27.3 percent) or are free standing (18.2 percent) in that they are in separate buildings.

Up until 3 years ago, the pharmacies operated under their original names but carried the PMPI logo. Dr. Gust recommended, and the board approved, changing the names of the pharmacies to a single name of "Professional Medical Pharmacies, Inc." This allowed them to benefit from name exposure and media advertising. No two pharmacies are closer than 5 miles from another PMPI pharmacy.

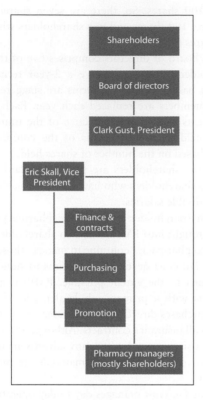

Figure VI.4.1 Organization of Professional Medical Pharmacies, Inc.

Days and hours of operation vary somewhat based on setting. Most of the pharmacies in the medical office buildings are open Monday through Friday only, and from 9 a.m. to 6:30 p.m. The five other pharmacies typically are open Monday through Saturday only, and from 9 a.m. to 7 p.m.

All of the pharmacies carry over-the-counter (OTC) medications. And all of the pharmacies located in medical office buildings and one other pharmacy carry home health supplies. None of the pharmacies located in medical office buildings carry health and beauty aids or gifts and cards. Two of the pharmacies located in medical office buildings also carry durable medical equipment.

Prescription activity

The prescription activity and services offered are summarized in Table VI.4.2. The prescription volumes varied considerably between pharmacies, with those in medical office buildings mostly dispensing fewer prescriptions than those in community settings. Overall, the average pharmacy dispensed about 45,760 prescriptions per year. Of these, over half (51.4 percent) were refills.

Because the pharmacies were located in different parts of the city, their patient mixes varied somewhat and this impacted the payment mix. However, the great majority of prescriptions (83.8 percent) were

Table VI.4.1 Pharmacy characteristics

Medical pharmacy characteristics	Average/ number	Range
Total square footage	1,987	1,523–2,806
Location		
Medical office building	6	
Shopping center	3	
Free standing	2	
Days open per week	5	5–6
Hours open per week	52	40–60
Non-prescription merchandise carried		
Over-the-counter medications	11	
Home health supplies	7	
Health and beauty aids	5	
Gifts and cards	4	
Durable medical equipment	2	

Table VI.4.2 Prescription characteristics

Prescription mix characteristics	Average/ number	Range
Number of prescriptions per week	45,760	39,798–67,920
Percent refills	51.4%	48.1–60.2%
Percent generic	67.9%	41.9–72.3%
Payment mix		
Medicare	11.3%	6.4–15.9%
Other third party	83.8%	71.9–91.6%
Cash	4.9%	3.8–6.4%
Services offered		
Prescription consultations	11	
Compounding	7	
Delivery	6	
Automatic refill	4	
Unit packaging	3	
Medication therapy management	2	

dispensed under third-party programs other than Medicare.

All of the pharmacies offered prescription consultations, and they generally reported that about 25 percent of the patients want the consults. The others either are getting refills or say they do not need or want consultations. All of the community pharmacies and one of the pharmacies located in a medical office building offer delivery. Four of the pharmacies located in the medical office buildings offer compounding services, as do three in community settings. The pharmacies with the highest refill percentages also do automatic refills and send reminders to their patients.

Financial characteristics

Selected financial characteristics of the pharmacies are presented in Table VI.4.3. The average pharmacy generated nearly $3.28 million in revenues last year. These revenues have grown an average of about 3.5 percent annually over the last 5 years. Despite the differences in locations, the ranges in revenues were reasonably close, ranging from a low of more than $2.6 million to a high of nearly $3.9 million. Prescription sales accounted for the vast majority of revenues, averaging 94.9 percent of total sales.

Costs of goods averaged 78.9 percent, with the range directly related to the mix of products sold. Since purchasing contracts were set by PMPI, no pharmacy did any better in buying than another. As Dr. Skall noted:

> When we look at differences between pharmacies, the costs of goods are a direct function of what sells in each pharmacy. We have different locations, so the prescription mix will vary, and a pharmacy that does 97 percent

of its business in prescriptions will have a different cost of goods percentage than one that does 10 percent of its business in OTCs or gifts and cards. Non-prescription sales can vary by what individual managers choose to buy and how well they lay out the merchandise. But, prescription activity is what it is, and the margin an individual pharmacy generates is partly set by our contract terms and to a much lesser extent by non-prescription purchase choices.

Average inventory levels (i.e. beginning inventory plus ending inventory divided by two) varied considerably, and averaged nearly $358,300. The variations in inventory were thought to be due to the sizes of the pharmacies, the value of the mix of merchandise, and how much each pharmacy kept on hand. Dr. Gust commented on inventory levels:

> Controlling inventory is one part of the job that drives me crazy. We don't have any control over the dollar value of some of the prescription inventory. Pharmacies that dispense more brand-name prescriptions are going to have higher investments in inventory, and there is a big difference among our pharmacies in that regard. I'm not sure if it is the location or just that our pharmacists don't look for opportunities to convert to generics when therapeutically appropriate. Or, some may just want to carry more units of inventory so they don't run out. But, this is a big problem area for us. We need to keep our dollars in inventory to an absolute minimum, and I am sure we are not doing as good a job with this as we could. Part of the problem is that the managers are shareholders and are used to doing things a certain way. And, I'm not sure there is much incentive for them to keep inventory levels down.

The expansion plan

Dr. Gust and members of the board of directors felt that there was a need to increase the size of the company in order to be in a better position to negotiate with suppliers and insurance companies. As Dr. Skall noted:

> We are not sure that going from 11 to 20 pharmacies will make us that much stronger

Table VI.4.3 Financial characteristics

Financial characteristics	Average/ number	Range
Annual revenues	$3,279,814	$2,619,719–$3,891,465
Prescription	94.9%	89.3–97.1%
Non-prescription	5.1%	2.9–10.7%
Costs of goods	78.9%	74.5–79.6%
Payroll as percent of revenues	14.8%	11.9–17.8%
Inventory	$358,284	$261,359–$448,763
Prescription	$298,645	$182,480–$416,663
Non-prescription	$59,639	$32,100–$78,879

when it comes to negotiating. But, at our current sales and costs of goods levels, this would represent more than $29.5 million in additional sales and nearly $23.3 million in purchasing. It also would represent nearly 412,000 more prescriptions dispensed per year. These are sizeable numbers in our minds, but would they make a big difference to a major wholesaler or to insurance companies? Maybe or maybe not.

What the board and Dr. Gust do know is that to get to be big enough to have more leverage, we have to grow. If we do this expansion well, I am sure we are going to do more down the road. Hopefully, this is just the first step in becoming a real player in the marketplace. We have to start somewhere.

This expansion also will give us more market coverage. This makes it more reasonable to advertise in the media if we have pharmacies in all parts of the city.

The general plan for expansion was to add nine pharmacies in the next 3 years. Some of this could be by acquisition by the company if it could obtain financing, and by bringing in current owners of medical pharmacies as new shareholders in much the same manner as was done in the past. Dr. Gust felt it was most likely that there would be six to nine new shareholders:

I really don't think we will just buy pharmacies as a company. PMPI does not have the money to do this, so it would have to come from additional investments from the current shareholders, and I doubt they will want to do that. Besides, that's not how we have done things in the past.

Nobody was quite certain how this would transpire. I think the goal is to find current owners who want to join our company and do so at the same 100 shares per pharmacy level we have used. The current shareholders know this would dilute their ownership interests, but it does build a bigger company. If we can find good locations that do not overly compete with the pharmacies we currently have, and owners who would like to join us, it would be ideal. I suspect that some owners are thinking of retirement in the next few years, and this may be a way to merge their pharmacies into a

company that will continue to pay shareholders over time.

Based on this, Dr. Gust and Dr. Skall wanted to set up a template for measuring the performance of pharmacies now and in the future after the expansion. In particular, they wanted to identify what measures should be used to assess quality, efficiency, and financial performance. They also felt it was important to set up a process for periodically measuring performance, but were unsure of how often this should take place or how it should be done. And they wanted to identify in advance how the data from the performance measures would be used. As Dr. Gust noted:

We need to put this all together so that it is standardized and consistent to the extent possible across all of our current and future pharmacies. But, most importantly, after we identify the performance measures we want to use, we have to know how we will use the data. There is no reason to do all of this if it's going to sit in a stack of paper somewhere. The measures have to be relevant and focus on things that we should be evaluating and activities we can change if the measures suggest we are not doing as well as we should. Guess that also means we need to set some goals for each measure as well. I'm not sure why these things always look like they will be easy to do, but when you get started, they are much more complex. Seems to happen that way every time.

Possible discussion questions

1 What should be the performance measures for: Quality? Efficiency? Financial success?

2 How often should the performance measures be taken, and what process should be used?

3 How should variations in performance be taken into account based on the differences in operations among the current pharmacy locations and prescription activity?

4 How should the results of performance monitoring be used?

Case VI.5 Sierra Oaks Pharmacy

On January 1st, Lynn Rosen and one of her staff pharmacists took inventory for Sierra Oaks Pharmacy. It was a ritual they had performed for many years.

With the pharmacy closed on New Year's Day, she always wanted to have a very accurate picture of the inventory in her pharmacy for tax purposes. Although her computer system maintained inventory levels, she liked being precise and did not want to take any chance that there were errors.

Now, four weeks later, her concerns about inventory levels and profits were confirmed. In glancing at the numbers, it appeared that this was the second year in a row that inventory levels in both the prescription department and front-end appeared to be high. The statements from her accountant showed that while sales had grown from the previous year, gross margins had declined. This was going to result in her making less profit for the past year, and profit from the year before had not been all that great. She commented on the numbers:

> I thought we had a pretty good year last year in terms of revenues. Prescription volume was up slightly despite some intense competition and third-party programs keeping reimbursements low. But, if the gross margin is low, it makes it very difficult to generate much profit. I already have tried to cut our operating costs as much as possible, so if things are going to get better, it is going to have to come from making better purchase decisions. And I think I may have too much inventory. This may be the result of poor purchasing or the need to shift some of the product lines I carry in both the prescription department and front-end.

Sierra Oaks Pharmacy

Dr. Rosen and her older brother opened Sierra Oaks Pharmacy nearly 28 years ago. After graduating from pharmacy school about 3 years apart, they took different career paths. Her brother went to work in a local hospital pharmacy, while she took a position in a chain pharmacy in a nearby town. After working for their respective employers for several years, they decided to pool money they received from an inheritance and created Sierra Oaks Pharmacy. Initially, they both wanted to be their own bosses, but soon realized that the pharmacy might not be sufficiently profitable to support both of their families. So, Dr. Rosen bought out her brother and he went to work for a pharmaceutical manufacturer in another part of the USA.

Located in the western part of the USA, Sierra Oaks Pharmacy is a relatively large community pharmacy with approximately 10,500 square feet of space. It is situated in a old shopping center with 26 outlets including the pharmacy. Although there are only three vacant sites in the center, it has experienced some turnover of retail stores. A current list of the stores in the center is shown in Table VI.5.1. Even though the center was built nearly 30 years ago, it has been owned by the same family and has been well maintained and looks more modern than its age would suggest. It originally started with a single strip of stores and has been expanded to now have space for 29 tenants. When the owners added another line of store space, they upgraded the fronts of all stores so that everything would match.

Sierra Oaks Pharmacy is situated near the middle of the shopping center. The general layout of the pharmacy is presented in Figure VI.5.1. The prescription department consumes about 1,100 square feet of space, and the rest is devoted to front-end merchandise, aisle space, waiting areas, and storage. The

Table VI.5.1 Mix of stores in shopping center

Type of outlet	Number of outlets in center
Sierra Oaks Pharmacy	1
Bank	1
Beauty salon	1
Dry cleaner	1
Fast food outlets	2
Fitness center	1
Florist	1
Gift shops	4
Jewelry store	1
Mail outlet/photocopy store	1
Men's store	1
Nail salon	2
Optical store	1
Pet store	1
Real estate office	1
Restaurants/pizza parlors	4
Shoe store	1
Women's store	1
Vacant sites	3
Total	29

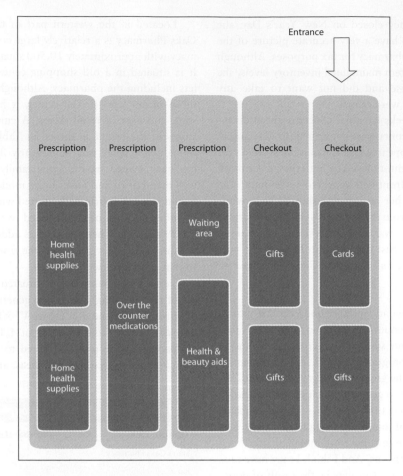

Figure VI.5.1 General layout of Sierra Oaks Pharmacy.

approximate allocation of space on a square footage basis other than storage is shown in Table VI.5.2.

The layout of the pharmacy and types of merchandise carried has not changed appreciably over the

Table VI.5.2 Allocation of floor space	
Area of the pharmacy	**Approximate square footage**
Prescriptions	1,100
Over-the-counter medicines	1,600
Health and beauty aids	1,050
Gift items	1,700
Cards	750
Home health supplies	1,500
Checkout, waiting area, aisle space	1,100
Storage, etc.	1,700
Total	10,500

years. Ms. Rosen commented about the store's layout and merchandise mix:

My pharmacy has been reasonably successful, although it is struggling more now than at any time since we got past the first few years of business. We were careful when we got started in terms of how we arranged the space and what merchandise we carried. Actually, my brother had a better eye for the front-end merchandise than I do, but it's my responsibility. Now, I know that there have been changes in the tenant mix in the shopping center and we have more competition from some of the stores than we did when it started. But, most of the people in the neighborhood have not moved so the majority of our customers are the same people we have been serving for the last 20 or more years. In thinking about it now, I guess I have been somewhat complacent in not making changes in the front-end. I know our prescription mix has changed over the years as our customers need different medications than they needed many years ago. So, it's probably time to look closely at how we do business.

The marketplace

The population surrounding the center has grown somewhat over the last 10 years. However, residents of the area tend not to move, so the neighborhoods have aged over time. Presented in Table VI.5.3 are selected demographics of the market area.

Over the last 10 years, the population in the immediate area has grown about 7.0 percent, averaging nearly 0.7 percent growth per year. The area has traditionally been a mix of ages and incomes. The outer edges of the area to the north and south have experienced the most fluctuation in residents with those in the north having higher incomes and those at the outer edge to the south being younger and less affluent.

The neighborhoods closest to the shopping center have experienced the least change in residents. Accordingly, most residents have shifted into older age categories. And household incomes in the $75,000–$149,999 range have declined as people have moved from being in the labor force to being retired.

Although the neighborhoods have not changed appreciably over the years, there has been some shift in the competition. Within a 3-mile area, at the current time there are three national/regional chain pharmacies, two supermarkets that have pharmacies, and four independent community pharmacies. The other major changes in the last 5 years have been the closing of two other community pharmacies and the addition of one of the three chain pharmacies. Of the four community pharmacies, two have relatively large front-end space and one is located in another neighborhood shopping center while the other is in a stand-alone building. The other two community pharmacies are very small and situated in medical office buildings.

According to Dr. Rosen, the two larger independent pharmacies present the most competition:

> The chain pharmacies do compete with us, especially for over-the-counter (OTC)

Table VI.5.3 Selected demographic charactistics of market area for current year and 10 years ago

	Current year	Ten years ago
Gender		
Male	45.2%	47.9%
Female	54.8%	52.1%
Total	100.0%	100.0%
Total population	18,611	17,389
Age		
Under 18 years	19.2%	22.2%
18–34 years	12.1%	15.5%
35–54 years	28.4%	28.2%
55–64 years	12.6%	10.5%
65–74 years	14.5%	12.1%
75 years and over	13.2%	11.5%
Total	100.0%	100.0%
Household income		
Less than $10,000	7.9%	6.0%
$25,000–$49,999	15.2%	14.9%
$50,000–$74,999	39.2%	36.9%
$75,000–$99,999	13.2%	16.2%
$100,000–$149,999	11.4%	12.1%
$150,000–$199,999	7.9%	8.2%
$200,000 or more	5.2%	5.7%
Total	100.0%	100.0%
Employment (18 and older)		
Employed full time	53.8%	62.8%
Employed part time	9.7%	7.8%
Unemployed but in labor market	9.3%	5.5%
Retired	26.1%	22.7%
Other	1.1%	1.2%
Total	100.0%	100.0%

medications and health and beauty aids. I cannot match their prices, but I can come close to matching the selections they offer. Neither of those sell much in the way of home health supplies, but they do have greeting cards, and their selection is probably bigger than ours. That's too bad, because the profit margin on cards is pretty good.

The two larger independent pharmacies are similar to us. I think they do pretty well, but they have not been in this area as long as I have. I have been here for nearly 30 years, and both of those opened up about 15 years ago. Their prices are about the same as mine, and they have good gift selections. They probably do a lot better than me with gifts because when I have gone into their stores, they are attractive. I have more gift items, but they must do well with theirs.

The two medical pharmacies are not really competitors except for prescriptions and home health supplies. I can beat both of them on price and selection for home health supplies because I have more space. Their stores are quite small. I suspect they just try to capture the business of patients of the physicians in their respective buildings. But, those are the people who also live in the neighborhoods, so I guess we do compete.

Sierra Oaks Pharmacy sales and gross margins

Dr. Rosen began looking in more detail at the financial results for the last 2 years. In particular, she was concerned about the declining gross margin (i.e. revenues minus costs of goods sold). She felt that it was critical to gain better control over this area if profits were to improve:

> Two years ago, I took a very hard look at our operating expenses and tried to make as many cuts as possible. While there always is room for improvement, I think the pharmacy is operating pretty efficiently at this time. Now the issue is how to improve my gross margin. If there is not enough left over after paying for the costs of goods, there is no chance to make a profit. And, I doubt that I can really raise prices to any meaningful extent. So, I need to try to either change the mix of front-end items or reduce the costs of what I buy, or both. This won't be easy, but I need to look at the contributions I am getting from every part of my pharmacy.

The revenues and costs of goods sold for the last 2 years are presented in Table VI.5.4. What was of particular concern to her was that revenues rose 2.9 percent but costs of goods sold rose 4.9 percent, resulting in a 1.8 percent decline in gross margin:

> The "bottom line" so to speak is that I sold more and made less. How can that be? With more sales, I should be able to get better terms or make larger purchases and get better

quantity discounts on what I buy. But, it looks like that didn't happen.

Her other concern was the increase in dollars invested in inventory. She noticed this when taking physical inventory several weeks ago, but it became even more evident when reviewing her financial statements. Presented in Table VI.5.5 are the average inventory levels in each merchandise category for the last 2 years. At Dr. Rosen's request, her accountant computed the average inventory by adding the inventory at the beginning of the year to the inventory at the end of the year, and then dividing by two. While this was not a perfect number with respect to average inventory, it did provide a basis for reviewing what has happened over the last 2 years. As Dr. Rosen noted:

> My average inventory rose nearly 10.4 percent this last year. But, my sales only increased by 2.9 percent. This suggests to me that I have too much inventory. However, my accountant said that it would be either too much inventory now or not enough inventory in the past. He recommended that I look at my inventory turnover in each category and see if I am doing a good job with buying and selling.

> I told him that I wasn't sure how to do this, so he gave me the formula to use to compute inventory turnover. It is costs of goods sold divided by average inventory. Then, he suggested I look at how many days it takes to sell the inventory. This is 365 days divided by the inventory turnover. His general feeling is that my prescription inventory should turn over about 10 or 11 times a year and the other merchandise should turn over about 8 or 9 times a year. I guess I can compare what I have with those numbers. He suggested that I use those to decide on a target amount of inventory to carry in each merchandise category. He said if I divide the costs of goods sold by a desirable inventory turnover rate, I can figure how much inventory I should keep on hand.

> I told him that this should be his job, but he said that I need to learn how to do all of this so it will make more sense to me in the long term. So, I guess I am paying him to tell me to do it myself. If he wasn't so good, I'd be mad.

Table VI.5.4 Revenues and costs of goods sold for last 2 years

	Last year	Two years ago	Percent change
Revenues			
Prescriptions	$3,038,309	$2,952,894	2.9%
Over-the-counter medicines	$302,987	$296,602	2.2%
Health and beauty aids	$342,654	$338,446	1.2%
Gift items	$234,203	$233,015	0.5%
Cards	$71,738	$82,048	−12.6%
Home health supplies	$229,983	$199,376	15.4%
Total	$4,219,874	$4,102,381	2.9%
Costs of goods sold			
Prescriptions	$2,412,418	$2,306,210	4.6%
Over-the-counter medicines	$94,229	$86,311	9.2%
Health and beauty aids	$188,460	$191,222	−1.4%
Gift items	$146,377	$139,809	4.7%
Cards	$39,097	$41,024	−4.7%
Home health supplies	$123,041	$99,688	23.4%
Total	$3,003,621	$2,864,264	4.9%
Gross margin			
Prescriptions	$625,892	$646,684	−3.2%
Over-the-counter medicines	$208,758	$210,291	−0.7%
Health and beauty aids	$154,194	$147,224	4.7%
Gift items	$87,826	$93,206	−5.8%
Cards	$32,641	$41,024	−20.4%
Home health supplies	$106,942	$99,688	7.3%
Total	$1,216,253	$1,238,117	−1.8%

Table VI.5.5 Average inventory levels for last 2 years

Average inventory[a]	Last year	Two years ago
Prescriptions	$262,219	$242,759
Over-the-counter medicines	$13,857	$11,823
Cosmetics	$33,063	$29,878
Gift items	$34,852	$27,414
Cards	$3,522	$4,022
Home health supplies	$23,662	$20,344
Total	$371,175	$336,241

[a] Computed by: [(inventory at beginning of year) plus (inventory at end of year)] divided by 2.

The future

Dr. Rosen decided that her accountant's advice would be the best place to start. She hoped that by doing this, she could identify areas in which inventory could be reduced and thereby free up cash. She also thought this may be a good place to start to assess whether she should try to change some merchandise lines if they are not selling as well as she would like.

In addition to trying to control inventory, Dr. Rosen's accountant suggested she look for better deals when purchasing. As a result, she contacted some of her secondary suppliers to see if there were any special deals that could help her improve her gross margin without creating more problems with the dollars invested in inventory.

Two suppliers responded almost immediately. Both were suppliers of non-prescription merchandise and they offered her deals on some merchandise.

One offered her a discount on an order if she paid cash on delivery. The offer was for some health and beauty aids. Dr. Rosen was considering purchasing about $15,000 in merchandise, and the supplier told her he could give her a 1.5 percent discount if she would pay in 10 days instead of the normal 30 days. He said that these types of deals arise every once in a while, and some were for the 1.5 percent and others were for 1.75 percent and still other for as much as 1.95 percent if she could pay in 10 rather than 30 days. Dr. Rosen was not sure if this was a good idea or not. She had a line of credit from her bank, and the interest rate on any borrowing she might do was at 8.5 percent.

Another supplier of gift items suggested that she consider purchasing in larger quantities to obtain better prices. This supplier told her to try to use "reorder points" in dollars for broad categories of merchandise such as gifts as a whole. It said that if she could make single orders with larger dollar values less often, there may be some opportunities to give her better prices. When Dr. Rosen looked over her sales of gift items, she found that the total sales remained quite stable over the year, rarely varying more than 15 percent from the average on any given day. The supplier suggested that she use the 15 percent as a figure for computing the safety stock. This supplier guaranteed delivery of all gift merchandise within seven days.

Dr. Rosen thought that all of this advice regarding inventory turnover and these two deals would be good to consider as well. If she could try to figure out how much inventory to keep on hand, she could make better decisions regarding how much to purchase and whether to take advantage of the deals. She knew that this would only give her the overall picture of what needed to be done, and individual items had to be scrutinized to decide specifically what to order and when. But at least it was a start:

> At this point, I need to try everything I can to get a better idea of what needs to be done. Looking at inventory levels overall may tell me where the problems are and where I need to focus my attention. Then, I can look at purchase deals and order quantities and reorder points to put more sound decision making into this. These are not going to be my favorite things to do over the next few weeks, but it may be the best use of my time for the pharmacy.

Possible discussion questions

1 What errors has Dr. Rosen made with respect to merchandising the front-end of her pharmacy? What changes should she make?

2 What are the turnover rates for the merchandise lines? How many days on the average is inventory held in the store? How do these compare with what Dr. Rosen's accountant recommended?

3 What would be good target levels for inventory for each merchandise line?

4 How should the deals offered by the suppliers be calculated? What is the value of the cash discount? What reorder points in dollars should be used for each merchandise line?

Case VI.6 Thompson's Stores, Inc.

Carl Thompson, president and chief executive officer of Thompson's Stores, Inc., was reviewing the minutes of a quarterly meeting he held the previous week with his regional and store managers. It had been a difficult and contentious two days as they met to discuss what appeared to be a loss of market share overall for the chain of mass merchandise stores. Sales were down for the second time in three fiscal quarters, and the only bright spot in operations was the performance of the chain's prescription departments. Mr. Thompson summed up his concerns:

> Competition is intense and we are up against some big national and regional players. Being smaller than some of these companies, we need to be much more flexible and adapt to local market conditions. We are not going to beat the national chains on a price basis, so we have to find some competitive advantage. When I showed the results of the third quarter to the managers, they all agreed that we need to do something before the competition totally eats our lunch.

Mr. Thompson asked all of the regional and store managers to make recommendations about how better to compete, and how to do so without unduly increasing expenses. Two of the more popular ideas coming at the end of the quarterly meeting were top on his list to consider. One was to extend store hours to be more accessible to customers. Even though this would add to the labor expense, he thought it was worth pursuing because that was the only cost increase and employees were stocking the shelves during times the stores were closed anyway. The other recommendation was to take advantage of the success of the pharmacy departments by expanding the consultation services staff pharmacists provide for both prescriptions and non-prescription products sold in the pharmacy department.

Based on the strong advocacy of these two recommendations, he asked Christine Singh, one of the regional managers for pharmacy operations and a pharmacist by training, to develop a plan based on expanding both store hours and pharmacy services. He commented about this:

> I like the managers' ideas, but we are going to test this out first. Changing store hours is relatively easy to do, even though it could be either very profitable or a little more expensive. My biggest concern is messing around with the pharmacy operations. If we can bring pharmacists closer to our customers, it could be a great way to build customer loyalty to our stores. But, pharmacists are the highest paid employees we have other than managers, and it's not always easy to hire more good ones. I want to be sure we are using their time wisely and efficiently. So, I asked Christine to develop a plan for expanding pharmacy hours and getting pharmacists more involved in counseling patients on everything from their prescriptions to the decongestants they buy. It will be interesting to see how receptive the pharmacists are to all of this. I would think they would like to use their knowledge to a greater extent, so it should be a positive all the way around.

Thompson's Stores, Inc.

Thompson's Stores is a chain of 28 mass merchandise stores located in two states in the southern USA. Although the chain has been in the Thompson family for nearly 30 years, it has undergone several transformations during this time.

Originally, Thompson's was a small chain of department stores. When one of the daughters of the founder married the son of an owner of another chain of apparel stores, the "in-laws" sat down and decided that it might be worth while to explore merging their stores into a larger chain so they could reduce some of their respective overhead expenses such as accounting and marketing. They still operated the two groups of stores separately, but they shared advertising space and centralized their headquarters operations.

Within 3 years, the Thompson family bought out their in-laws and put them all under the same name. At about the same time, the founder's son, Carl, married the daughter of the owner of four large gift stores. Again, the "in-laws" decided to merge their

businesses except this time they blended the merchandise between the stores and kept the Thompson's Stores name.

Over the next 10 years, the Thompson family expanded the number of stores and closed smaller ones that did not have the physical space for the growing amount of merchandise that was being added. Food items were added nearly 12 years ago, and pharmacy departments were started 6 years ago. Mr. Carl Thompson eventually became the president of the company when his father decided to retire. Members of his wife's family lost interest in the daily operations and were content to be shareholders in the company but not participate in the decisions. Carl Thompson commented on the evolution of the company:

> It's kind of sad. If my parents would have had more children than my sister and me, we probably would have a much larger and more diverse type of company. I think we needed two more siblings who would have married into families that owned grocery stores and pharmacies. Then, we would have been all set. Anyway, this company really just evolved based on family dynamics. My dad was a great businessman and he could see opportunities a mile away.
>
> The only real problem with all of this is that it has taken a while for the public to understand what we are. We sell a wide range of merchandise, like department stores, but we also added food and medications just because it seemed like a good idea. Until we added the pharmacies, we didn't really try to tell our story of what we offer and why customers should come to us instead of the many competitors that are out there.
>
> We got more serious when we opened the prescription departments. For one thing, they are much more expensive than nearly anything else in our stores. But, we know that people get prescriptions filled and shop, so this has worked out. We did put some effort into promoting our pharmacies and I think that is why these departments are doing much better than any other departments in the stores.

Carl Thompson took over all company operations nearly 10 years ago. He restructured the company to have four vice presidents and managers for each of the five geographic regions within which Thompson's

Stores operates. A condensed organizational chart is presented in Figure VI.6.1.

Store hours and sales

Thompson's Stores carried a broad array of merchandise, including:

- women's apparel
- men's apparel
- children's apparel
- infant apparel and equipment (e.g. strollers)
- shoes
- sporting goods
- household appliances
- electronics (e.g. cameras, radios, games)
- toys and games
- hardware
- garden supplies
- automotive supplies
- home furnishing (except furniture)
- packaged foods
- refrigerated foods

- pharmacy department (i.e. prescriptions, over-the-counter medications, health and beauty aids, lotions, eye care, vitamins, nutritional supplements).

Despite the stores being relatively large in size, they tended to carry a wider range of merchandise but limited selections with each. Mr. Thompson decided that it was better to have as many different types of items as possible even if it meant there was not as much selection among products:

> I really don't understand why my competitors want to carry a large assortment of the same products. All they end up doing is having one brand compete with another. I'm not sure consumers care that much. I prefer to carry just one or two brands of an item and then have more space for different merchandise. That way, I can order in larger quantities and get the advantage of quantity discounts. But, we have had complaints that we don't give our customers enough of a choice. If they cannot decide between two lines of the same item, then maybe they should go elsewhere.

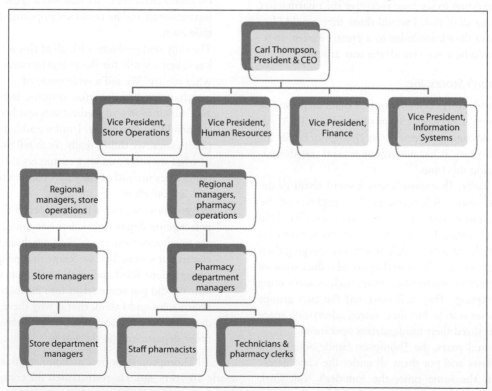

Figure VI.6.1 Organization of Thompson's Stores.

Average store sales by broad categories are presented in Table VI.6.1. These percentages have remained about the same over time except that prescription sales have grown from 5.1 percent to 6.4 percent of total sales in the last 2 years.

Thompson's Stores are open seven days a week, except for being closed on all national and state holidays. The stores are closed for these holidays approximately 12 days per year.

Comparatively, most of the mass merchandise competitors close for only 2–3 days per year. Store hours are Monday through Friday from 9 a.m. to 9 p.m., Saturdays from 10 a.m. to 6 p.m., and Sundays from 11 a.m. to 5 p.m. Mr. Thompson commented on the days and hours of operation:

Historically, we have tried to open and close at what we consider reasonable hours. I'm not sure why we need to open earlier or stay open later. All it seems to do is stretch out the sales through the day rather than increase sales. My managers, however, believe that with people working odd hours these days, they like to shop when they get off work or when the stores are not as crowded and the checkout lines are shorter. I'm not sure about this, but that is one of the reasons why we are going to test this out in one of the regions. I have a real problem with being open on holidays. If everybody else gets the day off, I don't see why our employees shouldn't have it off too. That seems only fair. It's expensive for us to close and pay them anyway, but it just seems like the right thing to do. My managers definitely don't agree with me on this. They say that I am complaining about our costs being too high, but still give the extra holidays. However, if we stayed open, we would be paying double or triple time. Now, that's expensive.

Average store sales by blocks of hours are presented in Table VI.6.2. The largest volumes of sales historically have occurred on Saturday mornings between 10 a.m. and 11:59 a.m., weeknights between 7 p.m. and 9 p.m., and Sunday mornings between 11 a.m. and 12:59 p.m. These three time periods account for about 27.4 percent of total weekly sales.

Pharmacy department hours and sales

The pharmacy departments in all stores were open from 9 a.m. to 7 p.m. Monday through Friday, and from 10 a.m. to 3 p.m. on Saturday. The departments were closed on Sundays. Dr. Singh explained the rationale for pharmacy hours:

Early on, Carl decided that the pharmacies did not need to be open the full time the stores were open. He felt that most people would have their prescriptions filled almost immediately after visiting their physicians. Since most of the prescriptions we get are sent electronically, and doctor's offices close around 6 p.m., we thought that this would give us enough time to fill the prescriptions and for people to come in to pick them up. It is a little tight in the evenings when

Table VI.6.1 Average store sales by product category

Overall store sales by category	Percent of total store sales
General merchandise/other	62.9%
Food	21.4%
Prescriptions	6.4%
Health and beauty aids	5.1%
Over-the-counter medications	4.2%
Total	100.0%

Table VI.6.2 Store sales by hours of operation

Hours of operation	Percent of weekly total	Percent of individual day
Monday through Friday		
9:00 a.m.–10:59 a.m.	6.0%	14.1%
11:00 a.m.–12:59 p.m.	7.8%	18.3%
1:00 p.m.–2:59 p.m.	6.6%	15.5%
3:00 p.m.–4:59 p.m.	4.9%	11.5%
5:00 p.m.–6:59 p.m.	8.2%	19.2%
7:00 p.m.–9:00 p.m.	9.1%	21.4%
Total	42.6%	100.0%
Saturday		
10:00 a.m.–11:59 a.m.	9.2%	29.0%
12:00 p.m.–1:59 p.m.	8.1%	25.6%
2:00 p.m.–3:49 p.m.	7.6%	24.0%
4:00 p.m.–6:00 p.m.	6.8%	21.5%
Total	31.7%	100.0%
Sunday		
11:00 a.m.–12:59 p.m.	9.1%	35.4%
1:00 p.m.–2:59 p.m.	8.7%	33.9%
3:00 p.m.–5:00 p.m.	7.9%	30.7%
Total	25.7%	100.0%

most people get off of work. But, on the flip side, if people see their doctors during the day, the odds are they are not going back to work for a while anyway. We all know that this is an expensive part of the store, so the push has been to limit the number of hours. Expanding the store hours and the hours the pharmacy department is open is a good idea. I'm glad Carl gave me the opportunity to experiment with this.

Weekly sales by an average pharmacy department are presented in Table VI.6.3. Although there is some variation in sales between departments based on their geographic areas, the averages are reasonably close for each one.

An average pharmacy dispenses nearly 57,000 prescriptions a year. The numbers of prescriptions dispensed by blocks of hours and days are presented in Table VI.6.4. These numbers have risen by 4.3 percent per year for the last 2 years—the main reason for the belief that the pharmacy departments can be a means of building overall store sales.

Normally, each store tries to have one or two staff pharmacists and one technician working each day. However, this varied somewhat because Mondays, Wednesdays, and Fridays were the busiest days for prescriptions. Of the prescriptions dispensed on weekdays, the percentage of prescriptions dispensed each day was as follows:

- Monday: 22.9 percent
- Tuesday: 13.1 percent

Table VI.6.4 Number of prescriptions dispensed in average week by hours of operation

	Number of Rx
Average number of prescriptions dispensed per week	
Monday through Friday	
9:00 a.m.–10:59 a.m.	93
11:00 a.m.–12:59 p.m.	191
1:00 p.m.–2:59 p.m.	129
3:00 p.m.–4:59 p.m.	174
5:00 p.m.–7:00 p.m.	254
Total	842
Saturday	
10:00 a.m.–11:59 a.m.	108
12:00 p.m.–1:59 p.m.	89
2:00 p.m.–3:00 p.m.	57
Total	254
Number of prescriptions dispensed per week	1,096
Total number of prescriptions dispensed per year	56,984

- Wednesday: 20.1 percent
- Thursday: 18.4 percent
- Friday: 25.5 percent.

Depending on the day and time, the average wait for a prescription that was brought into the store ranged from 7 to 45 minutes. The longer times were most likely to occur Monday and Friday afternoons and Saturday mornings. Dr. Singh estimated that about 25 percent of the customers who obtain prescriptions want medication consultations, and the average time to undertake the consult is between 2 and 4 minutes.

Thompson's Stores pharmacy departments also have responsibility for over-the-counter medications (OTCs) and health and beauty aids (HBAs). These non-prescription products account for 14.7 percent of total pharmacy department sales. The top selling OTCs and HBAs are presented in Table VI.6.5.

Dr. Singh and the other regional managers for pharmacy operations believe there might be opportunities to counsel customers on the best OTCs and HBAs to use. She commented about this:

I think all of the managers agree that opportunities exist to expand our OTC and HBA sales if we can get pharmacists involved with customers when they are in those aisles.

Table VI.6.3 Pharmacy sales by hours of operation

Hours of operation	Percent of weekly total	Percent of individual day
Monday through Friday		
9:00 a.m.–10:59 a.m.	8.5%	11.1%
11:00 a.m.–12:59 p.m.	17.4%	22.7%
1:00 p.m.–2:59 p.m.	11.8%	15.4%
3:00 p.m.–4:59 p.m.	15.9%	20.7%
5:00 p.m.–7:00 p.m.	23.2%	30.2%
Total	76.8%	100.0%
Saturday		
10:00 a.m.–11:59 a.m.	9.9%	42.7%
12:00 p.m.–1:59 p.m.	8.1%	34.9%
2:00 p.m.–3:00 p.m.	5.2%	22.4%
Total	23.2%	100.0%

Table VI.6.5 Top selling over-the-counter medications and health and beauty aids

Top HBA/OTC categories	Percent of total HBA and OTC sales
Nutritional supplements	7.2%
Pain remedies	7.1%
Hand and body lotions	5.1%
Shampoos	4.4%
Sanitary napkins	4.1%
Toothpaste	3.3%
Cold remedies	3.2%
Facial cleaners and lotions	3.1%
Antacids	2.9%
Razor blades	1.2%
Total	41.6%

Currently, they spend less than about 15 minutes a day consulting with patients on these products. Our security cameras show that many customers spend considerable time looking at the brands, reading some parts of the labels, and just appearing confused about what to buy. When this happens, about 75 percent of them walk away with no product in their hands or shopping cart.

We think it would be fantastic if we could have pharmacists move away from the prescription area and assist those customers. We all believe that our sell rate would increase from 25 to 80 percent if customers were given advice. Since an average OTC or HBA sells for between $8 and $15, this could generate significant dollars.

The problem, of course, is pharmacist time. This is where we really have to look at scheduling, possibly using additional part-time staff or maybe pharmacy students who are much less expensive to employ. Part-time pharmacists are about 20 percent less expensive, and would be an even lower cost if we could find some who only want to work a few hours and not receive benefits. Pharmacy students are at least 40 percent less expensive. But, there are issues of hiring and scheduling if we go this way. That's part of what I have to decide before submitting my recommendations to Carl.

The test market

After Carl Thompson gave her the assignment to run a test in her region, Dr. Singh selected a store in a suburb of a city in the center of her region of this southern state. She felt that this store and location would be reasonably representative of all of the company's stores.

The population of the suburban area was about 18,000 and selected demographic characteristics are presented in Table VI.6.6. Generally, Dr. Singh considered this a somewhat younger and more affluent area. In about 75 percent of the households, both the female and male heads of households were working, and at least one was in a professional position. Dr. Singh commented about the population in this suburb:

> I picked this one because it primarily consists of younger households with two incomes. These are hard working people who may want the

Table VI.6.6 Selected demographic characteristics of Thompson's Stores' customers and users of prescriptions

	Overall store	Rx dispensed[a]
Gender		
Women	65.0%	68.9%
Men	35.0%	31.1%
Total	100.0%	100.0%
Age		
Under 16	17.1%	19.8%
16–20	20.4%	12.5%
21–35	23.1%	20.6%
36–50	16.9%	15.9%
51–64	15.4%	18.1%
65 and above	7.1%	13.1%
Total	100.0%	100.0%
Household income		
Less than $35,000	9.1%	Not available
$35,000–$49,999	11.8%	Not available
$50,000–$74,999	14.8%	Not available
$75,000–$99,999	23.8%	Not available
$100,000–$149,999	21.7%	Not available
$150,000–$199,999	11.1%	Not available
$200,000 or more	7.7%	Not available
Total	100.0%	

[a] Demographic characteristics of user of the prescriptions.

extended hours because they cannot come in during the 8–5 time period. I also thought it would be a good test to see if doing more prescription consultations and OTC and HBA outreach could stimulate sales. These people have the money but not the time to fool around. Time is more valuable to them than money in some cases. So, I would like to attract them with a strong prescription counseling program, sell them the higher-end OTCs and HBAs, and make them loyal customers which will benefit all departments within the store. These are the most desirable customers we can have for the store.

My other option was to select a store that had a high percentage of older customers. We know they have a lot of prescriptions filled, and are big purchasers of OTCs and HBAs. But, they also are more price sensitive. So, I'm not sure which group would be better, but I had to make a decision and I did.

Competition in the area was keen. Within the suburban area, there was one other mass merchandise store, three chain pharmacies, and three independent pharmacies. Their days and hours of operation are presented in Table VI.6.7.

Dr. Singh was reading through the request Carl Thompson made. He was proposing to change the store hours to 8 a.m. to 10 p.m. Monday through Saturday, and 10 a.m. to 8 p.m. on Sunday. He indicated that he was receptive to a different schedule if Dr. Singh felt it was better to do something else.

Based on this, he wanted her to develop a plan to expand the hours of the pharmacy department, determine how many pharmacists and technicians to employ at various times of the day, recommend how

those positions be staffed between full- and part-time pharmacists. He also wanted plans for how to expand prescription consultations and have pharmacists spend some amount of time advising customers on OTCs and HBAs.

The more she read through his request, the more uncomfortable she became. Among the immediate concerns that came to mind were how much would the volume of prescriptions grow versus be shifted by the added time the pharmacy department was open, how much pharmacist time to allocate to activities other than dispensing prescriptions, and how to market the pharmacists' services:

> When Carl asked me to take the lead in testing all of this, I was honored. Now, just how many decisions that needs to be made is beginning to sink in. There is a lot of planning to do. Guess I should have sat lower in the chair and kept my head down when all of this came up at the quarterly meeting.

Possible discussion questions

1 What should be the operating schedule for the test pharmacy department?

2 How should pharmacists be scheduled and what mix of full-time and part-time pharmacists should be used?

3 How much time should the test pharmacy department allocate to prescription consultations and counseling on OTCs and HBAs? How can this time be scheduled to keep labor costs to a reasonable level?

4 How can the pharmacy encourage prescription customers to want and accept consultations on their medications? How can this be done for OTCs and HBAs?

Table VI.6.7 Competitors' hours of operation

Competing pharmacies	Monday through Friday	Saturday	Sunday
Thompson's current pharmacy schedule	9 a.m.–9 p.m.	10 a.m.–3 p.m.	Closed
Mass merchandiser "A"	8 a.m.–11 p.m.	8 a.m.–11 p.m.	9 a.m.–9 p.m.
Chain pharmacy "A"	9 a.m.–9 p.m.	9 a.m.–9 p.m.	10 a.m.–7 p.m.
Chain pharmacy "B"	9 a.m.–10 p.m.	9 a.m.–7 p.m.	9 a.m.–2 p.m.
Chain pharmacy "C"	8 a.m.–7 p.m.	8 a.m.–6 p.m.	10 a.m.–3 p.m.
Independent pharmacy "A"	9 a.m.–6 p.m.	10 a.m.–4 p.m.	Closed
Independent pharmacy "B"	9 a.m.–7 p.m.	Closed	Closed
Independent pharmacy "C"	8 a.m.–7 p.m.	10 a.m.–2 p.m.	Closed

Answers to self-test questions

Chapter 1

True/false statements

1	F
2	F
3	F
4	F
5	F
6	F
7	T
8	F
9	F
10	T

Chapter 2

True/false statements

1	F
2	T
3	F
4	F
5	T
6	T
7	F
8	F
9	F
10	T

Multiple choice questions

1	C
2	D
3	C
4	B
5	B

Multiple choice questions

1	A
2	C
3	D
4	D
5	A

Chapter 3

True/false statements

1	F
2	F
3	T
4	T
5	F
6	F
7	T
8	F
9	F
10	F

Multiple choice questions

1	A
2	D
3	D
4	B
5	C

Chapter 4

True/false statements

1	T
2	F
3	T
4	F
5	T
6	T
7	F
8	F
9	F
10	T

Multiple choice questions

1	C
2	D
3	B
4	B
5	B

Chapter 5

True/false statements

1	T
2	F
3	T
4	T
5	F
6	T
7	T
8	F
9	F
10	F

Multiple choice questions

1	A
2	B
3	A
4	D
5	A

Chapter 6

True/false statements

1	T
2	T
3	F
4	T
5	F
6	T
7	T
8	F
9	T
10	F

Multiple choice questions

1	C
2	B
3	B
4	B
5	B

Chapter 7

True/false statements

1 T
2 T
3 T
4 F
5 T
6 F
7 F
8 F
9 T
10 T

Multiple choice questions

1 D
2 C
3 C
4 A
5 A

Chapter 8

True/false statements

1 T
2 F
3 F
4 F
5 F
6 F
7 F
8 T
9 T
10 F

Multiple choice questions

1 C
2 B
3 C
4 D
5 D

Chapter 9

True/false statements

1 F
2 F
3 T
4 F
5 F
6 F
7 T
8 T
9 T
10 F

Multiple choice questions

1 C
2 D
3 D
4 C
5 D

Chapter 10

True/false statements

1 F
2 T
3 F
4 F
5 F
6 T
7 T
8 F
9 F
10 T

Multiple choice questions

1 D
2 B
3 B
4 C
5 B
6 C

Chapter 11

True/false statements

1	F
2	T
3	T
4	T
5	T
6	F
7	F
8	T
9	F
10	T

Multiple choice questions

1	D
2	C
3	D
4	A
5	D

Chapter 12

True/false statements

1	T
2	F
3	T
4	F
5	T
6	F
7	F
8	T
9	F
10	F

Multiple choice questions

1	B
2	C
3	A
4	C
5	B

Chapter 13

True/false statements

1	T
2	T
3	F
4	F
5	T
6	F
7	T
8	F
9	T
10	T

Multiple choice questions

1	D
2	A
3	A
4	C
5	D

Chapter 14

True/false statements

1	T
2	F
3	F
4	T
5	F
6	F
7	T
8	T
9	F
10	T

Multiple choice questions

1	B
2	A
3	A
4	B
5	A

Chapter 15

True/false statements

1 F
2 F
3 T
4 T
5 T
6 F
7 T
8 T
9 F
10 T

Multiple choice questions

1 D
2 B
3 C
4 B
5 D

Chapter 16

True/false statements

1 T
2 F
3 T
4 T
5 F
6 F
7 F
8 F
9 F
10 T

Multiple choice questions

1 B
2 D
3 B
4 D
5 D

Chapter 17

True/false statements

1 F
2 T
3 T
4 F
5 F
6 T
7 F
8 F
9 T
10 F

Multiple choice questions

1 A
2 C
3 B
4 A
5 C

Index